# Resources, Environment and Agricultural Development

**Series Editors**

**"Resources, Environment and Agricultural Development"** series aim to provide an in-depth study of the challenges facing the world today, such as resource shortages and environmental pollution, as well as opportunities in agricultural modernization, technological progress, and income distribution, to focus on the critical issues of the balanced development in overall environment. Based on the central theme of overall sustainable and inclusive development in agriculture, the series' coverage includes but is not limited to studies in development economics, environmental & resource economics, agricultural economics, and public administration.

The series are positioned as a collection of scholarly books that aims to explore sustainable and inclusive development of agriculture under the constraints of resources and environmental conditions, under various predisposition of the resource environment and national contexts. We have incorporated many vivid and realistic agricultural development experiences into the book, such as lessons from China's agriculture, which provide a glimpses of China's rich practices and pathways for other countries worldwide.

Linyi Zheng

# Cropland Abandonment in Rural China

Springer

Linyi Zheng
China Academy for Rural Development,
School of Public Affairs
Zhejiang University
Hangzhou, China

ISSN 3059-2216 ISSN 3059-2224 (electronic)
Resources, Environment and Agricultural Development
ISBN 978-981-95-8286-0 ISBN 978-981-95-8287-7 (eBook)
https://doi.org/10.1007/978-981-95-8287-7



This Springer imprint is published by the registered company Springer Nature Singapore Pte Ltd.
The registered company address is: 152 Beach Road, #21-01/04 Gateway East, Singapore 189721, Singapore

# Preface

Whenever I travel by high-speed train, I always make a point of glancing out the window. Most of the fleeting scenery fades away before it can leave a lasting impression, yet some images linger persistently in my mind, refusing to fade. As a scholar specializing in agricultural economics, the realities of agricultural production inevitably draw my attention. In recent years, what has struck me most profoundly is that across China—from east to west, north to south, and spanning plains and mountainous regions—it has become a common sight to see cropland gradually overgrown with weeds instead of crops. I have come to recognize that the phenomenon of farmers abandoning cropland in rural China is becoming increasingly prevalent. While this phenomenon may bring certain ecological benefits, it is undoubtedly detrimental to the sustainable use of cropland, to say nothing of national food security and the long-term development of agriculture.

In China, advancing effective governance of abandoned cropland carries both historical and contemporary imperatives. On one hand, China's history teaches us to prioritize food security. The nation has endured multiple famines throughout its past—such as the 1942 Henan famine—which claimed countless lives. To prevent such tragedies from recurring, the prudent use of every inch of land has become deeply ingrained in the Chinese consciousness, with land long regarded as the lifeblood of farmers. An ancient Chinese proverb, "Where there is land, there is grain," underscores the critical importance of land for food production. On the other hand, as a developing nation with a large population and scarce arable land resources, strengthening land protection and promoting its sustainable use have always been top policy priorities for ensuring national food security. According to World Bank data, China's per capita arable land in 2023 was a mere 0.08 hectares—less than half of the global average of 0.17 hectares. To feed nearly 20% of the world's population with only 9% of its arable land, prioritizing sustainable farming practices is imperative. Yet why do farmers still abandon their croplands? This is the first core question this book addresses head-on. Furthermore, as a social science, agricultural economics must not only answer the "why" but also the "how." Shifting from "why" to "how," the second question this book seeks to answer is: Based on identifying the key drivers of cropland abandonment, how can we scientifically evaluate the effectiveness of existing governance measures for addressing this issue?

To structure this book coherently and develop a clear narrative, the author attempts to distill a clear thread from the myriad strands: People-Land-Money-Rights. Here, "People" refers to agricultural producers——including countless smallholder farmers and emerging large-scale farmers (known as "new types of agricultural operating entities" in the Chinese context). They are the direct stakeholders in agricultural production and the core focus of this book. Only by understanding these people and their needs can we design viable institutional arrangements that sustain agricultural development. "Land" denotes to cropland itself, whose inherent characteristics exert a profound influence on how agricultural producers utilize it. Agricultural economics (especially land economics) is fundamentally a discipline centered on the relationships between people and between people and land. Thus, studying cropland use requires a deep understanding of the land's own conditions. "Money" represents the income generated from agricultural activities. In a market economy, farmers act as rational economic agents seeking to maximize profits, and their decisions are often shaped by the comparative returns of agricultural production. "Rights" refers to property rights—farmers' rights to land. The clear definition and effective protection of property rights constitute a fundamental institutional safeguard for sound economic development, and the security of land tenure exerts a profound impact on farmers' resource allocation decisions.

Overall, drawing on the "People-Land-Money-Rights" perspective, this book employs nationally representative large-sample data and modern econometric methods to empirically address two closely interrelated questions: First, why do farmers abandon their croplands? This addresses the "why" dimension. The book focuses on four key drivers of cropland abandonment: off-farm employment, land fragmentation, insufficient comparative returns from agriculture, and insecure land tenure. These topics form the content of Chapters 3 to 6. Second, how can we effectively address cropland abandonment caused by these drivers? This addresses the "how" dimension. The book examines the effectiveness of four types of governance measures: fostering new agricultural operating entities, constructing farmland water conservancy projects, reforming agricultural subsidy systems, and reforming land tenure. These form the content of Chapters 7 to 10. This book comprises 11 chapters in total, with the remaining three chapters being the Introduction, Literature Review, Analytical Framework, and Conclusion. The book aims to systematically examine the driving factors and governance measures behind cropland abandonment by Chinese farmers at the present stage.

The completion of this book would not have been possible without the support of many individuals. First and foremost, I would like to express my deepest gratitude to my family—my parents, who are genuine farmers and raised me through great hardships. It was their unwavering dedication that gave me the courage and opportunity to leave the mountains and rural areas to pursue my academic aspirations. My wife, Siqi Wang, who is also passionate about academic research, provided invaluable companionship and understanding—her support was crucial to the completion of this work. Second, I am deeply indebted to my teachers: in particular, my mentors

Yingliang Zhang, Wenrong Qian, Mingyong Hong, and Guanming Shi, as well as renowned land economists such as Shouying Liu and Songqing Jin. Their professional guidance and consistent support enabled me to delve deeply into the field of land economics with unwavering enthusiasm and perseverance. Furthermore, I would like to thank Professors Binlei Gong and Scott Rozelle, the editors of the READ series, whose enthusiastic invitation to contribute and generous recommendation have been a tremendous source of encouragement to me. Finally, I am grateful to my friends in the publishing industry—especially Nature Springer, who graciously accepted this manuscript despite its challenges. I am deeply honored by their willingness to publish this work. Simultaneously, some of the materials presented in this book have been previously published in international journals including *Food Policy, Canadian Journal of Agricultural Economics, China Agricultural Economic Review, Journal of Rural Studies, and Land Degradation & Development.* I extend my sincere gratitude to these journals for generously granting republishing permissions. Additionally, I would like to acknowledge the contributors of several chapters, including Liufang Su, Ziqing Zuo, Jiahao Zhang, Hanqi Zhao, and other colleagues, whose valuable efforts and contributions have laid a solid foundation for the completion of this work.

As this is my first English-language book and my knowledge remains limited, there are undoubtedly numerous shortcomings and errors within these pages. I would be deeply honored and grateful if scholars and experts worldwide would kindly offer their corrections and guidance.

December 15, 2025

Linyi Zheng
China Academy for Rural Development
School of Public Affairs
Zijingang Campus, Zhejiang University
Hangzhou, China

# Preface for The READ Series

In recent years, challenges such as resource depletion, environmental pollution and food scarcity have persistently posed a threat to the realization of the sustainable development goals of the United Nations. In terms of resources, the world has witnessed a threefold increase in the consumption of our planet's resources in the past five decades, with a growth rate that is still continuing to expand at an average annual pace that exceeds 2.3%. The direct impact of chemical pollution in the world's air, soil, water, and workplaces is estimated to be causing 2 million deaths each year. In terms of food scarcity, about 9.2 percent of the global population—735 million people—faced chronic hunger in 2022, 122 million more than in 2019. And many of these issues may be becoming even more severe as they are being exacerbated by climate change, natural disasters, severe epidemics, conflicts, and civil unrest, which in turn often leads to other issues such as economic stagnation, inequality and health risks.

In this context, there is an urgent need for systematic research and international communication to tackle these problems because we have only one planet. I am delighted to see that the Resource, Environment and Agricultural Development (READ) team at Zhejiang University has established a collaboration with Springer Nature, one of the world's leading academic publishers, to launch the Resource, Environment and Agricultural Development Book Series (READ Series). This series aims to provide in-depth studies of the most serious challenges facing the world today, such as resource scarcity and environmental pollution. The series will also seek to identify opportunities that can assist in the modernization of agriculture, help facilitate technological breakthroughs, and contribute to the reduction of income inequalities which are all needed to help the academic world to focus on the critical issues of the balanced development in the overall environment. Based on the central theme of overall sustainable and inclusive development in agriculture, the scope of the series includes, but is not limited to, studies in development economics, environmental and resource economics, agricultural economics, and public administration.

Resource, environment and agricultural development constitute a multi-dimensional, interdisciplinary research field that encompasses a wide range of issues from agricultural production practices and policy-making to technological innovation and environmental management. As our guide to the future, resource environment and agricultural development are key areas that we cannot overlook or choose to ignore. For instance, how can we, the world, ensure global food security and sustainable development in a long run? How can policymakers across the planet mitigate and begin to adapt to the inevitable negative impacts of climate change? How can nations around the world maintain food output levels worldwide while using less resources and creating less polluting spillovers. How can governments—in developing and developed nations launch successful and sustainable fights against poverty and hunger? How to enhance the sustainability and resilience of agri-food system? How can nations begin to accelerate the pace of green transition while simultaneously spurring economic growth? Is it possible to provide clean water and energy to everyone? These research questions relate to global challenges and to how to achieve future sustainable development goals. To achieve these goals, we need to work together across disciplinary boundaries to find solutions for the mutual development of resources, environment and agriculture, and to evaluate how the proposed solutions will affect the future of our world.

I am very pleased to see that Dr. Gong Binlei and Dr. Scott Rozelle will be serving as the editors of the READ Series. Dr. Gong is the Qiushi Chair Professor in the School of Public Affairs and serves as the Executive Vice Dean in the China Academy for Rural Development (CARD) at Zhejiang University. His own research agenda focuses on ways to optimize resource allocation and enhance the overall productivity growth in the economy as well as new approaches that can lead to successes in the green transition and rural development. Dr. Rozelle hold the Helen F. Farnsworth Professorship of International Agricultural Policy and is Senior Fellow in Freeman Spogli Institute for International Studies at Stanford University. His research focuses on China's agricultural policy, poverty alleviation and issues related to dealing with inequality, with an emphasis on the rural education, health and early childhood development. I am convinced that their rich experience and profound knowledge in the field of sustainable development will be major assets to grow the READ book series into an important source of information with excellent reputation under their leadership as editors.

In summary, I extend my sincerest wishes for the READ series to become a valuable resource, offering theoretical underpinnings, empirical insights, and policy recommendations that can significantly support the pursuit of global sustainable development. Beyond the insights it provides, I hope the opportunity that this series provides will also encourages scholars to join this journey of discovery, to explore the future of resources, environment, and agricultural development—and indeed submit their own work for publication in the READ series, thereby contributing to the growth of the academic community in this series. Hence, this series should not only help readers gain both a broad and deep understanding of these issues but also inspire the engagement of all into working on successful ways to achieve sustainable development.

Washington, DC, USA

Johan Swinnen
Director General of the International
Food Policy Research Institute (IFPRI)
Managing Director of Systems
Transformation, CGIAR

**Acknowledgments** This work was supported by the National Natural Science Foundation of China (Grant No. 72503220, 72141307), the Ministry of Science and Technology of China with the National Key Research and Development Program (Grant No. 2025YFE0111303), Humanities and Social Science Fund of Ministry of Education of China (Grant No. 23YJC790203, 2024JZDZ064), Zhejiang Provincial Philosophy and Social Sciences Planning Project (Grant No. ZKZD2024001, 24YJRC01ZD-1YB), and Fundamental Research Funds for the Central Universities (Grant No. S20250025).

**Competing Interests** The author has no competing interests to declare that are relevant to the content of this manuscript.

# Editor's Recommendation

"Rapid population growth, frequent extreme weather events, and the ongoing Russia-Ukraine conflict have led to the abandonment of cropland, a significant issue that exits an increasing negative impact on food security. Reducing cropland abandonment for food security has therefore become a policy priority for various countries. Using nationally representative micro-survey data and modern econometric methods, this book delves into the fundamental aspects of this issue, enabling an in-depth exploration of the drivers and governance strategies behind micro-scale cropland abandonment. This not only provides Chinese evidence for effective governance of global cropland abandonment, but also contributes Chinese wisdom to food security based on land protection."

—Helen F. Farnsworth, *Senior Fellow at Stanford University, Faculty Co-director of the Stanford Center on China's Economy and Institutions, Scott Rozelle*

"Cropland abandonment, a primary manifestation of land use and cover change (LUCC), exerts a profound impact on global food security. Utilizing detailed data, scientific methods, and innovative research designs, this book systematically examines the drivers and governance strategies of farmers' cropland abandonment, with "People-Land-Money-Rights" as the analytical framework, providing profound insights into land protection, food security, and sustainable agricultural development. With a clear problem orientation and important academic value, this book serves as a valuable academic resource for researchers and policy makers seeking to understand LUCC in China."

—Qiushi, *Chair Professor in School of Public Affairs at Zhejiang University, the Executive Vice Dean in China Academy for Rural Development (CARD), Binlei Gong*

# Contents

# List of Contributors

- Chapter 1. Introduction, Linyi Zheng
- Chapter 2. Literature review and analytical framework, Linyi Zheng
- Chapter 3. Off-farm employment and cropland abandonment, Linyi Zheng
- Chapter 4. Land fragmentation and cropland abandonment, Linyi Zheng, Liufang Su & Songqing Jin
- Chapter 5. Agricultural comparative return and cropland abandonment, Linyi Zheng, Songqing Jin & Liufang Su
- Chapter 6. Land tenure insecurity and cropland abandonment, Linyi Zheng, Jiahao Zhang, Hanqi Zhao & Liufang Su
- Chapter 7. New agricultural operating entities and cropland abandonment, Linyi Zheng
- Chapter 8. Farmland water conservancy project and cropland abandonment, Linyi Zheng, Yeyang Li & Ziqing Zuo
- Chapter 9. Agricultural subsidy reform and cropland abandonment, Linyi Zheng, Bin Yan & Wenrong Qian
- Chapter 10. Land tenure reform and cropland abandonment, Linyi Zheng & Wenrong Qian
- Chapter 11. Key findings and future agenda, Linyi Zheng

# Chapter 1
# Introduction

**Abstract** As the core carrier of grain production, the importance of protecting and sustainably utilizing farmland is undeniable. Taking food security as its logical starting point, this chapter analyzes the current status and hazards of cropland abandonment as well as the critical significance of addressing this issue. It particularly highlights the necessity of tackling cropland abandonment amid growing uncertainties in global food security, thereby clarifying the academic value and practical significance of this study. Results show that systematically examining the drivers of cropland abandonment and corresponding governance measures holds significant value both practically and academically. This is crucial for safeguarding food security and promoting sustainable agricultural development.

**Keywords** Cropland abandonment · Food security · Sustainable agricultural development

## 1.1 Background

Food security is vital to a nation's economy and people's livelihood, and stands as a top priority in national governance. However, in recent years, the global food security situation has been grim due to the continuous growth of the world population, frequent occurrences of extreme weather events, and the escalating Russia-Ukraine conflict (Zheng et al., 2023). According to the latest estimates from *The State of Food Security and Nutrition in the World,* released by the Food and Agriculture Organization (FAO) of the United Nations in 2025, 638 million to 720 million people worldwide faced hunger in 2024, with the global prevalence of food insecurity remaining as high as 8.2% (FAO, 2025). Although the number of hungry people globally decreased by 15 million compared to 2023 and 22 million compared to 2022 after the end of the COVID-19 pandemic, it still remained above the pre-pandemic level. Furthermore, factors such as high food price inflation in recent years have been hindering the recovery of the global food security situation. Faced with this series of

 
L. Zheng, *Cropland Abandonment in Rural China*, Resources, Environment and Agricultural Development, https://doi.org/10.1007/978-981-95-8287-7_1

severe challenges, achieving the "Zero Hunger" vision outlined in the United Nations Sustainable Development Goals (SDGs) by 2030 remains a long and arduous task.

Against the backdrop of significantly increased global food security uncertainties, the importance of strengthening cropland protection is self-evident for China, a country with a large population and limited arable land (Xin & Li, 2018; Xu et al., 2019; Zheng, 2024). In normal years, food supply in the era of globalization can be secured through market mechanisms such as international trade. However, when international circumstances undergo sudden changes and disrupt food supply chains, excessive reliance on foreign food supplies can trigger food crises and even threaten national security. For a large developing country like China, its own food security is intrinsically linked to the stability of the global food market. Safeguarding its own food security is, in itself, a contribution to global food security. Based on this understanding, and as a responsible major power, China has consistently taken strengthening cropland protection, promoting the sustainable use of cropland, and ensuring food supply for its 1.4 billion people as the primary task of national governance (Li & Li, 2017; Xin & Li, 2018; Xu et al., 2019; Zheng et al., 2023). It is widely recognized that cropland constitutes a natural resource and public good essential to human survival, serving as the most critical material carrier for food production (Zavalloni et al., 2021). All grains and foods required for human survival and development come directly or indirectly from cropland, which provides over 75% of the protein and more than 80% of the calories for human life activities, and 88% of human food is also produced from cropland (Chen, 2007).

Nevertheless, the problem of cropland abandonment in China has become increasingly prominent in recent years, posing severe challenges to food security. According to the China Rural Household Panel Survey (CRHPS) and the China Labor-force Dynamics Survey (CLDS), Fig. 1.1 shows that the incidence of cropland abandonment by farmers in China rose from 9.16% in 2013 to 19.92% in 2021. Further research indicates that the grain loss caused by cropland abandonment reached 49.23 million tons in 2020, accounting for approximately 7.36% of the national total grain output that year (Wang et al., 2023); furthermore, the annual grain loss due to cropland abandonment in China could even feed an additional 19.85 million people (Guo et al., 2023). Therefore, amid the challenging global food security situation, it is imperative to strengthen the protection of cropland quantity in agricultural production, maintain a certain amount of usable cropland, and strictly prevent, reduce, and curb the abandonment of cropland by farmers (Li et al., 2021; Deng et al., 2019; Zheng & Qian, 2022).

To safeguard national food security, the Chinese government attaches great importance to the issue of cropland abandonment and its governance. For instance: the *Opinions on Guiding the Orderly Transfer of Rural Land Management Rights and Developing Appropriate-Scale Agricultural Operations issued by the Central Government* in 2014 emphasized that local governments could reduce cropland abandonment by suspending agricultural subsidies; Article 64 of *the Rural Land Contracting Law of the People's Republic of China*, revised and adopted in 2018, clearly stipulates that the lessor has the right to terminate the land management right transfer contract if the lessee abandons the cropland for more than two consecutive

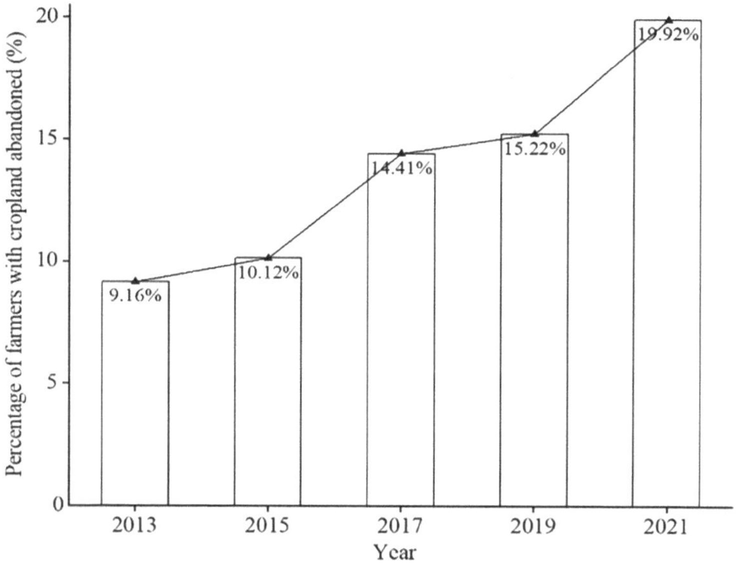


**Fig. 1.1** Percentage of farmers with cropland abandoned in China

years; in 2021, the Ministry of Agriculture and Rural Affairs specially issued the *Guiding Opinions on Coordinated Utilization of Abandoned Cropland to Promote Agricultural Production Development*, pointing out that cropland abandonment should be curbed by improving the subsidy mechanism, accelerating infrastructure construction, standardizing land transfer, and developing agricultural socialized services. The Central "No. 1 Document" for 2023 and 2024 successively emphasized the need to "strengthen the utilization of abandoned cropland" and "promote the utilization of abandoned cropland in light of local conditions." Therefore, how to curb the abandonment of cropland and thereby safeguard national food security has become one of the important issues urgently needing to be addressed at present and future in rural China.

Reviewing existing literature, while scattered studies have examined factors influencing cropland abandonment by households—such as natural disasters (Guo et al., 2020), terrain and land parcels (Luo et al., 2019; Mou et al., 2022; Wang et al., 2022), soil conditions (Han & Song, 2019), cropland area (Li & Dai, 2014; Hong, 2022), and agricultural labor force (Zhang et al., 2014)—no scholars have yet conducted a systematic exploration of key drivers of cropland abandonment and the effectiveness of its governance measures from a "People-Land-Money-Rights" perspective. In particular, few studies have focused on the potential impacts of off-farm employment, land fragmentation, low agricultural comparative return, and insecure land tenure on farmers' cropland abandonment from the perspective of "People-Land-Money-Rights." Based on this perspective, there is a lack of efforts to quantify and evaluate governance measures for cropland abandonment under different types of impacts, empirically test the inhibitory effects of different governance measures, and further propose optimized policy schemes to facilitate the effective governance of farmers' cropland abandonment. Consequently, it is of theoretical necessity to explore the driving factors behind cropland abandonment and corresponding governance measures from an academic standpoint.

## 1.2 Research Objectives and Significance

Given the current realities of rural China and existing research gaps, this book, guided by the "People-Land-Money-Rights" analytical framework, focuses on addressing two interrelated core questions in a logical sequence: first, answering the "why" behind cropland abandonment—i.e., what key factors drive farmers to abandon their croplands?—and second, exploring the "how" of effective governance—namely, are the existing measures for addressing cropland abandonment effective in curbing the problem rooted in these identified factors?

To elaborate, the book first systematically examines, in line with the "People-Land-Money-Rights" paradigm, the sequential impacts of off-farm employment ("People"), land fragmentation ("Land"), low agricultural comparative returns ("Money"), and land tenure insecurity ("Rights") on farmers' cropland abandonment behavior. Through this analysis, it identifies the key drivers of cropland abandonment, thereby thoroughly addressing the "why" question.

Building on this foundational analysis, the book then shifts its focus to the "how" question by directly quantifying the effectiveness of targeted governance measures. It further explores whether key intervention initiatives—aligned with the "People-Land-Money-Rights" framework—such as the development of new agricultural operating entities ("People"), the construction of farmland water conservancy projects ("Land"), reforms of agricultural subsidy policies ("Money"), and land tenure reforms ("Rights")—can effectively curb cropland abandonment. Ultimately, this research strives to provide a solid land protection guarantee for safeguarding national food security.

The research significance of this book thus manifests in two key dimensions: Theoretically, by anchoring in the "People-Land-Money-Rights" perspective, it clarifies the impact effects and action mechanisms of off-farm employment, land fragmentation, low agricultural comparative return, land tenure insecurity—along with their corresponding governance measures—on farmers' cropland abandonment behavior. This not only fills existing research gaps but also enriches and expands the theoretical system of cropland protection and sustainable agricultural development. Practically, on the basis of identifying the key driving factors of farmers' cropland abandonment, quantifying the inhibitory effects of different governance measures will provide empirical support for improving and optimizing relevant policies, thereby further consolidating the foundation for national food security. Additionally, empirical evidence from China will offer valuable lessons and policy insights for other developing and developed countries confronting similar cropland abandonment challenges.

## References

Chen, Y. X. (2007). *Agricultural environmental protection* (2nd ed.). Chemical Industry Press. (in Chinese).

Deng, X., Xu, D., Zeng, M., & Qi, Y. (2019). Does internet use help reduce rural cropland abandonment? Evidence from China. *Land Use Policy, 89*, 104243.

FAO, I., UNICEF, WFP, WHO. (2025). The State of Food Security and Nutrition in the World 2025. Retrieved from Rome.

Guo, A., Yue, W., Yang, J., Xue, B., Xiao, W., Li, M., He, T., Zhang, M., Jin, X., & Zhou, Q. (2023). Cropland abandonment in China: Patterns, drivers, and implications for food security. *Journal of Cleaner Production, 418*, 138154.

Guo, B. B., Fang, Y. L., & Zhou, Y. K. (2020). Influencing factors and spatial differentiation of cultivated land abandonment at the household scale. *Resources Science, 42*, 696–709. (in Chinese).

Han, Z., Song, W., 2019. Spatiotemporal variations in cropland abandonment in the Guizhou–Guangxi karst mountain area, China. *Journal of Cleaner Production, 238*, 117888.

Hong, W. J. (2022). Initial natural endowment and farmers' land abandonment behavior: Based on the investigation of the scale of contracted land. *Journal of Nanjing Agricultural University (Social Sciences Edition), 22*, 124–135. (in Chinese).

Li, S., & Li, X. (2017). Global understanding of farmland abandonment: A review and prospects. *Journal of Geographical Sciences, 27*, 1123–1150.

Li, W. H., & Dai, Z. L. (2014). A hypothesis of farmland abandoning based on the farmers' family characters. *China Population, Resources and Environment, 24*, 143–149. (in Chinese).

Li, Y. L., Ma, W. Q., Jiang, G. H., Li, G. Y., & Zhou, D. Y. (2021). The degree of cultivated land abandonment and its influence on grain yield in main grain producing areas of China. *Journal of Natural Resources, 36*, 1439–1454. (in Chinese).

Luo, B. L., Wan, Y. L., Hong, W. J., & Zhong, W. J. (2019). Fragmentation, service outsourcing and farmland abandonment—An empirical analysis based on questionnaires from 2704 households in 9 provinces. *Economic Review Journal*, 63–73. (in Chinese).

Mou, Y., Zhao, Y. L., Li, X. B., Ren, H. Y., & Liu, Y. (2022). The influence of plot quality characteristics on terrace abandonment in mountainous areas of Southwest China: A case study of Baidu Village in Jianhe County, Guizhou Province. *Geographical Research, 41*, 903–916. (in Chinese).

Wang, J., Yu, C., Fang, X., Li, G., & Cao, Y. (2022). Does land tenure fragmentation aggravate farmland abandonment? Evidence from big survey data in rural China. *Journal of Rural Studies, 91*, 126–135.

Wang, Y., Yang, A., & Yang, Q. (2023). The extent, drivers and production loss of farmland abandonment in China: Evidence from a spatiotemporal analysis of farm households survey. *Journal of Cleaner Production, 414*, 137772.

Xin, L., & Li, X. (2018). China should not massively reclaim new farmland. *Land Use Policy, 72*, 12–15.

Xu, D., Deng, X., Huang, K., Liu, Y., Yong, Z., & Liu, S. (2019). Relationships between labor migration and cropland abandonment in rural China from the perspective of village types. *Land Use Policy, 88*, 104164.

Zavalloni, M., D'Alberto, R., Raggi, M., & Viaggi, D. (2021). Farmland abandonment, public goods and the CAP in a marginal area of Italy. *Land Use Policy, 107*, 104365.

Zhang, Y., Li, X. B., Song, W., & Shi, T. C. (2014). Effect of agricultural laborer on cropland abandonment under land circulation at different levels in Wulong County, Chongqing City. *Progress in Geography, 33*, 552–560. (in Chinese).

Zheng, L. (2024). Does off-farm work induce farmland abandonment? Evidence from China. *China Agricultural Economic Review, 16*, 664–682.

Zheng, L., Li, L., Zhao, Z., & Qian, W. (2023). Does land certification increase farmers' use of organic fertilizer? Evidence from China. *Journal of Land Use Science, 18*, 39–54.

Zheng, L., & Qian, W. (2022). The impact of land certification on cropland abandonment: Evidence from rural China. *China Agricultural Economic Review, 14*, 509–526.

# Chapter 2
# Literature Review and Analytical Framework

**Abstracts** A literature review and the construction of an analytical framework are essential prerequisites and foundations for academic research. This chapter first systematically reviews a body of literature on cropland abandonment, engaging in academic dialogue with existing research to identify and clarify the marginal contributions of this study. On this basis, it further constructs the analytical framework for the entire research using the "People-Land-Money-Rights" as the analytical clue, thereby providing directional guidance for the advancement of subsequent research. Results show that while existing literature has extensively explored the conceptual connotation, driving factors, impact effects, and governance strategies associated with the phenomenon of empirically examine the drivers of cropland abandonment and corresponding governance measures from a "People-Land-Money-Rights" perspective.

**Keywords** Cropland abandonment · food security · sustainable agricultural development · literature review · analytical framework

A literature review and the construction of an analytical framework are essential prerequisites and foundations for academic research. This chapter first systematically reviews a body of literature on cropland abandonment, engaging in academic dialogue with existing research to identify and clarify the marginal contributions of this study. On this basis, it further constructs the analytical framework for the entire research using the "People-Land-Money-Rights" as the analytical clue, thereby providing directional guidance for the advancement of subsequent research.

 
L. Zheng, *Cropland Abandonment in Rural China*, Resources, Environment and Agricultural Development, https://doi.org/10.1007/978-981-95-8287-7_2

## 2.1 Literature Review

### 2.1.1 *Basic Status of Cropland Abandonment*

Cropland abandonment is a global economic and social issue. Since the mid-nineteenth century Industrial Revolution, European countries have had extensive early records related to large-scale cropland abandonment (Baldock, 1996; Mather, 2001). In the early twentieth century, the phenomenon of cropland abandonment also began to emerge in some countries in the Americas and Southeast Asia (Fox et al., 2009; Rhemtulla et al., 2009). After the collapse of socialism in the 1990s, former socialist countries in the former Soviet Union and Central and Eastern Europe, such as Albania (Deininger et al., 2012; Sikor et al., 2009), Russia, Ukraine, and Kazakhstan (Meyfroidt et al., 2016), also faced relatively high rates of cropland abandonment.

Entering the twenty-first century, the problem of cropland abandonment has become increasingly severe in France (San Roman Sanz et al., 2013), Portugal (Van Doorn & Bakker, 2007), Switzerland (Price et al., 2015), and Austria (Silber & Wytrzens, 2005). In recent years, the issue of cropland abandonment by farmers has also begun to stand out in some developing countries, such as Mexico (Schneider & Geoghegan, 2006), Chile (Díaz et al., 2011), Argentina (Izquierdo & Grau, 2009), and China (Yan et al., 2016; 2014; Zhang et al., 2019).

Overall, according to estimates and calculations by Campbell et al. (2008), the global area of abandoned cropland has reached approximately 3.85 to 4.72 million square kilometers since the twentieth century.

### 2.1.2 *Definition of Cropland Abandonment*

Cropland abandonment mainly refers to the idleness and waste of cropland resources, with similar expressions including the abandonment of cropland, cultivated land, or agricultural land. However, there is no unified academic consensus on the specific meaning of cropland abandonment, especially regarding the duration of idleness required for cropland resources to be classified as abandoned.

For example, the Food and Agriculture Organization (FAO) defines abandoned cropland as cropland that has not been used for agricultural production or other agricultural purposes for at least five years (Di Gregorio, 2005); the Ministry of Agriculture of Japan defines it as cropland that has not been cultivated in the past year and has no tendency to be cultivated in the future (Kobayashi et al., 2020); the International Symposium on Land Consolidation and Land Banking proposes that cropland abandonment can be judged from the following aspects: (1) cultivable but unused; (2) uncultivated for more than two years; (3) cultivable but damaged due to poor management (Chen & Zheng, 2018).

For the convenience of statistics and governance, in fact, academia has also classified cropland abandonment. For instance, based on the idleness status of cropland within a year, it is divided into seasonal abandonment and perennial abandonment (Tan, 2003); based on whether cropland is fully utilized, it is divided into explicit abandonment and implicit abandonment (Luo, 2012); based on the quality of farming conditions, it is divided into complete abandonment and incomplete abandonment (Huang & Li, 2021).

In summary, cropland abandonment generally refers to the behavior of farmers reducing or giving up the cultivation of existing cropland under the combined effect of a series of factors, resulting in the land being left barren or underutilized for a certain period (Luo, 2012; Yang & Xu, 2015).

### 2.1.3 *Influencing Factors of Cropland Abandonment by Farmers*

#### 2.1.3.1 Natural Environment Factors

Cropland is an important component of natural resources, and its utilization status is directly affected by natural environment factors. From existing literature, the natural environment factors influencing cropland abandonment by farmers mainly include the following categories: (i) Natural disasters and climatic conditions: Natural disasters and extreme weather such as droughts, floods, hailstorms, acid rain, landslides, and mudslides all increase the risk of cropland abandonment by farmers (Keenleysid et al., 2010; Ustaoglu & Collier, 2018; Guo et al., 2020); (ii) Terrain and topography of cropland, such as altitude, slope, and mountainous terrain: Altitude and slope have a strong correlation with cropland abandonment (Mottet et al., 2006; Müller et al., 2013), and abandonment is more likely to occur in mountainous areas (Aide & Grau, 2004; Chen & Zheng, 2018; Gellrich et al., 2007; Lieskovský et al., 2015); (iii) Status and soil conditions of cropland, such as cropland fragmentation, market value of cropland, soil fertility, soil pollution, soil erosion, and ridge collapse (Alix-Garcia et al., 2012; Bakker et al., 2005; Luo et al., 2019; Zhang et al., 2018; Zheng & Qian, 2022). In particular, cropland fragmentation is regarded as one of the key factors leading to cropland abandonment (Wang et al., 2022; Zhang et al., 2018); (iv) Accessibility of cropland, such as commuting distance and time, irrigation conditions, and difficulty of mechanized operation (Ma et al., 2022; Mou et al., 2022); (v) Wildlife: Cropland where crops are easily damaged by wildlife is more prone to abandonment, and the presence of wildlife has become a critical factor for cropland abandonment by farmers in mountainous areas of China (Li et al., 2014). Overall, relatively harsh natural environments can induce cropland abandonment by farmers.

#### 2.1.3.2 Socio-Economic Factors

Socio-economic factors are the primary driving forces behind cropland abandonment by farmers (Li & Li, 2017), and they can be sorted out at both macro and micro levels. From the macro perspective, the socio-economic factors contributing to cropland abandonment by farmers mainly include the following aspects: (i) Rural population outflow driven by industrialization and urbanization, leading to a shortage of agricultural labor (Chen & Zheng, 2018; Romero-Calcerrada & Perry, 2004). The rapid advancement of industrialization and urbanization, coupled with the booming development of the secondary and tertiary industries, has created a large number of non-agricultural jobs and employment opportunities. This has driven the continuous transfer of rural labor to non-agricultural sectors in cities and towns, resulting in the abandonment of marginal cropland (Benayas et al., 2007; Sikor et al., 2009); (ii) The increasingly severe aging population, with rural areas facing a more acute aging problem than urban areas. This has caused a shortage of agricultural labor in rural areas, further inducing cropland abandonment by farmers (Lin, 2015; Yang & Xu, 2015); (iii) Against the backdrop of globalization, changes in international and domestic markets have led to rising prices of agricultural production factors and falling prices of agricultural products. This has resulted in relatively low comparative agricultural benefits and the gradual marginalization of agriculture, posing challenges to the rational utilization of cropland (Aide & Grau, 2004; Gao & Yao, 2022; Kong, 2016); (iv) The underdeveloped markets for agricultural socialized services and cropland transfer, along with the relatively low level of large-scale agricultural operations. Cropland that some farmers are unable to cultivate can hardly be transferred out or obtain effective trusteeship services (Zheng, 2020).

From the micro perspective, the socio-economic factors of cropland abandonment by farmers can be summarized as follows: (i) The loss of agricultural labor due to farmers' non-agricultural employment (Abolina & Luzadis, 2015; Xie & Huang, 2022; Xu et al., 2019); (ii) High agricultural production costs that squeeze profit margins, such as rising labor costs (Strijker, 2005; Li & Li, 2017), increasing prices of agricultural materials (Alix-Garcia et al., 2012), and high costs of agricultural socialized services (Jiang, 2020); (iii) Low and volatile agricultural product prices, which increase the risks of farming (Cao et al., 2008; Zhang et al., 2019); (iv) A high dependency ratio (Khanal & Watanabe, 2006; Zheng & Qian, 2022).

#### 2.1.3.3 Political and Institutional Factors

Political and institutional factors such as inadequate land reform and imperfect land systems are also important incentives for cropland abandonment by farmers. A common case is that of Central and Eastern European countries in the 1990s (Sikor et al., 2009). After the collapse of the Soviet Union in 1991, the agricultural land property rights system in these countries began to shift from public ownership to private ownership, leading to increasing fragmentation of agricultural land ownership. A large amount of privatized cropland was owned by people without agricultural production experience (Deininger et al., 2012). This not only weakened large-scale agricultural operations but also caused a sharp rise in land transaction costs (Baumann et al., 2011; Prishchepov et al., 2012). Therefore, affected by the collapse of the Soviet Union, the rate of cropland abandonment in Central and Eastern European countries was particularly high (Bakker et al., 2011; Ioffe & Nefedova, 2004; Kuemmerle et al., 2008). Defects in the legal and policy framework, as well as inefficient land registration services, also contributed to large-scale cropland abandonment (Alix-Garcia et al., 2012; Deininger et al., 2012). From 1991 to 2000, approximately 31% of cropland (or 57 million hectares) was abandoned (Stefanski et al., 2014). Among these countries, Russia was the most severely affected by the Soviet Union's collapse in terms of cropland abandonment.

The imperfect agricultural land property rights system in China is also considered an important institutional factor for cropland abandonment by farmers (Zheng & Qian, 2022). Under the household contract system, adjustments to agricultural land have been repeatedly prohibited but remain prevalent, resulting in poor stability of agricultural land property rights and exacerbating cropland abandonment by farmers (Feng et al., 2013; Li et al., 2014; Liu, 2020; Xu et al., 2008; Yu et al., 2003). In addition, the rural social security system is also incomplete. To a certain extent, cropland still assumes the functions of employment and elderly support, serving as a fallback for farmers who fail to secure jobs in cities (He, 2017; Wen, 2009). Therefore, some farmers would rather abandon their cropland than transfer it out (Tan, 2003).

#### 2.1.3.4 Technological and Cultural Factors

The impact of agricultural production technology and farming culture on cropland abandonment by farmers cannot be ignored. The impact of technology on cropland abandonment by farmers is complex. Deng et al. (2019) used survey data from 8031 farmers across 27 provinces in China and an endogenous switching regression model to explore the impact of farmers' internet use on cropland abandonment. The study found that in terms of spatial distribution, the spatial agglomeration trend of farmers' internet use was opposite to that of the area of abandoned cropland; in terms of quantitative relationship, internet use reduced the probability of cropland abandonment by farmers by 43.20%. Based on evidence from the southern United States, Rudel, 2001 found that agricultural production technology had a negative impact on cropland abandonment. Specifically, between 1935 and 1970, agricultural counties with rapid increases in per mu yield experienced the abandonment of marginal cropland, while those with slow increases in per mu yield were in the stage of deforestation for cultivation. The possible reason why agricultural technology induces cropland abandonment is that under the trend of growing global food demand, agricultural technological progress reduces the demand for cropland, making it possible to shrink the scope of cropland utilization. This in turn leads to the intensive use of high-quality cropland and the irrational use of marginal cropland, potentially increasing the likelihood of cropland abandonment by farmers (Li & Li, 2017). At the same time, there is no conclusive finding on the impact of cultural factors on cropland abandonment by farmers. Based on a case study in Slovakia, Lieskovský et al. (2015) pointed out that cultural factors played a role in the governance of cropland abandonment by farmers, such as changes in rural culture, the attractiveness and diversity of agricultural production and lifestyles, the inheritance of traditions, and restrictions related to health and age. However, domestic studies have also noted that due to the deep "land attachment complex" of many Chinese farmers, after settling in cities, they would rather abandon their cropland than transfer it to others (Tan, 2003; Yang & Xu, 2015).

## 2.1.4 *Impact Effects of Cropland Abandonment by Farmers*

### 2.1.4.1 Impact on Food Security

Where there is land, there is grain. Cropland serves as the foundational carrier of food production, and changes in cropland area are closely tied to food output. Since cropland abandonment constitutes the idleness and waste of cropland resources, it directly reduces the area of usable cropland—thereby threatening food production, causing declines in local food output, and further triggering problems such as food shortages and malnutrition, all of which exert negative impacts on national or regional food security (Khanal & Watanabe, 2006; Queiroz et al., 2014; Verburg et al., 2008; Zhang et al., 2019). In this sense, cropland abandonment by farmers undoubtedly increases the difficulty for countries to respond to food security and food nutrition crises (Deng et al., 2018; Xu et al., 2019).

By constructing a mediating effect model of cropland abandonment, Li et al. (2021) empirically examined the impact of such abandonment on food output. The study found that cropland abandonment had a significant negative effect on food output: in 2017, it led to a food output loss of up to 22.656 million tons in major grain-producing areas, accounting for 4.69% of the national total food output.

However, some scholars have questioned whether cropland abandonment will inevitably harm food security, though these views currently lack empirical support. For instance, Luo (2012) argues that whether cropland abandonment triggers food security risks depends on multiple conditions: cropland abandonment does not equate to a reduction in total cropland area, as the reclamation of abandoned cropland can maintain stable cropland stocks; furthermore, a decline in grain-sown area does not necessarily lead to lower food output, since technological innovation and crop variety improvement can offset the reduction in sown area without decreasing yields. Huang and Li (2021) further point out that food security is essentially determined by the contradiction between human needs and land resources. In the short term, the abandonment of some cropland—driven by domestic and foreign market mechanisms and farmers' voluntary choices—will not threaten China's food security, as such cropland is mostly marginal land with poor farming conditions.

Therefore, overall, the claim that cropland abandonment triggers food security issues is largely based on the assumption of large-scale or long-term abandonment. Whether small-scale and short-term cropland abandonment affects food output still requires more empirical verification. Nevertheless, for a populous developing country like China with limited arable land, it is always necessary to prevent and mitigate the potential impact of cropland abandonment by farmers on food security (Li & Li, 2017; Zheng & Qian, 2022).

#### 2.1.4.2 Impact on Ecosystems

This semi-natural artificial ecosystem—deprived of human management—will gradually evolve into a natural ecosystem over time. Thus, cropland abandonment exerts a significant impact on ecosystems themselves (Stoate et al., 2009). Specifically, the impacts of cropland abandonment on ecosystems mainly include the following aspects: (i) Hydrological and soil effects: It alters surface runoff, reduces water availability (Rey Benayas et al., 2007), increases soil infiltration rates (Bakker et al., 2008), mitigates soil erosion and water loss (Jiao et al., 2007; Liu et al., 2012), and produces comparative effects on soil erosion processes (Ruiz-Flano et al., 1992; Stanchi et al., 2012); (ii) Carbon cycle and climate regulation: It enhances soil carbon storage, facilitates the carbon cycle of terrestrial ecosystems, and contributes to improving the global ecological environment and mitigating the greenhouse effect (Kuemmerle et al., 2011; Silver et al., 2000; Schierhorn et al., 2013; Kuemmerle et al., 2015; Kurganova et al., 2014; van der Zanden et al., 2017); (iii) Ecological risks: It promotes vegetation homogenization in abandoned areas, elevates the risk of wildfires, triggers forest fires, and induces natural disasters (Moreira & Russo, 2007); (iv) Ecological restoration potential: It boosts the potential for ecological restoration. By providing diverse ecosystem services (Bondeau et al., 2007; Knops & Tilman, 2000), it aids in the restoration of forest ecosystems (Bowen et al., 2007; Chazdon, 2008); (v) Biodiversity impacts: It affects biodiversity (Cramer et al., 2008; MacDonald et al., 2000), particularly land biodiversity (Plieninger et al., 2014; Queiroz et al., 2014). Cropland abandonment directly drives changes in the land system: abandoned cropland gradually converts to grassland, shrubland, and other land types (Zhang et al., 2019), which disrupts the habitats of birds and arthropods that originally inhabited the farmland system, leading to a substantial decline in wild populations (Doxa et al., 2010).

#### 2.1.4.3 Impact on Rural Development

In addition to its impacts on food security and ecosystems, cropland abandonment also exerts a strong negative impact on rural development. As a core element of rural development, cropland not only serves the function of agricultural production but also has other value dimensions such as leisure tourism, landscape aesthetics, and cultural inheritance (Buijs et al., 2006; Li & Li, 2017).

Moreover, with the transformation of economic and social development, people's living standards and consumption levels have continuously improved, and the consumption structure has become increasingly diversified. The development and utilization of the non-production functions of cropland have thus become a key driver for the integration of rural industries (Yang et al., 2019). Therefore, when cropland is abandoned, agricultural landscapes will degrade to varying degrees (Fischer et al., 2012), traditional farming culture and aesthetic values will be partially lost, and villages may face the risk of decline (Benjamin et al., 2007).

In addition, cropland abandonment is mostly caused by the decline in village population—especially labor outflow (Sikor et al., 2009; Xu et al., 2019). However, the long-term abandonment of cropland makes it difficult to effectively restore its production function (Strijker, 2005), which further accelerates labor outflow and reduces the attractiveness of villages. This traps these villages in a vicious cycle (Brouwer, 2008), hinders the sustainable development of agriculture (Liu & Xiong, 2018), and diminishes the contribution of the agricultural sector to rural economic development (Baumann et al., 2011).

### *2.1.5 Governance Measures for Cropland Abandonment by Farmers*

Although few studies have directly quantified governance measures for cropland abandonment, scholars have successively proposed a series of countermeasures to promote effective governance of the issue, based on its driving factors. To summarize, the governance measures for cropland abandonment by farmers mainly include the following:

Improving the agricultural land property rights system: The foundation of cropland protection lies in property rights protection, and farmers' cropland utilization behavior is largely closely tied to the agricultural land property rights system (Yu et al., 2003; Zheng et al., 2021). Ambiguity of agricultural land property rights subjects, unclear definition of property rights, unstable property rights, and incomplete property rights can all trigger cropland abandonment by farmers (Cao et al., 2008; Luo et al., 2017; Zheng & Qian, 2022).

Upgrading agricultural production conditions: Efforts should be made to advance land consolidation, maintain terrace walls, construct machine-cultivated roads, rebuild farmland water conservancy facilities, and promote contiguous and centralized cropland management (Inbar & Llerena, 2000; Shi & Li, 2013; Wang et al., 2022; Yang & Xu, 2015). These actions will continuously improve agricultural infrastructure and farming conditions, addressing cropland abandonment by farmers caused by marginal cropland issues such as cropland fragmentation and low cropland quality (Cao et al., 2008; Xie and Huang, 2021).

Improving the agricultural land transfer market: Farmers should be encouraged to participate in agricultural land transfer voluntarily, and cropland should be guided to concentrate in an orderly manner toward new agricultural business entities to develop appropriate-scale agricultural operations. This will enhance the marketization level of agricultural land transfer, improve the allocation and utilization efficiency of cropland resources (Ji & Qian, 2018; Li & Qin, 2022; Zhou et al., 2020), and prevent surplus cropland from being abandoned (Deininger et al., 2012; Guo et al., 2020; Zhang et al., 2014).

Developing agricultural socialized services, especially socialized agricultural machinery services: The construction of the agricultural socialized service system should be strengthened, agricultural socialized service organizations cultivated, and the market for outsourced agricultural services improved. Enhancing the level of agricultural socialized services to meet farmers' demand for outsourced services (Cao et al., 2008; Chen & Han, 2021; Xie & Huang, 2022) will help resolve cropland abandonment by farmers caused by labor shortages (Lu et al., 2022; Luo et al., 2019; Xue et al., 2022).

Increasing productive agricultural subsidies: Agricultural subsidies themselves function as an incentive and restraint mechanism: on the one hand, suspending subsidy payments can restrict farmers' cropland abandonment behavior; on the other hand, increasing agricultural subsidies can boost enthusiasm for agricultural production and operation (Strijker, 2005; Zheng & Qian, 2022). Empirical evidence from Europe and Japan has shown that providing agricultural subsidies to farmers can effectively alleviate cropland abandonment caused by low comparative agricultural benefits (Estel et al., 2015; Li & Li, 2017).

In addition, improving the level of village organization (Feng et al., 2021), increasing the adoption of agricultural technology (Xu et al., 2017), promoting agricultural branding (Baldock et al., 1996), and raising the grain purchase price (Yang & Xu, 2015) are also considered feasible measures to govern cropland abandonment by farmers.

### 2.1.6 Research Review and Prospect

In summary, existing literature has conducted extensive, rich, and valuable discussions on the conceptual connotation, influencing factors, and impact effects of cropland abandonment by farmers, as well as the governance measures derived therefrom. This provides sufficient literature support and a solid theoretical foundation for the in-depth development of this project. However, from the perspective of existing achievements, the following three aspects still require further deepening and exploration.

Firstly, in terms of research perspective. Although some studies have briefly mentioned the potential impacts of population aging, cropland marginalization, and agricultural marginalization on cropland abandonment by farmers (Cao et al., 2008; Lin, 2015; Wang et al., 2022; Zhang et al., 2016), few scholars have specifically explored the issue from the "People-Land-Money-Rights" perspective—especially in the Chinese context, where systematic examination of the aforementioned practical challenges facing current cropland abandonment by farmers is lacking. Meanwhile, there are also few academic studies that use large-sample survey data to analyze the temporal and spatial variation trends of cropland abandonment by farmers in China (Guo et al., 2020). To date, only Zhang et al. (2019) have conducted a meta-analysis by extracting literature on cropland abandonment from the CNKI database spanning 1992 to 2017.

Secondly, in terms of research content. Although some scholars have briefly mentioned farmland consolidation, agricultural machinery services, and agricultural subsidies in the policy implication section of their empirical studies—for example, Zhang et al. (2014) and Mou et al. (2022) proposed strengthening agricultural infrastructure construction in response to the reality that poor farming conditions in mountainous areas easily lead to cropland abandonment; Han and Song (2019) suggested increasing agricultural subsidies based on the situation that rising agricultural labor costs trigger abandonment; and Xu et al. (2019) argued that abandonment caused by non-agricultural employment of labor in plain areas can be addressed by promoting agricultural machinery—few scholars have directly quantified governance measures for cropland abandonment (including land consolidation, agricultural machinery services, and agricultural subsidies), conducted empirical research on the effectiveness of different governance measures, or further put forward policy recommendations for optimizing the governance of cropland abandonment by farmers.

Thirdly, in terms of research data and methods. Currently, most literature related to cropland abandonment uses cross-sectional data based on surveys in specific provinces and cities (Li & Dai, 2014; Luo et al., 2017, 2019; Yan et al., 2016; Zhang et al., 2014, 2018; Xie and Huang, 2021), which are relatively insufficient in terms of national representativeness and temporal variability. Meanwhile, most studies adopt Logit, Probit, and Tobit models (Xie & Huang, 2022; Xu et al., 2019; Xue et al., 2022; Yan et al., 2016), focusing on exploring the influencing factors of cropland abandonment by farmers and emphasizing correlations rather than causal relationships. This means the validity and credibility of some research conclusions remain open to further discussion.

In view of the above considerations, building on previous studies, this book will adopt the "People-Land-Money-Rights" perspective, comprehensively use nationally representative data from the China Rural Household Panel Survey (CRHPS) and the China Labor-force Dynamics Survey (CLDS), and apply modern econometric methods including panel fixed-effect models, the Instrumental Variable (IV) method, the Difference-in-Difference (DID) model, the Propensity Score Matching (PSM) model, and the Inverse Probability Weighted Regression Adjustment (IPWRA) model. It will examine the impacts of non-agricultural employment, cropland fragmentation, comparative agricultural benefits, and insecure land property rights on cropland abandonment by farmers, and identify the key driving factors of such abandonment. On this basis, it will further quantify the inhibitory effects of governance measures—such as the development of new agricultural business entities, the construction of farmland water conservancy projects, agricultural subsidy reforms, and land property rights reforms—on cropland abandonment, thereby providing decision-making references for promoting the effective governance of cropland abandonment.

## 2.2 Analytical Framework

Accurately identifying the key drivers behind farmers' abandonment of cropland is the prerequisite and foundation for effectively addressing this issue. As a land use phenomenon, cropland abandonment results from the combined effects of natural, economic, social, and political factors. However, from the perspective of "People-Land-Money-Rights," cropland abandonment by farmers is ultimately influenced by four key factors: labor, land, income, and land rights. Integrating existing research findings, the primary drivers of cropland abandonment in the Chinese context are off-farm employment ("People"), fragmented land ("Land"), low comparative returns in agriculture ("Money"), and insecure land tenure ("Rights").

### *2.2.1 Key Drivers of Cropland Abandonment by Farmers*

Off-farm employment is the direct cause of farmers abandoning their cropland. Theoretically, off-farm employment directly leads to a shortage of agricultural labor, thereby increasing the likelihood of cropland abandonment. Particularly after the Lewis turning point, the phenomenon of surplus rural labor has largely disappeared (Cai, 2018). Consequently, the continuous migration of large numbers of migrant workers from rural to urban areas has made the question of who will farm the cropland in rural areas increasingly pressing (Xu et al., 2019). According to data from the annual Migrant Worker Monitoring Survey Report released by the National Bureau of Statistics of China, the number of migrant workers has steadily increased. In 2010, the total number of migrant workers nationwide was 242 million; by 2015, it reached 277 million; and by 2024, it had surged to 299 million.[1]. This trend indicates that both the pace and scale of rural labor shifting to non-agricultural industries are expanding, leading to increasingly severe labor shortages in rural areas. Moreover, the rise in off-farm employment not only reduces the quantity of agricultural labor but also alters its quality (Zheng, 2024a). Younger and more skilled workers increasingly opt for off-farm jobs, leaving behind an aging workforce with lower educational attainment. This shift in labor composition further diminishes agricultural productivity, increases production costs, and weakens farmers' willingness to cultivate land, thereby exacerbating the abandonment of cropland (Lu, 2020). Therefore, when exploring effective governance strategies for cropland abandonment, it is essential to fully consider the potential negative impact of off-farm employment on this phenomenon. Mitigating the shortage of agricultural labor through the cultivation of new types of agricultural

[1] The data can be accessed from https://www.stats.gov.cn/sj/zxfb/202504/t20250430_1959523.html

business operating entities is crucial to achieving effective protection and sustainable utilization of cropland.

Land fragmentation is a key trigger for farmers abandoning cropland. Theoretically, fragmented land increases agricultural production costs, inadvertently raising the difficulty of farming and leading to cropland abandonment (Deininger et al., 2012; Zhang et al., 2018). In the Chinese context, land fragmentation is pronounced, with each household owning an average of about five plots of cropland (Zheng et al., 2023). These plots are small and scattered, a situation particularly pronounced in the hilly and mountainous regions of southern China (Wang et al., 2022). This highly fragmented land pattern not only restricts the adoption of agricultural mechanization and new technologies but also increases infrastructure costs for irrigation, drainage, and other systems (Xue et al., 2022). Consequently, agricultural production costs rise significantly (Kawasaki, 2010), reducing agricultural productivity (Latruffe & Piet, 2014; Lu et al., 2019), and complicates land transfers (Liu et al., 2019). Even when farmers are willing to offer land for free, finding willing tenants proves difficult. These factors ultimately drive farmers to abandon their croplands (Deininger et al., 2017; Zheng et al., 2025). When exploring effective governance of cropland abandonment, it is essential to fully consider the potential negative impact of land fragmentation on this phenomenon. Strengthening agricultural water conservancy projects to improve production conditions can help curb the expansion of cropland abandonment.

The low agricultural comparative returns are the economic root cause of farmers abandoning cropland. Theoretically, insufficient agricultural comparative returns weaken farmers' motivation for agricultural production, prompting them to shift toward higher-yielding non-agricultural industries and thereby exacerbating the phenomenon of abandoned cropland. According to data from the annual National Agricultural Product Cost and Revenue Data Compilation released by the National Development and Reform Commission of China, agricultural product prices have fluctuated significantly in recent years, while production costs have continued to rise. On one hand, prices for agricultural inputs such as seeds, fertilizers, and pesticides have steadily increased, raising the basic costs of agricultural production. On the other hand, labor costs in agriculture have significantly risen due to the migration of labor to non-agricultural industries in urban areas (Wu et al., 2024). Additionally, increased land transfer costs, particularly rising rents, have further squeezed the profit margins of agricultural production (Liu et al., 2019). For instance, between 2011 and 2022, the total cost per mu (1 mu = 1/15 ha) for rice cultivation increased from 896.98 yuan to 1361.91 yuan, a rise of approximately 51.83%. Within this, material and service expenses grew from 409.34 yuan per mu to 644.72 yuan per mu, labor costs from 327.96 yuan to 457.13 yuan per mu, and land costs from 159.68 yuan to 260.06 yuan per mu.[2] However, the increase in agricultural product prices during the same period lagged far behind the rise in costs, resulting in reduced actual income for farmers. Under these circumstances, farmers increasingly prefer off-farm

[2] The data can be accessed from https://www.weihengag.com/home/article/detail/id/22845

employment for higher economic returns, exacerbating the abandonment of cropland (Xu et al., 2019; Zheng, 2024b). Therefore, enhancing agriculture's comparative profitability and reducing production costs—particularly by curbing unreasonable increases in land transfer rents—are critical measures to mitigate cropland abandonment and safeguard food security.

Insecure land tenure is the institutional root cause of farmers abandoning cropland. Theoretically, land tenure insecurity encourages predatory land use practices, hinders the development of land rental markets, and ultimately leads to cropland abandonment (Deininger et al., 2012). Under conditions of insecure land tenure, farmers worry about the uncertain future returns on their land (Zheng, 2024), lacking motivation for long-term investments such as improving soil fertility or constructing irrigation facilities. This short-term behavior may degrade land quality, subsequently affecting agricultural productivity and income (Besley, 1995). Furthermore, insecure land tenure can lead to an inactive land rental market, making it difficult for farmers willing to transfer their land to find suitable tenants and increasing the risk of cropland abandonment (Margaret et al., 2022). In some regions, inadequate land rental mechanisms and poor information flow further complicate land transfers (Wang et al., 2015), exacerbating the problem of abandoned cropland. Therefore, deepening land tenure reforms to enhance the security of land tenure rights is a pivotal institutional safeguard for reducing abandoned cropland and ensuring food security.

### 2.2.2 Governance Measures for Farmers' Cropland Abandonment

Since off-farm employment, land fragmentation, agricultural comparative returns, and insecure land tenure are regarded as key drivers of cropland abandonment by farmers, it is particularly necessary to explore relevant governance measures that specifically address the conditions enabling such abandonment. The Chinese government has placed high priority on addressing cropland abandonment, implementing multiple measures to tackle the issue. Certain initiatives—particularly the cultivation of new agricultural business entities, construction of farmland water conservancy projects, agricultural subsidy reforms, and land tenure reforms—have the potential to block the conditions enabling cropland abandonment. This could mitigate the negative impacts of off-farm employment, land fragmentation, declining agricultural returns, and insecure land tenure on cropland abandonment. To this end, this book attempts to quantify the effectiveness of these governance measures. Adopting a "People-Land-Money-Rights" perspective, it empirically examines the impact of new agricultural operating entities ("People"), farmland water conservancy projects ("Land"), agricultural subsidy reforms ("Money"), and land tenure reforms ("Rights") on cropland abandonment. This analysis aims to evaluate the efficacy of these governance measures.

New agricultural operating entities can address the challenge of who will farm the land. Theoretically, they will alleviate the shortage of agricultural labor caused by off-farm employment, thereby reducing the occurrence of abandoned cropland. In the Chinese context, new agricultural operating entities refer to large-scale farming households, including professional operators, family farms, farming companies, and agricultural cooperatives (Huang & Liang, 2018). Professional operators derive their income primarily from agriculture, operating at a scale far exceeding that of ordinary smallholders. Family farms leverage household labor for scaled, intensive, and commercial production. Farming companies adopt modern corporate management practices, boasting strong economic capacity and technological advantages. Agricultural cooperatives achieve resource sharing and risk pooling through collective production. By implementing scaled operations and mechanized production, these entities reduce labor costs, thereby alleviating labor shortages. Simultaneously, these new agricultural entities leverage advanced technology and management expertise to provide technical guidance to surrounding farmers (Li, 2017), enhancing their agricultural skills and production efficiency. Thus, they not only mitigate labor shortages through scaled operations and mechanization but also strengthen neighboring farmers' production capacity and risk resilience through technical support, effectively reducing the likelihood of cropland abandonment.

The construction of farmland water conservancy projects can improve agricultural production conditions and, in theory, help mitigate the adverse effects of land fragmentation on land use. By establishing comprehensive infrastructure such as irrigation and drainage systems, power transmission and distribution networks, field roads, and farmland protection facilities, these projects promote contiguous and centralized land management (Hao et al., 2024). This approach reduces agricultural production costs and enhances efficiency. A well-developed irrigation system ensures crops receive adequate water even during dry seasons, minimizing yield risks caused by water shortages. Well-designed drainage facilities effectively prevent waterlogging, preserving soil structure and fertility. Power transmission and distribution infrastructure guarantees electricity supply for agricultural production, enabling the reliable operation of farm machinery and irrigation equipment. Improved field roads enhance the efficiency of agricultural product transportation while lowering logistics costs. Protective engineering measures effectively guard against natural disasters, shielding farmland from hazards like wind erosion and soil erosion. The enhancement of these infrastructure systems not only improves land utilization conditions but also facilitates land transfers and large-scale operations, further boosting land efficiency and economic returns (Xu et al., 2025). Consequently, agricultural water conservancy projects not only improve production conditions and promote contiguous land management but also provide robust support for reducing cropland abandonment, serving as a vital safeguard for sustainable land use.

Agricultural subsidy reforms will enhance farmers' access to subsidies and increase their income, thereby improving the comparative returns of agriculture and reducing the abandonment of cropland caused by insufficient agricultural income. In May 2015, China's Ministry of Finance and Ministry of Agriculture issued the

*Guiding Opinions on Adjusting and Improving the Three Agricultural Subsidy Policies*, launching pilot reforms of the agricultural subsidy system. In April 2016, the two ministries further issued the *Notice on Fully Launching the Reform of the Agricultural Three Subsidies*. This reform consolidated the original agricultural input subsidy, high-quality seed subsidy, and grain direct subsidy into a single agricultural support and protection subsidy. It explicitly states that subsidies go to those who cultivate the land and mandates that payments be disbursed to farmers in a single installment by June 30 each year. Simultaneously, subsidies are tied to farmland conservation: farmers who abandon their land or change its designated use will not receive subsidies. This reform enhanced the precision and timeliness of subsidies, ensuring farmers actively engaged in agricultural production receive timely support to alleviate financial pressures (Fan et al., 2023). Furthermore, the reform expanded the subsidy fund pool, increased farmers' subsidy income, and boosted the economic efficiency of agricultural production. Through these measures, the agricultural subsidy reform not only increased farmers' production motivation but also enhanced their agricultural comparative returns, thereby helping curb the phenomenon of cropland abandonment.

Land tenure reforms enhance the security of land rights by safeguarding farmers' subsistence and development rights, thereby incentivizing increased agricultural investment and reducing the likelihood of cropland abandonment. Secure land tenure is crucial for agricultural production, as farmers are only willing to make long-term investments to improve soil quality and boost agricultural productivity when they are confident their land rights are protected (Holden et al., 2009). When land tenure is insecure, farmers worry they may not recoup their investments from future land returns, making them more likely to abandon marginal lands with poorer cultivation conditions (Saint-Macary et al., 2010). However, land tenure reforms such as land certification can effectively address farmers' insecurity regarding land rights, strengthening their willingness to make long-term investments in the land (Kassa, 2014). Once farmers' land security is guaranteed, their future expectations become more stable, making them more likely to adopt long-term measures such as using organic fertilizers to improve soil fertility (Zheng et al., 2023). This not only enhances land productivity but also reduces the abandonment of cropland due to poor soil fertility. Therefore, by enhancing tenure security, land tenure reforms provide farmers with stable land use expectations, incentivizing increased agricultural investment and effectively reducing the likelihood of cropland abandonment.

In the light of the above discussion, the research ideas of this book can be summarized as follows: Using "People-Land-Money-Rights" as the analytical clue, this book leverages nationally representative household-level panel data and modern econometric approaches to empirically investigate two core issues regarding cropland abandonment: its driving factors (addressing the "why" question) and targeted governance measures (addressing the "how" question). To elaborate, by exploring why farmers abandon their croplands and how such abandonment can be effectively governed, this study aims to provide evidence-based decision-making support for

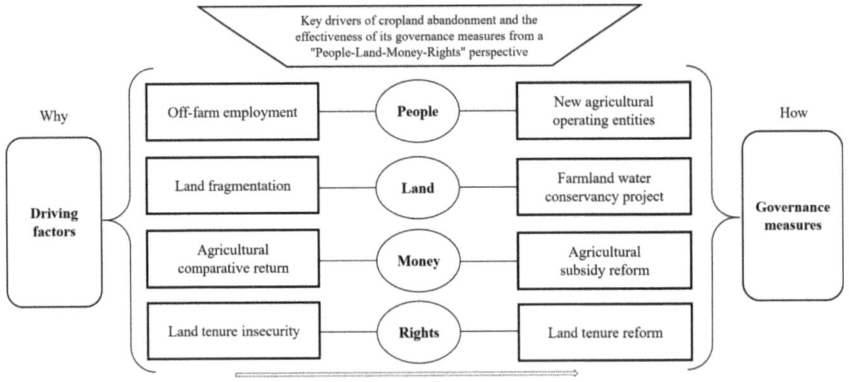


**Fig. 2.1** The analytical framework of this book

safeguarding national food security and advancing sustainable agricultural development through the efficient governance of cropland abandonment. Specifically, the analytical framework of this book is structured as follows Fig. 2.1.

## References


Abolina, E., & Luzadis, V. A. (2015). Abandoned agricultural land and its potential for short rotation woody crops in Latvia. *Land Use Policy, 49*, 435–445.

Aide, T. M., & Grau, H. R. (2004). Globalization, migration, and Latin American ecosystems. *American Association for the Advancement of Science, 305*, 1915–1916.

Alix-Garcia, J., Kuemmerle, T., & Radeloff, V. C. (2012). Prices, land tenure institutions, and geography: A matching analysis of farmland abandonment in post-socialist Eastern Europe. *Land Economics, 88*, 425–443.

Bakker, M. M., Govers, G., Kosmas, C., Vanacker, V., Van Oost, K., & Rounsevell, M. (2005). Soil erosion as a driver of land-use change. *Agriculture, Ecosystems & Environment, 105*, 467–481.

Bakker, M. M., Govers, G., van Doorn, A., Quetier, F., Chouvardas, D., & Rounsevell, M. (2008). The response of soil erosion and sediment export to land-use change in four areas of Europe: The importance of landscape pattern. *Geomorphology, 98*, 213–226.

Bakker, M. M., Hatna, E., Kuhlman, T., & Mücher, C. (2011). Changing environmental characteristics of European cropland. *Agricultural Systems, 104*, 522–532.

Baldock, D., (1996). Environmental impacts of Agri-environmental measures. *Subsidies and Environment: Exploring the Linkages*, 123–137.

Baldock, D., Brouwer, F. M., Beaufoy, G., & Godeschalk, F. (1996). *Farming at the margins: Abandonment or redeployment of agricultural land in Europe.* IEEP London.

Baumann, M., Kuemmerle, T., Elbakidze, M., Ozdogan, M., Radeloff, V. C., Keuler, N. S., Prishchepov, A. V., Kruhlov, I., & Hostert, P. (2011). Patterns and drivers of post-socialist farmland abandonment in Western Ukraine. *Land Use Policy, 28*, 552–562.

Benjamin, K., Bouchard, A., & Domon, G. (2007). Abandoned farmlands as components of rural landscapes: An analysis of perceptions and representations. *Landscape and Urban Planning, 83*, 228–244.

Besley, T. (1995). Property rights and investment incentives: Theory and evidence from Ghana. *Journal of Political Economy, 103*, 903–937.

Bondeau, A., Smith, P. C., Zaehle, S., Schaphoff, S., Lucht, W., Cramer, W., Gerten, D., Lotze-Campen, H., Müller, C., & Reichstein, M. (2007). Modelling the role of agriculture for the 20th century global terrestrial carbon balance. *Global Change Biology, 13*, 679–706.

Bowen, M. E., McAlpine, C. A., House, A. P., & Smith, G. C. (2007). Regrowth forests on abandoned agricultural land: A review of their habitat values for recovering forest fauna. *Biological Conservation, 140*, 273–296.

Brouwer, F., (2008). Sustainable land management: strategies to cope with the marginalisation of agriculture. Edward Elgar Publishing.

Buijs, A. E., Pedroli, B., & Luginbühl, Y. (2006). From hiking through farmland to farming in a leisure landscape: Changing social perceptions of the European landscape. *Landscape Ecology, 21*, 375–389.

Cai, F. (2018). The great exodus: How agricultural surplus laborers have been transferred and reallocated in China's reform period? *China Agricultural Economic Review, 10*, 3–15.

Campbell, J. E., Lobell, D. B., Genova, R. C., & Field, C. B. (2008). The global potential of bioenergy on abandoned agriculture lands. *Environmental Science & Technology, 42*, 5791–5794.

Cao, Z. H., Hao, J. M., & Liang, L. T. (2008). Economic analysis and strategy research on farmers cultivated land abandonment behavior. *Journal of Agrotechnical Economics*, 43–46. (in Chinese).

Chazdon, R. L. (2008). Beyond deforestation: Restoring forests and ecosystem services on degraded lands. *Science, 320*, 1458–1460.

Chen, J. S., & Han, Q. (2021). Effect of agricultural productive services on farmland abandonment. *Journal of South China Agricultural University (Social Science Edition)*, 23–34. (in Chinese).

Chen, X. Y., & Zheng, G. Q. (2018). Research progress on arable land abandonment in China and abroad. *China Population, Resources and Environment, 28*, 37–41. (in Chinese).

Cramer, V. A., Hobbs, R. J., & Standish, R. J. (2008). What's new about old fields? Land abandonment and ecosystem assembly. *Trends in Ecology & Evolution, 23*, 104–112.

Deininger, K., Monchuk, D., Nagarajan, H. K., & Singh, S. K. (2017). Does land fragmentation increase the cost of cultivation? Evidence from India. *The Journal of Development Studies, 53*, 82–98.

Deininger, K., Savastano, S., & Carletto, C. (2012). Land fragmentation, cropland abandonment, and land market operation in Albania. *World Development, 40*, 2108–2122.

Deng, X., Xu, D., Qi, Y., & Zeng, M. (2018). Labor off-farm employment and cropland abandonment in rural China: Spatial distribution and empirical analysis. *International Journal of Environmental Research and Public Health, 15*, 1808.

Deng, X., Xu, D., Zeng, M., & Qi, Y. (2019). Does internet use help reduce rural cropland abandonment? *Evidence from China. Land Use Policy, 89*, 104243.

Di Gregorio, A. (2005). *Land cover classification system: Classification concepts and user manual: LCCS*. Food & Agriculture Org.

Díaz, G. I., Nahuelhual, L., Echeverría, C., & Marín, S. (2011). Drivers of land abandonment in southern Chile and implications for landscape planning. *Landscape and Urban Planning, 99*, 207–217.

Doxa, A., Bas, Y., Paracchini, M. L., Pointereau, P., Terres, J. M., & Jiguet, F. (2010). Low-intensity agriculture increases farmland bird abundances in France. *Journal of Applied Ecology, 47*, 1348–1356.

Estel, S., Kuemmerle, T., Alcántara, C., Levers, C., Prishchepov, A., & Hostert, P. (2015). Mapping farmland abandonment and recultivation across Europe using MODIS NDVI time series. *Remote Sensing of Environment, 163*, 312–325.

Fan, P., Mishra, A. K., Feng, S., Su, M., & Hirsch, S. (2023). The impact of China's new agricultural subsidy policy on grain crop acreage. *Food Policy, 118*, 102472.

Feng, G. Q., Li, J., Sun, R., Chen, Z. J., Zhang, S. Y., Ren, X. L., 2021. Can the organizational degree of villages restrict farmers' behavior of land abandonment? Chinese Journal of Population, Resources and Environment, 165–172 (in Chinese).

Feng, L., Jiang, Y., Ye, J. P., & Zhu, K. L. (2013). Farmers' attitudes during the institutional change of rural land readjustment in China: An empirical analysis based on a survey of 17 provinces from 1999 to 2010. *Journal of Management World*, 44–58. (in Chinese).

Fischer, J., Hartel, T., & Kuemmerle, T. (2012). Conservation policy in traditional farming landscapes. *Conservation Letters, 5*, 167–175.

Fox, J., Fujita, Y., Ngidang, D., Peluso, N., Potter, L., Sakuntaladewi, N., Sturgeon, J., & Thomas, D. (2009). Policies, political-economy, and swidden in Southeast Asia. *Human Ecology, 37*, 305–322.

Gao, M., & Yao, Z. (2022). Ensure the benefits of grain farmers in China: Theoretical logic, key issues and mechanism design. *Journal of Management World, 38*, 86–102. (in Chinese).

Gellrich, M., Baur, P., Koch, B., & Zimmermann, N. E. (2007). Agricultural land abandonment and natural forest re-growth in the Swiss mountains: A spatially explicit economic analysis. *Agriculture, Ecosystems & Environment, 118*, 93–108.

Guo, B. B., Fang, Y. L., Zhou, Y. K., (2020). Influencing factors and spatial differentiation of cultivated land abandonment at the household scale. Resources Science 42, 696–709 (in Chinese).

Han, Z., Song, W., 2019. Spatiotemporal variations in cropland abandonment in the Guizhou–Guangxi karst mountain area, China. Journal of Cleaner Production 238, 117888.

Hao, S., Wang, G., Yang, Y., Zhao, S., Huang, S., Liu, L., & Zhang, H. (2024). Promoting grain production through high-standard farmland construction: Evidence in China. *Journal of Integrative Agriculture, 23*, 324–335.

He, X. F., (2017). Family farming in response to an aging society. The Journal of Humanities, 103–109 (in Chinese).

Holden, S. T., Deininger, K., & Ghebru, H. (2009). Impacts of low–cost land certification on investment and productivity. *American Journal of Agricultural Economics, 91*, 359–373.

Huang, S. A., Li, Y. M., (2021). Rational cognition of farmland abandonment and government supervision. Social Science Front, 67–77 (in Chinese).

Huang, Z., & Liang, Q. (2018). Agricultural organizations and the role of farmer cooperatives in China since 1978: Past and future. *China Agricultural Economic Review, 10*, 48–64.

Inbar, M., & Llerena, C. A. (2000). Erosion processes in high mountain agricultural terraces in Peru. *Mountain Research and Development, 20*, 72–79.

Ioffe, G., & Nefedova, T. (2004). Marginal farmland in European Russia. *Eurasian Geography and Economics, 45*, 45–59.

Izquierdo, A. E., & Grau, H. R. (2009). Agriculture adjustment, land-use transition and protected areas in northwestern Argentina. *Journal of Environmental Management, 90*, 858–865.

Ji, X. Q., & Qian, Z. H. (2018). How to promote the transfer of farmland management rights in a targeted way? *Journal of Management World, 87-97*, 183–184. (in Chinese).

Jiang, C. Y., 2020. On the four relations in the development of agricultural production trusteeship service. Issues in Agricultural Economy, 55–63 (in Chinese).

Jiao, J., Tzanopoulos, J., Xofis, P., Bai, W., Ma, X., & Mitchley, J. (2007). Can the study of natural vegetation succession assist in the control of soil erosion on abandoned croplands on the loess plateau, China? *Restoration Ecology, 15*, 391–399.

Kassa, W., (2014). Land titling and investment in Tanzania: An empirical investigation. Available at SSRN 2480216.

Kawasaki, K. (2010). The costs and benefits of land fragmentation of rice farms in Japan. *Australian Journal of Agricultural and Resource Economics, 54*, 509–526.

Khanal, N. R., & Watanabe, T. (2006). Abandonment of agricultural land and its consequences. *Mountain Research and Development, 26*, 32–40.

Knops, J. M., & Tilman, D. (2000). Dynamics of soil nitrogen and carbon accumulation for 61 years after agricultural abandonment. *Ecology, 81*, 88–98.

Kobayashi, Y., Higa, M., Higashiyama, K., & Nakamura, F. (2020). Drivers of land-use changes in societies with decreasing populations: A comparison of the factors affecting farmland abandonment in a food production area in Japan. *PLoS One, 15*, e0235846.

Kong, X. Z. (2016). The basic connotation and policy suggestions on the structural reform of agricultural supply side. *Reform*, 104–115. (in Chinese).

Kuemmerle, T., Hostert, P., Radeloff, V. C., van der Linden, S., Perzanowski, K., & Kruhlov, I. (2008). Cross-border comparison of post-socialist farmland abandonment in the Carpathians. *Ecosystems, 11*, 614–628.

Kuemmerle, T., Olofsson, P., Chaskovskyy, O., Baumann, M., Ostapowicz, K., Woodcock, C. E., Houghton, R. A., Hostert, P., Keeton, W. S., & Radeloff, V. C. (2011). Post-soviet farmland abandonment, forest recovery, and carbon sequestration in western Ukraine. *Global Change Biology, 17*, 1335–1349.

Kurganova, I., Lopes de Gerenyu, V., Six, J., & Kuzyakov, Y. (2014). Carbon cost of collective farming collapse in Russia. *Global Change Biology, 20*, 938–947.

Latruffe, L., & Piet, L. (2014). Does land fragmentation affect farm performance? A case study from Brittany, France. *Agricultural Systems, 129*, 68–80.

Li, J. Y., & Qin, F. (2022). How to overcome the demand dilemma of farmland transfer in China? Evidence from the development of new agricultural operators. *Journal of Management World, 84-99*, 6. (in Chinese).

Li, S., & Li, X. (2017). Global understanding of farmland abandonment: A review and prospects. *Journal of Geographical Sciences, 27*, 1123–1150.

Li, W. H., Dai, Z. L., (2014). A hypothesis of farmland abandoning based on the farmers' family characters. China Population, Resources and Environment 24, 143–149 (in Chinese).

Li, Y. L., Ma, W. Q., Jiang, G. H., Li, G. Y., & Zhou, D. Y. (2021). The degree of cultivated land abandonment and its influence on grain yield in main grain producing areas of China. *Journal of Natural Resources, 36*, 1439–1454. (in Chinese).

Li, Z. (2017). China's agricultural basic operating system. In Z. Li (Ed.), *Reform and development of agriculture in China* (pp. 65–79). Springer Singapore.

Li, Z. H., Yan, J. Z., Hua, X. B., Xin, L. J., Li, X. B., (2014). Factors influencing the cultivated land abandonment of households of different types: A case study of 12 typical villages in Chongqing municipality. Geographical Research 33, 721–734 (in Chinese).

Lieskovský, J., Bezák, P., Špulerová, J., Lieskovský, T., Koleda, P., Dobrovodská, M., Bürgi, M., Gimmi, U., (2015). The abandonment of traditional agricultural landscape in Slovakia–Analysis of extent and driving forces. Journal of Rural Studies 37, 75–84.

Lin, B. (2015). An analysis on the status and trend of old population without self-care ability in China. *Population & Economics*, 77–84.

Liu, S. Y. (2020). Micro-level land institution foundations of agricultural performance in China: A book review on rural land property rights and agricultural performance. *China Land Science*, 105–110. (in Chinese).

Liu, S. Y., Xiong, X. F., 2018. Implementation and institutional supply of China's rural revitalization strategy. China Review of Political Economy, 80–96 (in Chinese).

Liu, Y., Fu, B., Lü, Y., Wang, Z., & Gao, G. (2012). Hydrological responses and soil erosion potential of abandoned cropland in the loess plateau, China. *Geomorphology, 138*, 404–414.

Liu, Y., Yan, B., Wang, Y., & Zhou, Y. (2019). Will land transfer always increase technical efficiency in China?—A land cost perspective. *Land Use Policy, 82*, 414–421.

Lu, C. (2020). Does household laborer migration promote farmland abandonment in China? *Growth and Change, 51*, 1804–1836.

Lu, H., Xie, H., & Yao, G. (2019). Impact of land fragmentation on marginal productivity of agricultural labor and non-agricultural labor supply: A case study of Jiangsu, China. *Habitat International, 83*, 65–72.

Lu, H., Zhou, Y. H., Zhang, P. W., Geng, X. H., 2022. Impact of socialized agricultural services on farmland abandonment: Empirical evidence based on Chinese family database. China Land Science, 69–78 (in Chinese).

Luo, B. L., Wan, Y. L., Hong, W. J., Zhong, W. J., 2019. Fragmentation, service outsourcing and farmland abandonment—An empirical analysis based on questionnaires from 2704 households in 9 provinces. Economic Review Journal, 63–73 (in Chinese).

Luo, Y. H., 2012. Does farmland abandonment inevitably endanger national food security. Modern Economic Research, 64–69 (in Chinese).

Luo, M. Z., Liu, K., Zhu, W. J., 2017. Has land certification reduced farmland abandonment? An empirical analysis: Based on PSM from farmer questionnaire surveys in Sichuan, Henan and Shanxi provinces. Journal of Agrotechnical Economics, 15–27 (in Chinese).

Ma, W., Zhu, Z., & Zhou, X. (2022). Agricultural mechanization and cropland abandonment in rural China. *Applied Economics Letters, 29*, 526–533.

MacDonald, D., Crabtree, J. R., Wiesinger, G., Dax, T., Stamou, N., Fleury, P., Lazpita, J. G., & Gibon, A. (2000). Agricultural abandonment in mountain areas of Europe: Environmental consequences and policy response. *Journal of Environmental Management, 59*, 47–69.

Mather, A. (2001). The transition from deforestation to reforestation in Europe, agricultural technologies and tropical deforestation. *CAB International Wallingford UK.*, 35–52.

Meyfroidt, P., Schierhorn, F., Prishchepov, A. V., Müller, D., & Kuemmerle, T. (2016). Drivers, constraints and trade-offs associated with recultivating abandoned cropland in Russia, Ukraine and Kazakhstan. *Global Environmental Change, 37*, 1–15.

Moreira, F., & Russo, D. (2007). Modelling the impact of agricultural abandonment and wildfires on vertebrate diversity in Mediterranean Europe. *Landscape Ecology, 22*, 1461–1476.

Mottet, A., Ladet, S., Coqué, N., & Gibon, A. (2006). Agricultural land-use change and its drivers in mountain landscapes: A case study in the Pyrenees. *Agriculture, Ecosystems & Environment, 114*, 296–310.

Mou, Y., Zhao, Y. L., Li, X. B., Ren, H. Y., & Liu, Y. (2022). The influence of plot quality characteristics on terrace abandonment in mountainous areas of Southwest China: A case study of Baidu Village in Jianhe County, Guizhou Province. *Geographical Research, 41*, 903–916. (in Chinese).

Müller, D., Leitão, P. J., & Sikor, T. (2013). Comparing the determinants of cropland abandonment in Albania and Romania using boosted regression trees. *Agricultural Systems, 117*, 66–77.

Plieninger, T., Hui, C., Gaertner, M., & Huntsinger, L. (2014). The impact of land abandonment on species richness and abundance in the Mediterranean Basin: A meta-analysis. *PLoS One, 9*, e98355.

Price, B., Kienast, F., Seidl, I., Ginzler, C., Verburg, P. H., & Bolliger, J. (2015). Future landscapes of Switzerland: Risk areas for urbanisation and land abandonment. *Applied Geography, 57*, 32–41.

Prishchepov, A.V., Radeloff, V.C., Baumann, M., Kuemmerle, T., Müller, D., (2012). Effects of institutional changes on land use: Agricultural land abandonment during the transition from state-command to market-driven economies in post-soviet Eastern Europe. Environmental Research Letters 7, 024021.

Queiroz, C., Beilin, R., Folke, C., & Lindborg, R. (2014). Farmland abandonment: Threat or opportunity for biodiversity conservation? A global review. *Frontiers in Ecology and the Environment, 12*, 288–296.

Rey Benayas, J. M., Martins, A., Nicolau, J. M., & Schulz, J. J. (2007). Abandonment of agricultural land: An overview of drivers and consequences. *CABI Reviews, 14*, 1–12.

Rhemtulla, J. M., Mladenoff, D. J., & Clayton, M. K. (2009). Legacies of historical land use on regional forest composition and structure in Wisconsin, USA (mid-1800s–1930s–2000s). *Ecological Applications, 19*, 1061–1078.

Romero-Calcerrada, R., & Perry, G. L. (2004). The role of land abandonment in landscape dynamics in the SPA 'Encinares del río Alberche y Cofio, Central Spain, 1984–1999. *Landscape and Urban Planning, 66*, 217–232.

Rudel, T. K. (2001). Did a green revolution restore the forests of the American south?, agricultural technologies and tropical deforestation. *CAB International Wallingford UK*, 53–68.

Ruiz-Flano, P., Lasanta, T., García-Ruiz, J., 1992. Soil erosion in abandoned fields in relation to vegetation characteristics and management.

Saint-Macary, C., Keil, A., Zeller, M., Heidhues, F., & Dung, P. T. M. (2010). Land titling policy and soil conservation in the northern uplands of Vietnam. *Land Use Policy, 27*, 617–627.

San Roman Sanz, A., Fernandez, C., Mouillot, F., Ferrat, L., Istria, D., & Pasqualini, V. (2013). Long-term forest dynamics and land-use abandonment in the Mediterranean mountains, Corsica, France. *Ecology and Society, 18*.

Schierhorn, F., Müller, D., Beringer, T., Prishchepov, A. V., Kuemmerle, T., & Balmann, A. (2013). Post-soviet cropland abandonment and carbon sequestration in European Russia, Ukraine, and Belarus. *Global Biogeochemical Cycles, 27*, 1175–1185.

Schneider, L., & Geoghegan, J. (2006). Land abandonment in an agricultural frontier after a plant invasion: The case of bracken fern in southern Yucatán, Mexico. *Agricultural and Resource Economics Review, 35*, 167–177.

Shi, T. C., & Li, X. B. (2013). Farmland abandonment in Europe and its enlightenment to China. *Geography and Geo-Information Science*, 101–103. (in Chinese).

Sikor, T., Müller, D., & Stahl, J. (2009). Land fragmentation and cropland abandonment in Albania: Implications for the roles of state and community in post-socialist land consolidation. *World Development, 37*, 1411–1423.

Silber, R., Wytrzens, H.K., 2005. Modelling the probability of land abandonment at parcel level.

Silver, W. L., Ostertag, R., & Lugo, A. E. (2000). The potential for carbon sequestration through reforestation of abandoned tropical agricultural and pasture lands. *Restoration Ecology, 8*, 394–407.

Stanchi, S., Freppaz, M., Agnelli, A., Reinsch, T., & Zanini, E. (2012). Properties, best management practices and conservation of terraced soils in southern Europe (from Mediterranean areas to the Alps): A review. *Quaternary International, 265*, 90–100.

Stefanski, J., Chaskovskyy, O., & Waske, B. (2014). Mapping and monitoring of land use changes in post-soviet western Ukraine using remote sensing data. *Applied Geography, 55*, 155–164.

Stoate, C., Baldi, A., Beja, P., Boatman, N., Herzon, I., Van Doorn, A., De Snoo, G., Rakosy, L., & Ramwell, C. (2009). Ecological impacts of early 21st century agricultural change in Europe–a review. *Journal of Environmental Management, 91*, 22–46.

Strijker, D. (2005). Marginal lands in Europe—Causes of decline. *Basic and Applied Ecology, 6*, 99–106.

Tan, S. K. (2003). Extent description and index system of sustainability judgment and its pattern of cultivated land abandoning. *China Land Science*, 3–8. (in Chinese).

Ustaoglu, E., & Collier, M. J. (2018). Farmland abandonment in Europe: An overview of drivers, consequences, and assessment of the sustainability implications. *Environmental Reviews, 26*, 396–416.

van der Zanden, E. H., Verburg, P. H., Schulp, C. J., & Verkerk, P. J. (2017). Trade-offs of European agricultural abandonment. *Land Use Policy, 62*, 290–301.

Van Doorn, A. M., & Bakker, M. M. (2007). The destination of arable land in a marginal agricultural landscape in South Portugal: An exploration of land use change determinants. *Landscape Ecology, 22*, 1073–1087.

Verburg, P. H., Eickhout, B., & Van Meijl, H. (2008). A multi-scale, multi-model approach for analyzing the future dynamics of European land use. *The Annals of Regional Science, 42*, 57–77.

Wang, H., Riedinger, J., & Jin, S. (2015). Land documents, tenure security and land rental development: Panel evidence from China. *China Economic Review, 36*, 220–235.

Wang, J., Yu, C., Fang, X., Li, G., & Cao, Y. (2022). Does land tenure fragmentation aggravate farmland abandonment? Evidence from big survey data in rural China. *Journal of Rural Studies, 91*, 126–135.

Wen, T. J. (2009). Why rural land privatization cannot be implemented in China. *Red Flag Manuscript*, 15–17. (in Chinese).

Wu, J., Zhang, M., Yang, X., & Wu, B. (2024). Effects of land and labor costs growth on agricultural product prices and farmers' income. *Land, 2012*, 13.

Xie, H. L., & Huang, Y. Q. (2022). Impact of non-agricultural employment and land transfer on farmers' farmland abandonment behaviors: A case study in Fujian-Jiangxi-Hunan mountainous areas. *Journal of Natural Resources*, 408–423. (in Chinese).

Xu, D., Chen, M., & Li, R. (2025). How high-standard farmland construction can affect farmers' grain cultivation behavior: Evidence from rural China. *Habitat International, 160*, 103384.

Xu, D., Deng, X., Huang, K., Liu, Y., Yong, Z., & Liu, S. (2019). Relationships between labor migration and cropland abandonment in rural China from the perspective of village types. *Land Use Policy, 88*, 104164.

Xu, D., Guo, S., Xie, F., Liu, S., & Cao, S. (2017). The impact of rural laborer migration and household structure on household land use arrangements in mountainous areas of Sichuan Province, China. *Habitat International, 70*, 72–80.

Xu, Q., Tian, S. C., Xu, Z. G., Shao, T., (2008). Rural land system, land fragmentation and farmer's income inequality. Economic research journal, 83-92+105. (in Chinese).

Xue, P., Han, X., Wang, Y., & Wang, X. (2022). Can agricultural machinery harvesting services reduce cropland abandonment? *Evidence from rural China. Agriculture, 12*, 901.

Yan, J., Yang, Z., Li, Z., Li, X., Xin, L., & Sun, L. (2016). Drivers of cropland abandonment in mountainous areas: A household decision model on farming scale in Southwest China. *Land Use Policy, 57*, 459–469.

Yang, F., Zheng, L. Y., & Zhang, Y. L. (2019). Symbiotic patterns and evolutionary logic of agricultural management paradigms. *Rural Economy*, 22–28. (in Chinese).

Yang, G. Y., & Xu, W. X. (2015). Cultivated land abandoning and its governance: Literature review and research prospective. *Journal of China Agricultural University, 20*, 279–288. (in Chinese).

Yu, H., Huang, J. K., Rozelle, S., Brandt, L., Zhang, L. X., 2003. Use rights security, land transfer and resource degradation. Economic research journal, 82-91+95. (in Chinese).

Zhang, Q., Song, C., & Chen, X. (2018). Effects of China's payment for ecosystem services programs on cropland abandonment: A case study in Tiantangzhai township, Anhui, China. *Land Use Policy, 73*, 239–248.

Zhang, X., Zhao, C., Dong, J., & Ge, Q. (2019). Spatio-temporal pattern of cropland abandonment in China from 1992 to 2017: A meta-analysis. *Acta Geographica Sinica, 74*, 411–420. (in Chinese).

Zhang, Y., Li, X., & Song, W. (2014). Determinants of cropland abandonment at the parcel, household and village levels in mountain areas of China: A multi-level analysis. *Land Use Policy, 41*, 186–192.

Zhang, Y., Li, X., Song, W., & Zhai, L. (2016). Land abandonment under rural restructuring in China explained from a cost-benefit perspective. *Journal of Rural Studies, 47*, 524–532.

Zheng, L. (2024a). Does off-farm work induce farmland abandonment? Evidence from China. *China Agricultural Economic Review, 16*, 664–682.

Zheng, L. (2024b). Those with constant property rights have perseverance: China's land tenure reform promotes environment-friendly farming practices. *Humanities and Social Sciences Communications, 11*, 1–10.

Zheng, L., Jin, S., & Su, L. (2025). Of nothing comes nothing: The impact of agricultural comparative return on cropland abandonment. *Journal of Rural Studies, 119*, 103759.

Zheng, L., & Qian, W. (2022). The impact of land certification on cropland abandonment: Evidence from rural China. *China agricultural economic review, 14*, 509–526.

Zheng, L., Su, L., & Jin, S. (2023). Reducing land fragmentation to curb cropland abandonment: Evidence from rural China. *Canadian Journal of Agricultural Economics/Revue canadienne d'agroeconomie, 71*, 355–373.

Zheng, L. Y. (2020). China's agricultural management system: Evolutionary course, problem focus and reform orientation. *Rural Economy*, 88–95. (in Chinese).

Zheng, L. Y., Qian, W. R., Liu, Q., & Guo, X. L. (2021). The impact of the new round of farmland certification on the ecological protection of cultivated land: Taking the application of chemical fertilizers and pesticides as examples. *Chinese Rural Economy*, 76–93. (in Chinese).

Zhou, J. K., Wang, W. B., Gong, M. Y., & Huang, Z. X. (2020). Land transfers, occupational stratification and poverty reduction. *Economic Research Journal*, 155–171. (in Chinese).

# Chapter 3
# Off-Farm Employment and Cropland Abandonment

**Abstract** Curbing the abandonment of cropland is a critical measure to ensure national food security. This study investigates whether, how and under what circumstances off-farm employment induces cropland abandonment, which is of great importance for developing countries to cope with food security. Exploiting large-scale panel data from the newly released Chinese Family Database, this chapter employs a two-way fixed effects model to empirically estimate the causal relationship between off-farm employment and cropland abandonment. Results show that off-farm employment leads to an increase in the probability and area of cropland abandoned due to insufficient agricultural labor. However, off-farm employment does not harm farm households in plain areas, or villages with land rental markets, abundant agricultural labor, and agricultural machinery, while abandon their cropland than those in other areas. Additionally, when the number of off-farm workers in a household exceeds two, the probability and area of cropland abandonment will miraculously decline, as the household will no longer live entirely on agriculture. This study fills the gap in clarifying the relationship between off-farm employment and cropland abandonment, and identifies scenarios where off-farm employment may not cause cropland abandonment through multiple dimensions, providing insights into the governance of cropland abandonment during rural-urban transformation in developing countries.

**Keywords** Off-farm employment · Cropland abandonment · Labor economics · Rural-urban transformation · Food security

Curbing the abandonment of cropland is a critical measure to ensure national food security. This study investigates whether, how and under what circumstances off-farm employment induces cropland abandonment, which is of great importance for developing countries to cope with food security. Exploiting large-scale panel data

This chapter has been published. For more details, please see: Zheng L., Does off-farm work induce farmland abandonment? Evidence from China. China Agricultural Economic Review, 2024, 16(4):664–682.



L. Zheng, *Cropland Abandonment in Rural China*, Resources, Environment and Agricultural Development, https://doi.org/10.1007/978-981-95-8287-7_3

from the newly released Chinese Family Database, this chapter employs a two-way fixed effects model to empirically estimate the causal relationship between off-farm employment and cropland abandonment.

## 3.1 Introduction

Ending hunger, achieving food security, improving nutrition, and promoting sustainable agriculture is the second goal of the Sustainable Development Goals (SDGs) advocated by the United Nations in 2015. However, the current global food security situation does not usher optimism, especially due to the growing world population, frequent occurrence of extreme weather events, the global spread of coronavirus disease 2019 (COVID-19), and the intensification of the Russia-Ukraine conflict in recent years (Zheng, 2024). The State of Food Security and Nutrition in the World 2022, co-authored by the Food and Agriculture Organization (FAO) of the United Nations and several international agencies, shows that in 2021, 702 million to 828 million people worldwide suffered hunger, and the prevalence of undernourishment was as high as 9.8% globally (FAO, 2022).

Cropland is a valuable resource for food production, thus maintaining a certain amount of cropland is essential to ensuring food security in countries around the world (Lambin & Meyfroidt, 2010; Xu et al., 2019a; Zheng & Qian, 2021). However, the abandonment of cropland has gradually become a global socio-economic problem in recent years. Developed countries such as the United States (Queiroz et al., 2014), France (San Roman Sanz et al., 2013), Switzerland (Price et al., 2015), and Japan (Ito et al., 2016), as well as developing countries such as Albania (Deininger et al., 2012), Argentina (Izquierdo & Grau, 2009) and China (Yan et al., 2016; Zheng et al., 2023), all have various degrees of cropland abandonment (Deng et al., 2018). Cropland abandonment is the dormant or deserted state of cropland due to a lack of effective farming or management measures (Ojha et al., 2022). This phenomenon can be measured in empirical studies through indicators such as the probability of farm households abandoning cropland, the area of abandoned cropland, and the proportion of abandoned cropland to the total area (Deng et al., 2018; Ma et al., 2022; Zheng et al., 2023). Cropland abandonment exerts a direct and far-reaching consequence on agricultural output. Once cropland is no longer used for farming, food production in the region decreases and the overall food supply may also decline. As a result, cropland abandonment has aroused widespread concern and great attention from countries around the world.

Several scholars have highlighted industrialization and urbanization as one of the most important economic drivers of land use change (Chandrasekhar, 1993; Djoumessi et al., 2020; Lambin & Meyfroidt, 2010). Driven by the forces of industrialization and urbanization, off-farm employment has become an increasingly prominent manifestation of rural-urban transformation (Cai, 2018; Van den Broeck & Kilic, 2019). However, there has been little discussion about off-farm employment and cropland abandonment, especially in the Chinese context, although a large body of literature has highlighted the impacts of off-farm employment on outcomes such as land transfer (Wang et al., 2020), income growth (Cai, 2018; Rajkhowa & Qaim, 2022), consumption change (Zheng, 2023), rural poverty (Li et al., 2021) and agricultural productivity (Djoumessi et al., 2020). China is undergoing rapid industrialization and urbanization, and massive rural migrant workers are constantly shifting to urban non-agricultural industries (Xu et al., 2019a; Zhang et al., 2014). According to the 2022 Rural Migrant Workers Monitoring Survey Report released by the National Bureau of Statistics of China, the total number of rural migrant workers in China was 295.62 million in 2022, with an increase of 3.11 million or 1.1% over the previous year. The massive outflow of rural migrant workers leads to a gradual reduction in agricultural labor engaged in food production (MacDonald et al., 2000; Zhang et al., 2014), potentially increasing the likelihood of cropland abandonment.

Nevertheless, to our best knowledge, only a few studies have been conducted using the China Labor-force Dynamics Survey (CLDS) to investigate the link between off-farm employment and cropland abandonment in China (Deng et al., 2018; Xu et al., 2019a; Xu et al., 2019b; Lu, 2020). Despite their relevance, the findings may not hold up because the off-farm employment variable occurs after the cropland abandonment variable in the CLDS, suggesting a reverse causality problem. Additionally, these studies do not address the potential endogeneity problems introduced by omitted variables such as farmers' preferences and abilities, nor do they adequately explore the underlying mechanisms and assess heterogeneous effects from a labor and land endowment perspective.

Given this literature gap, we use newly released and large-scale panel data from the 2017 and 2019 Chinese Family Database (CFD) to examine the overall impact, mechanism, and heterogeneous effects of off-farm employment on cropland abandonment. Our study extends the existing literature in the following three aspects: First, we take advantage of CFD that off-farm employment occurs before cropland abandonment and large-scale panel data and adopt the panel two-way fixed effects model to rule out the endogeneity problem caused by reverse causality and omitted variables, respectively. Meanwhile, we also redefine the independent variable to exclude potential interference from measurement errors. This makes the estimates more credible. Second, by examining the heterogeneous effects and the nonlinear relationship between off-farm employment and cropland abandonment, this study pays particular attention to scenarios where off-farm employment does not cause cropland abandonment. This could fill the gap in clarifying the relationship between off-farm employment and cropland abandonment and provide a useful reference for the governance of cropland abandonment in the context of mass rural-urban migration in developing countries. Third, we also attempt to investigate the underlying mechanisms of how off-farm employment affects cropland abandonment, which helps to enrich previous studies.

## 3.2 Theoretical Basis and Analytical Framework

Lewis' dual economic theory argues that there exists a dual economic structure of the advanced industrial sector and the backward agricultural sector in developing countries. Among them, there is surplus labor in the traditional agricultural sector. Due to the obvious income gap between industry and agriculture, surplus agricultural labor will continue to flow to modern urban industrial sectors, forming a phenomenon of rural-urban labor migration. The result of absorbing surplus agricultural labor in the modern urban industrial sector is to expand production and accumulate profits. Simultaneously, with the continuous outflow of surplus agricultural labor in rural areas, the marginal productivity of agricultural labor gradually increased. Moreover, as the level of remuneration of agricultural workers approaches the level of industrial wages, the characteristics of the dual economic structure are slowly disappearing; and the transformation of industrialization and urbanization is basically realized (Lewis, 2016).

During this rural-urban transition, the effect of off-farm employment on cropland abandonment is complex. On the one hand, reduced agricultural labor caused by off-farm employment will theoretically exacerbate cropland abandonment. On the other hand, land rent-out promoted by off-farm employment will theoretically reduce cropland abandonment. Nevertheless, whether the above assumptions are true or not is also moderated by labor and land characteristics, respectively. In terms of labor characteristics, the assumption that off-farm employment will exacerbate cropland abandonment is primarily based on the fact that off-farm employment will cause insufficient household agricultural labor (Zheng, 2023). However, if there is surplus labor in the household itself or if the household has agricultural machinery, then farmers are less likely to abandon their cropland. Regarding land characteristics, the assumption that off-farm employment will reduce cropland abandonment is based mainly on the fact that off-farm employment will promote land rent-out (Wang et al., 2020). However, if farmers live in non-plain or mountainous areas where farming is inconvenient or in villages without land rental markets, it is still unclear whether off-farm employment will reduce cropland abandonment (Fig. 3.1).

Based on the above discussion, under the condition of farming, there are theoretically four scenarios where off-farm employment does not necessarily lead to cropland abandonment (see the dashed arrow in Fig. 3.1 for details). First, farm households have abundant agricultural labor. According to the New Economics of Labor Migration (NELM), farmers' migration behavior is a household decision rather than an individual decision (Rozelle et al., 1999). They usually consider whether to go out for off-farm employment to maximize household income (Deng et al., 2018). When there is surplus labor in farm households, this portion of workers engaged in off-farm employment will not increase cropland abandonment but will increase the source of household income. Second, farm households have agricultural machinery to make up for labor shortages. The fact that family members working off-farm can significantly increase household remittances (Taylor et al., 2003) and create conditions for purchasing agricultural machinery (Su et al., 2016) implies that even when off-farm

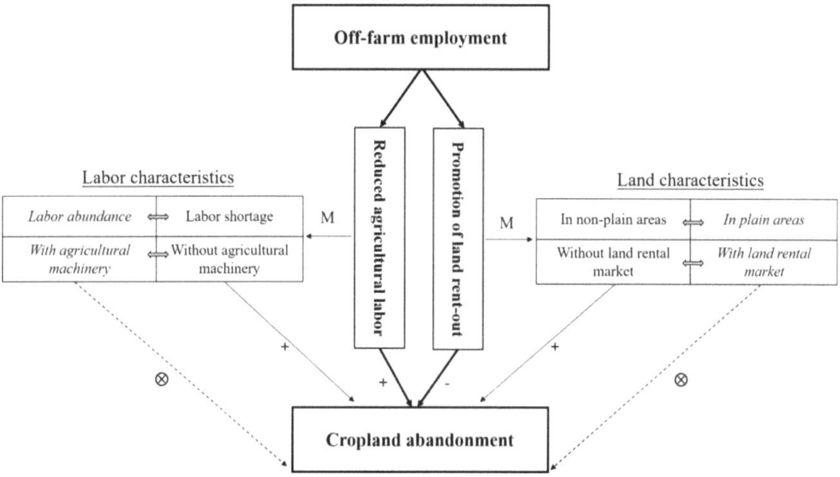


**Fig. 3.1** Theoretical framework of off-farm employment on cropland abandonment. *Note* M represents moderating effects. ⊗, +, and - denote unclear effect, positive effect, and negative effect under theoretical expectation, respectively

employment does lead to a decline in the number of agricultural workers, this decline can be offset by the application of agricultural machinery (MacDonald et al., 2000). Thus, as long as off-farm employment contributes to the purchase of agricultural machinery, then cropland may not be abandoned. Third, farmers live in plain areas where farming is easy. Compared with non-plain areas, plain areas have various advantages (Müller et al., 2013), such as high soil fertility (Zheng & Qian, 2021), convenient use of machinery (MacDonald et al., 2000) and easy renting of land out, etc. As a result, farmers in plain areas do not need to abandon their cropland (van der Zanden et al., 2017), even if off-farm employment has caused a serious shortage of agricultural labor (Zhang et al., 2014). Fourth, there is a land rental market in the village where the farmers live. When a farmer participates in off-farm employment, he can not only obtain wage income but also rent from leased cropland (Zheng & Qian, 2021). In this sense, as long as the village has a land rental market and farmers have the opportunity to rent out their cropland, there is no need for them to abandon it (Deng et al., 2018).

## 3.3 Research Design

### 3.3.1 Data Source

The research data used in this study are mainly drawn from the 2017 and 2019 CFD in 29 Chinese provinces (Fig. 3.2). To ensure data representativeness at multiple levels, a stratified, three-stage sampling method proportional to population size was applied to the survey (Qian, 2020). The dataset is comprehensive and informative, covering the basic structure of rural households, income and expenditure, agricultural production and operation, land use, and other aspects, which can provide first-hand information for the study of China's rural social economy (Zheng, 2024). Most importantly, this database has unique advantages for this study. On the one hand, information on cropland abandonment refers to the current year of the survey, while off-farm employment and most household characteristics refer to the previous year of the survey, which can rule out the problem of reverse causality to some extent. On the other hand, the database has two periods of panel data reflecting China's current economic and social status, which can alleviate the omitted variable bias by leveraging a fixed effects model. To examine the impact of off-farm employment on cropland abandonment, we retained key variables such as cropland abandonment, off-farm employment, individual characteristics of household heads, household characteristics of farmers, and some village characteristics. Subsequently, considering missing values in some variables, I deleted 147 samples with information loss from 15,248 original samples. Finally, an unbalanced panel of 15,101 farmer households with cropland across 29 provinces in China was used for the analysis.

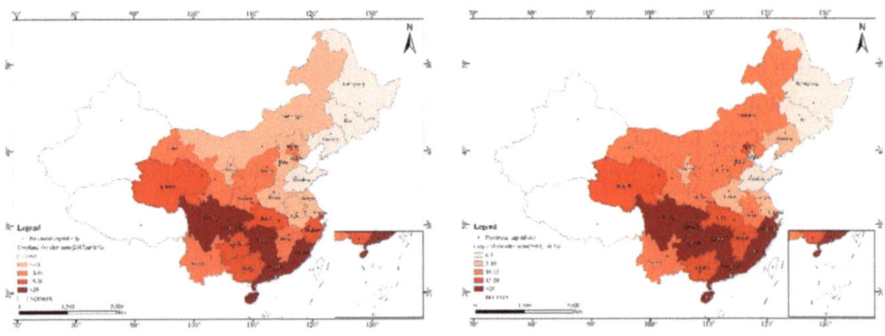

(a) 2017 (b) 2019

**Fig. 3.2** Distribution of cropland abandonment in China during 2017–2019. *Source* The 2017 and 2019 Chinese Family Database

### 3.3.2 Variables and Sample Characteristics

Table 3.1 presents the definitions of variables and sample statistical characteristics of the selected variables in the analysis. The dependent variable used in the study, mainly following Deng et al. (2018), refers to farmers' choice behavior whether to abandon cropland or not. Meanwhile, referring to Xu et al. (2019a), we select the ratio of farmers' off-farm employment as the core independent variable. As mentioned earlier, the interviewers asked about the occupation of the head of household in the previous year and the abandoned cropland of farm households in the current year. Thus, an important and unique advantage of this data is that endogeneity problems arising from reverse causality are excluded by taking advantage of the time difference that the core independent variable occurs before the dependent variable. In the meantime, to reduce the interference of the omission of observable factors on the estimated results, we also control for the following important characteristic variables by drawing on relative studies. In particular, we include age and age-squared terms, health, education of the head of farmer households (Xie & Lu, 2017; Zhang et al., 2014; Zheng, 2024), dependency ratio, income, comparative gain, land area, land fragmentation (Deininger et al., 2012; Latruffe & Piet, 2014; Lu, 2020), land value and land certificate of surveyed households (Deng et al., 2018; Xu et al., 2019a), as well as new agricultural operators and per capita disposable annual income of surveyed villages (Zheng et al., 2023; Zheng & Qian, 2021).

As Table 3.1 shows, about 11.8% of farmer households have abandoned their cropland. This result is highly close to Xu's descriptive statistics using the CLDS database (Xu et al., 2019a). In addition, Fig. 3.2 also illustrates that from 2017 to 2019, cropland abandonment by farmers showed an increasing trend, indicating the seriousness of cropland abandonment in China, especially in southern China. The off-farm rate for farm households is 22.5%, meaning that at least one worker in a household of five is not engaged in farming. It shows that off-farm employment in rural China is an extremely common phenomenon. With regard to the individual characteristics of householders, the average age of heads of household is almost 53.59 years. The health status of heads of household is relatively good, whereas most of them have only about 7 years of education. As for household characteristics, the annual per capita household income is 13,040 yuan, which is used to support 35.1% of children and the elderly. Comparative agricultural gains remain relatively low, with only 44.7% of respondents reporting that their farm income exceeds the average village wage. Most of the farmers in the sample are scattered smallholders, with a per capita land area of 3.023 mu and nearly 5.453 plots. Household heads estimate the logarithm of the market value of contracted land to be 7.295 per mu, and since 2009, 59.3% of households have obtained land certificates. In terms of village characteristics, there are approximately 8 new agricultural operators in each village on average, and the annual disposable per capita income of the sample villages is 8530 yuan.

**Table 3.1** Variable definition and descriptive statistics (N = 15,101)

| Variables | Definition and assignment | Mean | S.D. |
|---|---|---|---|
| Cropland abandonment | Whether farm households abandon cropland (yes = 1, no = 0) | 0.118 | 0.323 |
| Off-farm employment | Share of non-agricultural labor in the household last year (0—1) | 0.225 | 0.262 |
| Age | Age of the head of household in years (year) | 53.590 | 10.687 |
| Age square | Age square of the head of household in years (year) | 2986.059 | 1072.744 |
| Health | Physical status of heads of household (very bad = 1, bad = 2, average = 3, good = 4, very good = 5) | 3.141 | 1.054 |
| Education | Years of schooling of the head of household (year) | 7.414 | 3.372 |
| Dependency ratio | Share of the children and elderly in the household (0—1) | 0.351 | 0.477 |
| Income | Per capita household income last year (10 thousand yuan) | 1.304 | 2.242 |
| Comparative gain | Whether the farm income of households last year was higher than the average village wage income (yes = 1, no = 0) | 0.447 | 0.497 |
| Land area | Per capita land area of the household (mu) | 3.023 | 6.261 |
| Land fragmentation | Number of plots | 5.453 | 5.791 |
| Land value | Logarithm of the market value of the contracted land per mu estimated by the head of household (yuan) | 7.295 | 2.256 |
| Land certificate | Since 2009, whether farmer households have got a land certificate (yes = 1, no = 0) | 0.593 | 0.491 |
| Village agriculture | Number of new agricultural operator in village, including professional large-scale operator, household farm, specialized cooperative, and agricultural enterprise | 7.586 | 82.159 |
| Village economy | Per capita disposable annual income of the village (10 thousand yuan) | 0.853 | 0.686 |

*Notes* 1 mu = 1/15 ha. Yuan is Chinese currency (1 USD = 7.15 Yuan in 2024)

### 3.3.3 Econometric Method

To alleviate the endogeneity problems caused by the omitted variables and reverse causality, this study takes advantage of CFD and exploits a two-way fixed effects (TWFE) model to identify the causal effect of off-farm employment on cropland abandonment. Specifically, the econometric regression model is set as follows.

$$\text{Abandonment}_{it} = \beta_0 + \beta_1 \text{Off\_farm}_{it-1} + \gamma \mathbf{X}_{it,t-1} + \sigma_i + \varphi_t + \mu_{it} \tag{3.1}$$

Where, the subscripts of $i$ and $t$ represent the head of the farm household and the survey year, respectively. *Abandonment* is a dichotomous variable, in which the value of 1 stands for that the farm household has cropland abandonment behavior and 0 denotes otherwise. *Off_farm* indicates the share of non-agricultural labor in the household. $\boldsymbol{X}$ is a vector of control variables that may affect both off-farm employment and cropland abandonment. $\beta_0$ is the constant term; $\beta_1$, $\gamma$ are the parameters to be estimated; $\sigma_i$ represents the household-fixed effect that controls for time-invariant differences among farmers; $\varphi_t$ represents the time-fixed effect, eliminating unobserved characteristics that are common to all farmers, but vary across time; and $\mu_{it}$ is the random error term capturing other unexplained shocks.

## 3.4 Impact of Off-Farm Employment on Cropland Abandonment

### *3.4.1 Benchmark Regression*

The regression results of the impact of off-farm employment on cropland abandonment using the two-way fixed effects model are displayed in Table 3.2. Among them, column (1) reports the estimates without control variables, while column (2) reports the estimates with added control variables based on Eq. (3.1). Compared to column (2), column (3) elevates the level of standard error clustering from the previous household to the current village, and column (4) further considers the effect of changing with time and province simultaneously. Although the off-farm employment coefficients in column (1) are slightly higher than those in the other columns, across all four columns, they all remain around 7% and are positively significant at the 1% level. This indicates that off-farm employment exerts a positive and significant effect on cropland abandonment, and the estimated results are basically unaffected by observable factors. It can be observed that under the background of large-scale rural migrant workers from rural areas to cities, the current off-farm employment has harmed the use of cultivated land in general; and the labor shortage caused by off-farm employment has increased the probability of cropland abandonment (Xu et al., 2019a).

As far as control variables are concerned, taking the estimates in column (4) as an example, the following estimated results can be found. Age and its square are significant at the 1% level and have opposite signs, indicating a nonlinear relationship between householder's age and cropland abandonment. This finding is consistent with Deng et al. (2018). Health and education variables are insignificant, probably their changes over the two-year study period were almost negligible. The dependency ratio is positively and significantly associated with cropland abandonment, indicating

**Table 3.2** Off-farm employment and cropland abandonment: benchmark regression

| | Dependent variable: whether farm households abandon cropland | | | |
|---|---|---|---|---|
| | (1) | (2) | (3) | (4) |
| Off-farm employment | 0.072*** | 0.066*** | 0.066*** | 0.064*** |
| | (0.027) | (0.028) | (0.029) | (0.028) |
| Age | | −0.019*** | −0.019*** | −0.019*** |
| | | (0.006) | (0.006) | (0.006) |
| Age square | | 0.0002*** | 0.0002*** | 0.0002*** |
| | | (0.000) | (0.000) | (0.000) |
| Health | | −0.008 | −0.008 | −0.008 |
| | | (0.005) | (0.005) | (0.006) |
| Education | | −0.003 | −0.003 | −0.003 |
| | | (0.003) | (0.003) | (0.003) |
| Dependency ratio | | 0.039* | 0.039* | 0.040* |
| | | (0.021) | (0.021) | (0.021) |
| Income | | 0.003 | 0.003 | 0.003 |
| | | (0.003) | (0.003) | (0.003) |
| Comparative gain | | −0.028** | −0.028* | −0.029** |
| | | (0.013) | (0.015) | (0.013) |
| Land area | | 0.002** | 0.002** | 0.002** |
| | | (0.001) | (0.001) | (0.001) |
| Land fragmentation | | 0.004*** | 0.004*** | 0.004*** |
| | | (0.001) | (0.001) | (0.001) |
| Land value | | −0.004 | −0.004 | −0.003 |
| | | (0.003) | (0.003) | (0.003) |
| Land certificate | | −0.027* | −0.027* | −0.029** |
| | | (0.014) | (0.014) | (0.015) |
| Village agriculture | | −0.0001** | −0.0001** | −0.0001** |
| | | (0.000) | (0.000) | (0.000) |
| Village economy | | −0.013 | −0.013 | −0.015* |
| | | (0.008) | (0.012) | (0.009) |
| Household-fixed effect | Yes | Yes | Yes | Yes |
| Time-fixed effect | Yes | Yes | Yes | Yes |
| Province×time-fixed effect | No | No | No | No |
| Obs. | 15,101 | 15,101 | 15,101 | 15,101 |
| Cluster unit | Household | Household | Village | Household |
| R-squared | 0.870 | 0.873 | 0.873 | 0.874 |

*Notes* ***, **, and * denote significance at the 1%, 5%, and 10% levels, respectively; Robust standard errors are shown in parentheses that a shortage of young and middle-aged labor force will cause the abandonment of cropland (Zheng et al., 2023). We do not observe the significant impact of household income on cropland abandonment. One possible explanation is that the increase in household incomes may increase farmers' leisure and cause cropland abandonment, but it may also increase land investment and reduce cropland abandonment (Ma et al., 2018). Comparative agricultural gains appear to significantly reduce the likelihood of cropland abandonment, suggesting that the smaller the gap between agricultural income and non-agricultural wage income, the more active farmers are in farming, and the less likely they are to abandon cropland. This also shows from the side that low agricultural comparative income is an important driving factor for farmers to abandon cropland. The relationship between land area and cropland abandonment is significantly positive, suggesting that farmers with more cropland are more likely to abandon it (Zheng & Qian, 2021). The coefficient of land fragmentation is positive at the 1% significance level, implying that an increase in plot size is associated with statistically significant increases in cropland abandonment (Deininger et al., 2012; Latruffe & Piet, 2014). The variable representing land value shows no significant effect on cropland abandonment, which may be explained by the fact that farmers with a higher market value of cropland are more likely to cherish it, while it is difficult to maximize their income by using cropland for agriculture. Land certificate tends to have a negative and significant effect on cropland abandonment, which is related to land tenure security (Deininger et al., 2011). Additionally, the coefficients of village agriculture and village economy are significantly negative, which means that the more developed the village is in agriculture or economy, the less cropland will be abandoned. This finding is aligned with Zheng and Qian (2021) and can be partly explained by land scarcity.

### 3.4.2 Robustness Checks

Table 3.3 presents the estimated results of a series of robustness checks. First, to exclude the estimation bias that may be caused by measurement errors, this study uses the percentage of abandoned cropland area over total cropland area as the dependent variable, and whether the farmer had off-farm employment behavior last year (yes = 1, no = 0) as the core independent variable. As can be seen from the estimation results in columns (1) and (2), off-farm employment significantly increases the probability of cropland being abandoned by farmers. Next, considering that the dependent variable in this study is a dummy variable, we also employ a panel logit model and panel probit model to re-estimate Eq. (3.1), respectively. The average marginal effects presented in columns (3) and (4) show once again that off-farm employment gives rise to a significant increase in cropland abandonment. Third, to establish an academic dialogue with relevant existing research (Deng et al., 2018; Xu et al., 2019a), we utilize the ordinary least squares (OLS) model and cross-sectional 2017 and 2019 CFD data for estimation. Results in columns (5) and (6) show that off-farm employment still has a positive impact on cropland abandonment, although there is a slight decrease in its coefficients compared to column (2) of Table 3.2. Finally, the balanced panel has some advantages over the unbalanced panel in estimating validity, although it does suffer from loss of untracked samples and causes bias in sample selection. Therefore, this study attempts to employ a balanced panel to re-estimate Eq. (3.1). As shown in column (7), the coefficient for off-farm employment appears to be highly consistent with those using the unbalanced panel in column (2) of Table 3.2. To conclude, the above estimates strongly confirm the negative effect of off-farm employment on cropland abandonment in rural China.

### 3.4.3 Endogeneity Discussion

This study was designed to minimize the potential impact of endogeneity problems, mainly demonstrated in the following four aspects. First, the two-way fixed effects model used in this study eliminates the influence of factors that are not time-dependent in a short period, such as farmers' preferences and abilities. This model also excludes the impact of factors that do not vary with farmers, such as national economic policies. Moreover, based on this model, column (4) of Table 3.2 specifically controls for the interaction terms between provinces and time-fixed effects, further ruling out the influence of unobservable factors such as provincial economic policies and climate that vary with province and time. Second, with the advantage of CFD, this paper draws on existing research to include as many relevant control variables as possible, excluding other potential omitted variables. When comparing columns (1) and (2) in Table 3.2, it is clear that the effect of off-farm employment on cropland abandonment remains significantly positive, regardless of the inclusion of additional control variables. Third, this study employs the cropland abandonment variable from the current year to regress the off-farm employment variable from the previous year, reducing the potential reverse causality problem. Finally, by redefining the core independent variables, this study mitigates the endogeneity problem caused by measurement errors. The positive relationship between off-farm employment and cropland abandonment remains robust in the estimated results in column (2) of Table 3.3. Therefore, in general, there is little cause for concern about the endogeneity of this study.

### 3.4.4 Mechanism Tests

As mentioned earlier, off-farm employment theoretically exerts positive and negative effects on cropland abandonment by reducing agricultural labor and promoting land rent-out, respectively. However, the estimates in Tables 3.2 and 3.3 support that off-farm employment generally induces cropland abandonment, implying that the land rent-out mechanism may not hold water.

**Table 3.3** Off-farm employment and cropland abandonment: robustness checks

| | Redefining Y | Redefining X | Changing estimation method | | Using cross-sectional data | | Balanced panel data |
|---|---|---|---|---|---|---|---|
| | (1) | (2) | (3) Logit | (4) Probit | (5) 2017 | (6) 2019 | (7) |
| Off-farm employment | 0.027** | 0.032** | 0.040*** | 0.043*** | 0.055*** | 0.064*** | 0.066*** |
| | (0.014) | (0.013) | (0.008) | (0.009) | (0.016) | (0.017) | (0.028) |
| Control variables | Yes | Yes | Yes | Yes | Yes | Yes | Yes |
| Household-fixed effect | Yes | Yes | Yes | Yes | Yes | Yes | Yes |
| Time-fixed effect | Yes | Yes | Yes | Yes | Yes | Yes | Yes |
| Obs. | 15,101 | 15,101 | 15,101 | 15,101 | 7454 | 7647 | 6236 |
| Log likelihood | – | – | −4922.823 | −4921.975 | – | – | – |
| Wald chi2 | – | – | 436.13 | 428.22 | – | – | – |
| R-squared | 0.866 | 0.873 | – | – | 0.054 | 0.065 | 0.681 |

*Notes* ***, **, and * denote significance at the 1%, 5%, and 10% levels, respectively; Robust standard errors, clustered at the household level, are shown in parentheses

**Table 3.4** Off-farm employment and cropland abandonment: mechanism analysis

| | Dependent variable | | | |
|---|---|---|---|---|
| | (1) Agricultural labor | (2) Cropland abandonment | (3) Land rent-out | (4) Cropland abandonment |
| Off-farm employment | −0.402*** | 0.060** | 0.026* | 0.059** |
| | (0.088) | (0.028) | (0.014) | (0.028) |
| Agricultural labor | | −0.016*** | | −0.016*** |
| | | (0.005) | | (0.005) |
| Land rent-out | | | | 0.050 |
| | | | | (0.037) |
| Control variables | Yes | Yes | Yes | Yes |
| Household-fixed effect | Yes | Yes | Yes | Yes |
| Time-fixed effect | Yes | Yes | Yes | Yes |
| Obs. | 15,101 | 15,101 | 15,101 | 15,101 |
| R-squared | 0.851 | 0.873 | 0.974 | 0.873 |

*Notes* ***, **, and * denote significance at the 1%, 5%, and 10% levels, respectively; Robust standard errors, clustered at the household level, are shown in parentheses

To prove this strictly, we first use agricultural labor (measured by the number of agricultural labor in the household) to regress off-farm employment and directly include agricultural labor in Eq. (3.1), and then use land rent-out (yes = 1, no = 0) to regress off-farm employment and further incorporate agricultural labor and land rent-out in Eq. (3.1). As expected, the results in columns (1) and (2) in Table 3.4 show that off-farm employment significantly decreases agricultural labor, leading to cropland abandonment. Nevertheless, the estimates in columns (3) and (4) suggest that while off-farm employment facilitates land rent-out, land rent-out does not further reduce cropland abandonment. The likely reason is that the land rental market in rural China needs to be further improved. According to CFD, although 69.33% of villages across the country have a land rental market, only 21.61% of farmers rent their land out. These results indicate that the current off-farm employment affects cropland abandonment through the reduction of agricultural labor rather than land rent-out.

## 3.5 Heterogeneous Effects of Off-Farm Employment on Cropland Abandonment

Previous estimates have fully demonstrated that current off-farm employment, in aggregate, increases the likelihood of cropland being abandoned by farmers. Under the irreversible situation of industrialization and urbanization, how can the negative impact of off-farm employment on cropland abandonment be minimized? This is an increasingly important issue that deserves great attention. Given that labor and land are the most critical resource factors for farmers, especially in developing countries like China, we attempt to analyze this issue from the perspective of labor and land endowment, complementing the previous theoretical analysis.

### 3.5.1 Effect of Off-Farm Employment on Cropland Abandonment under the Condition of Labor Endowment

One of the key assumptions that off-farm employment will cause cropland abandonment is that, after some members of a farm household are employed off-farm, there is not only no surplus agricultural labor but even a shortage of agricultural labor. Therefore, if farmers' off-farm employment does not affect the supply of agricultural labor, then the impact of off-farm employment on cropland abandonment may be minimal. For this reason, we roughly divide all samples into labor abundance and labor shortage groups, based on whether the number of agricultural workers in a farm household is greater than its mean at the village level. As expected, estimates of off-farm employment in columns (1) and (2) of Table 3.5 show that it only affects farm households with labor shortages, not households with abundant labor. What's more, the result passes the test of the coefficient difference between groups. To a certain extent, this indicates that as long as off-farm employment does not interfere with the supply of agricultural labor, its impact on cropland abandonment can be negligible.

In recent years, China's agricultural mechanization has developed rapidly, which has provided important technical support for agricultural modernization and greatly changed the situation of a long-term dependence on human and animal power in agriculture. According to publicly available data, the overall mechanization rate of crop cultivation, planting, and harvesting exceeds 73% in 2023. Considering that agricultural machinery will form a substitute for labor in the process of agricultural production, thereby alleviating the labor shortage caused by off-farm employment. As such, the impact of off-farm employment on cropland abandonment cannot ignore the role of machinery (Ma et al., 2022). To test this hypothesis, all samples are divided into two groups according to whether the farm household owns agricultural machinery or not. As shown in columns (3) and (4) of Table 3.5, statistically, farmers without agricultural machinery are more likely to abandon their cropland than those with agricultural machinery. These results confirm the coefficient difference between groups and reveal that the current negative impact of off-farm employment on cropland abandonment can be mitigated to some extent through the development of agricultural machinery.

**Table 3.5** Off-farm employment and cropland abandonment: labor grouping and machinery grouping

| | Dependent variable: whether farm households abandon cropland | | | |
|---|---|---|---|---|
| | (1) Labor abundance | (2) Labor shortage | (3) With machinery | (4) Without machinery |
| Off-farm employment | 0.035 | 0.107* | −0.0002 | 0.119** |
| | (0.047) | (0.057) | (0.042) | (0.051) |
| Observed difference | −0.072*** | | −0.119** | |
| Empirical p-value | 0.003 | | 0.025 | |
| Control variables | Yes | Yes | Yes | Yes |
| Household-fixed effect | Yes | Yes | Yes | Yes |
| Time-fixed effect | Yes | Yes | Yes | Yes |
| Obs. | 8343 | 6758 | 8210 | 6891 |
| R-squared | 0.920 | 0.933 | 0.931 | 0.905 |

*Notes* ***, **, and * denote significance at the 1%, 5%, and 10% levels, respectively; Robust standard errors, clustered at the household level, are shown in parentheses

### 3.5.2 *Effect of Off-Farm Employment on Cropland Abandonment under the Condition of Land Endowment*

Numerous driving forces exist, of which terrain is one of the most important natural determinants affecting land use (Yan et al., 2016). In practice, the difficulty of cultivating land in non-plain areas is usually much greater than in plain areas, due to constraints such as inconvenient transportation, difficult implementation of machinery, and soil erosion. Consequently, the rentability of land in non-plain areas is also lower, especially in mountainous areas. As such, the impact of off-farm employment on cropland abandonment may vary with topographical conditions. To examine the heterogeneous effect of off-farm employment from a terrain perspective, we divided all samples into two groups according to whether farm households lived in plain areas. Results in columns (1) and (2) of Table 3.6 show that off-farm employment primarily has a positive and significant impact on cropland abandonment in non-plain areas, but has no effect on plain areas. This finding is further supported by the significant coefficient difference between groups. The underlying reason is that farming in plain areas is relatively convenient, while in non-plain areas, land use is more difficult due to terrain, transportation, machinery use, and other restrictions. As a result, farmers in non-plain areas typically face greater land rent-out challenges, exacerbating abandoned cropland.

**Table 3.6** Off-farm employment and cropland abandonment: terrain grouping and land leasing grouping

| | Dependent variable: whether farm households abandon cropland | | | |
|---|---|---|---|---|
| | (1) Plain areas | (2) Non-plain areas | (3) With land rental market | (4) Without land rental market |
| Off-farm employment | 0.034 | 0.089** | −0.006 | 0.156** |
| | (0.032) | (0.042) | (0.031) | (0.078) |
| Observed difference | −0.055* | | −0.162** | |
| Empirical p-value | 0.088 | | 0.031 | |
| Control variables | Yes | Yes | Yes | Yes |
| Household-fixed effect | Yes | Yes | Yes | Yes |
| Time-fixed effect | Yes | Yes | Yes | Yes |
| Obs. | 5503 | 9598 | 10,786 | 4315 |
| R-squared | 0.861 | 0.873 | 0.906 | 0.946 |

*Notes* ***, **, and * denote significance at the 1%, 5%, and 10% levels, respectively; Robust standard errors, clustered at the household level, are shown in parentheses

With the continued liberalization of land transfer rights in China, the land rental market in rural areas has become increasingly active since the implementation of *the Land Contract Law of the People's Republic of China* in 2003. Consequently, farm households are easy to access by renting out land they cannot cultivate, so the impact of off-farm employment on cropland abandonment may differ between farmers with and without land rental opportunities. To investigate the heterogeneous effect of off-farm employment from a land lease perspective, all samples are divided into two groups according to whether the village has a land rental market. As shown in columns (3) and (4) of Table 3.6, estimates of off-farm employment in villages with a land rental market are insignificant, while those without a land rental market are significantly positive, regardless of whether control variables are added. Moreover, the result passes the coefficient difference test between groups at the level of 5% significance. This may be because, in villages where there is a land rental market, farmers have more opportunities to rent out their land, making it less likely to abandon their cropland.

**Table 3.7** Off-farm employment and cropland abandoned area

| | Dependent variable: the logarithm of the area of abandoned croplands | | | |
|---|---|---|---|---|
| | (1) | (2) | (3) | (4) |
| Off-farm employment | 0.067** | 0.072** | 0.072** | 0.076** |
| | (0.032) | (0.033) | (0.035) | (0.033) |
| Individual characteristics | | Yes | Yes | Yes |
| Household characteristics | | Yes | Yes | Yes |
| Community characteristics | | Yes | Yes | Yes |
| Household-fixed effect | Yes | Yes | Yes | Yes |
| Time-fixed effect | Yes | Yes | Yes | Yes |
| Province × time-fixed effect | No | No | No | Yes |
| Obs. | 15,101 | 15,101 | 15,101 | 15,101 |
| Cluster unit | Household | Household | Village | Household |
| R-squared | 0.837 | 0.841 | 0.841 | 0.843 |

*Notes* ***, **, and * denote significance at the 1%, 5%, and 10% levels, respectively; Robust standard errors, clustered at the household level, are shown in parentheses

## 3.6 Extended Analysis

### *3.6.1 Impact of Off-Farm Employment on the Cropland Abandoned Area*

Off-farm employment will cause farmers to abandon their cropland, but it is still unknown how much of it will be abandoned. To comprehensively explore the impact of off-farm employment on farmers' cropland abandonment behavior. Referring to Zheng and Qian (2021), we further use the logarithm of the abandoned cropland area to regress off-farm employment. The estimated results in Table 3.7 indicate that off-farm employment increases the area of abandoned cropland by about 7%, and this result passes the statistical test at the 5% significant level.

### *3.6.2 Effects of Different Types of Off-Farm Employment on Cropland Abandonment*

Since different types of off-farm employment imply different working distances, their effects on cropland abandonment may also be inconsistent (Xu et al., 2019a; Lu, 2020). Given the availability of data, therefore, this study distinguishes between local and non-local/out-migration types of work based on whether they work outside the province (no = 1, yes = 0), intending to explore the impact of these distinct types

**Table 3.8** Different types of off-farm employment and cropland abandonment

| | Dependent variable: whether farm households abandon cropland | |
|---|---|---|
| | (1) Local work | (2) Non-local work |
| Off-farm employment | 0.059* | 0.086* |
| | (0.035) | (0.047) |
| Observed difference | −0.027** | |
| Empirical p-value | 0.035 | |
| Control variables | Yes | Yes |
| Household-fixed effect | Yes | Yes |
| Time-fixed effect | Yes | Yes |
| Obs. | 5193 | 9908 |
| R-squared | 0.879 | 0.893 |

*Notes* ***, **, and * denote significance at the 1%, 5%, and 10% levels, respectively; Robust standard errors, clustered at the household level, are shown in parentheses

of off-farm employment on cropland abandonment. Table 3.8 shows that farmers who work off-farm in the local area are less likely to abandon their cropland than those in other areas. One possible explanation is that farmers working outside the province are less likely to work part-time in agriculture due to the high cost of round-trip transportation, accommodation, etc., compared to their local counterparts.

### *3.6.3 Nonlinear Relationship between Off-Farm Employment and Cropland Abandonment*

The above discussion focuses mainly on the impact of off-farm employment on cropland abandonment when farmers are still dependent on agriculture for their livelihoods, but the question is, what if farmers no longer rely solely on agriculture for their economic source? In this case, it is quite necessary to explore the nonlinear relationship between off-farm employment and cropland abandonment. For a rural household, when a small part of the labor participates in off-farm employment, the household can meet basic living needs by engaging in both agricultural and non-agricultural industries at the same time and abandoning the less profitable farm operation on marginal cropland. What needs to be added is that, because of unstable income expectations, farm households are likely to retain the cropland they cannot fully cultivate and are unwilling to lease it to others, even if the cropland may be abandoned in the future. In this case, we may observe a positive association between the two types of behavior. However, when most of the labor force is involved in off-farm employment, the large increase in off-farm wages will make the household less dependent on-farm operations; and cropland will also be boldly leased to others due to the shortage of agricultural labor and the increase in expected income. Under this condition, we may find a negative correlation between off-farm employment and cropland abandonment.

To explore the nonlinear relationship between off-farm employment and cropland abandonment, "whether farm households abandon cropland" and "logarithm of the area of abandoned croplands" are respectively used to regress the size of household off-farm employment for ease of interpretation of estimates. As shown in Table 3.9, it is interesting that regardless of the dependent variable, the size of off-farm employment and its square have opposite effects and pass the statistical test. This means that there is an inverted U-shaped relationship between off-farm employment and farmers' cropland abandonment behavior, which is basically in line with Deng et al. (2018). According to column (1), the turning point occurs when the size of off-farm employment in the household accumulates to the level of 1.95 ($0.039/-2 \times (-0.010)$). As for column (2), when the size of off-farm employment in the household reaches the level of 1.80 ($0.54/-2 \times (-0.015)$), an inflection point occurs. In other words, when farmer households have fewer than two off-farm employment, fluctuating income expectations can cause cropland to be abandoned due to a lack of labor. However, once households have more than two off-farm employment, they no longer abandon their cropland. The main reason is that according to the CFD, the size of off-farm employment in households of less than three persons accounted for 92.88% of the total sample. As a result, more than two off-farm employment in a household generally means that the family is less dependent on farming, and they live mainly on off-farm income.

**Table 3.9** Nonlinear relationship between off-farm employment and cropland abandonment

| | Dependent variable | |
|---|---|---|
| | (1) Whether farm households abandon cropland | (2) The logarithm of the area of abandoned croplands |
| Off-farm employment | 0.039*** | 0.054*** |
| | (0.013) | (0.018) |
| Off-farm employment$^2$ | −0.010** | −0.015*** |
| | (0.004) | (0.005) |
| Control variables | Yes | Yes |
| Household-fixed effect | Yes | Yes |
| Time-fixed effect | Yes | Yes |
| Obs. | 15,101 | 15,101 |
| R-squared | 0.873 | 0.841 |

*Notes* ***, **, and * denote significance at the 1%, 5%, and 10% levels, respectively; Robust standard errors, clustered at the household level, are shown in parentheses

## 3.7 Conclusions and Discussion

### 3.7.1 Conclusions

With the rapid development of industrialization and urbanization, the problem of cropland abandonment in developing countries is becoming increasingly serious, posing an urgent threat to food security in the post-epidemic era. Based on two periods of nationally representative household-level data from the CFD in 2017 and 2019 across 29 provinces in rural China, this study adopts a two-way fixed effects panel model to estimate the impact of off-farm employment on cropland abandonment. After comprehensively excluding the possible endogeneity problems caused by reverse causality, omitted variables, and measurement errors, the following conclusions are drawn: the current off-farm employment in general significantly increases the probability and area of cropland being abandoned by farmers due to the reduction of agricultural labor rather than land rent-out. This finding still holds after an array of robustness tests. Meanwhile, the effect also varies considerably with land and labor characteristics. Specifically, off-farm employment mainly affects farmers with a shortage of agricultural labor, while it does not increase the abandonment of cropland by farmers with sufficient agricultural labor; Off-farm employment exerts a positive and significant impact on cropland abandonment for farmers without agricultural machinery, but little influence on other farmers; off-farm employment is more likely to exacerbate cropland abandonment in non-plain areas compared with farmers living in plain areas; Compared with those without land rental market, villages with a land rental market are less likely to be affected by off-farm employment. Furthermore, farmers who work off-farm in the local area are less likely to abandon their cropland than those in other areas. In addition, there is a nonlinear inverted U-shaped relationship between off-farm employment and cropland abandonment. For China's current family structure, once the number of off-farm employment in a household exceeds two, the probability and area of cropland abandonment of farmers will decline surprisingly. Since the household is no longer dependent on farming, it is comfortable to rent out the cropland rather than abandon it.

### 3.7.2 Policy Implications

Given that industrialization and urbanization are hardly irreversible, minimizing the abandonment of cropland is a common challenge for developing countries. In this context, it is imperative for policymakers to focus on the heterogeneous effects of off-farm employment on cropland abandonment and to grasp the dynamic balance of man-land relations within the household. Based on the above findings, targeted policy recommendations are as follows. First, the government needs to develop local industries and nurture the rural labor market to alleviate the shortage of agricultural labor, especially during the busy farming season. Meanwhile, encouraging mutual assistance and cooperation among villagers may also be a viable option. Second, it is equally important to develop the agricultural machinery market and encourage farmers to address the labor shortage problem by leasing or purchasing agricultural machinery services in the process of farming, planting, and harvesting. Third, compared to plain areas, land consolidation in mountainous areas should be strengthened to reduce farm costs. The main reason is that, for many developing countries, mountainous areas may account for a larger proportion of land area and require more time and energy to maintain. Fourth, the government should develop the land rental market so that farm households can rent out land that is inconvenient for farming. The simple reason is that if the land can be rented out freely, then there is no need for farm households to abandon it. Finally, the inverted U-shaped relationship between off-farm employment and cropland abandonment implies that the optimization of the family labor structure should be taken as the starting point to further promote the transfer of labor from rural to urban areas. This is because when farm households engaged in off-farm employment are no longer completely dependent on agriculture, the probability and degree of abandonment of cropland will decrease rather than increase.

### 3.7.3 Research Limitations and Prospects

Despite the strengths of this study, there are several limitations, due to data availability challenges, that require further improvement. For instance, the impact of off-farm employment stability on cropland abandonment needs to be investigated in depth. In theory, the more stable off-farm employment of family members, the less likely they are to engage in both farm and migrant work, and instead focus on off-farm employment. Consequently, stability in off-farm employment may reduce cropland abandonment, as farmers can no longer rely on agriculture and rent out their croplands with confidence. Secondly, it is helpful to clearly define different types of cropland abandonment to specify differentiated strategies for the management of cropland abandonment. Cropland abandonment can be divided into seasonal and perennial abandonment according to the idle state of cropland within a year, and it can also be divided into explicit and implicit abandonment based on whether cropland is fully utilized. Since different types of cropland abandonment imply different levels of labor demand, the impact of off-farm employment may differ. Finally, it is valuable to find a reasonable instrumental variable to address the underlying endogeneity issues. Although this study focuses on the sources of endogeneity, i.e., omitted variables, reverse causality, and measurement error, and minimizes the interference of endogeneity on estimates, the endogeneity problem has not been fundamentally solved. Therefore, it is still necessary to find a suitable instrumental variable to more robustly evaluate the causal relationship between off-farm employment and cropland abandonment.

## References


Cai, F. (2018). The great exodus: How agricultural surplus laborers have been transferred and reallocated in China's reform period? *China Agricultural Economic Review, 10*, 3–15.

Chandrasekhar, C. (1993). Agrarian change and occupational diversification: Non-agricultural employment and rural development in West Bengal. *The Journal of Peasant Studies, 20*, 205–270.

Deininger, K., Ali, D. A., & Alemu, T. (2011). Impacts of land certification on tenure security, investment, and land market participation: Evidence from Ethiopia. *Land Economics, 87*, 312–334.

Deininger, K., Savastano, S., & Carletto, C. (2012). Land fragmentation, cropland abandonment, and land market operation in Albania. *World Development, 40*, 2108–2122.

Deng, X., Xu, D., Qi, Y., & Zeng, M. (2018). Labor off-farm employment and cropland abandonment in rural China: Spatial distribution and empirical analysis. *International Journal of Environmental Research and Public Health, 15*, 1808.

Djoumessi, Y. F., Kamdem, C. B., & Ndeffo Nembot, L. (2020). Moving off agrarian societies: Agricultural productivity to facilitate economic transformations and non-agricultural employment growth in sub-Saharan Africa. *Journal of International Development, 32*, 324–341.

FAO, I., UNICEF, WFP, WHO. (2022), The state of food security and nutrition in the world 2022. Retrieved from Rome.

Ito, J., Nishikori, M., Toyoshi, M., & Feuer, H. N. (2016). The contribution of land exchange institutions and markets in countering farmland abandonment in Japan. *Land Use Policy, 57*, 582–593.

Izquierdo, A. E., & Grau, H. R. (2009). Agriculture adjustment, land-use transition and protected areas in northwestern Argentina. *Journal of Environmental Management, 90*, 858–865.

Lambin, E. F., & Meyfroidt, P. (2010). Land use transitions: Socio-ecological feedback versus socio-economic change. *Land Use Policy, 27*, 108–118.

Latruffe, L., & Piet, L. (2014). Does land fragmentation affect farm performance? A case study from Brittany, France. *Agricultural Systems, 129*, 68–80.

Lewis, W. A. (2016). Economic development with unlimited supplies of labour. *Paradigms in Economic Development. Routledge*, 59–97.

Li, S. P., Dong, Y. Q., Zhang, L. X., & Liu, C. F. (2021), Off-farm employment and poverty alleviation in rural China. *Journal of Integrative Agriculture, 20*(4), 943–952. https://doi.org/10.1016/s2095-3119(21)63616-x

Lu, C. (2020). Does household laborer migration promote farmland abandonment in China? *Growth and Change, 51*, 1804–1836.

Ma, W., Renwick, A., & Grafton, Q. (2018). Farm machinery use, off-farm employment and farm performance in China. *Australian Journal of Agricultural and Resource Economics, 62*, 279–298.

Ma, W., Zhu, Z., & Zhou, X. (2022). Agricultural mechanization and cropland abandonment in rural China. *Applied Economics Letters, 29*, 526–533.

MacDonald, D., Crabtree, J. R., Wiesinger, G., Dax, T., Stamou, N., Fleury, P., Lazpita, J. G., & Gibon, A. (2000). Agricultural abandonment in mountain areas of Europe: Environmental consequences and policy response. *Journal of Environmental Management, 59*, 47–69.

Müller, D., Leitão, P. J., & Sikor, T. (2013). Comparing the determinants of cropland abandonment in Albania and Romania using boosted regression trees. *Agricultural Systems, 117*, 66–77.

Ojha, R. B., Atreya, K., Kristiansen, P., Devkota, D., & Wilson, B. (2022). A systematic review and gap analysis of drivers, impacts, and restoration options for abandoned croplands in Nepal. *Land Use Policy, 120*, 106237.

Price, B., Kienast, F., Seidl, I., Ginzler, C., Verburg, P. H., & Bolliger, J. (2015). Future landscapes of Switzerland: Risk areas for urbanisation and land abandonment. *Applied Geography, 57*, 32–41.

Qian, W., Crowley-Vigneau. (2020). The economy of Chinese rural households. Springer.

Queiroz, C., Beilin, R., Folke, C., & Lindborg, R. (2014). Farmland abandonment: Threat or opportunity for biodiversity conservation? A global review. *Frontiers in Ecology and the Environment, 12*, 288–296.
Rajkhowa, P., & Qaim, M. (2022). Mobile phones, off-farm employment and household income in rural India. *Journal of Agricultural Economics, 73*, 789–805.
Rozelle, S., Taylor, J. E., & DeBrauw, A. (1999). Migration, remittances, and agricultural productivity in China. *American Economic Review, 89*, 287–291.
San Roman Sanz, A., Fernandez, C., Mouillot, F., Ferrat, L., Istria, D., & Pasqualini, V. (2013). Long-term forest dynamics and land-use abandonment in the Mediterranean mountains, Corsica, France. *Ecology and Society, 18*.
Su, W., Eriksson, T., Zhang, L., & Bai, Y. (2016). Off-farm employment and time allocation in on-farm work in rural China from gender perspective. *China Economic Review, 41*, 34–45.
Taylor, J. E., Rozelle, S., & De Brauw, A. (2003). Migration and incomes in source communities: A new economics of migration perspective from China. *Economic Development and Cultural Change, 52*, 75–101.
Van den Broeck, G., & Kilic, T. (2019). Dynamics of off-farm employment in sub-Saharan Africa: A gender perspective. *World Development, 119*, 81–99.
van der Zanden, E. H., Verburg, P. H., Schulp, C. J., & Verkerk, P. J. (2017). Trade-offs of European agricultural abandonment. *Land Use Policy, 62*, 290–301.
Wang, J., Xin, L., & Wang, Y. (2020). How farmers' non-agricultural employment affects rural land circulation in China? *Journal of Geographical Sciences, 30*, 378–400.
Xie, H., & Lu, H. (2017). Impact of land fragmentation and non-agricultural labor supply on circulation of agricultural land management rights. *Land Use Policy, 68*, 355–364.
Xu, D., Deng, X., Huang, K., Liu, Y., Yong, Z., & Liu, S. (2019a). Relationships between labor migration and cropland abandonment in rural China from the perspective of village types. *Land Use Policy, 88*, 104164.
Xu, D., Deng, X., Guo, S., & Liu, S. (2019b). Labor migration and farmland abandonment in rural China: Empirical results and policy implications. *Journal of Environmental Management, 232*, 738–750.
Yan, J., Yang, Z., Li, Z., Li, X., Xin, L., & Sun, L. (2016). Drivers of cropland abandonment in mountainous areas: A household decision model on farming scale in Southwest China. *Land Use Policy, 57*, 459–469.
Zhang, L. x. (2021). Off-farm employment and poverty alleviation in rural China. *Journal of Integrative Agriculture, 20*, 943–952.
Zhang, Y., Li, X., & Song, W. (2014). Determinants of cropland abandonment at the parcel, household and village levels in mountain areas of China: A multi-level analysis. *Land Use Policy, 41*, 186–192.
Zheng, L. (2023). Impact of off-farm employment on cooking fuel choices: Implications for rural-urban transformation in advancing sustainable energy transformation. *Energy Economics, 118*, 106497.
Zheng, L. (2024). Big hands holding small hands: The role of new agricultural operating entities in farmland abandonment. *Food Policy, 123*, 102605.
Zheng, L., & Qian, W. (2021). The impact of land certification on cropland abandonment: Evidence from rural China. *China Agricultural Economic Review, 14*, 509–526.
Zheng, L., Su, L., & Jin, S. (2023). Reducing land fragmentation to curb cropland abandonment: Evidence from rural China. *Canadian Journal of Agricultural Economics/Revue canadienne d'agroeconomie, 71*, 355–373.

# Chapter 4
# Land Fragmentation and Cropland Abandonment

**Abstracts** Reducing land fragmentation can theoretically curb cropland abandonment, thus ensuring food security. However, few studies have quantified this relationship using large-scale survey data at the household level. This chapter adopts a two-way fixed-effects (TWFE) model to examine the effect of land fragmentation on cropland abandonment using nationally representative panel data from the China Rural Household Panel Survey (CRHPS). The panel data set contains 15,138 households across 29 provinces in 2017 and 2019. Results show that land fragmentation has a significant and positive relationship with cropland abandonment. The mechanism analysis reveals that this relationship is due to high labor costs and difficulties in renting out the fragmented land. The heterogeneity analysis indicates that farmers with poor human capital and those living in non-plain areas are at a higher risk of abandoning their cropland due to land fragmentation. Furthermore, the association between land fragmentation and cropland abandonment tends to vary across different land rent-in scenarios. For instance, an increase in the number of plots in the case of land rent-in is not necessarily associated with cropland abandonment. These findings are conducive to correcting the underestimation of the role of land fragmentation in cropland abandonment, and their implications may be extended to various countries.

**Keywords** Land fragmentation · Cropland abandonment · Land economics · Land use policy · Food security

Reducing land fragmentation can theoretically curb cropland abandonment, thus ensuring food security. However, few studies have quantified this relationship using large-scale survey data at the household level. This chapter adopts a two-way fixed effects (TWFE) model to examine the effect of land fragmentation on cropland abandonment using nationally representative panel data from the China Rural Household Panel Survey (CRHPS). The panel data set contains 15,138 households across 29 provinces in 2017 and 2019.



L. Zheng, *Cropland Abandonment in Rural China*, Resources, Environment and Agricultural Development, https://doi.org/10.1007/978-981-95-8287-7_4

## 4.1 Introduction

Cropland abandonment contributes to increasing carbon storage (Kuemmerle et al., 2011; Silver et al., 2000), reducing soil erosion (Liu et al., 2012), and restoring forest ecosystems (Chazdon, 2008). However, cropland abandonment can also have impacts on food security (Queiroz et al., 2014). When cropland is no longer used for farming, the food production in that area decreases, which could reduce the overall food supply (Campbell, 2015). The global role of food security is increasingly prominent in the context of the COVID-19 pandemic, frequent extreme weather events, and the ongoing conflict between Russia and Ukraine (Zheng et al., 2023). Therefore, reducing cropland abandonment and maximizing cropland use to maintain food security have become many governments' policy priorities.

Cropland abandonment is a global phenomenon that occurs in both developed and developing countries. Since the beginning of the industrial revolution in the mid-nineteenth century, European countries have documented substantial cropland abandonment (Mather, 2001). At the beginning of the twentieth century, cropland abandonment began occurring in parts of the Americas and Southeast Asian countries (Fox et al., 2009; Rhemtulla et al., 2009). After the collapse of socialism in the 1990s, the former Soviet Union and former socialist countries in Central and Eastern Europe, such as Albania (Deininger et al., 2012; Sikor et al., 2009), Russia, Ukraine, and Kazakhstan (Meyfroidt et al., 2016), also faced a high rate of cropland abandonment. In the twenty-first century, the cropland abandonment in France (San Roman Sanz et al., 2013), Portugal (Van Doorn and Bakker, 2007), Switzerland (Price et al., 2015), and Austria (Silber and Wytrzens, 2006) has become increasingly severe. In recent years, there has been a significant increase in cropland abandonment in several developing countries, including China (Deng et al., 2019; Xu et al., 2021; Yan et al., 2016; Zhang et al., 2014), Chile (Díaz et al., 2011), and Argentina (Izquierdo & Grau, 2009). According to Campbell et al. (2008), the global abandoned cropland area has ranged from approximately 3.85 million to 4.72 million $km^2$ since the twentieth century.

Cropland abandonment is a complex and multidimensional phenomenon that is influenced by the interaction of environmental, economic, political, and social determinants (Lambin & Meyfroidt, 2010). Harsh natural conditions (e.g., steep topographies and poor soil conditions), parlous economic state (e.g., massive rural-urban labor migration and low agricultural income), imperfect land rental market (e.g., market failure and policy distortion), and unsatisfactory land reform (e.g., transfer rights limitation and inheritance rights subdivision), among others, affect cropland abandonment to varying degrees (Deininger et al., 2012; Lieskovsky and Lieskovska, 2021; MacDonald et al., 2000; Prishchepov et al., 2012; Xu et al., 2019; Zhou et al., 2020; Zhang et al., 2014). Specifically, land fragmentation is a critical driving force affecting cropland abandonment (Zhang et al., 2018). However, little attention has been devoted to exploring the nexus between land fragmentation and cropland abandonment, as well as its mechanisms and heterogeneous effects.

To the best of our knowledge, there have been only three quantitative studies exploring this correlation, but reach different conclusions, possibly due to difference in sample size, and the cross-sectional nature of the data that is difficult to deal with omitted variable biases. Specifically, based on 98 villages in Albania in 2004, Sikor et al. (2009) have found no evidence that land fragmentation causes cropland abandonment. In contrast, employing data from 1796 farms in the 2005 Albania Living Standards Survey, Deininger et al. (2012) have pointed out that approximately 10% of cropland is abandoned due to land fragmentation. Like in Albania and other countries, China also witnessed land fragmentation and cropland abandonment. From a geographical perspective, Wang et al. (2022) quantified the impact of land tenure fragmentation on cropland abandonment using 5479 observations from the Chinese Family Database in 2017. They found that the larger the average plot size, the less likely the cropland would be abandoned. While this is the most relevant paper for this study, they did not employ the latest panel data and fixed-effect models to rule out biases associated with unobserved factors that are correlated with both land fragmentation and cropland abandonment. Meanwhile, they did not discuss how land fragmentation affects cropland abandonment, nor did they explore the heterogeneous effects of land fragmentation on cropland abandonment from the perspective of labor and land endowment. Furthermore, while they examined the moderation effect of land rentals, they did not further distinguish between land rent-out and rent-in, although the latter could directly reduce the degree of land fragmentation.

Given this literature gap, we employ a two-way fixed effects model and nationally representative panel data from the China Rural Household Panel Survey between 2017 and 2019 to alleviate the potential omitted variable bias and the possible estimation biases due to small samples. By comprehensively examining the overall and heterogeneous associations between land fragmentation and cropland abandonment, and the underlying mechanisms, we deepen the current understanding of the relationship between land fragmentation and cropland abandonment. Given that land rental is an important factor that causes changes in the number of plots, we also discuss the potential measurement bias of using the number of plots as the core independent variable in the estimation process when households participate in land rental.

More specifically, this study aims to fill a gap in research by comprehensively answering the following research questions: (i) Does land fragmentation increase cropland abandonment? (ii) If so, how does land fragmentation associated with cropland abandonment? (iii) Is the relationship between land fragmentation and cropland abandonment consistent among households with different levels of human capital and living in different topographies? (iv) In the Chinese scenario, is the role of land fragmentation in cropland abandonment underestimated when land fragmentation is measured by the number of plots? From the perspective of agricultural and applied economics, this is the first study to address the above questions using the latest large-scale panel data in the Chinese context.

## 4.2 Background and Theory

Land fragmentation hinders agricultural production efficiency and threatens national food security in China. To explore the relationship between land fragmentation and cropland abandonment in the Chinese context, we first examine the causes and governance of land fragmentation. Then, based on the literature, we analyze how land fragmentation affects cropland abandonment from the perspective of the labor market and land rental market, laying a theoretical foundation for the mechanism analysis in the empirical section.

### *4.2.1 Causes and Governance of Land Fragmentation in China*

Cropland fragmentation is not a new phenomenon in China. It is closely related to the extreme scarcity of land and irreversible population growth. However, today's intense discussion about land fragmentation dates back to the late 1970s or early 1980s, when the Household Responsibility System (HRS) was introduced in China, profoundly influencing the current and future pattern of land fragmentation. The HRS prioritized fairness at its establishment. Before the HRS, farmers could not make their own decisions on agricultural production. Under collective production system and the principle of equal distribution of production, farmers' production enthusiasm was severely hindered, leading to agriculture stagnation for a long time. In this context, based on the independent exploration of grassroots farmers in Anhui province, the HRS was officially recognized by the Chinese government and gradually promoted nationwide. Although the HRS is a collective land tenure system, in essence, its land use rights have been assigned to farmers rather than collectives. Farmers have gained greater autonomy over agricultural production by signing land leases with collectives.

The allocation of land under the HRS has three characteristics. First, the collective allocates the farmland to each household in the village according to the size of the household labor force, the household population, or a combination of the two. The farmers may initially obtain 15 years of land use rights. Second, farmland allocated to farmers by lottery is usually based on careful consideration of distance and fertility to ensure a fair starting point (Tan et al., 2006). As a result, a household may occupy several plots of farmland of different sizes, shapes, and locations. Third, due to changes in the village population (e.g., births, deaths, migrations, and marriages), the village collective may carry out land redistribution every few years to guarantee fairness in the process. Specifically, households with an increased population may obtain an extra piece of land from the collective. In contrast, households with a decreased population may be asked to give back a share of the land to the collective. This mechanism assures that every farmer in the village detains roughly the same amount of farmland in the short run. The advantages and disadvantages of the HRS are apparent. On the one hand, it can improve farmers' enthusiasm for production and increase food output in the initial stage of implementation. On the other hand, it has aggravated land fragmentation and hindered agricultural modernization over time.

To alleviate land fragmentation, China has implemented various governance measures. First, it has adopted land consolidation, the most direct solution to land fragmentation, widely used in many countries. Land consolidation implies reducing the degree of land fragmentation and promoting the continuous management of land through engineering, biological, and other measures in a region, according to the objectives determined by a general plan for land use. Starting from the mid-1980s, local governments in some eastern coastal areas of China have begun implementing land consolidation projects, followed a few years later by some central provinces (Tan et al., 2006). In 1999, the Land Management Law officially stated that land consolidation should be encouraged. Since the beginning of the 2000s, China has successively implemented *the National Plan for Land Development and Consolidation (2001–2010), the National Plan for Land Consolidation (2011–2015)*, and *the National Plan for Land Consolidation (2016–2020)*, all of which require comprehensive consolidation of land to increase the area of effective cropland. Second, China has supported land rental, which emphasizes the integration of plots of land to new agricultural management subjects through the market-based rental of land elements. Doing so, the farmland may be transformed, switching from the original small-scale farmers' decentralized operations to the current large-scale farmers' operations. To promote land transfer, the Chinese government issued *the Administrative Measures for the Transfer of Rural Land Contractual Management Rights* in 2005, encouraging farmers to lease their land to others voluntarily. In 2014, the Chinese government issued *the Opinions on Guiding the Orderly Transfer of Rural Land Use Rights to Develop Appropriate-Scale Agricultural Operations*, and began to separate land rights into ownership, contracting rights, and use rights, so that land use rights may better serve large-scale farmers. The government also enacted the prohibition of land redistribution, which required that collectives could not, in principle, redistribute their land during the contract period, thus reducing the probability that land would be further divided. Moreover, the Chinese government required that the contract period of land be extended from the original 15 years to 30 years. In the newly revised *Land Contract Law of the People's Republic of China* in 2019, the Chinese government extended the land contract period for another 30 years to reach 75 years. Finally, the government has introduced land exchange, emphasizing that farmers in the village could exchange plots far away from their homes with plots of neighbors through private consultations to achieve continuous farming.

The above measures are internal breakthroughs under the HRS to reduce the fragmentation of arable land. Although they have helped curb land fragmentation, the agricultural situation in China, with abundant people and limited land, implies that land fragmentation may not be resolved in the short run. The empirical evidence suggests that the above measures need to be continuously applied in the future. However, under irreversible urbanization and population growth, the HRS, the root cause of the current land fragmentation, needs further reform and improvement.

### 4.2.2 Land Fragmentation and Cropland Abandonment

Land fragmentation, associated with land scattering, pulverization, and parcellization (Bentley, 1987), is generally defined as the state in which a single farm is divided into numerous spatially separated plots that belong to at least one property rights subject (King and Burton, 1982; McPherson, 1982; van Dijk, 2003). Land fragmentation is a common challenge in agricultural production in many countries (Campbell, 2015; Kuemmerle et al., 2006). Theoretically, it increases labor input and restrains land rent-out, making cropland easily abandoned (Fig. 4.1).

From the labor market perspective, land fragmentation may increase the probability of cropland abandonment due to the increase in the cost of own labor input and hired labor input. For rational farmers, the higher the cost of agricultural production, the more likely they are to abandon cropland (Lu et al., 2019). Especially under the condition of land fragmentation, the probability of cropland being abandoned will be greatly increased (Deininger et al., 2012). The main reason is that land fragmentation usually means plots are small, fragmented, and scattered (Tan et al., 2006); This not only limits farmers' access to machinery and new technologies but also hinders the development of agricultural infrastructure like irrigation and drainage, resulting in high agricultural production costs (Kawasaki, 2010; Deininger et al., 2011; Ma et al., 2022). In addition, the plots of a farm household are scattered in different locations, making the transportation cost of farmers from their homes to these plots relatively high as well (Wang et al., 2022). As a result, farmers need to invest more time and effort in cultivating these plots, and even hire agricultural labor when their own labor is insufficient (Huang et al., 2008; Lu et al., 2018; Wang et al., 2020a). In this sense, land fragmentation may increase the input of their own agricultural labor and the cost of hiring agricultural labor thereby increasing the probability of cropland being abandoned.

From the land rental market perspective, land fragmentation hinders the lessees from renting the arable land, making the lessors more likely to abandon their land when unable or unwilling to continue agricultural production (FAO, 2004). Compared with large and contiguous plots, small, fragmented, and scattered plots generate greater difficulties in farming, more investment, and low output (Latruffe & Piet,

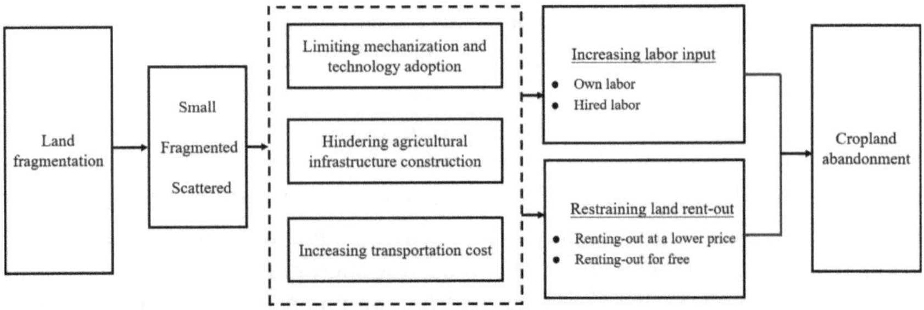


**Fig. 4.1** How land fragmentation affects cropland abandonment

2014; Liu et al., 2019; Veljanoska, 2018). The lessees usually avoid renting those plots, unless they can lease the land of multiple lessors and connect the small, fragmented, and scattered plots into a whole piece through land consolidation (Wang et al., 2022). However, doing so inevitably involves greater transaction costs (Jin and Deininger, 2009), and the initial investment is relatively high (Lu et al., 2018). Therefore, renting out small and scattered marginal land is generally challenging (Cao et al., 2020). Even if a farmer is willing to give their land to others to cultivate for free, sometimes no one is interested due to the relatively low agricultural income (Zhou et al., 2020; Zheng & Qian, 2021). In rural areas of China, it is common to lease farmland at a lower price, and farmers also offer their own land to others for free when they cannot cultivate it (Wang et al., 2015). Consequently, cropland abandonment is a reasonable choice for some farmers, especially for small, fragmented, and scattered plots. Hence, land fragmentation may make it more difficult for farmers to rent out land (at market prices), thus aggravating cropland abandonment.

## 4.3 Data and Methods

### *4.3.1 Methodology*

Our empirical analysis comprises three parts. In the first part, we empirically estimate the relationship between land fragmentation and farmers' crop abandonment behavior. To control for the interference of time-invariant unobservable factors at the household level, we specify the following two-way fixed effects (TWFE) model:

$$Y_{it} = \alpha_0 + \alpha_1 Frag_{it} + a_2 X_{it} + \varphi_t + \delta_i + \varepsilon_{it} \tag{4.1}$$

where the dependent variable $Y_{it}$ represents cropland abandonment of rural household $i$ in year $t$. It is a dichotomous variable that takes on a value of 1 if a rural household abandons cropland, and 0 if no cropland is abandoned (i.e., either under self-cultivation or leased to others). $Frag_{it}$ refers to the land fragmentation of rural household $i$ in year $t$. Land fragmentation is defined as the division of land into several distinct plots (Dovring, 2013). We employ the number of plots to proxy land fragmentation, one of the most commonly used measurements of land fragmentation (Cao et al., 2020; Sikor et al., 2009). The greater the number of plots, the higher the degree of land fragmentation is expected. As shown by Wan and Cheng (2001) and Latruffe and Piet (2014), this variable is more understandable than other complex descriptors for policymakers who are willing to implement a land consolidation program.

In line with the related literature, $X_{it}$ is a vector of control variable including the household head's age and its quadratic term (Zhang et al., 2014), the household head's education level (Xu et al., 2019), the dependency ratio, off-farm ratio (Deng et al., 2018; Xu et al., 2019), land certification, land size, land value, economic development and agricultural population characteristics of the village (Zheng & Qian, 2021). $\varphi_t$ is the time-fixed effect, controlling for the macroeconomic situation, national land policy and other time-varying factors that do not change with farmers. $\delta_i$ depicts the household-fixed effect, controlling for farmers' preferences, capabilities and other household-specific time-invariant factors. $\varepsilon_{it}$ is the error term, and $\alpha_0$, $\alpha_1$, $\alpha_2$ are the coefficients to be estimated. The proposed model controls the effect of unobservable factors at the household and time level, as well as the observable factors mentioned in previous studies, helping correct the estimation bias caused by omitted variables.

We assume that land fragmentation is accompanied by increased labor input and difficulties in land rent-out, causing farmers to abandon the land. Thus, in the second part of our analysis, we investigate the effect of land fragmentation on labor input and land rent-out to reveal the channels through which land fragmentation affects cropland abandonment. We specify a two-way fixed effects model as follows:

$$M_{it} = \beta_0 + \beta_1 Frag_{it} + \beta_2 X_{it} + \varphi_t + \delta_i + \varepsilon_{it}. \tag{4.2}$$

where $M_{it}$ represents labor input or land rent-out of rural household i in year t. Labor input is measured by either the quantity or the cost of self-employed and hired on-farm labor, while the degree of difficulty of renting out land is measured by the amount of rent received for per mu of land (RMB, logarithm),[1] whether the land is rented out for free, and whether the household rents out the land. $Frag_{it}$, $X_{it}$, $\varphi_t$, $\delta_i$ and $\varepsilon_{it}$ are defined as in Eq. (4.1) and $\beta_0$, $\beta_1$, $\beta_2$ are the coefficients to be estimated.

Finally, in the third part of our analysis, we investigate the potential heterogeneous relationship between land fragmentation and farmers' cropland abandonment behavior for different groups based on labor endowment, topography, and whether they rent-in land or not, respectively. We carry out heterogeneity analysis by grouping estimation. We compare the significance and magnitude of the coefficients in different groups to draw conclusions on the heterogeneity of land fragmentation affecting cropland abandonment.

### 4.3.2 Data Sources

We obtain household data from the China Rural Household Panel Survey (CRHPS), which is a combination of the China Household Finance Survey and the Chinese Family Database.[2] Since 2011, the CRHPS data have been collected every two years across the country, and five rounds of surveys have been conducted, namely, in 2011, 2013, 2015, 2017, and 2019. However, the data related to cropland abandonment have been collected since 2017; hence, we use the most recent two years of large-scale panel data for the empirical analysis.

---

[1] 1 mu = 1/15 hectare, and the exchange rate of the study period is approximately 1 dollar = 6.88 RMB.

[2] The data can be accessed from http://ssec.zju.edu.cn/sites/main/template/news.aspx?id=51035

The CRHPS collects data from 29 provinces (excluding Xinjiang and Tibet) across the country and employs a stratified, three-stage sampling method proportional to the population size to ensure data are nationally representative (Qian, 2020; Zheng et al., 2023). In the first stage, counties are divided into 10 layers according to per capita GDP, and counties are randomly selected by stratification. In the second stage, communities or villages are randomly selected at the county level. In the third stage, 20 households are randomly selected from each selected community or village. The 2017 survey comprised 11,085 samples from 527 communities, while the 2019 survey increased the number of observations to 11,306 farmer households from 776 communities. To investigate the impact of land fragmentation on cropland abandonment, we use a total number of 15,138 farmer households with cropland to form an unbalanced panel, excluding observations with missing information in the variables used for estimation. Note that there is no attrition in the CRHPS data.

### 4.3.3 Sample Characteristics

Table 4.1 reports the descriptive statistics of the variables used in the empirical analysis. Regarding the dependent variable, 12% of respondents exhibit cropland abandonment behavior. The number of plots of an average household is 5.49, suggesting that land fragmentation is severe in China. Concerning farmers' characteristics, the average age of the household's head is approximately 54, and only a small proportion of the heads (12.4%) have a high school diploma or higher. The mean dependency ratio of the elderly and children is 35.1%, and on average, 22.5% of working-age members are engaged in off-farm employment. An average sample household is endowed with 2.98 mu of cropland per capita, and the average unit value of agricultural land is 15,243 RMB per mu. In addition, 55.9% of respondents reported having obtained land certificates, suggesting that tenure insecurity is still a concern. An average sample household' earns between 5000–10,000 RMB. There are on average nearly eight types of large-scale farming operators in each surveyed village. Moreover, 21.4% of respondents exhibit land rent-out behavior, while 16.4% of respondents have land rent-in behavior.

### 4.3.4 Descriptive Statistics on Land Fragmentation and Cropland Abandonment

Based on the CRHPS data, Figs. 4.2 and 4.3 depict cropland abandonment and land fragmentation in 29 provinces in 2017 and 2019, respectively. Figure 4.2 shows that, from 2017 to 2019, cropland abandonment has become increasingly severe. This is especially the case in the southeastern coastal areas that have been experiencing better economic development, such as Guangdong and Fujian, the cropland abandonment

**Table 4.1** Definition of variables and data description (N = 15,138)

| Variable types | Variables | Definition and assignment | Mean | SD | Min | Max |
|---|---|---|---|---|---|---|
| Dependent variable | Cropland abandonment | Whether cropland is abandoned (0 = no; 1 = yes) | 0.120 | 0.324 | 0 | 1 |
| Key independent variable | Land fragmentation | Number of plots | 5.493 | 5.938 | 1 | 120 |
| Individual characteristics | Age | Age of householder | 53.568 | 10.699 | 16 | 69 |
| | $Age^2$ | Age square of the householder | 2983.942 | 1073.466 | 256 | 4761 |
| | Education | Whether the householder went to high school (0 = no; 1 = yes) | 0.123 | 0.329 | 0 | 1 |
| Household characteristics | Dependency ratio | The dependency ratio of the elderly and children (0—1) | 0.351 | 0.478 | 0 | 5 |
| | Off-farm ratio | The off-farm ratio of the household (0—1) | 0.225 | 0.262 | 0 | 1 |
| | Land certification | Whether farmers have obtained a land certificate (0 = no; 1 = yes) | 0.559 | 0.497 | 0 | 1 |
| | Land size | Per capita land area of the household (mu) | 2.979 | 6.179 | 0.001 | 360 |
| | Land value | Logarithm of land market value per mu estimated by the householder | 7.259 | 2.326 | 0 | 16.670 |
| Community characteristics | Village economy | The range of per capita disposable annual income (1 = lower than 1000 RMB, 2 = 1000–3000 RMB, 3 = 3000–5000 RMB, 4 = 5000–10,000 RMB, 6 = 15,000–20,000 RMB, 7 = 20,000–30,000 RMB, 8 = 30,000–50,000 RMB, 9 = 50,000–100000RMB) | 3.907 | 1.298 | 1 | 9 |

(continued)

**Table 4.1** (continued)

| Variable types | Variables | Definition and assignment | Mean | SD | Min | Max |
|---|---|---|---|---|---|---|
| | Village Agriculture | Number of large-scale farming operators in the village, including large-scale professional operators, household farms, specialized cooperatives, agricultural enterprises | 7.648 | 82.630 | 0 | 2563 |
| Land transfer | Rent-out | Whether the household rents out the land | 0.214 | 0.410 | 0 | 1 |
| | Rent-in | Whether the household rents in the land | 0.164 | 0.370 | 0 | 1 |

rate has increased significantly. Moreover, the spatial distribution of cropland abandonment shown in this study is consistent with that in Xu et al. (2019) using data from the China Labor-force Dynamics Survey in 2014, indicating the representativeness of the CRHPS data. Figure 4.3 reveals that the land fragmentation phenomenon is more severe in some southwestern provinces, such as Chongqing, Guizhou, and Guangxi. A high degree of overlap is observed between areas with high cropland abandonment rates and those with a high level of land fragmentation in both years, especially in the southwestern inland and southeastern coastal provinces. These data suggest a positive correlation between land fragmentation and cropland abandonment, which will be further tested by an empirical model in the following section.

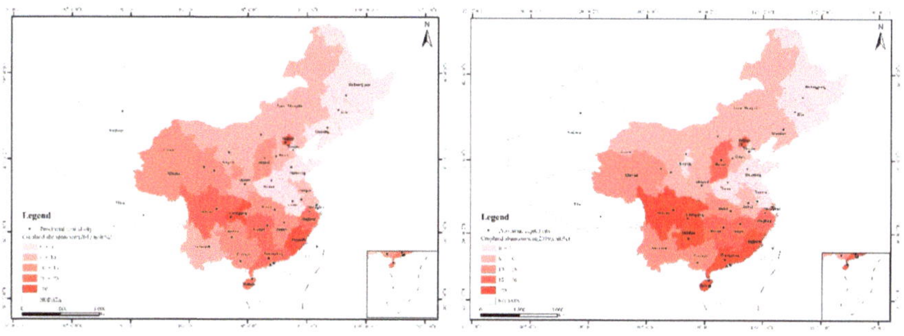

**(a) year 2017** **(b) year 2019**

**Fig. 4.2** Cropland abandonment in 29 provinces of China in 2017 and 2019

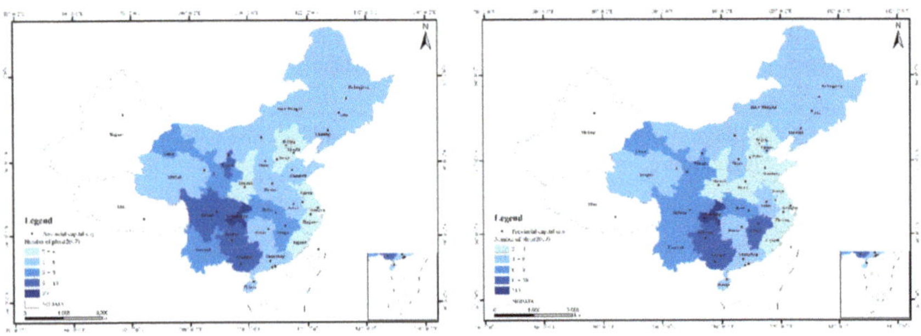

(a) year 2017 (b) year 2019

**Fig. 4.3** Land fragmentation in 29 provinces of China in 2017 and 2019

## 4.4 Empirical Results

### *4.4.1 Impact of Land Fragmentation on Cropland Abandonment*

As mentioned above, we employ a TWFE model to estimate the relationship between land fragmentation and farmers' cropland abandonment behavior. Table 4.2 reports the estimation results. In column (1), only the core independent variable (land fragmentation), the household-fixed effects, and time-fixed effects are included. In column (2), the household- and village-level time-varying variables are further included, to control for important time-varying unobservable factors. In column (3), the province×time-fixed effects are further included, to exclude potential interference from provincial land policies and weather risks (Ward and Shively, 2015). In all three models, the regression coefficients on land fragmentation are positive and significant at the 1% significance level. The coefficient is 0.005, suggesting that the probability of cropland being abandoned increases by 0.5% for an additional plot. The rationale is that smaller and more scattered plots are associated with greater difficulties in farming, requiring more investment, leading to lower output, and ultimately cropland abandonment (Latruffe & Piet, 2014; Liu et al., 2019; Veljanoska, 2018).

With regards to the results on control variables, they are also highly consistent across model specifications. We will focus our discussion using column (2) of Table 4.2 as an example. Age and its square term have significant coefficients that are equal to −0.023 ($p < 0.01$) and 0.0003 ($p < 0.01$), respectively, revealing a U-shaped relationship between householder's age and cropland abandonment. More specifically, when the household head's age is below a certain threshold (approximately 38 years old), the likelihood of cropland abandonment increases with farming experience. After this point, the probability of cropland abandonment increases with further increases in experience. This is not surprising, as it makes sense that further aging at certain age is associated with a decline in their technical and physical capacity. This

**Table 4.2** Effect of land fragmentation on cropland abandonment: Benchmark Results

| | Dependent variable: Whether cropland is abandoned | | |
|---|---|---|---|
| | (1) | (2) | (3) |
| Land fragmentation | 0.005*** | 0.005*** | 0.005*** |
| | (0.001) | (0.001) | (0.001) |
| Age | | −0.023*** | −0.023*** |
| | | (0.006) | (0.006) |
| $Age^2$ | | 0.0003*** | 0.0003*** |
| | | (0.000) | (0.000) |
| Education | | −0.068*** | −0.069*** |
| | | (0.025) | (0.025) |
| Dependency ratio | | 0.043** | 0.043** |
| | | (0.020) | (0.020) |
| Off-farm ratio | | 0.061** | 0.059** |
| | | (0.027) | (0.027) |
| Land certification | | −0.031** | −0.037** |
| | | (0.014) | (0.015) |
| Land size | | 0.002* | 0.002* |
| | | (0.001) | (0.001) |
| Land value | | −0.005** | −0.005* |
| | | (0.003) | (0.003) |
| Village economy | | −0.008* | −0.008 |
| | | (0.005) | (0.005) |
| Village agriculture | | −0.00006** | −0.00009*** |
| | | (0.000) | (0.000) |
| Household-fixed effect | Yes | Yes | Yes |
| Time-fixed effect | Yes | Yes | Yes |
| Province × time-fixed effect | No | No | Yes |
| Obs. | 15,138 | 15,138 | 15,138 |
| $R^2$ | 0.866 | 0.868 | 0.869 |

*Notes*: ***, **, and * denote significance at the 1%, 5%, and 10% levels, respectively; Robust standard errors clustered at the household level are presented in parentheses

finding is also in alignment with Zhang et al. (2014). We find that the education level is a negative and significant determinant of cropland abandonment, in contrast with Schneider and Geoghegan (2006). A plausible explanation may be that a household head with better education is more capable of managing farming activities; hence, they are less likely to abandon cropland (Yan et al., 2016).

The relationship between the dependency ratio and cropland abandonment is significant and positive, which may be explained by the fact that a high dependency ratio means limited labor availability for farming activities. The positive and significant coefficient on engagement in off-farm employment suggests that farmers with a higher level of off-farm engagement are associated with fewer labor resources to sustain the agricultural production on existing land. Land certification is negatively and significantly related to cropland abandonment, which is consistent with Zheng and Qian (2021); land with higher tenure security is less likely to be abandoned. Land size and land value are related to cropland abandonment positively and negatively, respectively, suggesting that the households endowed with a smaller size of land and land of higher value, are less likely to practice abandonment. Finally, the development of the village economy and agricultural development level are negatively correlated with cropland abandonment.

### 4.4.2 Robustness Check

We perform various robustness checks, and the results are presented in Table 4.3. First, instead of defining land abandonment as a dummy variable, we measure land abandonment by two continuous variables (i.e., *abandonment degree* and *abandonment ratio*) that measure the degree of cropland abandonment. The *abandonment degree* is an ordered categorical variable, equal to one, two, and three, depending on whether cropland is not, partially, or completely abandoned. The *abandonment ratio* refers to the ratio of the abandoned cropland area over the total cropland area. The results using these two alternative measures of land abandonment are reported in columns (1) and (2), respectively. The results are highly consistent with those in Table 4.2 as the coefficients of land fragmentation in both columns are positive and highly significant.

Next, we redefine land fragmentation by *Plot_Mean* and *Plot_Median*. *Plot_Mean* is a dichotomous variable, which equals one if the average plot area is lower than its mean at the village level, and zero otherwise. Similarly, *Plot_Median* equals one if the average plot area is lower than its median at the village level, and zero otherwise. Results in columns (3) and (4) of Table 4.3 show that both *Plot_Mean* and *Plot_Median* affect cropland abandonment positively and significantly.

Finally, we replace the TWFE model with a panel logit model and a panel probit model for estimation. The results are reported in column (5) and column (6) of Table 4.3, respectively. The coefficient on land fragmentation is positive and significant under different estimation models. Overall, the results obtained by redefining the dependent and the independent variables and changing the model specification are consistent with those in Table 4.2, confirming that land fragmentation is positively and significantly associated with cropland abandonment.

Additionally, we conduct other robustness checks in Table 4.4, such as employing subsamples that exclude households participating in land rentals, and adding the labor

**Table 4.3** Effect of land fragmentation on cropland abandonment: Results of robustness checks

| | Abandonment degree | Abandonment ratio | Whether cropland is abandoned | | Whether cropland is abandoned | |
|---|---|---|---|---|---|---|
| | (1) | (2) | (3) | (4) | (5) | (6) |
| Land fragmentation | 0.005*** | 0.002*** | | | 0.066*** | 0.037*** |
| | (0.002) | (0.001) | | | (0.006) | (0.004) |
| Plot_Mean | | | 0.063*** | | | |
| | | | (0.011) | | | |
| Plot_Median | | | | 0.051*** | | |
| | | | | (0.011) | | |
| Control variables | Yes | Yes | Yes | Yes | Yes | Yes |
| Household-fixed effect | Yes | Yes | Yes | Yes | No | No |
| Time-fixed effect | Yes | Yes | Yes | Yes | Yes | Yes |
| Obs. | 15,138 | 14,524 | 15,138 | 15,138 | 15,138 | 15,138 |
| Wald chi$^2$ | – | – | – | – | −5209.057 | −5209.452 |
| Log likelihood | – | – | – | – | 255.64 | 248.70 |
| $R^2$ | 0.878 | 0.863 | 0.869 | 0.868 | – | – |

*Notes* ***, **, and * denote significance at the 1%, 5%, and 10% levels, respectively; Robust standard errors clustered at the household level are presented in parentheses

migration variable. These estimates still support a positive and significant correlation between land fragmentation and cropland abandonment.[3]

### 4.4.3 Mechanism Tests

In this subsection, we investigate the effect of land fragmentation on labor input and land rent-out to explore the mechanisms underlying the positive relationship between land fragmentation and cropland abandonment.

Fragmented land holdings constrain farmers' mechanization ability and increase labor input (Wang et al., 2020b). Farmers who cannot afford high labor costs end up

[3] A review pointed out a possibility that local land policies affect land fragmentation and land abandonment. While this is unlikely for three reasons. First, a two-way fixed effects at household level control time invariant land policies at all levels. Second, there is only one year time gap between the two round panel data used in this study, so the chance for any village to implement a new local policy is very unlikely. Third, after careful review of the Rural Land Contract Law of the People's Republic of China, there is no legal provision for the village collective to reclaim the land's contractual rights without compensation. However, without information on localized village land policy, it is impossible for us to be exactly sure whether some villages implemented "illegal" land policies during the two survey rounds and how they may affect the results.

**Table 4.4** Relationship between land fragmentation and cropland abandonment: Further analysis

| | Dependent variable: Whether cropland is abandoned | | | |
|---|---|---|---|---|
| | (1) No rent-out | (2) No rent-in | (3) No transfer | (4) Adding a variable |
| Land fragmentation | 0.005*** | 0.007*** | 0.007*** | 0.005*** |
| | (0.001) | (0.002) | (0.002) | (0.001) |
| Labor migration | | | | −0.037 |
| | | | | (0.064) |
| Control variables | Yes | Yes | Yes | Yes |
| Household-fixed effect | Yes | Yes | Yes | Yes |
| Time-fixed effect | Yes | Yes | Yes | Yes |
| Obs | 11,906 | 12,653 | 9662 | 15,138 |
| $R^2$ | 0.880 | 0.875 | 0.887 | 0.868 |

*Notes* ***, **, and * denote significance at the 1%, 5%, and 10% levels, respectively; Robust standard errors clustered at the household level are presented in parentheses

choosing cropland abandonment. Therefore, the increased labor input may be one of the mechanisms through which land fragmentation is correlated with cropland abandonment. Regarding the number of on-farm workers reported in columns (1) and (2) in Table 4.5, land fragmentation is positively and significantly associated with the number of own and hired on-farm workers. Specifically, for every additional plot, the number of own on-farm workers and hired on-farm workers per unit of land increase by 0.015 and 0.176, respectively. We then replace the number of workers with the logarithm of the labor input value. The effects of land fragmentation on labor input are presented in columns (3) and (4) in Table 4.5. Again, the coefficients of land fragmentation are positive and statistically significant. More specifically, every additional plot is related to an increase in own labor input and hired on-farm labor input by 1.8% and 2.2%, respectively. The above empirical results confirm our hypothesis that land fragmentation generates high labor costs, thus increasing the likelihood of cropland abandonment.

In addition, in the context of urbanization and rural-urban labor migration, the Chinese government encourages land rental to improve the efficiency of land resource allocation. However, farmers find it challenging to rent out land with a high degree of fragmentation and often opt for cropland abandonment. Therefore, the decreased rent-out probability due to land fragmentation may be another driver of cropland abandonment. As shown in Table 4.6, land fragmentation has a negative and significant relationship with land rents and the likelihood of renting out land, and land fragmentation significantly increases the probability of renting out land for free. These results confirm another hypothesis that more fragmented cropland is less likely to be rented out (at market prices), which in turn increases the likelihood of cropland abandonment.

**Table 4.5** Effect of land fragmentation on labor input: Mechanism test I

| | Number of own on-farm workers | Number of hired on-farm workers | Own labor input in farming | Hired labor input in farming |
|---|---|---|---|---|
| | (1) | (2) | (3) | (4) |
| Land fragmentation | 0.015*** | 0.176*** | 0.018*** | 0.022*** |
| | (0.001) | (0.065) | (0.008) | (0.005) |
| Control variables | Yes | Yes | Yes | Yes |
| Household-fixed effect | Yes | Yes | Yes | Yes |
| Time-fixed effect | Yes | Yes | Yes | Yes |
| Obs. | 15,138 | 15,138 | 1638 | 15,138 |
| $R^2$ | 0.060 | 0.005 | 0.212 | 0.036 |

*Notes* ***, **, and * denote significance at the 1%, 5%, and 10% levels, respectively; Robust standard errors clustered at the household level are presented in parentheses

**Table 4.6** Effect of land fragmentation on land rent-out: Mechanism test II

| | (1) Land rents | (2) Land rent-out for free | (3) Land rent-out |
|---|---|---|---|
| Land fragmentation | −0.017*** | 0.003*** | −0.002*** |
| | (0.004) | (0.001) | (0.001) |
| Control variables | Yes | Yes | Yes |
| Household-fixed effect | Yes | Yes | Yes |
| Time-fixed effect | Yes | Yes | Yes |
| Obs. | 15,138 | 15,138 | 15,135 |
| $R^2$ | 0.031 | 0.015 | 0.052 |

*Notes*: ***, **, and * denote significance at the 1%, 5%, and 10% levels, respectively; Robust standard errors clustered at the household level are presented in parentheses

### 4.4.4 Heterogeneity Analysis

Changes in land and labor allocation do not occur independently. As shown in the previous subsection, land fragmentation increases labor input. Therefore, for households with more labor endowment (compared to those with less labor endowment), land fragmentation is likely to be less associated with cropland abandonment. To investigate this heterogeneity across labor endowment (human capital quality and quantity), we divide the sample into two groups according to the quality (i.e., health condition) of household labor. More specifically, any household whose share of unhealthy working-age members in total working-age members is lower than the sample mean of the share variable is considered part of the healthy labor group. Conversely, any household whose share of unhealthy working-age members in total working-age members is equal or greater than the sample mean of the share variable is considered part of the unhealthy labor group. In addition, we divide the sample into two other groups based on the number of workers. More specifically, we define any household whose number of workers is greater than the sample mean as part of the large labor group, and that with the number of workers smaller than the mean as part of the small labor group.

Figure 4.4 visually display the estimated heterogeneous relationship between land fragmentation on cropland abandonment by the health status and quantity of household labor. The estimated coefficients on land fragmentation for households belonging to the healthy labor group or the large labor group are insignificant, while they are positive and significant for the unhealth labor group or the small labor group. The rationale for these results is that farmers with healthier or more workers have a better capacity to cope with the increasing labor input need due to land fragmentation; in this scenario, cropland abandonment is not an inevitable option. In contrast, the increase in labor demand due to land fragmentation is difficult to overcome for rural households with poor labor endowments, which forces them to abandon their cropland.

Other endowment characteristics of land, such as its topography, may determine how land fragmentation is related to cropland abandonment. Intuitively, it is easier to implement land consolidation plans in plain areas than in mountainous areas. Therefore, the relationship between land fragmentation and cropland abandonment may vary among farmers in different topographies. To investigate this issue, we divide

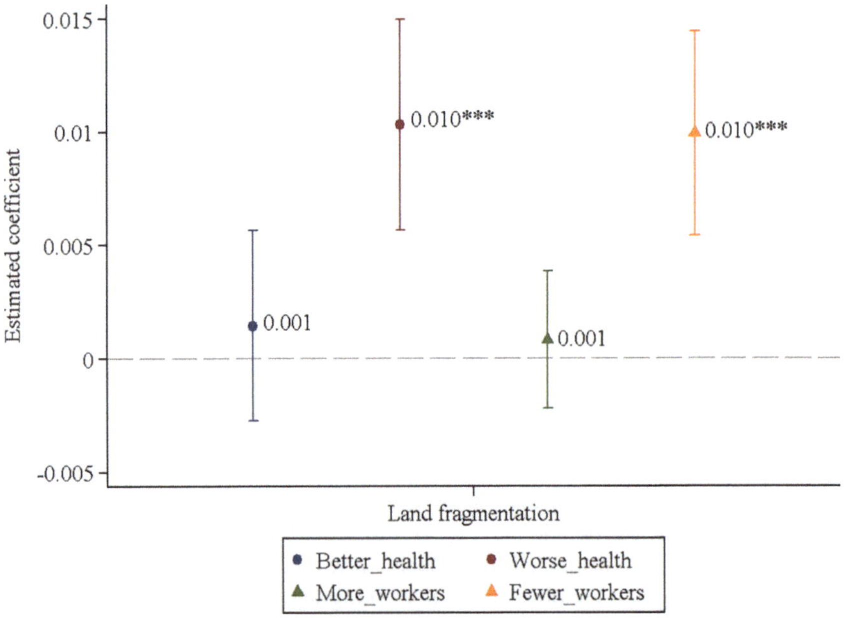


**Fig. 4.4** Heterogeneous effect of land fragmentation on cropland abandonment from the perspective of labor endowment. *Notes* ***, **, and * denote significance at the 1%, 5%, and 10% levels, respectively; The confidence level is 95%

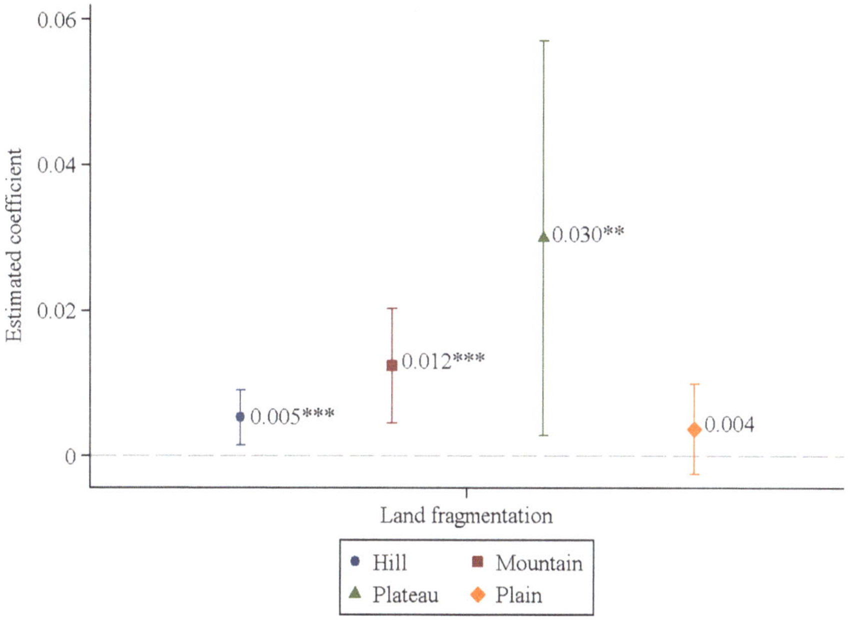


**Fig. 4.5** Heterogeneous effect of land fragmentation on cropland abandonment from the perspective of land topography. *Notes* ***, **, and * denote significance at the 1%, 5%, and 10% levels, respectively; The confidence level is 95%

the sample into four groups according to their topographical characteristics, namely, the hill group, mountain group, plateau group, and plain group. We estimate the relationship between land fragmentation and cropland abandonment for each of the four groups separately. As shown in Fig. 4.5, the estimated coefficients on land fragmentation in the hill, mountain, and plateau groups are all positive and significant, while that in the plain group is not significant. These results indicate that flat terrain alleviates the cultivation difficulties caused by land fragmentation; therefore, cropland abandonment is less practiced. This finding is consistent with the view that farmers in mountainous areas face an increased risk of cropland abandonment (Levers et al., 2018; Ustaoglu and Collier, 2018; Zhang et al., 2016).

## 4.5 Further Discussion

Although the number of plots has often been used to measure land fragmentation, in China, the increase in the number of plots involves two aspects that cannot be neglected. On the one hand, with the implementation of the HRS in China, the average land redistribution has increased the number of self-contracted land plots and land fragmentation. On the other hand, renting land from other households directly leads to an increase in the number of land plots. While the increase in the number of plots due to redistribution entails exogenous land fragmentation, the increase in the number of plots due to rent-in reflects farmers' intention for large-scale operation. In other words, if rational farmers rent-in land that is adjacent to their own contracted land, the plot number increase does not mean an increase in land fragmentation. Therefore, the contiguity of land plots should be considered when employing the number of plots to measure land fragmentation. Unfortunately, data to describe the contiguity of land plots are unavailable to us. To address this issue, we divide the sample into two separate groups depending on whether a household is engaged in renting in land or not. This strategy is a novel methodological attempt, and the empirical evidence has substantial policy implications and potential guidance for future research.

We separately estimate the relationship between land fragmentation and cropland abandonment for the above-mentioned two groups. As shown in columns (1) and (2) in Table 4.7, the estimated coefficients on land fragmentation in the rent-in group are not significant, while those in the non-rent-in group are positive and significant. In line with our expectation, an increase in the number of plots due to renting in land does not necessarily lead to cropland abandonment. On the contrary, they are likely to benefit from reducing the fragmentation through the geographical connection of their own land and the rented land. Addressing heterogeneity from the perspective of the land rental, our study innovatively distinguishes the increase in the number of plots due to geographical connection through renting in land from land fragmentation due to the administrative land redistribution of contracted land among village collectives, emphasizing the role of land rental in weakening the constraints of land fragmentation. In addition, this approach helps correct the underestimation of the impact of land fragmentation on cropland abandonment.

As mentioned earlier, the increase in the number of plots mainly involves land redistribution and land rental, while the decrease in the number of plots is usually attributed to land consolidation and land exchange, all of which are closely related to land certification. Specifically, by issuing legally effective land certificates with clear rights and multiple uses to farmers, China's new round of land certification reform, launched in 2013, significantly inhibited land redistribution and promoted land leasing and land exchange (Zheng & Qian, 2021). Moreover, the land certification reform, partly adopted the way of focusing on defining and strengthening the rights rather than the physical boundary of land, and transformed land rights into share rights, namely, land consolidation and titling policy (Hu et al., 2021). The fact that the new round of reform goes beyond the physical boundary of land is likely to increase the feasibility of land consolidation.

To indirectly test how the land certification program that strengthens tenure security and promotes land transfers and exchanges affects the relationship between land fragmentation and cropland abandonment, we separate the sample into two subgroups (i.e., certification group and non-certification group). Results in columns (3) and (4) of Table 4.7 show that no matter whether the land is certified or not, land fragmentation is significantly and positively correlated with the probability of cropland abandonment. However, the relationship is much weaker for certified households than the non-certified households (0.003 vs. 0.011). These results suggest that

**Table 4.7** Effect of land fragmentation on cropland abandonment: Further analysis

| | Dependent variable: Whether cropland is abandoned | | | |
|---|---|---|---|---|
| | (1) Land rent-in | (2) No rent-in | (3) Land certification | (4) No certification |
| Land fragmentation | 0.002 | 0.007*** | 0.003** | 0.011*** |
| | (0.002) | (0.002) | (0.002) | (0.002) |
| Control variables | Yes | Yes | Yes | Yes |
| Observed difference | −0.005 | | −0.008 | |
| Empirical p-value | 0.000 | | 0.020 | |
| Household-fixed effect | Yes | Yes | Yes | Yes |
| Time-fixed effect | Yes | Yes | Yes | Yes |
| Obs. | 2485 | 12,653 | 8464 | 6674 |
| $R^2$ | 0.827 | 0.875 | 0.894 | 0.907 |

*Notes* ***, **, and * denote significance at the 1%, 5%, and 10% levels, respectively; Robust standard errors clustered at the household level are presented in parentheses; Empirical p-value is obtained by using the bootstrap method after 100 repetitions

land certification program which promotes land transfer, land exchange, and land consolidation, prohibits land redistribution, is important in delinking the connection between land fragmentation and cropland abandonment.

## 4.6 Conclusion and Policy Implications

China is characterized by a vast population and scarce land resources. Under the HRS, the problems of land fragmentation and cropland abandonment have become increasingly severe, bringing challenges and threats to food security. This study disentangled the relationship between land fragmentation and farmers' cropland abandonment behavior using two-year panel data from CRHPS. Methodologically, we employed a two-way fixed effects model as the main method, which is further supplemented by various robustness checks (i.e., using alternative measures of fragmentation variable and panel logit/probit models). In addition, heterogeneity analysis and mechanism analysis were carried out to help understand how land fragmentation is related to cropland abandonment.

The empirical results show a significant and positive correlation between land fragmentation and cropland abandonment, and these results are robust to various robustness checks. More specifically, ownership of each additional plot of land is associated with an increase in the probability of cropland abandonment by 0.5 percentage points. We posit that more difficulty in farming, more investment needed, lower output, and more difficulty in renting are the main reasons for the positive relationship between land fragmentation (smaller and more scattered plots) and farmers' cropland abandonment behaviors. The results of the mechanism analysis confirm that the higher labor input and labor cost, and more difficult to rent out due to land fragmentation are among the important mechanisms underlying the positive relationship between fragmented cropland and cropland abandonment. In this scenario, fragmentation generates high self-management costs and great difficulties in land rent-out, ultimately leading to cropland abandonment.

The heterogeneity analysis further substantiates our expectations regarding the relationship between land fragmentation and cropland abandonment. First, we find that the positive relationship between land fragmentation and cropland abandonment is much weaker for households endowed with healthier and more abundant labor. This result further highlights the argument that the increase in labor cost due to land fragmentation is an important mechanism underlying the positive relationship between land fragmentation and cropland abandonment. Second, we find that farmers in hilly, mountainous, or plateau areas often need to abandon their cropland due to land fragmentation, but not in plain areas. Land fragmentation is easier to address in plain regions, as the increase in input cost and the difficulties of land rent-out generated by land fragmentation is relatively smaller in the plain regions than in the other regions. Again, these results indirectly support the argument that the labor cost and difficulty in renting out land are two important mechanisms for the positive relationship between land fragmentation and cropland abandonment.

Further analysis reveals that an increase in the number of plots due to renting in land from other households may not necessarily lead to cropland abandonment. The argument is that renting in land that is connected to his/her own plot could even improve the fragmentation conditions. This finding has practical and methodological implications. Using the number of plots as a measure of land fragmentation without accounting for the fact of how the plot is obtained could lead to biased estimates on the relationship between land fragmentation and cropland abandonment. Our results also highlight the importance of promoting the land rental market to reduce land fragmentation, and hence cropland abandonment.

Dealing with cropland abandonment is essential to guarantee national and global food security. Therefore, our findings that land fragmentation is positively correlated with cropland abandonment have valuable implications for China and other developing countries where land fragmentation is increasingly prevalent. First, land fragmentation affects and depends on the land tenure system; hence, the government should reduce land redistribution to avoid further aggravation of land fragmentation. At the same time, policies to promote land consolidation and land exchange can help alleviate land fragmentation. Specifically, cropland with improper allocation, unreasonable use, as well as scattered, idle, and not fully utilized land may be integrated through the comprehensive regulation of field, water, and road resources to achieve contiguous integration. Second, developing countries must improve labor and land rental markets to better manage the need for high labor input and the difficulty of land rent caused by land fragmentation. Third, to weaken the positive association between land fragmentation and cropland abandonment among farmers who are endowed with limited labor resources and located in the non-plain area, the government should take measures (e.g., providing them with small machines, improving their human capital) to reduce the negative consequences of land fragmentation. In doing so, a protective barrier to food security will be gradually established.

## References


Bentley, J. W. (1987). Economic and ecological approaches to land fragmentation: In defense of a much-maligned phenomenon. *Annual Review of Anthropology, 16*, 31–67.

Campbell, J. E., Lobell, D. B., Genova, R. C., & Field, C. B. (2008). The global potential of bioenergy on abandoned agriculture lands. *Environmental Science & Technology, 42*, 5791–5794.

Campbell, J. R. (2015). Development, global change and traditional food security in Pacific Island countries. *Regional Environmental Change, 15*, 1313–1324.

Cao, Y., Zou, J., Fang, X., Wang, J., Cao, Y., & Li, G. (2020). Effect of land tenure fragmentation on the decision-making and scale of agricultural land transfer in China. *Land Use Policy, 99*, 104996.

Chazdon, R. L. (2008). Beyond deforestation: Restoring forests and ecosystem services on degraded lands. *Science, 320*, 1458–1460.

Chandrasekhar, C. (1993). Agrarian change and occupational diversification: Non-agricultural employment and rural development in West Bengal. *The Journal of Peasant Studies, 20*, 205–270.

Deininger, K., Ali, D. A., & Alemu, T. (2011). Impacts of land certification on tenure security, investment, and land market participation: Evidence from Ethiopia. *Land Economics, 87*, 312–334.

Deininger, K., Savastano, S., & Carletto, C. (2012). Land fragmentation, cropland abandonment, and land market operation in Albania. *World Development, 40*, 2108–2122.

Díaz, G. I., Nahuelhual, L., Echeverría, C., & Marín, S. (2011). Drivers of land abandonment in Southern Chile and implications for landscape planning. *Landscape and Urban Planning, 99*, 207–217.

Deng, X., Xu, D., Qi, Y., & Zeng, M. (2018). Labor off-farm employment and cropland abandonment in rural China: Spatial distribution and empirical analysis. *International Journal of Environmental Research and Public Health, 15*, 1808.

Deng, X., Xu, D., Zeng, M., & Qi, Y. (2019). Does internet use help reduce rural cropland abandonment? Evidence from China. *Land Use Policy*, 89, 104243.

Djoumessi, Y. F., Kamdem, C. B., & Ndeffo Nembot, L. (2020). Moving off agrarian societies: Agricultural productivity to facilitate economic transformations and non-agricultural employment growth in sub-Saharan Africa. *Journal of International Development, 32*, 324–341.

Dovring, F. (2013). *Land and labor in Europe 1900–1950: A comparative survey of recent Agrarian history*. Springer.

FAO (2004). *Operations manual for land consolidation pilot projects in Central and Eastern Europe*. Food and Agriculture Organization of the United Nations.

FAO, I., UNICEF, WFP, WHO. 2022, The state of food security and nutrition in the world 2022. Retrieved from Rome.

Fox, J., Fujita, Y., Ngidang, D., Peluso, N., Potter, L., Sakuntaladewi, N., Sturgeon, J., & Thomas, D. (2009). Policies, political-economy, and swidden in Southeast Asia. *Human Ecology, 37*, 305–322.

Hu, X., Su, K., Chen, W., Yao, S., & Zhang, L. (2021). Examining the impact of land consolidation titling policy on farmers' fertiliser use: Evidence from a quasi-natural experiment in China. Land Use Policy, 109, 105645.

Huang, J., Tao, R., & Xu, Z. (2008). *Institutional change and sustainable development: 30 years of Chinese agriculture and rural areas*: Shanghai People's Publishing Agency and Gezhi Press.

Jin, S., & Deininger, K. (2009). Land rental markets in the process of rural structural transformation: Productivity and equity impacts from China. *Journal of Comparative Economics, 37*, 629–646.
Kawasaki, K. (2010). The costs and benefits of land fragmentation of rice farms in Japan. *Australian Journal of Agricultural and Resource Economics, 54*, 509–526.
King, R., & Burton, S. (1982). Land fragmentation-notes on a fundamental rural spatial problem. Progress in Human Geography, 6, 475–494.
Kuemmerle, T., Radeloff, V. C., Perzanowski, K., & Hostert, P. (2006). Cross-border comparison of land cover and landscape pattern in Eastern Europe using a hybrid classification technique. *Remote Sensing of Environment, 103*, 449–464.
Meyfroidt, P., Schierhorn, F., Prishchepov, A. V., Müller, D., & Kuemmerle, T. (2016). Drivers, constraints and trade-offs associated with recultivating abandoned cropland in Russia, Ukraine and Kazakhstan. *Global Environmental Change, 37*, 1–15.
Ito, J., Nishikori, M., Toyoshi, M., & Feuer, H. N. (2016). The contribution of land exchange institutions and markets in countering farmland abandonment in Japan. *Land Use Policy, 57*, 582–593.
Izquierdo, A. E., & Grau, H. R. (2009). Agriculture adjustment, land-use transition and protected areas in northwestern Argentina. *Journal of Environmental Management, 90*, 858–865.
Lambin, E. F., & Meyfroidt, P. (2010). Land use transitions: Socio-ecological feedback versus socio-economic change. *Land Use Policy, 27*, 108–118.
Latruffe, L., & Piet, L. (2014). Does land fragmentation affect farm performance? A case study from Brittany, France. *Agricultural Systems, 129*, 68–80.
Levers, C., Schneider, M., Prishchepov, A. V., Estel, S., & Kuemmerle, T. (2018). Spatial variation in determinants of agricultural land abandonment in Europe. *Science of the total environment, 644*, 95-111.
Lewis, W. A. (2016). Economic development with unlimited supplies of labour. *Paradigms in Economic Development. Routledge*, 59–97.
Lieskovsky, J., & Lieskovska, D. (2021). Cropland abandonment in Slovakia: Analysis and comparison of different data sources. *Land, 10*, 334.
Liu, Y., Fu, B., Lü, Y., Wang, Z., & Gao, G. (2012). Hydrological responses and soil erosion potential of abandoned cropland in the Loess Plateau br/China. *Geomorphology*, 138, 404–414.
Liu, J., Jin, X., Xu, W., Sun, R., Han, B., Yang, X., Gu, Z., Xu, C., Sui, X., & Zhou, Y. (2019). Influential factors and classification of cultivated land fragmentation, and implications for future land consolidation: A case study of Jiangsu province in eastern China. *Land Use Policy, 88*, 104185.
Lu, C. (2020). Does household laborer migration promote farmland abandonment in China? *Growth and Change, 51*, 1804–1836.
Lu, H., Xie, H., He, Y., Wu, Z., & Zhang, X. (2018). Assessing the impacts of land fragmentation and plot size on yields and costs: A translog production model and cost function approach. *Agricultural Systems, 161*, 81–88.
Lu, H., Xie, H., & Yao, G. (2019). Impact of land fragmentation on marginal productivity of agricultural labor and non-agricultural labor supply: A case study of Jiangsu, China. Habitat International, 83, 65–72.
Ma, W., Renwick, A., & Grafton, Q. (2018). Farm machinery use, off-farm employment and farm performance in China. *Australian Journal of Agricultural and Resource Economics, 62*, 279–298.
Ma, W., Zhu, Z., & Zhou, X. (2022). Agricultural mechanization and cropland abandonment in rural China. *Applied Economics Letters, 29*, 526–533.
MacDonald, D., Crabtree, J. R., Wiesinger, G., Dax, T., Stamou, N., Fleury, P., Lazpita, J. G., & Gibon, A. (2000). Agricultural abandonment in mountain areas of Europe: Environmental consequences and policy response. *Journal of Environmental Management, 59*, 47–69.
Mather, A. (2001). The transition from deforestation to reforestation in Europe. *Agricultural Technologies and Tropical Deforestation*, 35–52.
McPherson, M. F. (1982). Land fragmentation: A selected literature review: Cambridge Mass.

Müller, D., Leitão, P. J., & Sikor, T. (2013). Comparing the determinants of cropland abandonment in Albania and Romania using boosted regression trees. *Agricultural Systems, 117*, 66–77.

Ojha, R. B., Atreya, K., Kristiansen, P., Devkota, D., & Wilson, B. (2022). A systematic review and gap analysis of drivers, impacts, and restoration options for abandoned croplands in Nepal. *Land Use Policy, 120*, 106237.

Price, B., Kienast, F., Seidl, I., Ginzler, C., Verburg, P. H., & Bolliger, J. (2015). Future landscapes of Switzerland: Risk areas for urbanisation and land abandonment. *Applied Geography, 57*, 32–41.

Prishchepov, A. V., Radeloff, V. C., Baumann, M., Kuemmerle, T., & Müller, D. (2012). Effects of institutional changes on land use: Agricultural land abandonment during the transition from state-command to market-driven economies in Post-Soviet Eastern Europe. *Environmental Research Letters, 7*, 024021.

Ustaoglu, E., & Collier, M. J. (2018). Farmland abandonment in Europe: an overview of drivers, consequences, and assessment of the sustainability implications. *Environmental Reviews, 26*, 396–416.

Qian, W., Crowley-Vigneau, 2020. The economy of Chinese rural households. Springer.

Queiroz, C., Beilin, R., Folke, C., & Lindborg, R. (2014). Farmland abandonment: Threat or opportunity for biodiversity conservation? A global review. *Frontiers in Ecology and the Environment, 12*, 288–296.

Rajkhowa, P., & Qaim, M. (2022). Mobile phones, off-farm employment and household income in rural India. *Journal of Agricultural Economics, 73*, 789–805.

Rhemtulla, J. M., Mladenoff, D. J., & Clayton, M. K. (2009). Legacies of historical land use on regional forest composition and structure in Wisconsin, USA (mid-1800s–1930s–2000s). *Ecological Applications, 19*, 1061–1078.

Rozelle, S., Taylor, J. E., & DeBrauw, A. (1999). Migration, remittances, and agricultural productivity in China. *American Economic Review, 89*, 287–291.

San Roman Sanz, A., Fernandez, C., Mouillot, F., Ferrat, L., Istria, D., & Pasqualini, V. (2013). Long-term forest dynamics and land-use abandonment in the Mediterranean mountains, Corsica, France. *Ecology and Society, 18*.

Silber, R., & Wytrzens, H. K. (2006). *Modelling the probability of land abandonment at parcel level*. Citeseer.

Sikor, T., Müller, D., & Stahl, J. (2009). Land fragmentation and cropland abandonment in Albania: Implications for the roles of state and community in post-socialist land consolidation. *World Development, 37*, 1411–1423.

Su, W., Eriksson, T., Zhang, L., & Bai, Y. (2016). Off-farm employment and time allocation in on-farm work in rural China from gender perspective. *China Economic Review, 41*, 34–45.

Tan, S., Heerink, N., & Qu, F. (2006). Land fragmentation and its driving forces in China. *Land Use Policy, 23*, 272–285.

Taylor, J. E., Rozelle, S., & De Brauw, A. (2003). Migration and incomes in source communities: A new economics of migration perspective from China. *Economic Development and Cultural Change, 52*, 75–101.

Van Dijk, T. (2003). Scenarios of Central European land fragmentation. *Land Use Policy, 20*, 149–158.

Van den Broeck, G., & Kilic, T. (2019). Dynamics of off-farm employment in sub-Saharan Africa: A gender perspective. *World Development, 119*, 81–99.

van der Zanden, E. H., Verburg, P. H., Schulp, C. J., & Verkerk, P. J. (2017). Trade-offs of European agricultural abandonment. *Land Use Policy, 62*, 290–301.

Van Doorn, A. M., & Bakker, M. M. (2007). The destination of arable land in a marginal agricultural landscape in South Portugal: An exploration of land use change determinants. *Landscape Ecology, 22*, 1073–1087.

Veljanoska, S. (2018). Can land fragmentation reduce the exposure of rural households to weather variability. *Ecological Economics*, 154, 42–51.

Wan, G. H., & Cheng, E. (2001). Effects of land fragmentation and returns to scale in the Chinese farming sector. *Applied Economics*, 33, 183–194.

Wang, H., Riedinger, J., & Jin, S. (2015). Land documents, tenure security and land rental development: Panel evidence from China. *China Economic Review, 36*, 220–235.

Wang, J., Cao, Y., Fang, X., Li, G., & Cao, Y. (2022). Does land tenure fragmentation aggravate farmland abandonment? Evidence from big survey data in rural China. *Journal of Rural Studies, 91*, 126–135.

Wang, X., Yamauchi, F., Huang, J., & Rozelle, S. (2020a). What constrains mechanization in Chinese agriculture? Role of farm size and fragmentation. *China Economic Review, 62*, 101221.

Wang, Y., Li, X., Lu, D., & Yan, J. (2020b). Evaluating the impact of land fragmentation on the cost of agricultural operation in the southwest mountainous areas of China. *Land Use Policy*, 99, 105099.

Wang, J., Xin, L., & Wang, Y. (2020). How farmers' non-agricultural employment affects rural land circulation in China? *Journal of Geographical Sciences, 30*, 378–400.

Ward, P. S., & Shively, G. E. (2015). Migration and land rental as responses to income shocks in rural China. *Pacific Economic Review, 20*(4), 511–543.

Xie, H., & Lu, H. (2017). Impact of land fragmentation and non-agricultural labor supply on circulation of agricultural land management rights. *Land Use Policy, 68*, 355–364.

Xu, D., Deng, X., Guo, S., & Liu, S. (2019). Labor migration and farmland abandonment in rural China: Empirical results and policy implications. *Journal of Environmental Management, 232*, 738–750.

Xu, W., Jin, X., Liu, J., & Zhou, Y. (2021). Analysis of influencing factors of cultivated land fragmentation based on hierarchical linear model: A case study of Jiangsu Province China. *Land Use Policy*, 101, 105119.

Xu, D., Deng, X., Huang, K., Liu, Y., Yong, Z., & Liu, S. (2019). Relationships between labor migration and cropland abandonment in rural China from the perspective of village types. *Land Use Policy, 88*, 104164.

Yan, J., Yang, Z., Li, Z., Li, X., Xin, L., & Sun, L. (2016). Drivers of cropland abandonment in mountainous areas: A household decision model on farming scale in Southwest China. *Land Use Policy, 57*, 459–469.

Zhang, Y., Li, X., Song, W., & Zhai, L. (2016). Land abandonment under rural restructuring in China explained from a cost-benefit perspective. *Journal of Rural Studies, 47*, 524–532.

Zhang, Q., Song, C., & Chen, X. (2018). Effects of China's payment for ecosystem services programs on cropland abandonment: A case study in Tiantangzhai Township, Anhui China. *Land Use Policy*, 73, 239–248.

Zhang, L. X. (2021). Off-farm employment and poverty alleviation in rural China. *Journal of Integrative Agriculture, 20*, 943–952.

Zhang, Y., Li, X., & Song, W. (2014). Determinants of cropland abandonment at the parcel, household and village levels in mountain areas of China: A multi-level analysis. *Land Use Policy, 41*, 186–192.

Zheng, L. (2023). Impact of off-farm employment on cooking fuel choices: Implications for rural-urban transformation in advancing sustainable energy transformation. *Energy Economics, 118*, 106497.

Zheng, L. (2024). Big hands holding small hands: The role of new agricultural operating entities in farmland abandonment. *Food Policy, 123*, 102605.

Zheng, L., & Qian, W. (2021). The impact of land certification on cropland abandonment: Evidence from rural China. *China Agricultural Economic Review, 14*, 509–526.

Zheng, L., Su, L., & Jin, S. (2023). Reducing land fragmentation to curb cropland abandonment: Evidence from rural China. *Canadian Journal of Agricultural Economics/Revue canadienne d'agroeconomie, 71*, 355–373.

Zhou, T., Koomen, E., & Ke, X. (2020). Determinants of farmland abandonment on the urban–rural fringe. *Environmental Management, 65*, 369–384.

# Chapter 5
# Agricultural Comparative Return and Cropland Abandonment

**Abstract** Cropland abandonment exerts far-reaching consequences for food security and sustainable agricultural development. However, while it is generally believed that low agricultural comparative return (ACR) is the main cause of cropland abandonment, the magnitude of such effects and their underlying mechanisms are not well understood. On the basis of constructing a mathematical model and analysis framework, this chapter employs a large-scale farm-level panel data from Chinese Family Databases during 2015–2021 and a panel high-dimensional fixed effects model to investigate the impact of ACR on cropland abandonment. Results show that ACR has a positive impact on the proportion of abandoned cropland area to total cropland area, with an average coefficient of 0.016. This effect is mainly achieved through reductions in long-term land investment, agricultural capital input, and agricultural labor input. Nevertheless, it is also moderated by the effects of rural factor markets and government agricultural subsidies. In particular, the agricultural machinery market, the land rental market and the level of agricultural subsidies can weaken ACR's negative impact on land use, while current agricultural subsidies have little effect. Our findings also reveal that the effects of ACR on cropland abandonment vary significantly across geographical regions, grain areas, and terrain zones. Specifically, ACR is not harmful to households in northeastern and central China or major grain producing areas, while it harms others. Overall, this study provides a better understanding of the quantitative relationship between ACR and cropland abandonment in rural China, and valuable insights for other developing countries in formulating targeted measures to curb cropland abandonment in low ACR situations.

**Keywords** Agricultural comparative return · Cropland abandonment · Agricultural subsidies · Food security · Sustainable agricultural development

This chapter has been published. For more details, please see: Zheng, L., Jin, S., Su, L. Of nothing comes nothing: The impact of agricultural comparative return on cropland abandonment. Journal of Rural Studies, 2025, 119:103759.

 
L. Zheng, *Cropland Abandonment in Rural China*, Resources, Environment and Agricultural Development, https://doi.org/10.1007/978-981-95-8287-7_5

## 5.1 Introduction

Land produces a wide array of foods, making it a key contributor to global sustenance. As the world's population continues to grow at a rapid pace and its consequent increased food demand, the protection and responsible use of limited land resources is emerging as a universal challenge for humanity (Stehfest et al., 2019). Nevertheless, cropland abandonment is widespread in both developing and developed countries and has transformed into a global economic and social concern (Blair et al., 2018; Deng et al., 2019; Ito et al., 2016; Ojha et al., 2022; Zheng et al., 2023a; Zavalloni et al., 2021). A recently published study, drawing upon ESA-CCI land-cover time-series data, reveals that an alarming 1.01 million hectares of cropland were abandoned globally between 1992 and 2020, equivalent to an average of 36,000 hectares of cropland being abandoned each year (Zheng et al., 2023b). The expansion of cropland abandonment not only heightens public concern about food security, but also undermines sustainable agricultural development (Guo et al., 2023; Wang et al., 2023). In certain instances, cropland abandonment may yield certain environmental benefits, such as increased carbon sequestration and regeneration of forest ecosystems (Kuemmerle et al., 2011; Zheng et al., 2023b). However, due to the escalating impact of the COVID-19 pandemic, extreme weather events, and the ongoing conflict between Russia and Ukraine on global food security (Andrianarimanana et al., 2023; Zheng, 2024a), the detrimental effects of cropland abandonment on agriculture have gradually intensified in recent years. In this regard, it is of critical importance to explore the multiple drivers of cropland abandonment, with a view to enhancing targeted management of cropland abandonment and thus ensuring food security.

There is widespread academic discussion about why farmers abandon cropland. A growing body of scholarly literature indicates that cropland abandonment is primarily attributed to the following factors: (i) adverse natural conditions, such as remote mountainous areas (Hong et al., 2024), fragmented land (Deininger et al., 2012; Zheng et al., 2023a), and poor soil fertility (Ojha et al., 2022); (ii) unfavorable economic conditions, such as non-agricultural employment (Zheng, 2024b) and low agricultural income (Zavalloni et al., 2021); (iii) inadequate institutional arrangements, such as insecure land tenure (Zheng & Qian, 2022) and limited land transfer rights (Deininger et al., 2012). Notably, economic factors, particularly low farm incomes, have been identified as the primary cause of farmers' decision to abandon cropland (Guo et al., 2023; Wang et al., 2022). However, it is important to note that the level of agricultural income is a relative concept due to differences in the frame of reference, and it is more specific to low agricultural comparative returns (Wang et al., 2023). Provided that other conditions remain constant, farmers' decision to abandon cropland depends primarily on the level of agricultural comparative return (ACR), which is widely recognized as the most critical economic factor in the Chinese context (Zhang et al., 2019). For a rational farmer, if their agricultural income and non-agricultural wage income are both relatively low, they are unlikely to abandon cropland for survival; conversely, if non-agricultural wage income is higher or even substantially higher than agricultural income, then they are highly likely to abandon cropland (Ma & Zhu, 2020).

Regrettably, despite the recognition by a subset of academics that ACR plays a pivotal role in instigating cropland abandonment (Wang et al., 2023), there is a notable lack of literature that directly investigates whether and how ACR triggers cropland abandonment, perhaps due to the fact that ACR is a counterfactual state, making it challenging to measure. For most developing countries, increasing agricultural income beyond non-agricultural wage income is not an easy task; especially in the context of rural–urban transformation, low ACR is likely to persist for an extended period. As the world's largest developing country, it is an undeniable fact that China's agricultural income is currently lower than non-agricultural wage income. According to the National Bureau of Statistics of China, since 2015, Chinese farmers' non-agricultural wage income has superseded agricultural income as the primary source of household income. In recent years, the influx of rural workers to urban areas for employment has escalated every year, reaching a total of 297.53 million by 2023. It also suggests that the gap between agricultural and non-agricultural earnings may persist and widen, with higher non-agricultural earnings acting as a catalyst for rural–urban migration (Zheng, 2024b). Concurrently, the issue of cropland abandonment in rural China is not encouraging. According to the Chinese Social Survey (CSS), the proportion of farmers abandoning cropland has risen from 9.80% in 2011 to 12.35% in 2021. The aforementioned preliminary evidence suggests an underlying positive correlation between ACR and cropland abandonment, but the extent to which ACR will induce farmers to abandon cropland remains to be further empirically examined.

In light of the above considerations, this study will seek to examine the main factors contributing to cropland abandonment by conducting an empirical analysis of the impact of ACR on cropland abandonment. Compared with the existing literature, the potential marginal contributions to this study mainly include the following three aspects. Firstly, we take the lead in developing an analytical framework to elucidate how ACR affects cropland abandonment, and our empirical design aligns well with theoretical derivation, thereby addressing the limitations of previous studies that only indirectly mention ACR. More importantly, we adopt a measurement approach for ACR using the value of the previous year and off-farm wage income at the village level. This effectively addresses endogenous issues caused by reverse causality and enables us to obtain unbiased estimation results. Secondly, using panel tracking data from Chinese Family Databases with national representation, the panel high-dimensional fixed effects model will be employed to assess the overall effects, mechanisms, and heterogeneous effects of ACR on cropland abandonment, thereby enabling a comprehensive investigation of the relationship between ACR and cropland abandonment. Thirdly, starting from agricultural subsidies, agricultural machinery markets, and land rental markets, we focus on land use change in the context of rural–urban transformation, and explore the governance strategies of abandoned cropland under the situation of low ACR, so as to contribute Chinese solutions to food security based on land protection in developing countries.

The remainder of the study is structured as follows. Section 5.2 discusses how ACR affects cropland abandonment. Section 5.3 introduces the data, selected variables and empirical strategy, and describes the descriptive statistics of the samples employed. Section 5.4 presents empirical findings on the impacts and mechanisms of ACR on cropland abandonment. Section 5.5 provides an analysis of the heterogeneous effects observed. Section 5.6 concludes with policy implications and research outlooks.

## 5.2 Theoretical Analysis and Research Hypothesis

### 5.2.1 *The Effect of ACR on Cropland Abandonment*

Dualistic economic theory suggests that the higher wage benefits in modern industrial sectors compared to traditional agricultural sectors induce large numbers of agricultural laborers to continuously migrate to urban areas (Lewis, 1954). Changes in the allocation of labor factors also lead to the reconfiguration of land resources by farmers. In order to analyze the impact of ACR on farmers' cropland abandonment behavior clearly, this study constructs the following theoretical model. Suppose the efficiency of agricultural production technology is $A$, and the inputs of labor, land, and capital are $L_f, N_f, K_f$, respectively. Using the technique of Chari et al. (2021) and Adamopoulos and Restuccia (2014) for agricultural production, the corresponding production function can be expressed as follows:

$$\begin{aligned} &Y = f\left(N_f, L_f, K_f\right) = A^{1-\partial}\left(N_f^{\alpha} L_f^{\beta} K_f^{\gamma}\right)^{\partial} \\ &\alpha + \beta + \gamma = 1, \partial < 1 \end{aligned} \tag{5.1}$$

where $Y$ is the output of agricultural production. $\partial$ represents the scale return of agricultural production, and $\partial < 1$ indicates decreasing returns to scale. This inequality condition is based on the claim in most literature that increasing returns to scale in agricultural production do not exist at all except in some very special cases (Berry & Cline, 1980; Binswanger et al., 1995; Johnson & Ruttan, 1994). In developing countries in particular, diminishing returns to scale are more common. $\alpha$, $\beta$, and $\gamma$ measure the relative importance of land, labor, and capital respectively, while $\partial\alpha$, $\partial\beta$, and $\partial\gamma$ represent the output elasticity of land, labor, and capital respectively. Meanwhile, it is assumed that the agricultural production function satisfies the Inada conditions (Inada, 1963), that is $f'(0) = \infty, f'(\infty) = 0, f'(x) > 0, f''(x) < 0$, where $f'(\cdot)$ and $f''(\cdot)$ denote the first derivative and the second derivative, respective, and $x$ can refer to either $L_f$, $N_f$ or $K_f$.

The agricultural household model, with the dual constraints of labor and land, aiming to maximize income $\pi$, can be demonstrated as follows:

$$
\begin{aligned}
\underset{N_f,L_f,K_f}{Max\pi} &= pf\left(N_f, L_f, K_f\right) - uK_f + rN_r + wL_n + T\left(N_f\right) \\
&s.t. N_f + N_r \le \overline{N} \\
&L_f + L_n \le \overline{L}
\end{aligned}
\tag{5.2}
$$

where $p$ is the price of agricultural products. $r$, $w$, and $u$ represent land rent, labor wages, and capital interest rates, respectively. Additionally, $L_n$ signifies the number of non-agricultural employment labor force while $N_r$ denotes the area of land transferred out. $\overline{N}$ indicates household land resource constraints and $\overline{L}$ refers to household labor force constraints. Furthermore, $T\left(N_f\right)$ symbolizes government subsidies to farmers for agricultural production, which are calculated according to the land area cultivated by farmers ($N_f$). Based on Eq. (5.2), we take the first order derivative for $L_f$, $N_f$ and $K_f$ yields respectively (see Appendix A for more details of the derivation):

$$
\frac{\partial \pi}{\partial N_f} = pf'_{N_f} - r + \frac{\partial T\left(N_f\right)}{\partial N_f} = 0 \tag{5.3}
$$

$$
\frac{\partial \pi}{\partial L_f} = pf'_{L_f} - w = 0 \tag{5.4}
$$

$$
\frac{\partial \pi}{\partial K_f} = pf'_{K_f} - u = 0 \tag{5.5}
$$

The core essence of the decline in comparative agricultural returns is reflected in the decrease in agricultural income and the increase in non-agricultural income. The decline in agricultural income can be attributed to a reduction in grain profits, often caused by a decrease in agricultural product prices or an increase in input costs. Therefore, the analysis of the impact of declining comparative agricultural returns can be conducted from three aspects: decreasing agricultural product prices, increasing input costs, and rising non-agricultural income.

Firstly, we analyze the impact of the decrease in the ACR caused by the decline in agricultural product prices on land allocation. Equation (5.3) can be rewritten as:

$$
pf'_{N_f} = r - \frac{\partial T\left(N_f\right)}{\partial N_f} \tag{5.6}
$$

Assuming that government subsidies are implemented according to a fixed per acre subsidy standard, $\frac{\partial T\left(N_f\right)}{\partial N_f}$ is a constant that remains unchanged. In the event of a decrease in $p$, Eq. (5.6) can only be maintained by increasing $f'_{N_f}$ while keeping $r$ constant. Moreover, considering $f''(x) < 0$ implies that $N_f$ will exhibit a decline. This derivation can be proved by the total differentiation of Eq. (5.6) shown in Appendix B.

Next, we turn to discuss the impact of the decrease in ACR due to higher input costs on land allocation. The input costs increase, that is, $u$ in Eq. (5.5) increases. To ensure that Eq. (5.5) still holds true while $p$ remains unchanged, it is necessary to increase $f'_{K_f}$ and correspondingly decrease $K_f$. This derivation can be proved by the total differentiation of Eq. (5.5) shown in Appendix C. We further expand Eq. (5.6) in a specific manner (see Appendix D for more details of the derivation):

$$pA^{1-\partial}\alpha\partial N_f^{\alpha\partial-1}L_f^{\beta\partial}K_f^{\gamma\partial} = r - \frac{\partial T(N_f)}{\partial N_f} \tag{5.7}$$

Under the condition of holding other factors constant, a decrease in $K_f$ necessitates a corresponding decrease in $N_f$ to maintain the Eq. (5.7). This derivation can be demonstrated by the total differentiation of Eq. (5.7) shown in Appendix E.

Lastly, the decline in ACR may also be due to an increase in non-agricultural income, which is reflected in the rise of wages for non-agricultural employment ($w$). In order to maintain Eq. (5.4) while $w$ increases and other factors remain constant, it is necessary to increase $f'_{L_f}$ and decrease $L_f$ accordingly. This derivation can be proved by the total differentiation of Eq. (5.4) shown in Appendix F. Furthermore, it can be inferred that a decrease in $L_f$ requires a corresponding decrease in $N_f$ to ensure the validity of Eq. (5.7).

In conclusion, it can be inferred that a decline in ACR will lead to a reduction in land use. Ideally, farmers would opt to rent their surplus cropland out to generate rental income. However, due to the homogeneous factor allocation logic among farmers in the same land rental market, when farmers collectively decide to transfer their croplands, an oversupply situation arises. Consequently, farmers may face the dilemma of transferring their land with zero rent. To mitigate losses from potential damage beyond crop yields, farmers are more likely to abandon their croplands. Alternatively, imperfect land rental markets and high transaction costs for land rental may lead to cropland abandonment. Therefore, we propose the first research hypothesis as follows:

**Hypothesis 1** A decrease in ACR increases the farmers' cropland abandonment.

### 5.2.2 *The Mediation Mechanism of ACR Affecting Cropland Abandonment*

Based on the previous analysis, it becomes evident that the decline in ACR can be manifested by a decrease in $p$, coupled with an increase in $u$ and $w$. To attain equilibrium conditions as stated in Eqs. (5.4) and (5.5), it is imperative to augment $f'_{L_f}$ and $f'_{K_f}$, while correspondingly diminishing $L_f$ and $K_f$. In this scenario, combining Eq. (5.7) reveals that the decrease in $L_f$ and $K_f$ will further result in a decrease in variable $N_f$. This can also be explained by the complementary relationship between labor and capital with land (Chari et al., 2021; Sazama & Davis, 1973). Therefore, it can be inferred that a decrease in ACR reduces capital and labor inputs in agricultural production, which have been proved by previous studies to exert a negative relationship with cropland abandonment (Chen et al., 2025; Deininger et al., 2012; Zheng, 2024b).

Especially for investments that take a long time to show returns, such as those related to improving land quality, including investments in straw and manure returns, the costs are high and the effectiveness period is long. Therefore, in situations where ACR decreases, farmers are even less likely to implement these types of investments. However, in the long run, the lack of these investments would degrade land quality and subsequently decrease agricultural productivity (referred to as $A$) (Zhang et al., 2023). According to Eq. (5.7), it can be inferred that when other factors remain constant, the decrease in $A$ leads to a decrease in $N_f$ thus promoting cropland abandonment. To sum up, we propose the following hypotheses:

**Hypothesis 2-1** A decline in ACR leads to cropland abandonment through reduced long-term land investment.

**Hypothesis 2-2** A decrease in ACR results in cropland abandonment through reduced agricultural capital input.

**Hypothesis 2-3** A decline in ACR leads to cropland abandonment through reduced agricultural labor input.

### 5.2.3 The Moderation Mechanism of ACR Affecting Cropland Abandonment: A Dual Perspective of Market Development and Government Subsidies

The above two hypotheses may not necessarily hold true, as there may be certain influential factors that hinder the mechanism of ACR affecting cropland abandonment or affecting ACR itself. We therefore attempt to further identify these powerful moderating factors. Generally speaking, the development of the agricultural machinery market and the land rental market, as well as government subsidies, can all play an effective role in moderating the impact of ACR on cropland abandonment, with the former two from the market perspective and the latter from the government perspective. Thus, we discuss these moderating effects further from the dual perspectives of market and government based on the theoretical framework mentioned above.

#### 5.2.3.1 The Role of Agricultural Machinery Market and Land Rental Market

One of the mechanisms through which ACR induces cropland abandonment is off-farm labor migration, resulting in insufficient agricultural labor. However, if there is an external force that can address this issue, it can weaken the positive impact of ACR on cropland abandonment. This external force should be able to effectively address the problem of imbalanced allocation between land and labor. The development of the agricultural machinery market and the land rental market has the potential to address this problem. The former involves replacing labor with machinery to compensate for labor shortages, while the latter involves reallocating land resources by transferring them to households with more agricultural labor.

First, the moderating role of the agricultural machinery market on cropland abandonment resulting from the reduction of ACR is dissected. On the one hand, agricultural machinery can be perceived as an input factor in the short run, denoted as part of $K_f$. As a production factor, agricultural machinery affects cropland abandonment through two moderating pathways: (1) Serving as a substitute factor for labor input, the presence of agricultural machinery can alleviate the issue of inadequate agricultural workforce and ensure that $N_f$ does not experience significant or even any decline due to reduced ACR, thereby assisting in mitigating cropland abandonment; (2) As a complementary factor to land, agricultural machinery drives farmers to expand operational scales to achieve economies of scale (Feder et al., 1985; Takeshima et al., 2020), thereby reducing cropland abandonment. On the other hand, in the long run, when agricultural machinery incorporates breakthrough technological innovations, it helps reduce resource waste, improve land quality, and optimize planting cycles, thereby enhancing total factor productivity $A$ (Cui, 2023; Ma et al., 2022). Similarly, an increase in $A$ leads to an increase in $f'_{N_f}$, further promoting an increase in $N_f$, thus helping to prevent cropland abandonment.

Next, we focus on the moderating role of the land rental market on cropland abandonment resulting from the reduction of ACR. In the Eq. (5.2), land rent $r$ can be defined as a function of the development level $z$ of the land rental market, where a more mature and standardized land rental market corresponds to a higher value of $z$. The advancement of the land rental market development level facilitates the following mechanisms: From the lessor's perspective, it promotes the transition of land from informal and relationship-based transactions to market-oriented transactions, thus reducing the probability of zero-rent arrangements and elevating rent level (Tang et al., 2019; Zheng et al., 2025); From the lessee's perspective, a well-developed land rental market can decrease transaction cost, enhance contractual stability, and encourage acceptance of higher rent (Li & Ito, 2021). Thus, $\frac{\partial r}{\partial Z} > 0$ can be obtained. Based on Eq. (5.2), we take the first order derivative with respect to $N_r$ yields:

$$-pA^{1-\partial}\alpha\partial\left(\overline{N} - N_r\right)^{\alpha\partial-1}L_f^{\beta\partial}K_f^{\gamma\partial} + r - s = 0 \tag{5.8}$$

where $s = \frac{\partial T(N_f)}{\partial N_f}$. Equation (5.8) can be rewritten as:

$$r = pA^{1-\partial}\alpha\partial\left(\overline{N} - N_r\right)^{\alpha\partial-1}L_f^{\beta\partial}K_f^{\gamma\partial} + s \tag{5.9}$$

According to Eq. (5.9), taking the partial derivative of the first order with respect to $r$, we can get:

$$\frac{\partial r}{\partial Nr} = -pA^{1-\partial}\alpha\partial(\alpha\partial - 1)\left(\overline{N - N_r}\right)^{\alpha\partial-2}L_f^{\beta\partial}K_f^{\gamma\partial} > 0 \quad (5.10)$$

Thus, $\frac{\partial Nr}{\partial r} > 0$ can be obtained. In order to verify the moderating role of the land rental market on cropland abandonment, we identify $\frac{\partial Nr}{\partial Z}$ as follows:

$$\frac{\partial Nr}{\partial Z} = \frac{\partial Nr}{\partial r} \cdot \frac{\partial r}{\partial Z} > 0 \quad (5.11)$$

This indicates that with the development of land rental markets, farmers tend to rent out land they are unwilling to cultivate due to low ACR rather than abandon it. Therefore, we propose the following hypotheses:

**Hypothesis 3-1** The development of agricultural machinery market curbs cropland abandonment caused by ACR reduction.

**Hypothesis 3-2** The development of land rental market reduces cropland abandonment due to reduced ACR.

#### 5.2.3.2 The Role of Government Agricultural Subsidies

Government subsidies for agricultural production play a crucial role in China. According to statistical data, China's subsidies for safeguarding cropland encompass 220 million farming households and nearly 1.3 billion mu of contracted land, with an average subsidy amounting to approximately 95 yuan per mu and approximately 564 yuan per household.[1] This inclusive approach effectively boosts farmers' incomes, facilitates the transition of supportive agricultural policies from "yellow box" to "green box," and expands the policy space for promoting agricultural development and augmenting farmers' earnings. Consequently, we aim to reveal the moderating role of government agricultural subsidies in mitigating cropland abandonment caused by reduced ACR.

Here, we discuss agricultural subsidies linked to production. Since 2015, China has linked the decoupled direct subsidies to land fertility conservation, explicitly excluding abandoned cropland from subsidy eligibility. As subsidies are contingent on agricultural production, they generate a production incentive effect, directly shaping land resource allocation. However, as an income-raising policy, agricultural subsidies also induce an income effect, indirectly affecting land allocation by altering labor allocation through leisure consumption. To disentangle these dual effects, we introduce the utility function of farmers, that is $U = U(\pi, L)$, where $\pi$ is income

[1] https://www.mof.gov.cn/zhengwuxinxi/caijingshidian/zgcjb/202109/t20210916_3753468.htm.

and $L$ is leisure time. To simplify the analysis, we disregard land renting out, which complicates subsidy implementation due to regional variations in criteria, e.g., subsidies based on contracted area versus actual cultivated area, and simplify income $\pi$ shown in Eq. (5.2) as:

$$\pi = pf\left(N_f, L_f, K_f\right) - uK_f + wL_n + N_f \cdot s \tag{5.12}$$

The land constraint condition is $N_f \leq \overline{N}$, and the area of abandoned land is $D = \overline{N} - N_f$. By considering leisure, the time constraint condition can be expressed as $L_f + L_n + L = \overline{L}$. Land and labor are allocated to maximize utility:

$$\begin{aligned} & MaxU = U\left(pf\left(N_f, L_f, K_f\right) - uK_f + wL_n + N_f \cdot s, T - L_f - L_n\right) \\ s.t. \quad & N_f \leq \overline{N}, \end{aligned} \tag{5.13}$$

We introduce Lagrangian multiplier $\lambda \geq 0$ to construct Lagrangian function as follows:

$$\mathcal{L} = U\left(pf\left(N_f, L_f, K_f\right) - uK_f + wL_n + N_f \cdot s, T - L_f - L_n\right) + \lambda\left(\overline{N} - N_f\right) \tag{5.14}$$

Based on Eq. (5.14), taking the first order derivative with respect to $N_f$ and $L_f$, respectively, we can get:

$$\frac{\partial \mathcal{L}}{\partial N_f} = U_\pi \cdot \left(pf'_{N_f} + s\right) - \lambda = 0 \tag{5.15}$$

$$\frac{\partial \mathcal{L}}{\partial L_f} = U_\pi \cdot pf'_{L_f} - U_L = 0 \tag{5.16}$$

where $U_\pi$ and $U_L$ denote the first partial derivative of the utility with respect to $\pi$ and $L$, respectively.

Next, a comparative static analysis is conducted. First, the production incentive effect of agricultural subsidies can be identified based on Eq. (5.15). If utility remains unchanged through compensatory income adjustments and the subsidy $s$ increases such that Eq. (5.15) still holds, then $f'_{N_f}$ must decrease. In the case of $f''_{N_f} < 0$, $N_f$ will increase, thereby reducing abandoned land area $D$. Second, the income effect of agricultural subsidies can be identified based on Eq. (5.16). Agricultural subsidies enhance total income $\pi$, leading to a reduction in $U_\pi$ due to diminishing marginal utility. For Eq. (5.16) to remain valid, $f'_{L_f}$ needs to increase, and in the case of $f''_{L_f} < 0$, $L_f$ will decrease. Due to the complementary relationship between $L_f$ and $N_f$, without considering changes in mechanical input, $N_f$ will decrease, which in turn increases the abandoned land area $D$. In summary, the overall effect of agricultural subsidies on cropland abandonment can be decomposed into a negative production incentive effect and a positive income effect. However, China's growing level of agricultural mechanization development weakens the income effect while strengthening the production incentive effect. Additionally, given the relatively low current income levels of farmers, their preference for leisure is not strong, further weakening the income effect. Therefore, in absolute terms, the production incentive effect outweighs the income effect, resulting in a net negative impact of agricultural subsidies on cropland abandonment. Consequently, we put forward the following hypotheses:

**Hypothesis 4-1** The availability of agricultural subsidies mitigates cropland abandonment caused by ACR reduction.

**Hypothesis 4-2** The increase in the level of agricultural subsidies curbs ACR reduction-induced cropland abandonment.

Finally, to enhance the clarity of the theoretical logic presented in this study, a theoretical framework diagram (Fig. 5.1) is included. This diagram effectively illustrates the impact of ACR on cropland abandonment, along with its underlying mediating and moderating mechanisms that have been derived and substantiated in previous sections.

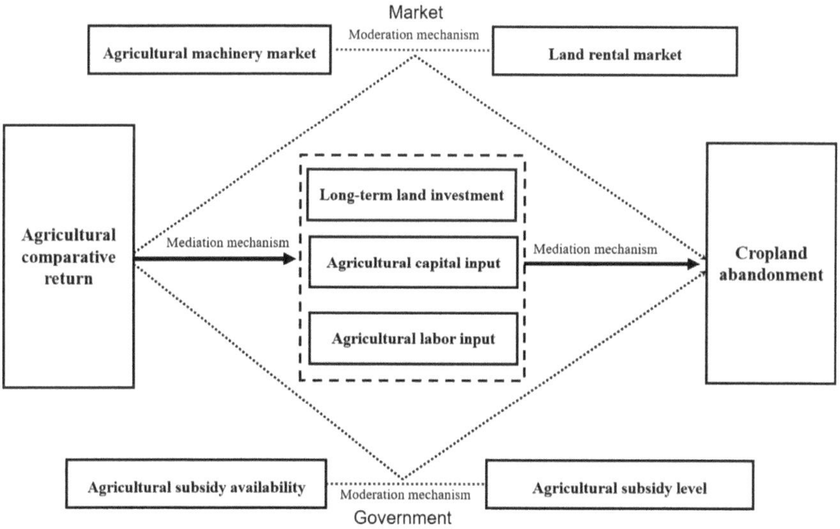


**Fig. 5.1** Analytical framework

## 5.3 Research Design

### 5.3.1 *Data Sources*

The data employed in this study were sourced from the Chinese Family Database (CFD).[2] The database has been built by conducting field surveys every two years since 2011. The survey was mainly led by Zhejiang University in 2011, 2013, 2015, 2017, and 2019, in conjunction with other universities such as Anhui University, Southwestern University of Finance and Economics, while in 2021, it was jointly conducted by South China Agricultural University and Southwestern University of Finance and Economics. Since information on cropland abandonment is only available from 2013 onwards, we only used data for 2015, 2017, 2019 and 2021.

During the survey, to ensure the national representativeness of the dataset, a stratified, three-stage, proportional population size (PPS) sampling method was employed to collect data from farm households and village directors in 29 provinces in China (excluding Xinjiang and Xizang). Specifically, in the first stage, counties were divided into 10 tiers based on GDP per capita, and counties were randomly selected in tiers. In the second stage, villages were randomly selected at the county level. In the third stage, 20 farm households were randomly selected from each selected village (Zheng, 2024c). The data is nationally representative at multiple levels, including provincial, county, and village (Zheng & Qian, 2022), and is by far one of the most informative large-scale micro-databases on agricultural production variables in China. Based on this database, there have been high-level articles published in Nature and Proceedings of the National Academy of Sciences (PNAS) as well as monographs published in Springer Press (Qian, 2020; Ren et al., 2023; Wu et al., 2018).

To estimate the impact of ACR on cropland abandonment, we conducted a data cleansing process for the empirical purpose of this study. Firstly, households without their own cropland (contracted land, in the Chinese context) were weeded out. Secondly, because older heads of households may have biased responses to the questionnaire, we excluded samples with heads of households over 70 years old. Thirdly, key variables including farm income, off-farm wage income, cropland abandonment, land transfer, agricultural machinery, agricultural subsidies, individual characteristics of household heads, family demographic characteristics, and land characteristics were retained. Observations with missing or invalid information pertaining to these variables were deleted. Ultimately, an unbalanced panel dataset spanning four years was obtained, consisting of 24,843 observations for empirical research.

[2] The data can be accessed from http://ssec.zju.edu.cn/sites/main/template/news.aspx?id=51035.

### 5.3.2 Empirical Strategy

Utilizing panel data, this study employs a high-dimensional fixed effects model to examine the impact of ACR on cropland abandonment, thereby mitigating potential estimation bias resulting from omitted variables. The model is constructed as follows:

$$Abandonment_{jt} = \alpha_0 + \alpha_1 ACR_{jvt-1} + \beta \boldsymbol{X}_{jt} + \mu_j + \delta_t + \omega_{ct} + \varepsilon_{jt} \tag{5.17}$$

where *j*, *v*, *c*, and *t* denote the farm household, village, county, and year, respectively. $Abandonment_{jt}$ is the dependent variable, which is specifically defined as the proportion of abandoned cropland area to total cropland area in year *t* for farm household *j*, and takes a value between 0 and 1. According to cobweb theory (Poitras, 2023) and the seasonal and cyclical nature of agricultural production, $ACR_{jvt-1}$ serves as the core independent variable in this study, which is a binary variable defined by comparing the farm income of the household *j* with the average wage income of other farmers in the same village *v* last year. When the former exceeds the latter, $ACR_{jvt-1}$ is assigned a value of 0, indicating comparative advantage in agricultural returns; when the former is less than the latter, $ACR_{jvt-1}$ is assigned a value of 1, indicating no comparative advantage in agricultural returns. Note that ACR measurement in this study has three favorable features: (1) the village-level measurement overcomes the issue of self-selection bias to some extent; (2) the core independent variable, as per the CFD questionnaire, occurs before the dependent variable, thus mitigating the occurrence of endogenous problems related to reverse causality; and (3) farm income specifically refers to gross income that is not included in agricultural production costs rather than net income, which can avoid the interference affecting agricultural production costs, such as the agricultural machinery market, land rental market, and agricultural subsidies.

Additionally, $\boldsymbol{X}_{jt}$ represents a series of control variables that may influence farmers' decision to abandon cropland. Based on previous literature and data availability, this study incorporates several control variables including individual characteristics such as the age of the household head and its quadratic term (Deng et al., 2019), education level (Ma & Zhu, 2020), as well as family characteristics like dependency ratio (Zheng, 2024a), health status of family members (Zheng & Qian, 2022), engagement in off-farm employment (Xu et al., 2019b; Zheng, 2024b), land size (Deng et al., 2019; Wang et al., 2023), land fragmentation (Deininger et al., 2012; Zheng et al., 2023a), and land certification (Deng et al., 2019; Zheng & Qian, 2022). These control variables are also employed to mitigate potential endogeneity issues arising from omitted variables. Furthermore, the high-dimensional fixed effects of this model primarily manifest in three dimensions: firstly, individual fixed effects represented by $\mu_j$, which address the issue of omitted variables caused by observable and unobservable factors that remain constant over time; secondly, time-fixed effects denoted as $\delta_t$ to control for influences on each year that are consistent across individuals, such as macroeconomic fluctuations; thirdly, the interaction effect between county-level fixed effects and time-fixed effects indicated by $\omega_{ct}$ to account for county-level factors that change over time, such as local land policy and extreme weather. $\alpha_0$ is the intercept term, $\alpha_1$ and $\beta$ are the parameters to be estimated, and $\varepsilon_{jt}$ is the random disturbance term.

### 5.3.3 *Sample Characteristics and Descriptive Statistics*

Table 5.1 provides definitions and descriptions of the selected variables. For the dependent variable, the average abandoned cropland per sample farmer accounted for 4.7% of the total cropland area. Approximately 9.3% of the sample farmers engaged in cropland abandonment behavior. The descriptive statistics for the core explanatory variable ACR indicate that approximately 54.9% of the sampled households have lower farm incomes compared to the average wage incomes of other farmers in the same village, suggesting a lack of comparative advantage in agricultural returns.

Next, we proceed to the descriptive statistics of the control variables. The mean age of the household head is approximately 53 years old. Merely 14.1% of heads of households have completed high school education, indicating a relatively low level of educational attainment. Concerning family demographic characteristics, the average elderly dependency ratio stands at around 0.14, suggesting that there is an average support burden of about 0.14 elderly individuals per labor force, which falls below one person. The average proportion of healthy individuals in the family population amounts to roughly 76.7%, implying a relatively favorable health status among the sample households. The average proportion of non-farm employment in total household labor is approximately 22.4%, signifying potential for further non-farm labor transferability. In terms of household land characteristics, the mean per capita cropland area measures about 2.82 mu, revealing a certain disparity compared to the global per capita cropland area (4.8 mu), thereby reflecting the issue of cropland scarcity in China. The average number of cropland plots reaches 5.45, indicating a significant problem of land fragmentation in China. Approximately 67.5% of farmers reported having obtained land certificates.

### 5.3.4 *Descriptive Statistics on ACR and Cropland Abandonment*

Before estimating the econometric model, we present the correlation between ACR and cropland abandonment by plotting a grouped bar chart by year (Fig. 5.2). According to the previous definition, the sample group when $ACR_{jvt-1} = 1$ is named as the more wage income; Conversely, when $ACR_{jvt-1} = 0$, the sample group is named more farm income. It is evident that from 2015 to 2021, there has been a consistent annual increase in the proportion of abandoned cropland areas for sampled households, regardless of comparative advantage in farm income compared to wage

**Table 5.1** Variable definitions and descriptive statistics (N = 24,843)

| Variables | Definition | Mean | SD | Min | Max |
|---|---|---|---|---|---|
| Cropland abandonment | Proportion of abandoned cropland area to total cropland area (0–1) | 0.047 | 0.172 | 0 | 1 |
| | Whether cropland is abandoned (yes = 1, no = 0) | 0.093 | 0.290 | 0 | 1 |
| ACR | Whether the household farm income last year was lower than the average wage income of other farmers in the village (yes = 1, no = 0) | 0.549 | 0.498 | 0 | 1 |
| Age | Age of household head | 53.178 | 10.877 | 16 | 69 |
| Education | Did the head of the household attend high school (yes = 1, no = 0) | 0.141 | 0.348 | 0 | 1 |
| Dependency ratio | Dependency ratio of the elderly (0–3) | 0.144 | 0.327 | 0 | 3 |
| Family health | Proportion of healthy people in the household (0–1) | 0.767 | 0.311 | 0 | 1 |
| Off-farm employment | Proportion of off-farm employment in the household (0–1) | 0.224 | 0.260 | 0 | 1 |
| Land size | Household cropland area per capita (mu) | 2.819 | 6.938 | 0.001 | 500 |
| Land fragmentation | Number of cropland plots | 5.450 | 6.058 | 1 | 120 |
| Land certification | Whether farmers have obtained a land certificate (yes = 1, no = 0) | 0.675 | 0.468 | 0 | 1 |

*Notes* 1 mu = 1/15 hectare. Yuan is Chinese currency (1 USD = 7.25 Yuan in 2025)

income. This underscores the escalating severity of the cropland abandonment issue and emphasizes its significance in our study. Furthermore, in each year, households lacking a comparative advantage in farm income exhibit a higher average proportion of abandoned cropland compared to those with such an advantage. Hence, it can be tentatively inferred that the absence of ACR may contribute to increased cropland abandonment. However, this analysis does not account for other factors and necessitates further rigorous empirical testing to establish causality between ACR and cropland abandonment.

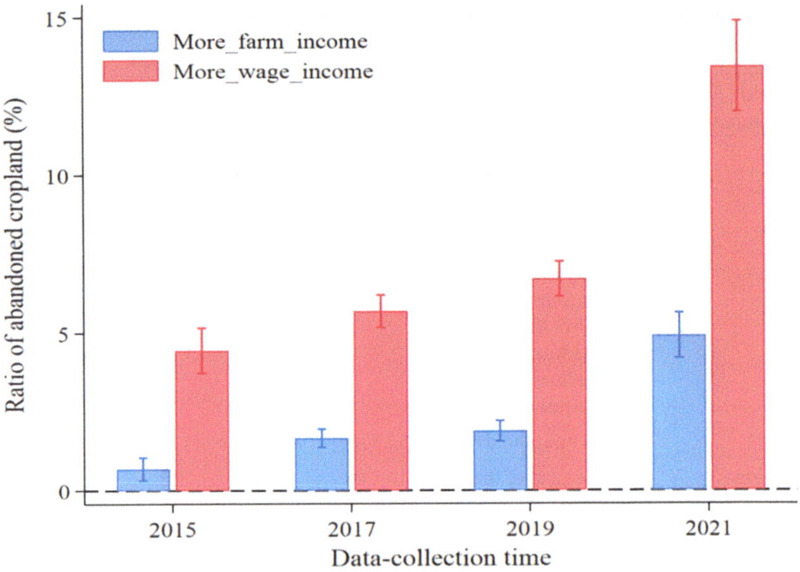


**Fig. 5.2** Correlation between ACR and cropland abandonment

## 5.4 Impact of ACR on Cropland Abandonment

### 5.4.1 Baseline Results

The baseline results of the impact of ACR on cropland abandonment, as estimated using the high-dimensional fixed effects model, are presented in Table 5.2. The three columns in Table 5.2 control the household-fixed effect, the year-fixed effect, as well as the interactive fixed effects of the county and year simultaneously. Column (1) includes only the core explanatory variable ACR, and the results indicate a significant positive impact of ACR on the proportion of abandoned cropland area to total cropland area, with a coefficient of 0.016. This indicates that farmers with lower agricultural return relative to non-agricultural return exhibit a 0.016 increase in the proportion of abandoned cropland area, which accounts for approximately 34% of the average proportion of abandoned cropland area to total cropland (0.047) observed in the sample households. This is a large impact effect, highlighting the importance of ACR to farmers' cropland use decisions. In columns (2) and (3), the personal characteristics of the head of household and family characteristics are included, respectively. The results demonstrate that ACR still has a significant positive impact on the proportion of abandoned cropland areas, with an almost unchanged coefficient compared to column (1). Consequently, the significant positive impact of ACR on cropland abandonment can be empirically proved, thereby confirming hypothesis 1 posited in our study.

**Table 5.2** ACR and cropland abandonment: baseline results

| Variables | Proportion of abandoned cropland area to total cropland area | | |
|---|---|---|---|
| | (1) | (2) | (3) |
| ACR | 0.016*** | 0.016*** | 0.016*** |
| | (0.004) | (0.004) | (0.004) |
| Age | | −0.001 | −0.001 |
| | | (0.002) | (0.002) |
| Age2 | | 5.01e−06 | 0.00001 |
| | | (0.00002) | (0.00002) |
| Education | | −0.015* | −0.015* |
| | | (0.008) | (0.008) |
| Dependency ratio | | | 0.019** |
| | | | (0.009) |
| Family health | | | −0.014* |
| | | | (0.008) |
| Off-farm employment | | | 0.026*** |
| | | | (0.009) |
| Land size | | | 0.001*** |
| | | | (0.0002) |
| Land fragmentation | | | 0.002** |
| | | | (0.001) |
| Land certification | | | −0.010** |
| | | | (0.005) |
| Household FE | Yes | Yes | Yes |
| Year FE | Yes | Yes | Yes |
| County × Year FE | Yes | Yes | Yes |
| Mean of dependent variable | 0.047 | 0.047 | 0.047 |
| Observations | 24,843 | 24,843 | 24,843 |
| R-squared | 0.684 | 0.684 | 0.685 |

*Notes* ***, **, and * denote significance at the 1%, 5%, and 10% levels, respectively; Robust standard errors are presented in parentheses

In terms of control variables, the age of the household head and its quadratic term do not exhibit a significant impact on cropland abandonment, which contradicts the significant nonlinear relationship identified by Zheng et al. (2023b). The education level of the household head is inversely correlated with cropland abandonment, aligning with the findings reported by Ma and Zhu (2020). This can be attributed to improved agricultural management skills associated with higher education, thereby leading to a reduction in cropland abandonment. Older dependency ratios are emerging as a pivotal determinant of cropland abandonment, while the health status of family members plays a crucial role in mitigating cropland abandonment. This finding is consistent with research conducted by Zheng and Qian (2022), which posits that households with poor labor endowments are more likely to abandon cropland. The higher the proportion of off-farm workers, the greater the extent of cropland abandonment, which can be attributed to a decline in farm labor due to the shift to off-farm employment (Xu et al., 2019a; Zheng, 2024b). From the perspective of land characteristics, cropland abandonment increases with the increase in per capita land size, because limited labor may choose to cultivate land of better quality and are more likely to abandon other marginal land in the face of large land sizes. Land fragmentation has a significant positive impact on cropland abandonment, which can be attributed to increased agricultural production costs (Wang et al., 2022; Zheng et al., 2023b). The confirmation of land property rights can effectively mitigate cropland abandonment, primarily due to the policy's reinforcement of farmers' awareness and recognition of property rights, thus fostering a greater sense of value for their cropland.

### 5.4.2 *Robustness Checks*

To assess the robustness of the baseline results, a series of rigorous robustness checks are conducted, and the corresponding results are demonstrated in Table 5.3. One approach to robustness checking is to replace variables. In column (1), the core independent variable ACR is replaced by ACRC. It is defined as whether the household farm income last year was lower than the average wage income of other farmers in the county. The results show that ACRC also has a significantly positive effect on cropland abandonment. Column (2) replaces the dependent variable in baseline regression with a binary variable, denoting whether the cropland is abandoned or not. The results indicate that the positive impact of ACR remains valid. Compared to farmers with a comparative advantage in agricultural returns, those without such an advantage exhibited an increased likelihood of cropland abandonment by 0.015.

The second approach involves replacing the estimation model. Given that a significant proportion of sample households do not exhibit cropland abandonment behavior, the dependent variable is treated as a censored variable (Zheng, 2024a). To obtain an unbiased estimate, we employ a panel Tobit model. As depicted in column (3), the estimated results from the panel Tobit model continue to support the positive impact of ACR on cropland abandonment.

The third approach is to add more control variables. Despite controlling for individual and household characteristics as much as possible in the previous section, it is still difficult to rule out the problem of omitted variables, such as land production conditions and village characteristics. For this reason, we further incorporate the following variables: land market value, per capita income, new agricultural operators, and land water conservancy project. Results in column (4) indicate that the positive

**Table 5.3** ACR and cropland abandonment: robustness checks

| Variables | Replacing variables | | Replacing model | Adding variables | Adjusting sample | |
|---|---|---|---|---|---|---|
| | (1) | (2) | (3) | (4) | (5) | (6) |
| ACR | | 0.015** | 0.070*** | 0.015** | 0.013*** | 0.071*** |
| | | (0.007) | (0.004) | (0.007) | (0.005) | (0.008) |
| ACRC | 0.011** | | | | | |
| | (0.005) | | | | | |
| Control variables | Yes | Yes | Yes | Yes | Yes | Yes |
| Other variables | – | – | – | Yes | – | – |
| Household FE | Yes | Yes | – | Yes | Yes | – |
| Year FE | Yes | Yes | – | Yes | Yes | – |
| County × Year FE | Yes | Yes | – | Yes | Yes | – |
| Observations | 24,843 | 24,843 | 24,843 | 12,428 | 20,932 | 3,911 |
| Log likelihood | – | – | −7717.433 | – | – | – |
| Wald chi2 | – | – | −603.07 | – | – | – |
| R-squared | 0.685 | 0.696 | – | 0.820 | 0.776 | 0.045 |

*Notes* ***, **, and * denote significance at the 1%, 5%, and 10% levels, respectively; Robust standard errors and delta-method standard errors are presented in parentheses. In column (4), land market value is defined as logarithm of land market value per mu estimated by the household head; per capita income is defined as per capita disposable annual in the village; new agricultural operators are defined as logarithm of the number of large-scale agricultural operators in the village, including professional operators, family farms, agricultural cooperatives, and farming companies; land water conservancy construction is measured by whether the village has carried out cropland water conservancy construction. Due to space limitations, estimates of other control variables are available from the authors upon request

association between ACR and cropland abandonment remains significant, although some variables in different years are missing, leading to a decline in observations.

The last approach is to adjust the samples. To mitigate the influence of COVID-19, we excluded sampled households in 2021 and focused solely on regression analysis using 2015–2019 samples. The result, presented in column (5), still demonstrates a significant impact of ACR on cropland abandonment. Furthermore, we conducted separate analyses among sampled households in 2021, as depicted in column (6), revealing that even amidst the shock of COVID-19, ACR still exerts a noteworthy positive effect on cropland abandonment.

To sum up, the results of various robustness checks consistently support the reliability and robustness of the baseline results, allowing us to scientifically and accurately assert that lower agricultural return compared to non-agricultural employment income is a significant factor leading to cropland abandonment.

### 5.4.3 Endogeneity Discussion

As mentioned earlier, this study was designed to minimize potential endogeneity concerns arising from omitted variables, measurement errors, and reverse causality. First, based on data availability, we drew on existing research to include as many relevant control variables as possible, excluding other potential omitted variables. When comparing columns (1)–(3) in Table 5.2, it is clear that the impact of ACR on cropland abandonment remains significantly positive with robust coefficients, regardless of the inclusion of additional control variables. Second, by redefining the core independent variables, this study mitigated the endogeneity problem caused by measurement errors of the core independent variable. The positive relationship between ACR and cropland abandonment remains robust in the estimated results in column (1) of Table 5.3. Third, with the benefit of the CFD, reverse causality in this study could be avoided by defining ACR using income variables from the previous year rather than the current year, and at the village/county level rather than the household level.

However, there are also other endogeneity concerns caused by selection bias in this study. In particular, more capable farmers may select better off-farm employment opportunities, and farmers with better land conditions may be more likely to choose farming. In this regard, we employ a Propensity Score Matching (PSM) approach to estimate the impact of ACR on cropland abandonment. Specifically, we utilize three commonly used matching methods, such as one-to-one nearest neighbor (NN) matching, NN matching within caliper, and kernel matching, for estimation. The results in Table 5.4 indicate that regardless of the matching method used, the average treatment effects (ATT) for ACR remain positive and significant regardless of the matching method used, indicating that our findings are consistent with previous estimates. Therefore, there is no need to worry too much about endogeneity in this study.

**Table 5.4** ACR and cropland abandonment: PSM estimates

| PSM methods | Cropland abandonment | | ATT | S.E. | *T*-value | Common support | |
|---|---|---|---|---|---|---|---|
| | Treat | Control | | | | Treat | Control |
| Nearest neighbor matching ($n$ = 1) | 0.068 | 0.020 | 0.048*** | 0.003 | 18.85 | 11,199 | 13,625 |
| NN matching with caliper ($n$ = 4, $r$ = 0.05) | 0.068 | 0.020 | 0.048*** | 0.002 | 20.60 | 11,199 | 13,625 |
| Kernel matching (bandwidth = 0.03) | 0.068 | 0.021 | 0.047*** | 0.002 | 21.19 | 11,199 | 13,625 |

*Notes* ***, **, and * denote significance at the 1%, 5%, and 10% levels, respectively

### 5.4.4 Mechanism Analysis

Based on theoretical analysis, we subsequently examined the internal mechanism by which ACR influences cropland abandonment by focusing on changes in input factors of land, capital, and labor. The estimated results are presented in Table 5.5.

Column (1) exhibits the estimated result of ACR's impact on long-term land investment. We defined a binary variable to characterize the long-term land investment of farmers, assigning a value of 1 when farmers engage in straw or manure return practices, and 0 otherwise. It can be found that compared to farmers with a comparative advantage in agricultural returns, the probability of implementing long-term land investment decreases by 0.026 for farmers without a comparative advantage in agricultural returns. This observed effect accounts for 4.27% of the proportion of sampled households (0.608) that have implemented long-term investments in land, which can be treated as a relatively obvious effect. The findings demonstrate that a comparative disadvantage in agricultural returns leads to an increase in cropland abandonment due to a reduction in long-term investment in land, which has been proved to help curb cropland abandonment by Ma and Zhu (2020). This is primarily attributed to the lack of cost-effectiveness associated with implementing long-term land investments under conditions of low comparative agricultural returns. Such investments not only require substantial input costs, but also necessitate several years for the beneficial effects of returning straw and manure on land quality to become apparent (Abdulai et al., 2011; Wang et al., 2021; Zheng, 2024c). Therefore, a reduction in long-term land investment produces corresponding reduction in the cost of cropland abandonment, making cropland abandonment easier to occur.

The estimate in Column (2) illustrates the impact of ACR on agricultural capital input, which is estimated using logarithm. The results show that the input of agricultural capital by farmers with comparative agricultural returns increased by 1.88 times

**Table 5.5** ACR and cropland abandonment: mechanism analysis

| Variables | Dependent variable | | |
|---|---|---|---|
| | (1) Long-term land investment | (2) Agricultural capital input | (3) Agricultural labor input |
| ACR | −0.026*** | −1.880*** | −0.074*** |
| | (0.009) | (0.072) | (0.006) |
| Control variables | Yes | Yes | Yes |
| Household FE | Yes | Yes | Yes |
| Year FE | Yes | Yes | Yes |
| County × Year FE | Yes | Yes | Yes |
| Observations | 23,204 | 24,843 | 24,843 |
| R-squared | 0.847 | 0.839 | 0.853 |

*Notes* ***, **, and * denote significance at the 1%, 5%, and 10% levels, respectively; Robust standard errors are presented in parentheses

more than that of farmers without comparative agricultural returns. This implies that ACR may enhance cropland abandonment by diminishing agricultural capital input. This phenomenon arises primarily from rational farmers' tendency to allocate their capital solely to high-yield projects (Huang & Shi, 2021). Consequently, the reduction in capital input for agricultural production corresponds to a decrease in cropland allocation, ultimately leading to an increase in cropland abandonment (Chen et al., 2025; Deininger et al., 2012).

The third column demonstrates the estimated impact of ACR on agricultural labor input, which is depicted as the proportion of agricultural labor to the total household population. The results indicate that farmers without comparative agricultural returns experience a reduction of approximately 7.4 percentage points in the proportion of agricultural labor to the total household population compared to those with comparative agricultural returns. This accounts for about 18.97% of the mean proportion of agricultural labor in the total household population (0.39) in the sampled households. The findings provide evidence that ACR increases cropland abandonment by diminishing agricultural labor input primarily due to the allure of high-yield off-farm livelihood activities (Xu et al., 2019a; Zheng, 2024b), resulting in an out-transfer of labor and subsequent suspension of land management due to workforce shortage and eventual cropland abandonment.

To conclude, we provide empirical evidence that ACR leads to cropland abandonment primarily through the reduction of long-term land investment, agricultural capital input, and agricultural labor input. The hypotheses 2-1, 2-2, 2-3 proposed by the aforementioned theory have been validated.

### 5.4.5 *Further Discussion*

#### 5.4.5.1 Moderating Effect of Factor Market Development

Based on the analysis in the previous section, it is of great significance to further explore how to alleviate the problem of cropland abandonment caused by low ACR. We first examine from a market perspective whether the development of factor markets in agricultural production can suppress cropland abandonment due to low ACR, and the results are shown in Table 5.6.

The estimates in columns (1) to (3) reveal the moderating effect of agricultural machinery market development. Using a subsample regression method, columns (1) and (2) examine the impact of ACR on cropland abandonment in villages with and without agricultural machinery markets, respectively. It is found that ACR has a significant positive effect on cropland abandonment in both cases, but the estimated coefficient for ACR is smaller in villages with agricultural machinery markets (0.013) compared to those without (0.060). To further identify the significance of this difference, we next include an interaction term between ACR and the village agricultural machinery market variable (assigned as 1 for villages with agricultural machinery markets and 0 for those without) in the regression model, as shown in

**Table 5.6** ACR and cropland abandonment: Moderating effect of factor market development

| Variables | Proportion of abandoned cropland area to total cropland area | | | | | |
|---|---|---|---|---|---|---|
| | Moderating effect of agricultural machinery market | | | Moderating effect of land rental market | | |
| | (1) | (2) | (3) | (4) | (5) | (6) |
| ACR | 0.013*** | 0.060** | 0.056*** | 0.008 | 0.028* | 0.030*** |
| | (0.005) | (0.028) | (0.021) | (0.005) | (0.016) | (0.010) |
| ACR × Agricultural machinery market | | | −0.042** | | | |
| | | | (0.021) | | | |
| ACR × Land rental market | | | | | | −0.018* |
| | | | | | | (0.010) |
| Control variables | Yes | Yes | Yes | Yes | Yes | Yes |
| Household FE | Yes | Yes | Yes | Yes | Yes | Yes |
| Year FE | Yes | Yes | Yes | Yes | Yes | Yes |
| County × Year FE | Yes | Yes | Yes | Yes | Yes | Yes |
| Observations | 20,412 | 1,847 | 22,259 | 19,294 | 5,549 | 24,843 |
| R-squared | 0.702 | 0.814 | 0.692 | 0.739 | 0.832 | 0.685 |

*Notes* ***, **, and * denote significance at the 1%, 5%, and 10% levels, respectively; Robust standard errors are presented in parentheses

column (3). The interaction term is statistically significant at a 5% level and has an estimated coefficient of −0.042. This indicates that compared to villages without agricultural machinery markets, villages with such markets can mitigate the promotion effect of low comparative returns on cropland abandonment by approximately 0.042. The main reason for this is that agricultural machinery replaces labor at a much lower cost, alleviating the labor shortage in agricultural production (Ma et al., 2022). This confirms Hypothesis 3-1. The development of agricultural machinery markets effectively mitigates cropland abandonment caused by low comparative returns in agriculture.

The estimates in columns (4) and (5) represent the moderating effects of land rental market. Similarly, we initially employ a subsample regression method to examine the impact of ACR on cropland abandonment in villages with and without land rental markets, as depicted in columns (4) and (5). It can be observed that in the presence of a land rental market, ACR does not exert a significant effect on cropland abandonment. Conversely, in villages without a land rental market, ACR exhibits a significantly positive effect on cropland abandonment, with an estimated coefficient larger than that under a land rental market. In column (6), we introduce an interaction term between ACR and variables related to the land rental market (where villages with land rental markets are assigned 1; otherwise, 0) to further investigate their disparities. This disparity is examined by the statistically significant negative coefficient (-0.018) at the 10% significance level for the interaction term. One possible explanation is that the development of land rental markets can not only provide opportunities for the reuse of idle cropland, but also allow farmers to earn a share of rental income (Ito et al., 2016; Zheng et al., 2025). This makes it unnecessary for farmers to abandon their croplands. Hypothesis 3-2 is verified, and the development of land rental markets (Zhang et al., 2014), effectively mitigates instances of low ACR-induced abandoned croplands.

#### 5.4.5.2 Moderating Effect of Government Subsidies

Subsequently, we investigate from a government perspective whether agricultural subsidies provided by the government to farmers can mitigate cropland abandonment resulting from low ACR. To delve deeper into the moderating role of government agricultural subsidies, this study conducts a comprehensive analysis from two perspectives: the availability and level of agricultural subsidies.

Columns (1) to (3) in Table 5.7 present estimates of how the availability of agricultural subsidies moderates the impact of ACR on cropland abandonment. The results indicate that, regardless of whether agricultural subsidies are available or not, low comparative returns have a significant and positive effect on cropland abandonment. However, under conditions where agricultural subsidies exist, the positive impact of ACR (0.009) is smaller than without any agricultural subsidy (0.048). To test whether this difference is significant, we considered the interaction term between ACR and agricultural subsidy availability. Column (3) shows that this interaction term is not significant, indicating that the moderating effect of agricultural subsidy availability has not been effectively utilized. Hypothesis 4-1 is falsified. This may be due to the fact that under China's latest agricultural subsidy policy (Fan et al., 2023), most farmers actually engaged in agricultural production can receive agricultural subsidies.

Columns (4) to (6) provide estimates of how the level of agricultural subsidies moderates the impact of ACR on cropland abandonment. To facilitate group comparisons, we redefined the continuous variable representing the level of agricultural subsidies as a binary variable. A value of 1 is assigned if the subsidy level exceeds the average subsidy level of other households in the same village; otherwise, a value of 0 is assigned. Results from grouped regression disclose that when a farmer household receives a higher agricultural subsidy per mu than others in the same village, the positive impact of ACR on cropland abandonment (0.006) is insignificant and lower compared to scenarios where a farmer receives significantly less agricultural subsidy than others in the same village (0.032). Moreover, this difference has also been proven to be statistically significant by column (6), confirming Hypothesis 4-2 and indicating that agricultural subsidy level is effective in suppressing the promotion of cropland abandonment caused by low agricultural returns. To sum up, it is not enough to address the availability of subsidies for farmers in order to reduce the impact of cropland abandonment caused by low ACR. Full consideration should be given to the level of subsidies, allowing farmers to receive higher subsidies than the average level of other farmers in the same village, thereby maximizing the moderating effect of agricultural subsidies.

**Table 5.7** ACR and cropland abandonment: Moderating effect of agricultural subsidy from government

| Variables | Proportion of abandoned cropland area to total cropland area | | | | | |
|---|---|---|---|---|---|---|
| | Moderating effect of agricultural subsidy availability | | | Moderating effect of agricultural subsidy level | | |
| | (1) | (2) | (3) | (4) | (5) | (6) |
| ACR | 0.009* | 0.048*** | 0.024*** | 0.006 | 0.032*** | 0.022*** |
| | (0.005) | (0.014) | (0.007) | (0.009) | (0.009) | (0.006) |
| ACR × agricultural subsidy availability | | | −0.012 | | | |
| | | | (0.008) | | | |
| ACR × agricultural subsidy level | | | | | | −0.013* |
| | | | | | | (0.007) |
| Control variables | Yes | Yes | Yes | Yes | Yes | Yes |
| Household FE | Yes | Yes | Yes | Yes | Yes | Yes |
| Year FE | Yes | Yes | Yes | Yes | Yes | Yes |
| County × Year FE | Yes | Yes | Yes | Yes | Yes | Yes |
| Observations | 15,398 | 9,445 | 24,843 | 12,855 | 11,988 | 24,843 |
| R-squared | 0.803 | 0.827 | 0.685 | 0.834 | 0.827 | 0.685 |

*Notes* ***, **, and * denote significance at the 1%, 5%, and 10% levels, respectively; Robust standard errors are presented in parentheses

## 5.5 Heterogeneous Effects of ACR on Cropland Abandonment

The previous section demonstrated a positive correlation between ACR and cropland abandonment. However, given the significant variations in regional development levels, functional positioning, and terrain across China, further investigation is required to establish the validity of this relationship. Therefore, in this section, this study aims to analyze the heterogeneity effects of ACR on cropland abandonment from three dimensions: geographical regional heterogeneity, heterogeneity in the functional positioning of grain production, and terrain heterogeneity.

### *5.5.1 Heterogeneity of Different Geographical Regions*

Considering the ascending level of economic development in China from west to east, along with the disparity among the northeastern, eastern, central, and western regions, a subsample was selected from each region, strictly adhering to the classification criteria set by the National Bureau of Statistics of China.[3] Carrying out regressions among the four subsamples respectively enables us to unveil geographical heterogeneity in how ACR influences cropland abandonment.

The estimated coefficient results of ACR are shown in Fig. 5.3, which reveals that ACR has a significant positive impact on cropland abandonment in the central and western regions. However, there is no significant effect of ACR on cropland abandonment in the northeastern and central regions. One possible reason is that the eastern region has the most developed economy with abundant off-farm employment opportunities and high wages (Han et al., 2021; Zheng & Qian, 2022), resulting in much higher non-agricultural returns compared to agricultural returns. This implies relatively lower ACR, resulting in a larger marginal effect of ACR on cropland abandonment. The western region, being economically underdeveloped, exhibits lower levels of agricultural development and consequently lower ACR, hence showing a significant impact of ACR on cropland abandonment as well. In contrast, there may not be a substantial difference between off-farm employment and agricultural production income in the northeastern and central regions due to their primary agricultural activities (Xu et al., 2019a); therefore, whether or not there is a low ACR does not significantly affect farmers' decision to abandon their cropland. Moreover, in the northeastern and central regions, favorable land conditions have facilitated the development of both the agricultural machinery market and the land rental market (Duan et al., 2022; Niu et al., 2025). Simultaneously, agricultural subsidy policy in the northeastern and central regions is relatively well established (Fan et al., 2023). These factors collectively contribute to mitigating the impact of low ACR on land abandonment.

### 5.5.2 *Heterogeneity of Different Grain Areas*

The previously insignificant effect of ACR on cropland abandonment in the northeastern and central regions may also be related to the fact that many major grain provinces are located in these two regions. In rural China, the policy of major grain areas is a fundamental measure to ensure food security (Zheng & Qian, 2022). This can potentially result in heterogeneity between major and non-major grain areas. Therefore, we categorize our samples into two sub-groups: those from major grain areas and those from non-major grain areas based on each province's positioning in terms of their contribution to grain production function.[4] Subsequently, grouped regression will be conducted for these two subsamples.

Figure 5.4 illustrates the estimated coefficients of ACR on cropland abandonment in the two subgroups. It is evident that ACR does not exert a significant impact

[3] http://www.stats.gov.cn/zt_18555/zthd/sjtjr/dejtjkfr/tjkp/202302/t20230216_1909741.htm#:~:text.

[4] https://news.cctv.com/2022/12/22/ARTI6EJkerwO4t3oUaHw6GUE221222.shtml.

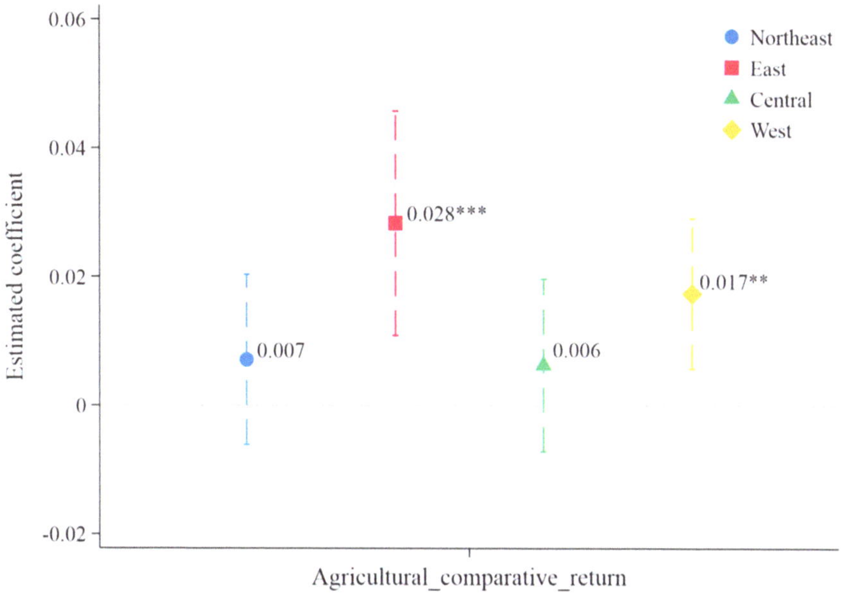


**Fig. 5.3** ACR and cropland abandonment: Regional heterogeneity

on cropland abandonment among farmers in major grain areas. Conversely, in non-major grain areas, ACR demonstrates a significantly positive effect on cropland abandonment, with an estimated coefficient higher than that of the whole sample. This can be attributed to two aspects: firstly, compared to non-major grain areas, major grain areas benefit from a range of supportive policies implemented by the government such as pricing mechanisms, insurance coverage, subsidies, and other measures (Ye et al., 2023; Zhang et al., 2021). These initiatives can compensate for lower ACR and enhance farmers' motivation to cultivate crops (Fan et al., 2023) while mitigating the issue of cropland abandonment due to low agricultural returns. The government offers substantial subsidies to farmers in major grain regions, and Sect. 4.4.2 has fully demonstrated the moderating effect of agricultural subsidies on mitigating the impact of ACR on cropland abandonment; secondly, unlike non-major grain areas, major grain areas are subject to relevant government restrictive policies, including strict prohibitions on abandoning cropland (Zheng & Qian, 2022). For example, the penalty criteria for abandoning cropland are implemented more strictly in major grain areas: no subsidies if cropland is abandoned for one year; and land use rights will be taken back if cropland is abandoned for more than two years. Consequently, farmers in major grain areas are less likely to abandon their croplands due to low agricultural returns.

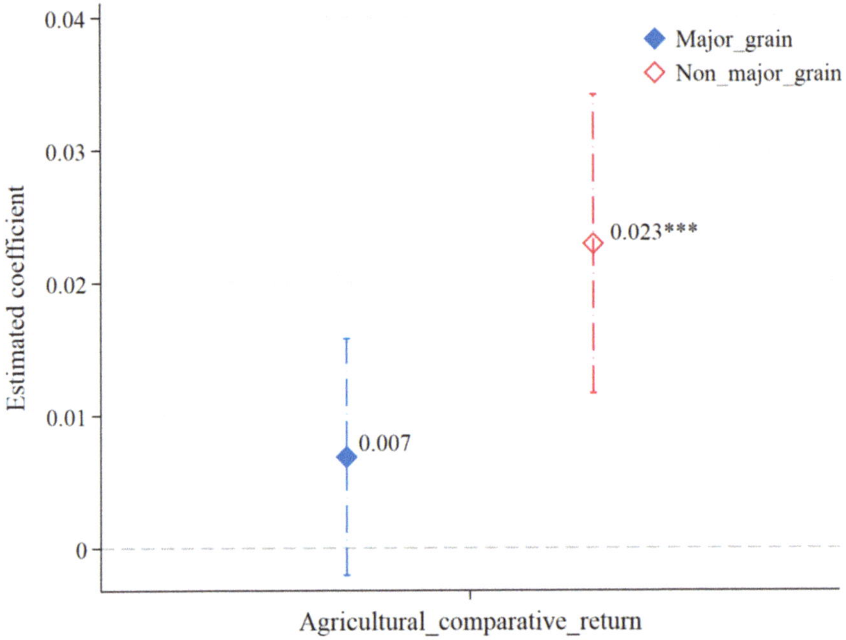


**Fig. 5.4** ACR and cropland abandonment: Major grain area heterogeneity

### *5.5.3 Heterogeneity of Different Terrain Zones*

The land use behavior of farmers may vary due to differences in terrain, as the terrain determines the difficulty of land production, with plains being more favorable for cultivation compared to mountains (Xu et al., 2019b). Therefore, based on the terrain information of the sample households, we divided them into two groups: those with plain-type land and those with mountain-type land, estimating separately the impact of ACR on cropland abandonment within each group to explain this heterogeneity.

Estimated results, as shown in Fig. 5.5, indicate that ACR has a significant positive impact on cropland abandonment among both plain and mountain-type farmers. However, the estimation coefficient of ACR is higher among farmers with mountain-type land. This disparity stems from three factors: First, mountain terrain inherently increases farming costs due to steep slopes that prevent mechanization and require more labor (Hong et al., 2024). Second, small, scattered plots in the mountains face market disadvantages. They are more difficult to rent out or consolidate, reducing profitability compared to large contiguous plains (Zheng et al., 2023b). Third, ecological limits on mountain slopes (e.g., soil erosion risks) restrict yield improvements, making farmers more likely to abandon cropland (Deng et al., 2019). Additionally, mountain areas often lack infrastructure (e.g., irrigation) to buffer climate shocks, worsening the effect of ACR on cropland abandonment (Deng et al., 2019). Once abandoned, mountain land faces higher ecological recovery costs (e.g., reversing

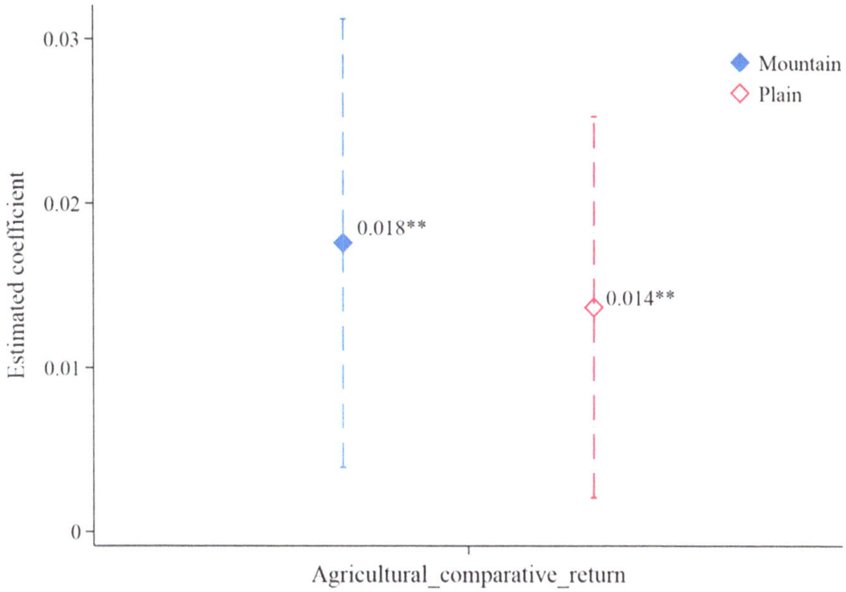


**Fig. 5.5** ACR and cropland abandonment: Terrain heterogeneity

erosion), creating a "lock-in" effect where recultivation becomes impractical, unlike reversible abandonment patterns in plains.

## 5.6 Conclusions and Discussion

### *5.6.1 Conclusions*

In the ongoing rural–urban transformation, the opportunity cost of farming has gradually increased, resulting in a widening gap between agricultural income and non-agricultural wage income. Consequently, these low ACRs have contributed to a substantial outflow of rural production factors to urban areas, potentially posing serious challenges to global food security and sustainable agricultural development. Against this background, this study employs the 2015–2021 CFD and panel high-dimensional fixed-effects models to examine the impact of ACR on cropland abandonment.

Our empirical results show that ACR significantly aggravated farmers' cropland abandonment behavior, increasing the ratio of abandoned cropland areas by 1.6%. This significant and positive correlation between ACR and cropland abandonment was still established after various robustness checks, including substitution of dependent variable, core independent variable, model, and samples. The mechanism analysis suggests that the decline in long-term land investment, input of agricultural capital and input of agricultural labor was an important channel for farmers to abandon cropland due to low ACR. However, the agricultural machinery market and the land rental market could reduce the negative impact of ACR on land use to some extent, while current agricultural subsidies have little effect. Heterogeneity analysis further reveals that the effects of ACR on cropland abandonment vary significantly across geographical regions, grain areas, and terrain zones. Specifically, regarding different geographical regions, ACR mainly increased cropland abandonment in eastern and western China. With regard to different grain areas, ACR increased cropland abandonment in non-major grain areas, but had no effect on major grain areas. For different terrain zones, the effect of ACR on cropland abandonment in mountainous areas was slightly higher than that in plains.

### 5.6.2 Policy Implications

Reducing cropland abandonment, strengthening land quantity protection, and promoting sustainable land use are important choices for food security and sustainable agricultural development. In this sense, the above findings of our study have important reference value for policymakers in developing countries.

Firstly, we must give priority to agriculture and rural areas, encourage the return of rural production factors to urban and rural areas, and block the mechanism of ACR that triggers cropland abandonment. In rural–urban transformation, urban expansion and rural decay are common practical problems in most developing countries. Appropriate government intervention is therefore needed to guide the flow of land, capital, and labor to rural areas, thus creating opportunities for the sustainable use of cropland.

Secondly, there is also an urgent need to jointly promote the construction of agricultural machinery markets and land rental markets in rural communities. On the one hand, replacing labor with machinery can effectively compensate for the shortage of agricultural labor due to rural–urban migration, thereby reducing cropland abandonment. On the other hand, by enhancing the market for rural land rentals, developing countries can benefit from transferring cropland from inefficient to efficient producers through land marketization, thereby preventing idle and unnecessary waste of valuable land resources.

Finally, substantial intensification of the reform of agricultural subsidies is an essential element in enhancing ACR and reducing cropland abandonment. Developing countries can improve their agricultural support and protection mechanisms, increase farmers' access to and income from agricultural subsidies, and thus stimulate their enthusiasm for agricultural pursuits. Fifth, developing countries should pay attention to the heterogeneity of different regions and promote the effective management of abandoned cropland according to local conditions. For example, for developed regions, there is a need to establish a feedback mechanism for secondary and tertiary industries to feed agriculture and cities to support rural areas; for less-developed regions and non-major grain areas, it is essential to increase support for agricultural subsidies.

### 5.6.3 Research Deficiencies and Prospects

Cropland abandonment represents a complex socio-economic challenge with a multi-dimensional research landscape around the world. Numerous studies have pointed out that cropland abandonment is the result of a combination of factors (Ojha et al., 2022; Xu et al., 2019a; Zavalloni et al., 2021), of which low ACR is considered the most important driving factor (Zhang et al., 2019). Unlike prior studies that mostly mention ACR indirectly (Guo et al., 2023; Ma & Zhu, 2020), or quantify non-economic factors of cropland abandonment (Deininger et al., 2012; Deng et al., 2019), this study directly explores the impacts and mechanisms of ACR on cropland abandonment by constructing ACR measurement indicators. This not only provides an indicator reference for ACR-related quantitative research, but also makes up for the lack of attention to key economic factors in the existing literature on cropland abandonment. However, due to data limitations and divergent research foci, the following aspects still warrant further investigation.

First and foremost, as pivotal policy instruments to influence farmers' production input decisions, the direct impact of agricultural subsidies and credit constraint relaxation on cropland abandonment cannot be ignored. While this research has illuminated the moderating effect of agricultural subsidies on the relationship between ACR and cropland abandonment, future studies could directly examine how these subsidies affect cropland abandonment behavior through income effects or substitution effects. Simultaneously, exploring the causal relationship between credit constraint relaxation and cropland abandonment, alongside strategies to deepen financial and credit system reforms for abandonment reduction, would provide valuable insights into policy formulation.

Moreover, under improved data accessibility conditions, future studies could delve into post-2021 cropland abandonment problems and governance strategies. This emphasis arises from the Chinese government's implementation of a series of policy initiatives since 2021, most notably the Guiding Opinions on the Coordinated Utilization of Abandoned Cropland to Promote Agricultural Production Development, which highlights a heightened policy focus on this issue compared to previous periods.

Lastly, while substantial efforts have been invested to mitigate potential endogeneity issues at their source, this study cannot guarantee the full elimination of such concerns. As such, future research is encouraged to identify appropriate instrumental variables that enable robust causal identification of the relationship between ACR and cropland abandonment, thereby advancing theoretical understanding and policy relevance. In addition, a more nuanced discussion of the various sources of endogeneity would be valuable. For example, the construction of new ACR measures and the re-estimation of their impact on cropland abandonment.

## Appendix: Complementary Derivation Processes of Theoretical Analysis

### *Appendix A*

$$\underset{N_f, L_f, K_f}{Max\pi} = pf\left(N_f, L_f, K_f\right) - uK_f + rN_r + wL_n + T\left(N_f\right)$$

$$s.t. N_f + N_r \leq \overline{N}$$

$$L_f + L_n \leq \overline{L}$$

To take the constraints condition into the objective function:

$$\underset{N_f, L_f, K_f}{Max\pi} = pf\left(N_f, L_f, K_f\right) - uK_f + r\left(\overline{N} - N_f\right) + w\left(\overline{L} - L_f\right) + T\left(N_f\right)$$

Based on the above equation, taking the first order derivative with respect to $L_f$, $N_f$ and $K_f$ respectively yields:

$$\frac{\partial \pi}{\partial N_f} = pf'_{N_f} - r + \frac{\partial T\left(N_f\right)}{\partial N_f} = 0$$

$$\frac{\partial \pi}{\partial L_f} = pf'_{L_f} - w = 0 \qquad \frac{\partial \pi}{\partial K_f} = pf'_{K_f} - u = 0$$

### *Appendix B*

$$pf'_{N_f} = r - \frac{\partial T\left(N_f\right)}{\partial N_f}$$

where $r$ and $\frac{\partial T(N_f)}{\partial N_f}$ is exogenous parameter. Take the total differential of the above equation as follows:

$$f'_{N_f}dp + pf''_{N_f}dN_f = 0$$
$$\Rightarrow \frac{dN_f}{dp} = -\frac{f'_{N_f}}{pf''_{N_f}} > 0$$

## Appendix C

$$\frac{\partial\pi}{\partial K_f} = pf'_{K_f} - u = 0 \qquad \Rightarrow pf'_{K_f} = u$$

Take the total differential of the above equation as follows:

$$pf''_{K_f}dK_f = du$$
$$\Rightarrow \frac{dK_f}{du} = \frac{1}{pf''_{K_f}} < 0$$

## Appendix D

$$f\left(N_f, L_f, K_f\right) = A^{1-\partial}\left(N_f^{\alpha}L_f^{\beta}K_f^{\gamma}\right)^{\partial}$$
$$\Rightarrow f'_{N_f} = A^{1-\partial}\alpha\partial N_f^{\alpha\partial-1}L_f^{\beta\partial}K_f^{\gamma\partial}$$

By substituting the aforementioned formula into $pf'_{N_f} = r - \frac{\partial T(N_f)}{\partial N_f}$, we can get:

$$pA^{1-\partial}\alpha\partial N_f^{\alpha\partial-1}L_f^{\beta\partial}K_f^{\gamma\partial} = r - \frac{\partial T\left(N_f\right)}{\partial N_f}$$

## Appendix E

$$pA^{1-\partial}\alpha\partial N_f^{\alpha\partial-1}L_f^{\beta\partial}K_f^{\gamma\partial} = r - \frac{\partial T\left(N_f\right)}{\partial N_f}$$

Under the condition of holding other factors constant, take the total differential of the above equation with respect to as follows:

$$pA^{1-\partial}\alpha\partial(\alpha\partial-1)N_f^{\alpha\partial-2}L_f^{\beta\partial}K_f^{\gamma\partial}dN_f+pA^{1-\partial}\alpha\partial N_f^{\alpha\partial-1}\gamma\partial L_f^{\beta\partial}K_f^{\gamma\partial-1}dK_f=0$$

$$\Rightarrow \qquad \frac{dN_f}{dK_f}=-\frac{pA^{1-\partial}\alpha\partial N_f^{\alpha\partial-1}\gamma\partial L_f^{\beta\partial}K_f^{\gamma\partial}}{pA^{1-\partial}\alpha\partial(\alpha\partial-1)N_f^{\alpha\partial-2}L_f^{\beta\partial}K_f^{\gamma\partial}}=-\frac{\gamma\partial N_f K_f}{(\alpha\partial-1)}>0$$

## Appendix F

$$\frac{\partial\pi}{\partial L_f}=pf'_{L_f}-w=0 \quad \Rightarrow pf'_{L_f}=w$$

Take the total differential of the above equation as follows:

$$pf''_{L_f}dL_f=dw$$

$$\Rightarrow \frac{dL_f}{dw}=\frac{1}{pf''_{L_f}}<0$$

## References


Abdulai, A., Owusu, V., & Goetz, R. (2011). Land tenure differences and investment in land improvement measures: Theoretical and empirical analyses. *Journal of Development Economics, 96*, 66–78.

Adamopoulos, T., & Restuccia, D. (2014). The size distribution of farms and international productivity differences. *American Economic Review, 104*, 1667–1697.

Andrianarimanana, M. H., Yongjian, P., & Rabezanahary Tanteliniaina, M. F., (2023). Assessment of the importance of climate, land, and soil on the global supply for agricultural products and global food security: Evidence from Madagascar. *Food Policy, 115*, 102403.

Berry, R. A., & Cline, W. R. (1980). Agrarian structure and productivity in developing countries. *Land Economics, 56*, 495–502.

Binswanger, H. P., Deininger, K., & Feder, G. (1995). Chapter 42 Power, distortions, revolt and reform in agricultural land relations. In *Handbook of development economics* (pp. 2659–2772). Elsevier.

Blair, D., Shackleton, C. M., & Mograbi, P. J. (2018). Cropland abandonment in South African smallholder communal lands: Land cover change (1950–2010) and farmer perceptions of contributing factors. *Land, 7*(4), 121.

Chari, A., Liu, E. M., Wang, S.-Y., & Wang, Y. (2021). Property rights, land misallocation, and agricultural efficiency in China. *The Review of Economic Studies, 88*, 1831–1862.

Chen, M., Han, Q., Zhang, C., & Chen, J. (2025). Valuing the effect of capital goes to countryside on cropland abandonment: Evidence from rural China. *Habitat International, 156*, Article 103299.

Cui, Y. (2023). Mechanization's impact on agricultural total factor productivity. *Agricultural Economics, 69*, 446–457.

Deininger, K., Savastano, S., & Carletto, C. (2012). Land fragmentation, cropland abandonment, and land market operation in Albania. *World Development, 40*, 2108–2122.

Deng, X., Xu, D., Zeng, M., & Qi, Y. (2019). Does Internet use help reduce rural cropland abandonment? Evidence from China. *Land Use Policy, 89*, Article 104243.

Duan, J. K., Ren, C. N., Wang, S. T., Zhang, X. M., Reis, S., Xu, J. M., & Gu, B. J. (2022). Consolidation of agricultural land can contribute to agricultural sustainability in China. *Nature Food, 3*, 179–179. https://doi.org/10.1038/s43016-021-00415-5

Fan, P., Mishra, A. K., Feng, S., Su, M., & Hirsch, S. (2023). The impact of China's new agricultural subsidy policy on grain crop acreage. *Food Policy, 118*, Article 102472.

Feder, G., Just, R. E., & Zilberman, D. (1985). Adoption of agricultural innovations in developing countries: A survey. *Economic Development and Cultural Change, 33*, 255–298.

Guo, A., Yue, W., Yang, J., Xue, B., Xiao, W., Li, M., He, T., Zhang, M., Jin, X., & Zhou, Q. (2023). Cropland abandonment in China: Patterns, drivers, and implications for food security. *Journal of Cleaner Production, 418*, Article 138154.

Han, W., Wei, Y., Cai, J., Yu, Y., & Chen, F. (2021). Rural nonfarm sector and rural residents' income research in China. An empirical study on the township and village enterprises after ownership reform (2000–2013). *Journal of Rural Studies, 82*, 161–175.

Hong, C., Prishchepov, A. V., & Bavorova, M. (2024). Cropland abandonment in mountainous China: Patterns and determinants at multiple scales and policy implications. *Land Use Policy, 145*, Article 107292.

Huang, J., & Shi, P. (2021). Regional rural and structural transformations and farmer's income in the past four decades in China. *China Agricultural Economic Review, 13*, 278–301.

Inada, K.-I. (1963). On a two-sector model of economic growth: Comments and a generalization. *The Review of Economic Studies, 30*, 119–127.

Ito, J., Nishikori, M., Toyoshi, M., & Feuer, H. N. (2016). The contribution of land exchange institutions and markets in countering farmland abandonment in Japan. *Land Use Policy, 57*, 582–593.

Johnson, N. L., & Ruttan, V. W. (1994). Why are farms so small? *World Development, 22*, 691–706.

Kuemmerle, T., Olofsson, P., Chaskovskyy, O., Baumann, M., Ostapowicz, K., Woodcock, C. E., Houghton, R. A., Hostert, P., Keeton, W. S., & Radeloff, V. C. (2011). Post-Soviet farmland abandonment, forest recovery, and carbon sequestration in western Ukraine. *Global Change Biology, 17*, 1335–1349.

Lewis, W. A. (1954). Economic development with unlimited supplies of labour. *The Manchester School, 22*, 139–191.

Li, X., & Ito, J. (2021). An empirical study of land rental development in rural Gansu, China: The role of agricultural cooperatives and transaction costs. *Land Use Policy, 109*, Article 105621.

Ma, W., & Zhu, Z. (2020). A note: reducing cropland abandonment in China—Do agricultural cooperatives play a role? *Journal of Agricultural Economics, 71*, 929–935.

Ma, W., Zhu, Z., & Zhou, X. (2022). Agricultural mechanization and cropland abandonment in rural China. *Applied Economics Letters, 29*, 526–533.

Niu, W., Luo, L., Shi, Y., Chai, C., Wang, H., Tian, Q., Jin, Y., Kong, X., Yu, Q., Ren, L., & Zhang, B. (2025). Impacts of "One Household One Plot" and "One Village Group One Plot" fragmentation consolidation models on cultivated land use transition from perspective of human-land system. *Habitat International, 156*, Article 103252.

Ojha, R. B., Atreya, K., Kristiansen, P., Devkota, D., & Wilson, B. (2022). A systematic review and gap analysis of drivers, impacts, and restoration options for abandoned croplands in Nepal. *Land Use Policy, 120*, Article 106237.

Poitras, G. (2023). Cobweb theory, market stability, and price expectations. *Journal of the History of Economic Thought, 45*, 137–161.

Qian, W. (2020). *The economy of Chinese rural households*. Springer.

Ren, C., Zhou, X., Wang, C., Guo, Y., Diao, Y., Shen, S., Reis, S., Li, W., Xu, J., & Gu, B. (2023). Ageing threatens sustainability of smallholder farming in China. *Nature, 616*, 96–103.

Sazama, G. W., & Davis, H. (1973). Land taxation and land reform. *Economic Development and Cultural Change, 21*, 642–654.

Stehfest, E., van Zeist, W.-J., Valin, H., Havlik, P., Popp, A., Kyle, P., Tabeau, A., Mason-D'Croz, D., Hasegawa, T., Bodirsky, B. L., Calvin, K., Doelman, J. C., Fujimori, S., Humpenöder, F., Lotze-Campen, H., van Meijl, H., & Wiebe, K. (2019). Key determinants of global land-use projections. *Nature Communications, 10*, 2166.
Takeshima, H., Hatzenbuehler, P. L., & Edeh, H. O. (2020). Effects of agricultural mechanization on economies of scope in crop production in Nigeria. *Agricultural Systems, 177*, Article 102691.
Tang, L., Ma, X., Zhou, Y., Shi, X., & Ma, J. (2019). Social relations, public interventions and land rent deviation: Evidence from Jiangsu Province in China. *Land Use Policy, 86*, 406–420.
Wang, J., Cao, Y., Fang, X., Li, G., & Cao, Y. (2022). Does land tenure fragmentation aggravate farmland abandonment? Evidence from big survey data in rural China. *Journal of Rural Studies, 91*, 126–135.
Wang, Y., Wu, P., Mei, F., Ling, Y., Qiao, Y., Liu, C., Leghari, S. J., Guan, X., & Wang, T. (2021). Does continuous straw returning keep China farmland soil organic carbon continued increase? A meta-analysis. *Journal of Environmental Management, 288*, Article 112391.
Wang, Y., Yang, A., & Yang, Q. (2023). The extent, drivers and production loss of farmland abandonment in China: Evidence from a spatiotemporal analysis of farm households survey. *Journal of Cleaner Production, 414*, Article 137772.
Wu, Y., Xi, X., Tang, X., Luo, D., Gu, B., Lam, S. K., Vitousek, P. M., & Chen, D. (2018). Policy distortions, farm size, and the overuse of agricultural chemicals in China. *Proceedings of the National Academy of Sciences, 115*, 7010–7015.
Xu, D., Deng, X., Guo, S., & Liu, S. (2019a). Labor migration and farmland abandonment in rural China: Empirical results and policy implications. *Journal of Environmental Management, 232*, 738–750.
Xu, D., Deng, X., Huang, K., Liu, Y., Yong, Z., & Liu, S. (2019b). Relationships between labor migration and cropland abandonment in rural China from the perspective of village types. *Land Use Policy, 88*, Article 104164.
Ye, D., Zhen, S., Wang, W., & Liu, Y. (2023). Spatial double dividend from China's main grain-producing areas policy: Total factor productivity and the net carbon effect. *Humanities and Social Sciences Communications, 10*, 459.
Zavalloni, M., D'Alberto, R., Raggi, M., & Viaggi, D. (2021). Farmland abandonment, public goods and the CAP in a marginal area of Italy. *Land Use Policy, 107*, Article 104365.
Zhang, D., Wang, H., & Lou, S. (2021). Research on grain production efficiency in China's main grain-producing areas from the perspective of grain subsidy. *Environmental Technology & Innovation, 22*, Article 101530.
Zhang, X., Hu, L., & Yu, X. (2023). Farmland leasing, misallocation reduction, and agricultural total factor productivity: Insights from rice production in China. *Food Policy, 119*, Article 102518.
Zhang, X., Zhao, C., Dong, J., & Ge, Q. (2019). Spatio-temporal pattern of cropland abandonment in China from 1992 to 2017: A meta-analysis. *Acta Geographica Sinica, 74*, 411–420.
Zhang, Y., Li, X., & Song, W. (2014). Determinants of cropland abandonment at the parcel, household and village levels in mountain areas of China: A multi-level analysis. *Land Use Policy, 41*, 186–192.
Zheng, L. (2024a). Big hands holding small hands: The role of new agricultural operating entities in farmland abandonment. *Food Policy, 123*, Article 102605.
Zheng, L. (2024b). Does off-farm work induce farmland abandonment? Evidence from China. *China Agricultural Economic Review, 16*, 664–682.
Zheng, L. (2024c). Those with constant property rights have perseverance: China's land tenure reform promotes environment-friendly farming practices. *Humanities and Social Sciences Communications, 11*, 763.
Zheng, L., Li, L., & Jin, S. (2025). Opening the village door: China's agricultural e-commerce facilitates the transformation of land rental markets. *Agricultural Economics, 56*(4), 622–636.
Zheng, L., & Qian, W. (2022). The impact of land certification on cropland abandonment: Evidence from rural China. *China Agricultural Economic Review, 14*, 509–526.

Zheng, L., Su, L., & Jin, S. (2023a). Reducing land fragmentation to curb cropland abandonment: Evidence from rural China. *Canadian Journal of Agricultural Economics/Revue canadienne d'agroeconomie, 71*, 355–373.

Zheng, Q., Ha, T., Prishchepov, A. V., Zeng, Y., Yin, H., & Koh, L. P. (2023b). The neglected role of abandoned cropland in supporting both food security and climate change mitigation. *Nature Communications, 14*, 6083.

# Chapter 6
# Land Tenure Insecurity and Cropland Abandonment

**Abstract** Property rights systems serve as foundational institutional arrangements underpinning economic and social operations. Land tenure security exerts a profound influence on factor allocation efficiency and the behavioral decisions of economic agents. Nevertheless, few scholars have examined the quantitative relationship between land tenure insecurity and farmers' cropland abandonment behavior—despite the fact that rural China is currently confronting both challenges concurrently. To address this research gap, this chapter adopts a panel random effects model to empirically investigate the impact of land tenure insecurity on cropland abandonment, utilizing three waves of panel data from the China Rural Household Panel Survey (2015–2019). Results show that land tenure insecurity significantly exacerbates cropland abandonment, increasing the proportion of abandoned cropland by an average of 0.70 percentage points. This effect is primarily driven by the fact that land tenure insecurity suppresses agricultural capital investment, reduces agricultural labor input, and impedes land transfer, thereby accelerating the spread of cropland abandonment. However, the impact of land tenure insecurity on cropland abandonment exhibits heterogeneity across horizontal income differentiation and vertical intergenerational disparities. Specifically, the adverse effects are more pronounced among higher-income farmers and the older generation, whereas lower-income farmers and the younger generation remain largely unaffected. Furthermore, formal institutions—exemplified by land certification—help mitigate the adverse effects of land tenure insecurity on cropland abandonment, while informal institutions, represented by village regulations, prove ineffective. Accordingly, future efforts should focus on strengthening the land tenure system, improving factor allocation efficiency, implementing tailored policies for different farm household groups, and advancing institutional coordination. This integrated approach will help alleviate the negative impacts of land tenure insecurity on land utilization and promote the sustainable development of agriculture.

**Keywords** Land tenure insecurity · Cropland abandonment · Land economics · Land use policy · Food security

 
L. Zheng, *Cropland Abandonment in Rural China*, Resources, Environment and Agricultural Development, https://doi.org/10.1007/978-981-95-8287-7_6

Property rights systems serve as foundational institutional arrangements underpinning economic and social operations. Land tenure security exerts a profound influence on factor allocation efficiency and the behavioral decisions of economic agents. Nevertheless, few scholars have examined the quantitative relationship between land tenure insecurity and farmers' cropland abandonment behavior—despite the fact that rural China is currently confronting both challenges concurrently. To address this research gap, this chapter adopts a panel random effects model to empirically investigate the impact of land tenure insecurity on cropland abandonment, utilizing three waves of panel data from the China Rural Household Panel Survey (2015–2019).

## 6.1 Introduction

Property rights systems are universally recognized as the cornerstone of institutional frameworks that govern economic and social operations, with their completeness and stability directly determining the efficiency of resource allocation and the sustainability of economic development (North, 1990). Among the multiple dimensions of property rights systems, tenure security stands out as a core element that exerts a profound and far-reaching impact on the behavioral decisions of economic agents, particularly in the agricultural sector where land serves as the fundamental means of production (Deininger & Jin, 2009). For farm households, secure land tenure not only provides a stable expectation of long-term returns from land use but also affects their willingness to allocate critical production factors such as capital, labor, and technology to agricultural production activities (Besley, 1995). In contrast, land tenure insecurity tends to induce short-sighted behavior among farmers, disrupting the optimal allocation of agricultural resources and potentially undermining the stability of agricultural development (Place et al., 1994; Zheng, 2024a).

The concept of land tenure security is multidimensional and can be defined and measured from three interrelated yet distinct perspectives: the legal, factual, and perceptual dimensions (Van Gelder, 2010). Legally defined tenure security refers to the degree to which farmers' land rights are protected by formal laws and regulations, including the clarity of property rights ownership, the enforceability of land contracts, and the availability of legal remedies for rights violations. Factual tenure security, on the other hand, reflects the actual status of land rights exercise in practice, i.e., whether farmers can freely use, transfer, mortgage, or inherit their land without arbitrary interference from external parties such as local governments or village collectives. Perceptual tenure security focuses on farmers' subjective judgments and expectations regarding the stability of their land rights, which are shaped by both legal provisions and practical experiences and are often more directly associated with their daily decision-making processes. Despite the differences among these dimensions, they collectively constitute the comprehensive connotation of land tenure security and jointly influence farmers' economic behaviors (Ma et al., 2015).

Against this backdrop, a large body of existing literature has explored the economic implications of land tenure security, with research focuses primarily concentrated on four major areas: agricultural investment, land rental markets, labor mobility, and agricultural productivity. In terms of agricultural investment, numerous empirical studies have confirmed that secure land tenure significantly enhances farmers' willingness to make long-term investments in land, such as agroforestry, soil improvement, the use of organic fertilizer, and the adoption of high-yield crop varieties (Mengesha et al., 2019; Zhou et al., 2022). For instance, Deininger et al. (2011) found that the issuance of land tenure certificates in Ethiopia increased farmers' investment in soil and water conservation by approximately 30%. In the context of land rental markets, tenure security reduces the transaction costs of land transfers by mitigating the risk of contract breaches, thereby promoting the concentration of land resources to more efficient farmers (Deininger & Jin, 2009; Wang et al., 2015). Regarding labor mobility, secure land tenure provides a safety net for rural households, enabling farmers to engage in off-farm employment with greater confidence without the fear of losing their land rights, which in turn facilitates the transfer of surplus agricultural labor (Wang et al., 2020; Adamopoulos et al., 2024). In terms of agricultural productivity, the positive impacts of tenure security on factor allocation efficiency and long-term investment ultimately translate into improvements in agricultural output and productivity (Abdulai et al., 2011; Gao et al., 2021). Despite the extensive exploration of tenure security in the aforementioned fields, a critical research gap remains: few studies have systematically examined the relationship between land tenure insecurity and cropland abandonment. Cropland abandonment, as a prominent issue in agricultural development in many developing countries, is inherently closely linked to the resource allocation behaviors (e.g., labor migration, capital investment, land rentals) that have been the focus of existing tenure security research. Although some scholars have briefly mentioned the potential association between land property rights reforms and cropland abandonment (Prishchepov et al., 2012), they have not further empirically tested the causal impact of tenure insecurity—especially the subjective perception of insecurity—on cropland abandonment.

To date, the research most relevant to this study primarily focuses on the impact of land certification (a core component of legal tenure security) on cropland abandonment. For example, Zheng and Qian (2022) found that land certification reduced cropland abandonment in China's rural areas by enhancing tenure security. However, these studies implicitly take tenure insecurity as a given premise and only examine the role of legal-level tenure security (represented by land certification) in mitigating cropland abandonment. A series of fundamental questions remain unanswered: Does tenure insecurity actually trigger cropland abandonment? Can land certification truly improve tenure security? If so, what are the underlying mechanisms? Are there heterogeneous effects across different farmer groups? Moreover, tenure security encompasses not only the legal and factual dimensions but also the perceptual dimension, which has a more direct impact on farmers' behavioral decisions (Van Gelder, 2009). Yet, existing research has paid insufficient attention to the perceptual dimension of tenure security, leaving its role in cropland abandonment unexplored. Additionally, land certification is essentially a formal institutional arrangement. In rural areas, informal institutions such as village regulations also play an important role in regulating land use behaviors (Ho, 2005). However, whether informal institutions can influence the relationship between tenure insecurity and cropland abandonment has not been empirically tested. This gap is particularly notable given that informal institutions often complement or interact with formal institutions in shaping rural economic outcomes.

In view of the above research gaps, this chapter employs three waves of panel data from the China Rural Household Panel Survey (CRHPS) covering the period 2015–2019 and adopts a panel random effects model to empirically examine the impact of land tenure insecurity on cropland abandonment, as well as its underlying mechanisms and heterogeneous effects. This study aims to extend the existing literature in three key aspects: First, by shifting the research perspective from tenure security to tenure insecurity, it directly addresses the hypothetical premise that land certification enhances tenure security and focuses on the impact of farmers' perceived tenure insecurity on cropland abandonment, thereby remedying the deficiency of existing research that predominantly focuses on legal and factual tenure security. Second, it investigates the potential mechanisms and heterogeneous effects of land tenure insecurity on cropland abandonment from the perspectives of factor allocation and farmer differentiation, systematically revealing the conditions under which cropland abandonment occurs in the context of tenure insecurity. Third, it explores governance solutions for cropland abandonment under tenure insecurity by focusing on the interaction between formal and informal institutions, providing policy references for developing countries that simultaneously face the challenges of land tenure insecurity and cropland abandonment.

## 6.2 Theoretical Analysis and Analytical Framework

Land tenure security serves as the rational basis for farmers' behavioral choices, it shapes farmers' expectations regarding agricultural production and management, thereby motivating them to reallocate agricultural land factors (Demsetz, 1967; Feder & Feeny, 1991). Ultimately, such factor reallocation manifests in distinct economic outcomes, specifically in the form of diverse land use behaviors such as cultivation, transfer, or abandonment. As illustrated in Fig. 6.1, land tenure insecurity undermines farmers' long-term expectations, introduces uncertainty into agricultural production, and raises transaction costs, thereby distorting the allocation of agricultural production factors. In theory, these distortions will influence farmers' cropland abandonment behavior through three key channels: suppressing agricultural capital investment, reducing agricultural labor input, and hindering land transfer activities.

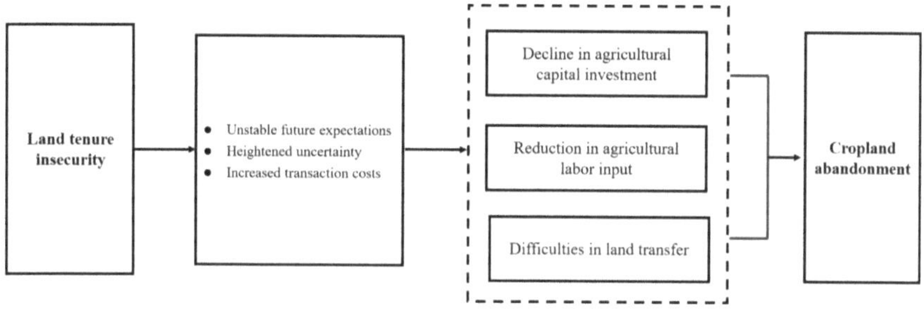


**Fig. 6.1** Analytical framework

### *6.2.1 Land Tenure Insecurity, Agricultural Capital Investment, and Cropland Abandonment*

Theoretically, land tenure insecurity suppresses agricultural capital investment and increases cropland abandonment by farmers due to low investment returns. Land tenure insecurity is typically associated with heightened uncertainty regarding arbitrary adjustments, expropriations, requisitions, and infringements of cropland rights, thereby amplifying investment risks for farmers (Jacoby et al., 2002). Although long-term agricultural investments exhibit higher marginal productivity elasticity and tend to yield greater returns under stable conditions free from external threats, their value is inherently tied to the land itself and closely linked to the natural attributes of specific plots. This gives rise to high asset specificity, non-transferability, and prolonged investment return cycles—such as investments in organic fertilizer application or soil quality improvement (Yami & Snyder, 2016). This characteristic of long-term agricultural investments renders it difficult for farmers to recover, transfer, or obtain compensation for private land investments, which ultimately become sunk costs. This potential risk of property loss is equivalent to imposing a random tax on farmers' investment returns (Besley, 1995), significantly discounting the future benefits of long-term agricultural investments and reducing farmers' expected returns.

Furthermore, the diminished expected returns resulting from land tenure insecurity alter farmers' risk aversion and time preferences (Kahneman & Tversky, 1979). This not only suppresses their willingness to engage in long-term, improvement-oriented investments but also compels them to opt for investments with shorter payback periods or even adopt predatory farming practices to mitigate uncertainty risks and secure substantial short-term gains. When confronting such risks, farmers' time preferences shift toward short-term investments to promptly recover costs and secure returns (Zheng, 2024a). Consequently, investment horizons shorten while discount rates for future returns rise, which further devalues the future payoffs of land-related capital investments and significantly erodes the net present value of the long-term returns from agricultural capital investments (Chen et al., 2025). Thus, land tenure insecurity suppresses agricultural capital input. When farmers perceive that the sum of the marginal cost of agricultural investment and the marginal expected loss due to land tenure insecurity exceeds the marginal expected return of agricultural investment, they will reduce total agricultural investment and shift toward short-term investment structures. Instead, farmers redirect limited resources to other sectors with higher marginal returns until the marginal returns across sectors are equalized. Ultimately, the lack of long-term capital investment to drive technological progress inhibits the growth of agricultural total factor productivity. This reduces the comparative returns of agriculture and confines production to inefficient levels by preventing the expansion of the production possibility frontier. When the marginal cost of cropland cultivation exceeds the marginal benefit, farmers will choose to abandon cropland.

### 6.2.2 Land Tenure Insecurity, Agricultural Labor Input, and Cropland Abandonment

Land tenure insecurity theoretically reduces agricultural labor input, increasing the likelihood of cropland abandonment by farm households due to labor shortages. As rational economic agents, rural households aim to maximize total expected household utility under the constraint of land tenure insecurity, allocating family labor based on the marginal returns of different productive activities. Farmers must simultaneously strive to raise the expected level of total household income and mitigate the uncertainty risk associated with that income, leading them to determine an optimal labor allocation ratio between the agricultural and non-agricultural sectors to secure both agricultural and non-agricultural income streams (Mullan et al., 2011).

In the process of labor allocation, households not only pursue the maximization of expected total income but also inherently seek to reduce income uncertainty—a risk-averse trait that is particularly pronounced in agriculture, given its heavy reliance on natural conditions and susceptibility to institutional constraints such as land tenure security. Land tenure insecurity directly undermines farm households' stable expectations of long-term agricultural returns, exerting a negative impact on the expected utility of agricultural production through two key channels: First, it heightens uncertainty about farmers' future income. Land tenure insecurity exposes farmers to risks such as forced cropland expropriation, arbitrary adjustments to land contracts by village collectives, or land disputes with other parties (Benjamin & Brandt, 2002). If these risks materialize, farmers may lose their cropland use rights or agricultural income, rendering the returns on their agricultural labor inputs highly uncertain; Second, it diminishes farmers' expected returns from full agricultural input. Agricultural production is characterized by long production cycles and irreversible labor inputs—farmers must continuously invest labor throughout the entire production process, including land preparation, sowing, field management, and harvesting.

However, if land tenure is insecure, farmers may fail to fully secure the returns commensurate with these labor inputs. Therefore, holding other factors constant, land tenure insecurity will drive households to allocate more labor to the non-agricultural sector to achieve an optimal utility level, thereby maximizing household utility and boosting total household income (Adamopoulos et al., 2024). Consequently, as the supply of agricultural labor becomes insufficient, land tenure insecurity will force many croplands—especially marginal croplands—to lie fallow.

### 6.2.3 *Land Tenure Insecurity, Land Transfer, and Cropland Abandonment*

Theoretically, land tenure insecurity hinders the development of land transfer markets and increases the likelihood of cropland abandonment resulting from inefficient land transfers. A sound and stable agricultural property rights system serves as the foundation for the efficient operation of land transfer markets (Deininger et al., 2011). In contrast, land tenure insecurity reinforces institutional constraints such as high transaction costs and unstable expectations, impeding the development of land transfers and leading to inefficient cropland allocation (Chen, 2017).

Specifically, in the context of land transfers, land tenure insecurity affects farmers' land transfer willingness. When making decisions between self-cultivation and land transfer, transferors adopt strategies with lower opportunity costs and higher comparative returns based on cost-benefit analysis. Land tenure insecurity increases the risks of long-term agricultural investment for farmers, thereby reducing their expected returns from cropland investment. Meanwhile, compared to the unstable income from self-cultivation, farmers may seek more stable earnings through non-agricultural employment, which offers higher comparative returns. When facing potential infringement of cropland rights, the longer farmers are separated from the actual control of their cropland, the greater the risk of permanently losing these rights (Rupelle et al., 2009). Consequently, farmers' objectives tend to shift from long-term profit maximization to short-term profit maximization. To mitigate potential losses from self-cultivation while retaining nominal collective membership rights, farmers prefer short-term transfer contracts to earn rental income and spread risks through periodic contract renewals.

However, the smooth operation of land transfers depends not only on the supply-side willingness of transferors but also on the demand-side demand of transferees. Such short-term contracts introduce uncertainty regarding future renewals (Lovo, 2016), and for transferees, land tenure insecurity suppresses their willingness to acquire cropland. Transferees decide whether to acquire additional cropland from other farmers based on the expected net returns from managing the land to achieve economies of scale, making them highly sensitive to the potential risks associated with land tenure insecurity. The core reason why land tenure insecurity inhibits land transfers lies in its amplification of information asymmetry regarding cropland rights allocation among transaction parties, which fragments the land transfer market and reduces the efficiency of cropland resource allocation (Feder & Feeny, 1991).

This is manifested in three aspects: First, land tenure insecurity increases information costs. Transactors need to invest additional resources in searching for and verifying transaction-related information such as cropland area, quality, boundaries, and ownership. Second, land tenure insecurity raises contract costs. Due to ambiguous rights and obligations, transactors must engage in complex negotiations and design detailed formal contracts to mitigate potential default risks and protect their interests. Third, land tenure insecurity increases enforcement costs. When ownership and responsibilities are unclear, both parties face the risk of opportunistic default during contract execution, leading to deviations from the original transaction agreements.

Land tenure insecurity is also prone to triggering cropland disputes, including ownership conflicts, contractual disputes, and land use disputes, thereby reducing the tradability of cropland. Consequently, the increased non-productive costs incurred in the process of competing for cropland control lead to rent dissipation (Barzel, 1974), prompting potential transactors to withdraw from the market. The underdevelopment of the land transfer market means that cropland cannot be effectively transferred to efficient operators, ultimately resulting in cropland abandonment when landowners lack the willingness or capacity for cultivation.

## 6.3 Research Design

### *6.3.1 Data Sources*

The data utilized in this study are derived from the China Rural Household Panel Survey (CRHPS) database, jointly initiated and implemented by Zhejiang University and Southwestern University of Finance and Economics. Officially launched in 2011, the CRHPS conducts nationwide surveys every two years, and to date, five waves of publicly available panel tracking datasets covering the period 2011–2019 have been released. This survey encompasses all 29 provincial-level administrative regions in China and adopts a stratified three-stage probability-proportional-to-size (PPS) sampling method, which ensures the nationwide representativeness of the data. The sampling procedure is specifically designed as follows: Stage 1: Counties (districts, county-level cities) are stratified into 10 tiers based on per capita GDP, with random selections conducted within each stratum. Stage 2: Villages are randomly sampled from the selected counties (districts, county-level cities). Stage 3: Households are randomly selected from the sampled villages. For rural samples, the final sampling protocol specifies randomly selecting approximately 20 farming households per sampled village as the survey respondents.

The CRHPS provides comprehensive and detailed rural household data, covering dimensions such as basic household structure, agricultural production and management, land use and transfer, income and consumption expenditure, labor mobility and migration, as well as village-level socioeconomic characteristics. It serves as a valuable source of primary data for investigating the socioeconomic development of rural households in China (Qian & Crowley-Vigneau, 2020). Characterized by a rigorous sampling design, rich content coverage, and long-term tracking, the survey data meet the requirements of scientific rigor, representativeness, and continuity in academic research, laying a solid foundation for micro-level long-term panel tracking studies on farming households.

To empirically estimate the impact of land tenure insecurity on cropland abandonment, a systematic data cleansing process was conducted for the purposes of this study. The specific steps are as follows: First, households without contracted cropland (a unique form of land ownership in the Chinese context) were excluded. Second, samples where the household head was over 70 years old were eliminated, as older household heads may exhibit response biases in questionnaire surveys. Third, key variables were retained, including land tenure insecurity, cropland abandonment, agricultural capital investment, agricultural labor input, land transfer, off-farm employment, individual characteristics of household heads, and household- and village-level characteristics. Observations with missing or invalid information for these key variables were deleted. Notably, since data on cropland abandonment are only available from 2013 onwards, this study only employs data from 2015, 2017, and 2019. Ultimately, an unbalanced panel dataset spanning three years with 20,267 observations was obtained for the empirical analysis.

### 6.3.2 Empirical Strategy

The core independent variable in this study is perceived land tenure insecurity, which reflects the deep-seated cognitive structure of individuals. The formation of such cognitive traits is typically shaped by long-term factors such as institutional environments, historical experiences, and socio-cultural norms, and thus tends to be stable and difficult to change in the short term. From the perspective of econometric theory, the panel fixed effects (FE) model relies primarily on within-group variation (i.e., changes in variables over time within the same individual) for parameter estimation. However, for variables with weak time variability, the FE model will fail to capture sufficient effective variation, leading to inefficient estimation results. In contrast, the panel random effects (RE) model incorporates both within-group variation and between-group variation (i.e., differences across individuals) into the estimation process, making it more suitable for scenarios where core independent variables exhibit long-term stability. Therefore, this study adopts the panel random effects model to empirically examine the impact of land tenure insecurity on cropland abandonment. To further ensure the reliability of the estimation results, we will conduct the Hausman test to formally verify the rationality of the model selection between fixed effects and random effects. The benchmark regression model is set as follows:

$$Abandonment_{it} = \alpha_0 + \alpha_1 Insecurity_{it} + \gamma \mathbf{Z}_{it} + \varphi_t + \varepsilon_{it} \tag{6.1}$$

Where: the subscripts $i$ and $t$ represent the household head and the survey year (2015, 2017, 2019), respectively; *Abandonment* denotes the dependent variable, representing the cropland abandonment status of the household, which is specifically defined as the ratio of abandoned cropland area to total cropland area; *Insecurity* is a dichotomous variable: if the surveyed household believes that land certification can clarify property rights or resolve land disputes, it is considered to have secure land tenure and coded as 0; otherwise, it is regarded as having land tenure insecurity and coded as 1; $\boldsymbol{Z}$ is a vector of control variables, including individual characteristics of the household head (e.g., age, education level) and household-level characteristics (e.g., family health, dependency ratio, off-farm employment participation, cropland size, cropland fragmentation); $\alpha_0$ is the constant term; $\alpha_1$ and $\gamma$ are the coefficients to be estimated; $\varphi_t$ represents the time dummy variable; and $\varepsilon_{it}$ is the random error term, which is assumed to follow a normal distribution with a mean of 0 and constant variance.

### 6.3.3 Descriptive Statistics

Table 6.1 presents the definitions and descriptive statistical results of the main variables in this study. Regarding the dependent variable, the average cropland abandonment ratio of sample households is 4.0%, and the average abandoned cropland area is 0.255 mu. From the perspective of abandonment degree, the mean value is 1.090, indicating that approximately 9.0% of sample households have engaged in cropland abandonment behavior, which is consistent with the overall low-level cropland abandonment status reflected by the abandonment ratio. For the core independent variable—land tenure insecurity—the mean value is 0.294. This indicates that 29.4% of the sampled households perceive land tenure insecurity, while the remaining 70.6% believe land certification can effectively guarantee their land rights, reflecting that most farmers have formed positive expectations for formal land tenure systems represented by land certification. Regarding household head characteristics, the average age of household heads is 53.125 years, with a standard deviation of 10.835. The mean value of educational level is 2.604, indicating that the overall educational attainment of rural household heads in the sample is relatively low. In terms of household demographic characteristics, the average ratio of healthy individuals in the household is 76.2%, suggesting that the overall health status of family members in the sample households is relatively favorable. The average elderly dependency ratio is 14%, meaning that there is an average support burden of approximately 0.14 elderly individuals per labor force in the sample households. The average proportion of off-farm employment in total household labor is 22.4%, indicating that a considerable portion of rural labor is still engaged in agricultural production. Regarding household land characteristics, the average per capita cropland area of sample households is 2.818 mu, reflecting the prominent issue of cropland scarcity in China. The average number of cropland plots is 5.536, with a standard deviation of 6.246 and a maximum of 120 plots, indicating that Chinese rural cropland is highly fragmented, which may pose constraints on large-scale agricultural operations. For village-level control variables, the mean value of the village agriculture variable is 0.662, meaning that 66.2% of the sampled villages have new agricultural operating entities, reflecting the continuous advancement of agricultural modernization at the village level. The mean value of the logarithm of village per capita income is 8.729, indicating that the actual average per capita income of the sampled villages is approximately 6192 yuan (calculated as e^8.729), which reflects the basic level of rural economic development in the sample areas.

### *6.3.4 Correlation Between Land Tenure Insecurity and Cropland Abandonment*

Prior to formal econometric analysis, we constructed grouped bar charts to explore the preliminary relationship between land tenure insecurity and cropland abandonment. Figure 6.2 presents the descriptive results based on the CRHPS data. As shown in the bar chart, from 2015 to 2019, the proportion of abandoned cropland area among sample households exhibited a consistent annual upward trend, regardless of whether their land tenure was secure or insecure. This trend underscores the increasingly severity of the cropland abandonment issue in rural China, highlighting the practical significance of this study. Furthermore, in each of the surveyed years, households with land tenure insecurity had a higher average proportion of abandoned cropland than those with secure land tenure. Based on this descriptive evidence, it can be tentatively inferred that land tenure insecurity may contribute to the expansion of cropland abandonment.

## 6.4 Empirical Results

### *6.4.1 Baseline Results*

Table 6.2 presents the baseline results investigating the relationship between land tenure insecurity and cropland abandonment, estimated via a panel random effects model. Specifically, Column (1) reports the regression results for land tenure insecurity without incorporating control variables. Column (2) adds household head individual characteristics to the specification in column (1), while column (3) further includes household-level control variables based on column (2). The results consistently demonstrate that the estimated coefficient of land tenure insecurity is significantly positive at the 1% level across all three model specifications, with minimal variations in magnitude. Specifically, the coefficients of land tenure insecurity are approximately 0.007, indicating that households perceiving land tenure insecurity have an average cropland abandonment rate 0.7 percentage points higher than those with a

**Table 6.1** Variable definitions and descriptive statistics (N = 20,267)

| Variables | Definition | Mean | SD | Min | Max |
|---|---|---|---|---|---|
| Abandonment ratio | Ratio of abandoned cropland area to total cropland area (0–1) | 0.040 | 0.153 | 0 | 1 |
| Abandonment area | Abandoned cropland area(mu) | 0.255 | 1.656 | 0 | 100 |
| Abandonment degree | Degree of cropland abandonment: None = 1, partial = 2, complete = 3 | 1.090 | 0.308 | 1 | 3 |
| Land tenure insecurity | Whether land certification can clarify property rights or resolve land disputes (yes = 0, no = 1) | 0.294 | 0.456 | 0 | 1 |
| Age | Age of household head | 53.125 | 10.835 | 16 | 69 |
| Age square | Age square of household head | 2939.696 | 1080.19 | 256 | 4761 |
| Education | Educational level: Illiteracy = 1, primary school = 2, junior high school = 3, senior high school = 4, vocational high school = 5, junior college = 6, bachelor = 7, master = 8, doctor = 9 | 2.604 | 1.016 | 1 | 9 |
| Family health | Ratio of healthy people in the household (0–1) | 0.762 | 0.311 | 0 | 1 |
| Dependency ratio | Dependency ratio of the elderly (0–3) | 0.140 | 0.322 | 0 | 3 |
| Off-farm employment | Ratio of off-farm employment in the household (0–1) | 0.224 | 0.259 | 0 | 1 |
| Land size | Household cropland area per capita (mu) | 2.818 | 6.800 | 0.001 | 500 |
| Land fragmentation | Number of cropland plots | 5.536 | 6.246 | 1 | 120 |
| Village agriculture | Whether there are new agricultural operating entities in the village (yes = 1, no = 0) | 0.662 | 0.473 | 0 | 1 |
| Village economy | Logarithm of village per capita income (yuan) | 8.729 | 0.978 | 0 | 11.695 |

*Notes* 1 mu = 1/15 hectare; Yuan is Chinese currency (1 USD = 7.25 Yuan in 2025); The observed values for village agricultural variables and village economic variables are 18,760 and 20,039, respectively

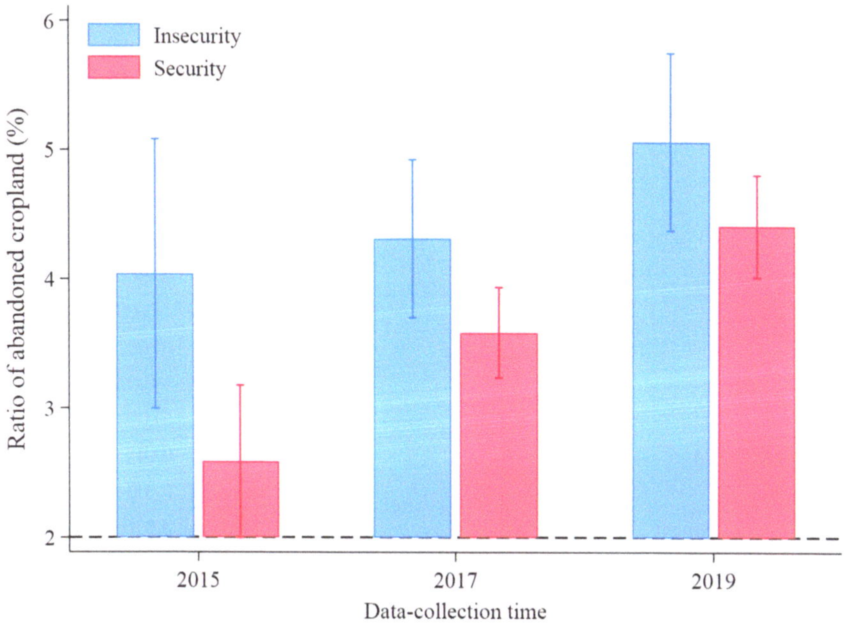


**Fig. 6.2** Land tenure insecurity and cropland abandonment: Correlation analysis

stronger sense of tenure security. Combined with the mean value of the dependent variable (cropland abandonment ratio) of 0.040, this implies that land tenure insecurity increased cropland abandonment in rural China by approximately 17.5% (calculated as 0.007/0.040 × 100) during the 2015–2019 period. This confirms that land tenure insecurity exerts a significantly positive impact on cropland abandonment, which is largely consistent with the correlational pattern observed in Fig. 6.2.

Regarding the control variables, the age of the household head and its quadratic term both exert a significantly negative and positive impact on cropland abandonment at the 1% significance level, respectively. This indicates a nonlinear relationship between the household head's age and cropland abandonment—cropland abandonment decreases first and then increases as the household head ages (Zheng, 2024b). The education level of the household head is significantly and inversely correlated with cropland abandonment at the 5% level, which aligns with the findings reported by Ma and Zhu (2020). This can be attributed to the fact that higher education helps improve farmers' agricultural management skills and resource allocation capabilities, thereby reducing the willingness and probability of cropland abandonment. From the perspective of household demographic characteristics, the elderly dependency ratio is a pivotal determinant of cropland abandonment, with a significantly positive coefficient at the 1% level—indicating that a heavier elderly support burden increases the likelihood of cropland abandonment. In contrast, the health status of family members plays a crucial role in mitigating cropland abandonment, as evidenced by its significantly negative coefficient at the 1% level. This finding is consistent with research

**Table 6.2** Land tenure insecurity and cropland abandonment: Baseline results

| | (1) | (2) | (3) |
|---|---|---|---|
| Insecurity | 0.008*** | 0.007*** | 0.007*** |
| | (0.003) | (0.003) | (0.003) |
| Age | | −0.005*** | −0.005*** |
| | | (0.001) | (0.001) |
| Age$^2$ | | 0.00005*** | 0.00005*** |
| | | (0.000) | (0.000) |
| Education | | −0.003** | −0.003** |
| | | (0.001) | (0.001) |
| Family health | | | −0.022*** |
| | | | (0.004) |
| Dependency ratio | | | 0.017*** |
| | | | (0.004) |
| Off-farm employment | | | 0.036*** |
| | | | (0.005) |
| Land size | | | −0.001*** |
| | | | (0.000) |
| Land fragmentation | | | 0.002*** |
| | | | (0.000) |
| Mean of dependent variable | 0.040 | 0.040 | 0.040 |
| Observations | 20,267 | 20,267 | 20,267 |
| Adjust-$R^2$ | 0.002 | 0.005 | 0.017 |

*Notes* ***, **, and * denote significance at the 1%, 5%, and 10% levels, respectively; Robust standard errors are presented in parentheses; This study also estimated results using a panel data two-way fixed effects model; however, Hausman tests indicated that the panel random effects model was superior. Relevant results are available from the authors upon request

conducted by Zheng and Qian (2022), which posits that households with poor labor endowments are more likely to abandon cropland due to insufficient effective labor supply. The proportion of off-farm workers is significantly and positively associated with the extent of cropland abandonment. This can be attributed to the decline in agricultural labor supply caused by the shift of labor to off-farm employment, which hinders normal agricultural production activities (Xu et al., 2019). In terms of land characteristics, land size has a significantly negative impact on cropland abandonment at the 1% level, which contradicts the initial inference that larger land size may lead to more abandonment. This may be because sufficient per capita cropland enables economies of scale in agricultural production, enhancing farmers' motivation to cultivate and reducing abandonment behavior (Zheng et al., 2025). Land fragmentation has a significantly positive impact on cropland abandonment, which can be attributed to the increased agricultural production costs caused by fragmented land (Wang et al., 2022; Zheng et al., 2023).

### 6.4.2 Robustness Checks

To ensure the reliability of the estimation results, this study conducted a series of rigorous robustness tests, including replacing the core independent variable, altering the dependent variable, adjusting the sample scope, and adding additional control variables. The relevant estimation results are detailed in Table 6.3.

First, we replaced the core independent variable to mitigate potential measurement errors. Unlike the previous approach, we further decomposed the core independent variable (land tenure insecurity) into two separate variables: (1) Insecurity1, defined as whether farmers believe land certification clarifies property rights (yes = 0, no = 1); and (2) Insecurity2, defined as whether farmers believe land certification facilitates resolving land disputes (yes = 0, no = 1). We then re-estimated the model using these two decomposed variables to replace the original core independent variable, respectively. The estimation results in columns (1) and (2) indicate that the positive effect of land tenure insecurity on cropland abandonment remains statistically

**Table 6.3** Land tenure insecurity and cropland abandonment: Robustness checks

| | Replacing X | | Replacing Y | | Replacing sample | | Adding variables |
|---|---|---|---|---|---|---|---|
| | (1) | (2) | (3) | (4) | (5) | (6) | (7) |
| Insecurity | | | 0.014** | 0.011** | 0.005** | 0.009*** | 0.006** |
| | | | (0.006) | (0.005) | (0.003) | (0.003) | (0.003) |
| Insecurity1 | 0.006** | | | | | | |
| | (0.002) | | | | | | |
| Insecurity2 | | 0.007*** | | | | | |
| | | (0.002) | | | | | |
| Village agriculture | | | | | | | −0.010*** |
| | | | | | | | (0.003) |
| Village economy | | | | | | | −0.002** |
| | | | | | | | (0.001) |
| Control variables | Yes | Yes | Yes | Yes | Yes | Yes | Yes |
| Observations | 20,267 | 20,267 | 20,267 | 20,267 | 16,895 | 13,506 | 18,614 |
| Adjust-$R^2$ | 0.017 | 0.017 | 0.024 | 0.021 | 0.021 | 0.018 | 0.019 |

*Notes* ***, **, and * denote significance at the 1%, 5%, and 10% levels, respectively; Robust standard errors are presented in parentheses

significant. This confirms that the prior findings are not altered by changes in the measurement approach of the core independent variable.

Second, we replaced the dependent variable to test the sensitivity of the results to variable definitions. We substituted the original cropland abandonment ratio with the logarithm of abandoned cropland area and the degree of cropland abandonment for re-estimation, respectively. The estimates in columns (3) and (4) once verify that the positive association between land tenure insecurity and cropland abandonment remains robust, further validating the reliability of the baseline findings.

Third, we adjusted the sample scope to address issues related to representativeness and underlying selection bias. On the one hand, considering that the 2015 cropland abandonment data were primarily derived from calculations rather than direct surveys of farmers, we excluded the 2015 sample to eliminate potential measurement bias. On the other hand, since this study focuses on the land tenure security of households with contracted cropland, and the diverse sources of property rights for new agricultural operators may interfere with the estimation, we excluded this group for re-estimation. The results in columns (5) and (6) based on the adjusted samples reaffirm the validity of the baseline conclusions.

Fourth, we added control variables to alleviate omitted variable bias. Due to the high missing rate of village-level data, the benchmark regression only controlled for household head and household-level variables, which may lead to confounding effects from unobserved village characteristics. Therefore, we further incorporated the village-level variables (Village agriculture and Village economy from Table 6.1) into the model for re-estimation. The corresponding results in column (7) show that even though the sample size decreased by 1653 observations due to data missingness, land tenure insecurity still significantly exacerbates cropland abandonment.

In summary, the results of the four robustness tests consistently confirm that the positive impact of land tenure insecurity on household cropland abandonment is stable and reliable. Thus, we have sufficient reason to conclude that land tenure insecurity is a key driver of rural household cropland abandonment.

### *6.4.3 Endogeneity Discussion*

Although concerns about endogeneity arising from omitted variables, measurement bias, and sample selection bias have been successively addressed through methods such as progressively adding control variables, replacing the core independent variable, and adjusting the sample scope, endogeneity issues stemming from self-selection may still exist between land tenure insecurity and cropland abandonment. To address this, we further leverage the propensity score matching (PSM) method to match households with similar observable characteristics, thereby estimating the difference in cropland abandonment between matched households under different land tenure security conditions. This approach helps mitigate the confounding effect of observable heterogeneity and enhances the robustness of causal inference (Zheng et al., 2025). Specifically, three common matching strategies in

**Table 6.4** Land tenure insecurity and cropland abandonment: Endogeneity tests

| PSM methods | Ratio of abandoned cropland area to total cropland area | | ATT | S.E. | T-value | Common support | |
|---|---|---|---|---|---|---|---|
| | Treat | Control | | | | Treat | Control |
| NN matching (n = 1) | 0.046 | 0.038 | 0.008** | 0.003 | 2.45 | 5959 | 14,306 |
| NN matching within caliper (n = 4, r = 0.05) | 0.046 | 0.038 | 0.008*** | 0.003 | 2.82 | 5959 | 14,305 |
| Kernel matching (bandwidth = 0.03) | 0.045 | 0.039 | 0.006** | 0.003 | 2.27 | 5457 | 13,152 |

*Notes* ***, **, and * denote significance at the 1%, 5%, and 10% levels, respectively

PSM—nearest neighbor matching, caliper matching, and kernel matching—were adopted for estimation. The results presented in Table 6.4 indicate that regardless of the matching method employed, the average treatment effect (ATT) of land tenure insecurity on cropland abandonment remains significantly positive, which is highly consistent with the findings of the benchmark regression.

### 6.4.4 Mechanism Test

From the perspective of factor allocation, the preceding theoretical analysis posits that land tenure insecurity affects farmers' cropland abandonment behavior through three channels: suppressing agricultural capital investment, reducing agricultural labor input, and hindering land transfers. Therefore, after confirming the positive relationship between land tenure insecurity and cropland abandonment, we further examine its underlying mechanisms. Specifically, regarding agricultural capital investment, we use the logarithms of two indicators for measurement: (1) agricultural fixed asset investment (including the value of agricultural machinery, livestock, and other durable production assets); and (2) agricultural variable asset investment (including productive inputs such as fertilizers, pesticides, and seeds). For agricultural labor input, we measure it as the proportion of family members engaged in farming relative to the total household population. For land transfers, we utilize whether farm households transferred out land (yes = 1, no = 0) and whether farm households transferred in land (yes = 1, no = 0).

Table 6.5 presents the estimation results. Columns (1) and (2) show that land tenure insecurity significantly inhibits both agricultural fixed and variable assets investment.

**Table 6.5** Land tenure insecurity and cropland abandonment: Mechanism test

| | Agricultural capital investment | | Agricultural labor input | Land transfer | |
|---|---|---|---|---|---|
| | (1) fixed capital | (2) variable capital | (3) labor input | (4) transfer-out | (5) transfer-in |
| NAOE | −0.547*** | −0.398*** | −0.020*** | 0.015** | −0.012* |
| | (0.067) | (0.052) | (0.005) | (0.007) | (0.007) |
| Control variables | Yes | Yes | Yes | Yes | Yes |
| Observations | 20,267 | 20,267 | 20,267 | 19,316 | 20,263 |
| Adjust-$R^2$ | 0.066 | 0.120 | 0.350 | 0.057 | 0.070 |

*Notes* ***, **, and * denote significance at the 1%, 5%, and 10% levels, respectively; Robust standard errors are presented in parentheses. For consistency, all estimates controlled for the same covariates

This finding aligns with existing research (Lovo, 2016) and reflects rational household decision-making: once insecure land tenure may expose agricultural investments to potential losses, farm households tend to reduce all forms of agricultural capital investment to avoid sunk costs, which ultimately leads to cropland abandonment. Column (3) reveals that land tenure insecurity significantly reduces agricultural labor input. This indicates that the uncertainty about future returns associated with insecure land tenure weakens farmers' willingness to commit labor to agricultural production, thereby exacerbating cropland abandonment driven by labor shortages. Columns (5) and (6) show that land tenure insecurity increases the probability of land transfer-out cropland by 1.5%, while reducing the probability of land transfer-in by 1.2%. This suggests that land tenure insecurity prompts farmers to transfer-out their cropland; however, insecure land tenure fails to attract potential transferees—especially for marginal land with relatively poor cultivation conditions. Consequently, marginal land that cannot be transferred out is ultimately abandoned. These findings confirm validates the theoretical mechanism proposed in this study.

### *6.4.5 Heterogeneity Analysis*

The aforementioned estimates have confirmed that, overall, land tenure insecurity leads to cropland abandonment. However, in practice, farm households in rural China have exhibited significant differentiation—particularly in terms of horizontal income disparities and vertical intergenerational differences. This implies that the impact of land tenure insecurity on cropland abandonment may also exhibit heterogeneous characteristics. Therefore, this study further examines the heterogeneous effects of land tenure insecurity on cropland abandonment from these two perspectives. Specifically, regarding horizontal income differentiation, we divided the full sample into higher-income and lower-income groups based on whether a household's per capita income exceeded the average per capita income of its village. For vertical intergenerational differences, we categorized the full sample into younger and older-generation groups, with the division criterion being whether the household head was born after 1980. The corresponding estimation results are detailed in Table 6.6.

Regarding income differentiation, the estimation results in columns (1) and (2) show that land tenure insecurity significantly exacerbates cropland abandonment among higher-income farmers, while exerting insignificant effect on lower-income farmers. This may be attributed to the fact that higher-income farmers typically have diversified income sources to mitigate risk shocks, resulting in relatively lower opportunity costs of exiting agricultural production. Consequently, when confronted with land tenure insecurity, they are more inclined to directly withdraw from farming and pursue alternative off-farm employment with more stable returns. In contrast, lower-income farmers exhibit distinctly different survival rationality. Even when facing higher risks associated with land tenure insecurity, their lack of sufficient capital accumulation prevents them from seeking off-farm livelihoods in urban areas. This compels them to maintain agricultural production as a basic livelihood safeguard, until they can gradually expand their agricultural operations and accumulate adequate capital. From an intergenerational perspective, the results in columns (3) and (4) indicate that, compared to older-generation farmers, land tenure insecurity does not lead to cropland abandonment among younger-generation farmers. A plausible explanation is that older farmers, constrained by physical limitations and reduced energy levels, are compelled to abandon cropland that they are unable to cultivate. In contrast, younger farmers possess greater vitality and labor capacity, making them less likely to abandon cropland solely due to land tenure insecurity.

**Table 6.6** Land tenure insecurity and cropland abandonment: Heterogeneity analysis

| | Horizontal income differentiation | | Vertical intergenerational differences | |
|---|---|---|---|---|
| | (1) higher-income | (2) lower-income | (3) younger generation | (4) older generation |
| Insecurity | 0.009** | 0.005 | 0.004 | 0.007*** |
| | (0.004) | (0.004) | (0.009) | (0.003) |
| Control variables | Yes | Yes | Yes | Yes |
| Observations | 10,818 | 9449 | 1769 | 18,498 |
| Adjust-$R^2$ | 0.019 | 0.015 | 0.036 | 0.015 |

*Notes* ***, **, and * denote significance at the 1%, 5%, and 10% levels, respectively; Robust standard errors are presented in parentheses

## 6.5 Extended Analysis

The previous findings have confirmed that land tenure insecurity exacerbates cropland abandonment, and such impacts remain valid after a series of tests. Given this, how to mitigate this negative effect has become an urgent practical issue to be addressed. In addressing this problem, the importance of institutional supply is self-evident. As emphasized by New institutional economist Douglass North (1990), institutions constitute a complex and extensive system of rules, consisting of formal and informal institutions. These two types of institutions interact with and influence each other: they not only form the basic framework for economic activities but also subtly shape people's behaviors and guide their decision-making in economic activities. Against this backdrop, this study further attempts to examine the governance of cropland abandonment under the condition of land tenure insecurity from the perspective of formal and informal institutions.

### *6.5.1 The Regulatory Role of Land Certification from a Formal Institutional Perspective*

Land certification, as a formal institutional arrangement, is widely recognized as a key measure to enhance land tenure security and has been implemented globally (de Janvry et al., 2015). Since 2013, the Chinese government has also launched a new round of land certification reforms, requiring clear delineation of the location, boundaries, size, and rights-responsibilities of cropland, followed by the issuance of legally binding land property certificates to farmers (Zheng, 2024a). To examine whether land certification can mitigate the negative impact of land tenure insecurity on cropland abandonment, we divided the full sample into certified and uncertified groups based on whether farmers had obtained land title certificates since 2013.

As shown in Fig. 6.3, the estimated coefficient of land tenure insecurity for certified farmers is 0.009 ($p < 0.01$), while that for uncertified farmers is 0.006 ($p > 0.1$). This indicates that land tenure insecurity only significantly exacerbates cropland abandonment among uncertified farmers, with no significant effect on certified farmers. Thus, deepening land tenure reforms—particularly advancing land certification—is undoubtedly an effective approach to alleviate the adverse impact of land tenure insecurity on cropland abandonment. However, it should be noted that the statistical difference between the two groups is insignificant. The likely reason is that by 2019, the vast majority of Chinese farmers had completed land certification, resulting in increasingly narrowed differences between certified and uncertified farmer groups, thereby weakening the statistical distinction between the two groups. According to the CRHPS database, by the summer of 2019, 79.27% of farm households nationwide had obtained land property certificates.

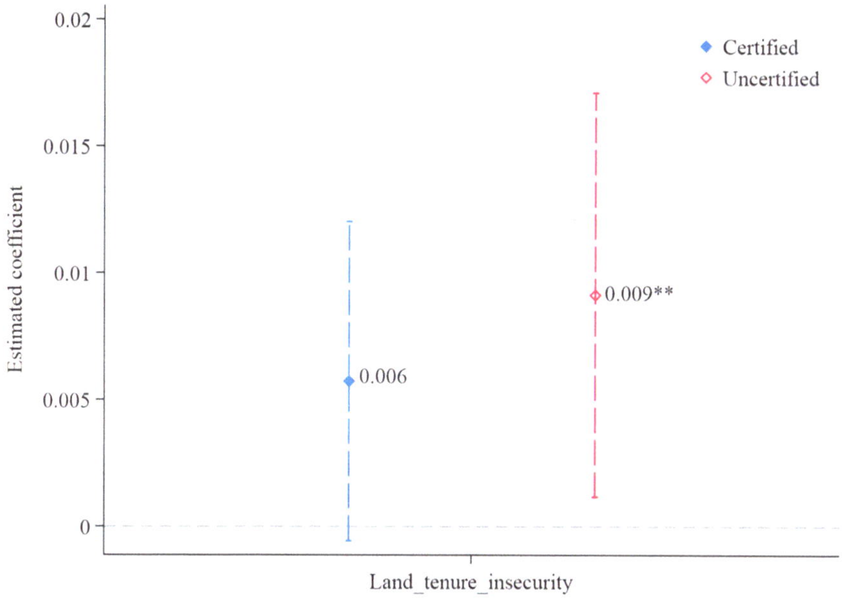


**Fig. 6.3** Land tenure insecurity and cropland abandonment: The role of formal institutions

### 6.5.2 *The Regulatory Role of Village Regulations from an Informal Institutional Perspective*

Informal institutions, also known as informal constraints or informal rules, refer to behavioral norms that have gradually formed through long-term social interactions and gained societal recognition as customary practices collectively abided by. In rural societies, village regulations are the most prevalent informal institutions. They serve as norms and guidelines for farmers' daily behaviors and play a prominent role in rural governance (Ho, 2005). Therefore, we divided the full sample into a regulated group and an unregulated group based on whether the village where the household resides has established village regulations. This grouping enables us to examine whether such informal institutions can constrain farmers' irrational land use practices.

The estimated coefficients of land tenure insecurity are presented in Fig. 6.4. The results show that land tenure insecurity exerts a significantly positive impact on cropland abandonment in villages with regulations, whereas its impact on cropland abandonment in villages without such regulations is statistically insignificant. Although the difference between the two groups is not statistically significant, this finding is somewhat inconsistent with expectations. A possible explanation is that village regulations, as informal institutions, perform dual functions: protection and exclusion. The protective function safeguards the rights and interests of community members through internal rules, while the exclusionary function preserves collective interests by establishing boundaries between the community and external parties. Under conditions of land tenure insecurity, this dual nature often institutionalizes and solidifies the boundaries between insiders and outsiders of the village. This not only intensifies internal competition over land property rights but also enhances exclusion from external land markets, thereby amplifying the negative effects of land tenure insecurity and leading to an imbalance in the functions of informal governance. Specifically, once a village formulates regulations and conventions, collective decision-making power is institutionally strengthened. Particularly when these regulations implicitly embody a simplistic pursuit of equal distribution to all, land allocation becomes more dependent on collective consensus rather than market efficiency principles. This creates opportunities for arbitrary land adjustments, which exacerbate farmers' perceptions of land tenure insecurity. By allocating land property rights through this non-market approach of equal land holdings among community members, villages weaken the land rights that farmers originally possessed, ultimately hindering the flexible allocation of land resources and further exacerbating cropland abandonment under conditions of land tenure insecurity.

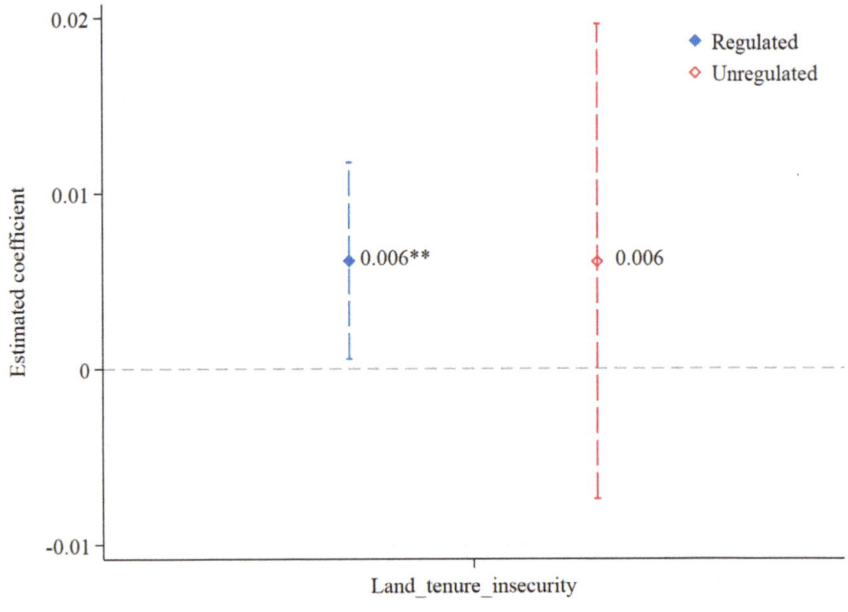


**Fig. 6.4** Land tenure insecurity and cropland abandonment: The role of informal institutions

## 6.6 Conclusions and Policy Implications

### 6.6.1 Conclusions

Land tenure security is closely linked to farmers' land use behavior. This chapter employs a panel random effects model to systematically examine the impact of land tenure insecurity on cropland abandonment, using nationally representative household-level panel data covering rural areas across 29 provinces in China from 2015 to 2019. The results indicate that land tenure insecurity significantly increases cropland abandonment overall, and this finding remains robust across various tests. On average, insecure land tenure leads to a 0.7 percentage point increase in the ratio of cropland abandonment by farm households.

Mechanism analysis reveals that land tenure insecurity induces farmers to abandon cropland primarily by reshaping the logic of factor allocation through three channels: capital, labor, and land. Specifically: First, land tenure insecurity suppresses agricultural capital investment, exerting significant negative effects on both fixed and variable capital investment. This hinders the long-term improvement of agricultural total factor productivity, ultimately exacerbating cropland abandonment. Second, land tenure insecurity reduces agricultural labor input, leading to labor shortages in agricultural production and thereby triggering cropland abandonment. Third, land tenure insecurity distorts the development of the land transfer market: while it facilitates land transfer-out, it inhibits land transfer-in. This hinders the flow of cropland resources to efficient farmers, further intensifying cropland abandonment.

Furthermore, group-specific regression analysis from the perspective of farmer differentiation shows heterogeneous effects of land tenure insecurity on cropland abandonment. In terms of income differentiation, land tenure insecurity primarily triggers cropland abandonment among higher-income farmers, while exerting no significant impact on lower-income farmers. Regarding intergenerational differences, older-generation farmers exhibit high sensitivity to land tenure insecurity in their cropland abandonment behavior, whereas younger-generation farmers remain unaffected.

In addition, institutional analysis indicates that formal institutional arrangements such as land certification effectively mitigate the negative impact of land tenure insecurity on cropland abandonment. However, informal institutions represented by village regulations fail to alleviate this adverse effect; instead, they may amplify the negative impact of land tenure insecurity under certain conditions.

### 6.6.2 Policy Implications

Curbing cropland abandonment is a crucial measure for safeguarding national food security and promoting sustainable agricultural development. The aforementioned findings clarify the impact, mechanisms, and heterogeneous characteristics of land tenure security on cropland abandonment, thereby providing important policy implications for advancing effective governance of cropland abandonment.

First, deepen land tenure system reforms to enhance land tenure security, and further optimize the allocation and utilization efficiency of land resources. Since land tenure insecurity is the institutional root cause of cropland abandonment, addressing this issue requires prioritizing institutional construction—establishing a land tenure system featuring clear ownership, efficient operation, and robust protection. This will help stabilize farmers' expectations of land rights, stimulate their enthusiasm for agricultural investment and production, and fundamentally curb cropland abandonment driven by insecure tenure.

Second, systematically optimize the market-oriented allocation mechanism of rural production factors to eliminate the conditions that induce cropland abandonment. Specifically, refine the agricultural subsidy policy to improve its accessibility and income-increasing effect, thereby enhancing farmers' motivation to engage in agricultural production and narrowing the income gap between agricultural and non-agricultural sectors. Meanwhile, strengthen the construction of the land transfer market, improve supporting service systems (such as property rights confirmation, contract registration, and dispute mediation), alleviate the concerns of both land transferors and transferees, and facilitate the market-oriented and orderly flow of cropland resources.

Third, recognize the objective reality of farmer differentiation and formulate targeted policies for cropland abandonment governance. For example, guide higher-income farmers to voluntarily transfer their idle cropland by improving the land transfer compensation mechanism; for older-generation farmer households, accelerate the development of labor-saving agricultural social services (such as mechanized cultivation, unified harvesting, and pest control) to help them overcome the constraints of physical capacity and fully leverage the role of agricultural mechanization in reducing production pressure.

Finally, objectively recognize the functional positioning of both formal and informal institutions, and emphasize their coordinated synergy in cropland abandonment governance. It is crucial to recognize that informal institutions are not universally effective in mitigating cropland abandonment; in cases where informal institutions fail or even backfire, formal institutional arrangements should be utilized to correct their deficiencies. By promoting the complementary and coordinated development of formal and informal institutions, the effectiveness of cropland abandonment governance can be comprehensively enhanced.

## References

Abdulai, A., Owusu, V., & Goetz, R. (2011). Land tenure differences and investment in land improvement measures: Theoretical and empirical analyses. *Journal of Development Economics, 96*, 66–78.

Adamopoulos, T., Brandt, L., Chen, C., Restuccia, D., & Wei, X. (2024). Land security and mobility frictions. *The Quarterly Journal of Economics, 139*, 1941–1987.
Barzel, Y. (1974). A theory of rationing by waiting. *The Journal of Law and Economics, 17*, 73–95.
Benjamin, D., & Brandt, L. (2002). Property rights, labour markets, and efficiency in a transition economy: The case of rural China. *Canadian Journal of Economics*, 689–716.
Besley, T. (1995). Property rights and investment incentives: Theory and evidence from Ghana. *Journal of political Economy, 103*, 903–937.
Chen, C. (2017). Untitled land, occupational choice, and agricultural productivity. *American Economic Journal: Macroeconomics, 9*, 91–121.
Chen, M., Han, Q., Zhang, C., & Chen, J. (2025). Valuing the effect of capital goes to countryside on cropland abandonment: Evidence from rural China. *Habitat International, 156*, 103299.
de Janvry, A., Emerick, K., Gonzalez-Navarro, M., & Sadoulet, E. (2015). Delinking land rights from land use: Certification and migration in Mexico. *American Economic Review, 105*, 3125–3149.
Deininger, K., Ali, D. A., & Alemu, T. (2011). Impacts of land certification on tenure security, investment, and land market participation: Evidence from Ethiopia. *Land Economics, 87*, 312–334.
Deininger, K., & Jin, S. (2009). Securing property rights in transition: Lessons from implementation of China's rural land contracting law. *Journal of Economic Behavior & Organization, 70*, 22–38.
Demsetz, H. (1967). Towards a theory of property rights. *The American Economic Review, 57*, 347–359.
Feder, G., & Feeny, D. (1991). Land tenure and property rights: Theory and implications for development policy. *The World Bank Economic Review, 5*, 135–153.
Gao, X., Shi, X., & Fang, S. (2021). Property rights and misallocation: Evidence from land certification in China. *World Development, 147*, 105632.
Ho, P. (2005). *Institutions in transition: Land ownership, property rights and social conflict in China.* Oxford University Press.
Jacoby, H. G., Li, G., & Rozelle, S. (2002). Hazards of expropriation: Tenure insecurity and investment in rural China. *American Economic Review, 92*, 1420–1447.
Kahneman, D., & Tversky, A. (1979). Prospect theory: An analysis of decision under risk. *Econometrica, 47*, 263–292.
Lovo, S. (2016). Tenure insecurity and investment in soil conservation. Evidence from Malawi. *World Development, 78*, 219–229.
Ma, W., & Zhu, Z. (2020). A note: Reducing cropland abandonment in China—Do agricultural cooperatives play a role? *Journal of Agricultural Economics, 71*, 929–935.
Ma, X., Heerink, N., Feng, S., & Shi, X. (2015). Farmland tenure in China: Comparing legal, actual and perceived security. *Land Use Policy, 42*, 293–306.
Mengesha, A. K., Mansberger, R., Damyanovic, D., & Stoeglehner, G. (2019). Impact of land certification on sustainable land use practices: Case of gozamin district. *Ethiopia. Sustainability, 11*, 5551.
Mullan, K., Grosjean, P., & Kontoleon, A. (2011). Land tenure arrangements and rural–urban migration in China. *World Development, 39*, 123–133.
North, D. C. (1990). *Institutions, institutional change and economic performance.* Cambridge University Press.
Place, F., Roth, M., & Hazell, P. (1994). Land tenure security and agricultural performance in Africa: Overview of research methodology. *Searching for land tenure security in Africa*, 15–39.
Prishchepov, A. V., Radeloff, V. C., Baumann, M., Kuemmerle, T., & Müller, D. (2012). Effects of institutional changes on land use: Agricultural land abandonment during the transition from state-command to market-driven economies in post-Soviet Eastern Europe. *Environmental Research Letters, 7*, 024021.
Qian, W., & Crowley-Vigneau, A. (2020). *The economy of Chinese rural households.* Springer.
Rupelle, M. D. L., Quheng, D., Shi, L., & Vendryes, T. (2009). *Land rights insecurity and temporary migration in rural China.* IZA Discussion Papers, Bonn.

Van Gelder, J. L. (2009). Legal tenure security, perceived tenure security and housing improvement in Buenos Aires: An attempt towards integration. *International Journal of Urban and Regional Research, 33*, 126–146.
Van Gelder, J. L. (2010). What tenure security? The case for a tripartite view. *Land Use Policy, 27*, 449–456.
Wang, H., Riedinger, J., & Jin, S. (2015). Land documents, tenure security and land rental development: Panel evidence from China. *China Economic Review, 36*, 220–235.
Wang, J., Cao, Y., Fang, X., Li, G., & Cao, Y. (2022). Does land tenure fragmentation aggravate farmland abandonment? Evidence from big survey data in rural China. *Journal of Rural Studies, 91*, 126–135.
Wang, J., Xin, L., & Wang, Y. (2020). How farmers' non-agricultural employment affects rural land circulation in China? *Journal of Geographical Sciences, 30*, 378–400.
Xu, D., Deng, X., Huang, K., Liu, Y., Yong, Z., & Liu, S. (2019). Relationships between labor migration and cropland abandonment in rural China from the perspective of village types. *Land Use Policy, 88*, 104164.
Yami, M., & Snyder, K. A. (2016). After all, land belongs to the state: Examining the benefits of land registration for smallholders in Ethiopia. *Land Degradation & Development, 27*, 465–478.
Zheng, L. (2024a). Those with constant property rights have perseverance: China's land tenure reform promotes environment-friendly farming practices. *Humanities and Social Sciences Communications, 11*, 763.
Zheng, L. (2024b). Does off-farm work induce farmland abandonment? Evidence from China. *China Agricultural Economic Review, 16*, 664–682.
Zheng, L., Jin, S., & Su, L. (2025). Of nothing comes nothing: The impact of agricultural comparative return on cropland abandonment. *Journal of Rural Studies, 119*, 103759.
Zheng, L., & Qian, W. (2022). The impact of land certification on cropland abandonment: evidence from rural China. *China Agricultural Economic Review, 14*, 509–526.
Zheng, L., Su, L., & Jin, S. (2023). Reducing land fragmentation to curb cropland abandonment: Evidence from rural China. *Canadian Journal of Agricultural Economics/Revue canadienne d'agroeconomie, 71*, 355–373.
Zhou, N., Cheng, W., & Zhang, L. (2022). Land rights and investment incentives: Evidence from China's latest rural land titling program. *Land Use Policy, 117*, 106126.

# Chapter 7
# New Agricultural Operating Entities and Cropland Abandonment

**Abstract** It is crucial to address cropland abandonment to achieve Zero Hunger according to the United Nations' sustainable development goals. However, quantitative research examining the governance of abandoned croplands from the perspective of agricultural operating entities remains relatively scarce. Based on a large sample of panel data from the Chinese Family Database, this chapter applies a panel Tobit model to examine the relationship between new agricultural operating entities (NAOEs) and cropland abandonment. Results show that NAOEs are negatively and significantly correlated with the ratio of abandoned cropland areas. The cultivation of NAOEs in villages could help deter farmers from abandoning their cropland. This effect is achieved through channels such as promoting land leasing, providing technical guidance, and facilitating the sale of agricultural products. Moreover, relative to farming companies, the contributions of the other three types of NAOEs, are more significant. Additionally, the effects of NAOEs on cropland abandonment vary significantly across regions, villages, and households. NAOEs benefit more from China's central and western regions, mountainous areas, villages with better land tenure security, and households with poorer human resource endowments. These findings provide valuable insights for policymakers to ensure food security and promote sustainable development by cultivating various large-scale farmers.

**Keywords** New agricultural operating entities · Smallholders · Cropland abandonment · Farm economics · Food security

It is crucial to address cropland abandonment to achieve Zero Hunger according to the United Nations' Sustainable Development Goals. However, quantitative research examining the governance of abandoned croplands from the perspective of agricultural operating entities remains relatively scarce. Based on a large sample of panel data from the Chinese Family Database, this chapter applies a panel Tobit model to

This chapter has been published. For more details, please see: Zheng L., Big hands holding small hands: The role of new agricultural operating entities in farmland abandonment. Food Policy, 2024, 123:102605.



L. Zheng, *Cropland Abandonment in Rural China*, Resources, Environment and Agricultural Development, https://doi.org/10.1007/978-981-95-8287-7_7

examine the relationship between new agricultural operating entities (NAOEs) and cropland abandonment.

## 7.1 Introduction

Zero Hunger, which encompasses ending hunger, ensuring food security, and promoting sustainable agriculture, is a crucial component of the United Nations Sustainable Development Goals. However, the current state of food security and nutrition is concerning, and meeting the Zero Hunger target by 2030 presents a formidable challenge. Despite the gradual fading of the impact of the COVID-19 pandemic since 2022, the global food supply chain continues to face significant disruptions due to frequent extreme weather events, the ongoing conflict between Russia and Ukraine, and the growing prevalence of food trade protectionism (Andrianarimanana et al., 2023; Hasegawa et al., 2021; Olabisi et al., 2021; Zheng et al., 2023a). According to the State of Food Security and Nutrition in the World 2023, released jointly by the Food and Agriculture Organization of the United Nations, the World Food Programme, and other international organizations, approximately 2.4 billion people, or 29.6% of the world's population, experienced severe food insecurity in 2022. Furthermore, the number of hungry individuals worldwide increased by 735 million, reflecting an increase of 122 million since the pre-pandemic period of 2019 (FAO, 2023).

The importance of croplands for food security and nutrition cannot be overstated. Cropland is the foundation of food production and directly or indirectly provides all food needed for human survival and development. On average, 83% of the 697 kg of food individuals consume yearly, 93% of the 2884 kcal consumed daily, and 80% of the 81 g of protein consumed daily come from croplands (FAOSTAT, 2018). However, owing to rapid industrialization and urbanization, cropland abandonment has become a major global problem (Zheng et al., 2023b). Campbell et al. (2008) estimated that, since the twentieth century, the area of abandoned cropland worldwide ranged from 385 million to 472 million ha. Cropland abandonment not only wastes land resources but also has serious negative impacts on food security. Recent empirical evidence from China reveals that, in 2020, approximately 49.23 million tons of food were lost owing to cropland abandonment, which accounted for 7.36% of total grain production that year (Wang et al., 2023).

The severe situation of cropland abandonment and its far-reaching impacts have garnered significant attention from scholars worldwide, resulting in a wealth of research. In summary, the literature on cropland abandonment focuses mainly on two aspects: driving factors and various impacts. Numerous studies have indicated that factors such as harsh terrain conditions (Han & Song, 2019; Zavalloni et al., 2021), remote geographical location (Lieskovsky & Lieskovska, 2021; Xu et al., 2019; Zhang et al., 2014), land fragmentation (Deininger et al., 2012; Zheng et al., 2023b), labor shortages (Meyfroidt et al., 2016; Xu et al., 2019), low agricultural returns (Yan et al., 2016), and imperfect land markets and land systems (Deininger et al., 2012; Zheng & Qian, 2022) all contribute to farmers abandoning their cropland. Additionally, it is important to note that besides food security, cropland abandonment also exerts significant negative effects on biodiversity (Müller et al., 2013; Queiroz et al., 2014), as well as cultural and aesthetic values (Elbakidze & Angelstam, 2007; Tseng et al., 2021).

Although a few scholars have attempted to assess cropland abandonment in terms of technology, machinery, and institutions (Deng et al., 2019; Ma et al., 2022; Zheng & Qian, 2022), little is known regarding solutions for curbing cropland abandonment, especially from the perspective of agricultural operators. Only Ma and Zhu (2020) have quantified the relationship between agricultural cooperatives and cropland abandonment in China. Employing data from the 2016 China Labor-Force Dynamics Survey, they found that establishing agricultural cooperatives in villages could help reduce the likelihood of cropland abandonment by 0.8% and the abandonment rate by 0.2%. Although their study provides a basis for this study, it also highlights areas for further improvement. Ma and Zhu (2020) did not thoroughly investigate the relevant mechanisms and heterogeneous effects at the village and household levels, leaving some questions unanswered. Simultaneously, although the proportion of farmers who did not abandon croplands was as high as 85% in their data, they did not address potential censored data issues, which could skew their findings. Moreover, they focused solely on agricultural cooperatives, neglecting the roles of other agricultural operators.

The New Agricultural Operating Entity (NAOE) is a large-scale farming entity in the Chinese context; in addition to agricultural cooperatives, it also includes professional operators, family farms, and farming companies (Huang & Liang, 2018). The NAOE was proposed in contrast to traditional smallholder farmers, characterized by small-scale, semi-subsistence farming. Compared with smallholder farmers, NAOEs usually have a larger scale of operation, better material equipment conditions, and strong management capabilities. They are agricultural business organizations with commercial production and profit maximization as their main objectives. Theoretically, when NAOEs help farmers benefit from agricultural activities, farmers are less likely to abandon their cropland. According to public information reports,[1] all kinds of NAOE currently operate approximately 30% of cropland, and support 127 million farmers, increasing farmers' average annual income by over 3500 yuan (1 dollar = 7.23 yuan). Therefore, developing various types of NAOEs, including professional operators, family farms, farming companies, and agricultural cooperatives, helps curb cropland abandonment and ensure food security, thus contributing to achieving Zero Hunger as per United Nations Sustainable Development Goals.

Given the diversity and importance of NAOEs in rural China, our study evaluates their impact of NAOE on cropland abandonment using newly released panel data from the Chinese Family Database (CFD), to enrich existing studies and provide references for other countries in order to solve the problem of cropland abandonment. Specifically, I add to the existing literature in three ways. The first is the

[1] The data can be accessed from http://www.npc.gov.cn/npc/c30834/202112/e0995f9916d747e38bcc7deafda97048.shtml

research perspective; unlike existing studies that focus on the driving factors and various impacts of cropland abandonment, this study is one of the few to focus on the governance of cropland abandonment, especially from the perspective of various agricultural operators. The second aspect concerns the research content; I estimate whether and how NAOEs affect cropland abandonment, and its heterogeneous effects across regions, villages, and households. The third aspect concerns research data and methodology; I employ two-period nationally representative farm-level data and a panel Tobit model to address censored data issues, making estimates more accurate and realistic.

## 7.2 Background and Theoretical Analysis

### *7.2.1 Development of NAOE in China*

Since the reform and opening up in 1978, China has witnessed accelerated industrialization and urbanization, adjustment of its agricultural industry, and changes in the basic rural management system (Anderson & Strutt, 2014; Li, 2017). Consequently, farm households in rural China have gradually divided, with some smallholder farmers withdrawing from agricultural production, and others evolving into various types of NAOEs characterized by large-scale market-oriented operations (Huang & Liang, 2018). Smallholder farmers and various types of NAOEs constitute all agricultural operators in China.

NAOE is a general term for professional operators, family farms, farming companies, and agricultural cooperatives, as defined by the Chinese government. Table 7.1 presents the differences and connections between the four types of NAOEs. Among them, professional operators are agricultural operators whose family labor time is mostly spent in one agricultural industry; their income accounts for over 80% of the total household income. Moreover, their production scale for planting or breeding is significantly larger than that of the local smallholder farmers. Family farms are agricultural operation organizations registered with local governments and engaged in large-scale, intensive, and commercialized agricultural production and operations using the family's labor as a business unit. Compared with professional operators, family farms not only require government recognition but also have higher requirements for intensification, management, and stability of production and operation. Farming companies are economic organizations that adopt modern enterprise management methods, engage in large-scale, intensive, commercialized agricultural production, and implement independent management and self-financing strategies. Compared with other NAOEs, farming companies usually have strong economic strength, advanced production technology, and modern management personnel, and have significant advantages in adapting to volatile market environments and responding to fierce international competition. Agricultural cooperatives are mutual economic organizations organized by operators of similar agricultural products and

**Table 7.1** Comparison of various types of NAOEs in rural China

| Types | Sources | Enrollment | Characteristics | Advantages |
|---|---|---|---|---|
| Professional operator | Smallholder farmers | No | Family labor dominates; it is engaged in farming or breeding | Specialized production |
| Family farm | Smallholder farmers, large professional farmers | Yes | Family labor dominates; it is engaged in farming, breeding, processing agricultural products, or leisure tourism | Diversification |
| Farming company | Smallholder farmers, large professional families, family farms, entrepreneurs | Yes | Wage labor dominates; it is engaged in planting, breeding, processing and selling agricultural products, agricultural technology research and development | Strong capital, advanced technology, efficient management |
| Agricultural cooperative | Association of numerous small farmers with village collective economic organizations or new agricultural operating entities | Yes | Wage labor dominates; it is engaged in planting, breeding, processing, and marketing agricultural products, and provides agricultural socialization services | Mutual assistance in production, benefit and risk-sharing |

*Notes* The distinctions between various types of NAOEs in China and other countries, especially developed countries in Europe and the United States, are as follows: first, NAOEs are built on non-private land property rights, predominantly through leasing rather than purchasing land to expand production scale; second, NAOEs are restrained by the limited resource endowment of a larger population and less land, resulting in a relatively small land size; third, due to the geographical constraints of more mountains and fewer plains, small and medium-sized agricultural machinery dominates.

providers and users of similar agricultural production factors or services under the principles of voluntary association and democratic management and registered with the local government. Through cooperation and collaboration among farmers, agricultural cooperatives can address the inefficiencies of traditional family-based operations and achieve mutual production assistance, benefit-sharing, and risk-sharing, thus promoting sustainable agricultural development.

With the strong support of the Chinese government, various types of NAOEs have developed rapidly and gradually grown into important main bodies and backbone forces for China to develop modern agriculture, ensure national food security, and drive smallholder farmers to become rich together. According to public data from China's Ministry of Agriculture and Rural Affairs,[2] by the end of September 2021, there were more than 3.8 million family farms nationwide, with an average of 134.3

[2] The data can be accessed from http://www.npc.gov.cn/npc/c30834/202112/e0995f9916d747e38bcc7deafda97048.shtml.

mu (1 mu = 1/15 ha) of cropland per family farm and a total annual operating income of nearly 890 billion yuan; Simultaneously, 2.23 million agricultural cooperatives, with a total annual operating income of more than 588 billion yuan, driving nearly half of the smallholder farmers across China, and 90,000 farming companies at or above the county level, created jobs for 17 million rural households. This evidence indirectly reveals the potential impact of NAOEs on land use, agricultural production, and farmers' well-being. Therefore, it is of great practical significance to investigate the role of NAOEs in reducing cropland abandonment.

### 7.2.2 *Potential Channels for NAOEs to Curb Cropland Abandonment*

Cropland abandonment results from the combined effects of multiple factors, including natural, economic, social, cultural, institutional, and technological factors (Díaz et al., 2011; Meyfroidt et al., 2016; Müller et al., 2013). In the Chinese context, numerous studies have shown that cropland abandonment among farmers is mainly due to poor land leases (Zheng & Qian, 2022), insufficient labor (Ma et al., 2022; Xu et al., 2019), low productivity (Yan et al., 2016), and difficulties in selling agricultural products (Han & Song, 2019). Fortunately, various types of NAOEs can theoretically help farmers break the above restrictions by promoting land leases, increasing the adoption of machinery, strengthening technical guidance, and assisting in agricultural product sales, thus curbing cropland abandonment (Fig. 7.1).

First, NAOEs can help reduce abandoned cropland by promoting land leases. Compared with smallholder farmers, NAOEs tend to have a higher demand for land and operate more land areas, making it easier to obtain economies of scale. Thus, NAOEs create demand for land and establish a platform for land trading (Ito et al., 2016). Therefore, when farmers do not want to cultivate their cropland, they can rent it to the NAOE instead of leaving it unproductive. Furthermore, previous studies indicate that farmers can receive higher land rents by renting cropland to NAOEs rather than nearby smallholders (Fu et al., 2022; Qiu et al., 2020). Consequently, the emergence of NAOEs can create conditions and incentives for farmers to rent

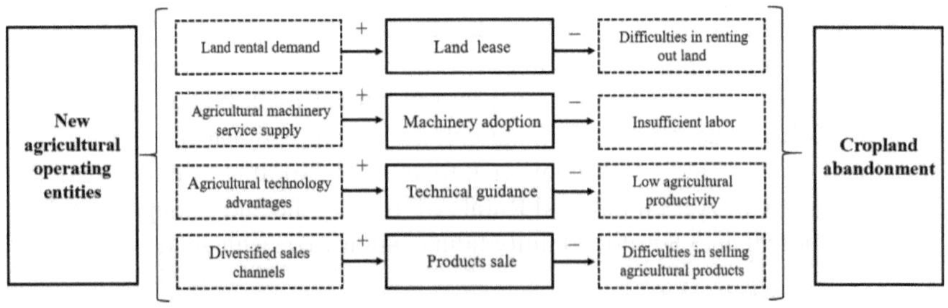


**Fig. 7.1** Analytical framework

their cropland, thereby reducing the probability of cropland abandonment (Liu et al., 2023). Based on this, I propose the following hypothesis:

**Hypothesis 1:** NAOEs promote farmers' land leases, reducing the likelihood of cropland abandonment.

Second, NAOEs can curb cropland abandonment through increased adoption of agricultural machinery. Various types of NAOEs, with their superior economic strength compared to smallholder farmers, typically purchase a variety of agricultural machinery and equipment covering all aspects of crop cultivation, planting, and harvesting to meet the needs of mechanized agricultural production and further improve agricultural productivity (Ma et al., 2022). Therefore, when an NAOE's agricultural machinery is idle, nearby farmers can also rent it or purchase their agricultural machinery services for agricultural production. Moreover, when farmers realize that an NAOE's certain agricultural machinery equipment is more cost-effective, they may also imitate them and purchase this type of agricultural equipment independently (Liu et al., 2022). By using agricultural machinery, farmers can effectively alleviate the shortage of labor in agricultural production, thereby reducing the occurrence of abandoned cropland (Zheng et al., 2023b). Therefore, I propose the following hypothesis:

**Hypothesis 2:** NAOEs increase farmers' adoption of agricultural machinery, reducing the likelihood of cropland abandonment.

Third, NAOEs can strengthen their technical guidance for curbing cropland abandonment. NAOEs possess a more contemporary business management philosophy and superior production technology than smallholder farmers, thus effectively using resource factors. Consequently, the agricultural productivity of these entities is relatively high (Huang & Liang, 2018). Owing to NAOE's unique technological advantages, the Chinese government has successively issued a series of documents, such as *the Opinions on Accelerating the Construction of a Policy System for Fostering New Agricultural Operating Entities, the Opinions on Promoting the Organic Connection between Smallholder Farmers and Modern Agricultural Development, and the Notice on Implementing Actions to Enhance New Agricultural Operating Entities*, encouraging NAOEs to drive the development of smallholder farmers (Zheng et al., 2023b). In this scenario, nearby smallholder farmers can receive agricultural technical guidance from NAOEs, enabling them to improve their agricultural skills through learning and imitation (Li, 2017). Applying advanced agricultural technologies can significantly increase agricultural productivity, potentially reducing farmers' likelihood of abandoning cropland due to farming challenges. Thus, I postulate the following hypothesis:

**Hypothesis 3:** NAOEs provide technical guidance to farmers, reducing the likelihood of cropland abandonment.

Finally, NAOEs can reduce cropland abandonment by helping farmers sell their produce. NAOEs have greater bargaining power in the agricultural market than smallholder farmers. They effectively organize agricultural production activities according to market demand and market their products through multiple channels, including e-commerce and live broadcasting of agricultural products. This approach has enabled them to commercialize agricultural products and obtain more stable economic returns (Huang & Liang, 2018). Consequently, with the aid and influence of NAOEs, farmers are likely to diversify their agricultural product sales channels, thus alleviating the challenges they face in selling agricultural products to various extents (Tadesse et al., 2019). Farmers can ensure their farm income when most agricultural products enter the market, making it less likely for them to abandon their cropland (Ma & Zhu, 2020). This is because when agricultural products cannot be transformed into income-generating commodities, they negatively affect farmers' enthusiasm for farming. Based on this understanding, the final hypothesis is proposed as follows:

**Hypothesis 4:** NAOEs help farmers sell their agricultural products, reducing the likelihood of cropland abandonment.

## 7.3 Research Design

### *7.3.1 Data Sources*

The data employed in this study were obtained from the 2017 and 2019 Chinese Family Databases (CFD), which are available on the website (source: http://ssec.zju.edu.cn/sites/main/template/news.aspx?id=51027) for public applications. The survey was led by Zhejiang University and implemented in conjunction with other Chinese universities, such as Anhui University and Fujian Agriculture and Forestry University. To ensure the national representativeness of the dataset, the survey adopted a sampling method that used a combination of stratified, three-stage, and proportional population size (PPS) sampling to collect data from farm households and village directors (grassroots leaders) in 29 provinces (excluding Xinjiang and Xizang) across the country. Given the focus of this study, I excluded households without cropland from data cleansing. Meanwhile, I retained key variables including NAOE, cropland abandonment, land leases, agricultural machinery, technical guidance, sales of agricultural products, individual characteristics of household heads, and family characteristics. Additionally, we deleted observations with missing information from these variables. Finally, we obtained unbalanced panel data over two periods with a sample of 15,680 farm households for the estimation. Of these, 1438 farm households reported abandoning cropland, whereas the remaining 14,242 did not, accounting for 9.17% and 90.83%, respectively.

### 7.3.2 Empirical Strategy

As indicated previously, the vast majority of farm households in the sample used in this study did not abandon their cropland, implying that the dependent variable is truncated and restricted, so that the Ordinary Least Squares (OLS) estimate with a censored dependent variable may be inconsistent and biased. To avoid this, Tobin (1958) proposed a Tobit model with Maximum Likelihood Estimation (MLE) to address censored dependent variables. The Tobit model, also known as the restricted dependent variable model and the sample selection model is a model in which the dependent variable takes the value if it satisfies certain constraints. Furthermore, panel data for which some dependent variable observations are compressed to a single point can be fitted using a panel Tobit model. Thus, we used a panel Tobit model that accounts for the distributional characteristics of the dependent variable and the type of panel data. Note that there are two types of panel Tobit models: fixed effects and random effects; however, Tobit models with unconditional fixed effects tend to be biased. Therefore, we followed the research of Shuai and Fan (2020) and adopted a random effects model for maximum likelihood estimation. Specifically, assuming that the panel data has J farm households and T periods, the panel Tobit model can be specified as follows:

$$Y_{vjt}^{*} = \alpha_0 + \alpha_1 NAOE_{vt} + \beta Z_{vjt} + \varepsilon_{vjt} \tag{7.1}$$

$$Y_{vjt} = \begin{cases} Y_{vjt}^{*},\ Y_{vjt}^{*} \geq 0 \\ 0,\ Y_{vjt}^{*} < 0 \end{cases} \quad j = 1, \ldots, \text{J and } t = 1, \ldots, \text{T} \tag{7.2}$$

$$\varepsilon_{vjt} \sim \text{N}\ (0, \sigma2) \tag{7.3}$$

where $j$ denotes the farm household, $v$ denotes the village, and $t$ denotes the year. $Y_{vjt}^{*}$ indicates potential cropland abandonment, whereas $Y_{vjt}$ is actually occurred; the latter is the dependent variable in this study, which is specifically defined as the ratio of abandoned cropland area to total cropland area in year $t$ for farm household $j$ in village $v$, and takes a value between 0 and 1. When the value of $Y_{vjt}$ is greater than or equal to 0, the actual observation is considered, and vice versa, the observation is left-truncated to zero. Regarding the core independent variable, using NAOE at the household level is prone to self-selection, resulting in biased estimates. Therefore, we use NAOE at the village level to investigate its impact on cropland abandonment. Specifically, NAOE represents the four types of NAOEs, including professional operators, family farms, agricultural cooperatives, and farming companies. When there are one or more types of NAOEs in a village, it takes the value of 1, and vice versa, it takes the value of 0. $\alpha_0$ is the intercept term, $\alpha_1$ and $\beta$ are the parameters to be estimated, and $\varepsilon_{vjt}$ is the random disturbance term.

Additionally, $Z_{vjt}$ is a series of control variables that may affect farmers' cropland abandonment behavior. Based on prior literature and data availability, the control variables selected in this study include individual characteristics, such as the gender of the head of household (Ma & Zhu, 2020), age and its square (Zhang et al., 2014), and educational status (Deininger et al., 2012), as well as family characteristics such as dependency ratio (Zheng & Qian, 2022), family size (Zavalloni et al., 2021), off-farm employment (Xu et al., 2019), land size (Wang et al., 2023), land fragmentation (Zheng et al., 2023b), and agricultural assets (Deng et al., 2019). These control variables also help alleviate the endogeneity problem caused by omitted variables.

### 7.3.3 Sample Characteristics and Descriptive Statistics

Table 7.2 provides the definitions and descriptions of the selected variables. For the dependent variable, the average abandoned cropland for each sample farmer accounted for 4.3% of the total cropland area. With regard to the core independent variable, approximately 67% of the sampled villages nationwide had various types of NAOEs, such as professional operators, family farms, agricultural cooperatives, and farming companies. Concerning individual characteristics, approximately 85% of the heads of households in the survey sample were male. The mean age of heads of households was approximately 54, and only 12% of them had attended high school. Regarding household characteristics, the average dependency ratio of the sample farmers was 34.9%. On average, each sample farm household comprised approximately four family members, one-fifth of whom were engaged in non-farm work. The sample farmers had poor land endowments, with an average household of 5.6 plots and less than 3 mu of cropland per household member. Additionally, the survey showed that each sample farmer owned approximately 5000 farm assets.

### 7.3.4 Descriptive Statistics on NAOE and Cropland Abandonment

Before conducting the formal econometric analysis, I drew group bars and scatter charts to explore the relationship between NAOE and cropland abandonment. Figure 7.2 shows the results obtained using CFD. The bar chart on the left shows that in both 2017 and 2019, the ratio of abandoned cropland areas in villages with NAOEs was lower than that in villages without NAOEs. Moreover, from 2017 to 2019, regardless of whether villages had NAOEs, the ratio of abandoned cropland areas increased. Additionally, the scatter chart on the right shows that cropland abandonment negatively correlates with NAOE. The above evidence suggests that the development of NAOEs may help curb the expansion of cropland abandonment.

**Table 7.2** Variable definitions and descriptive statistics (N = 15,680)

| Variables | Definition | Mean | SD | Min | Max |
|---|---|---|---|---|---|
| Cropland abandonment | Ratio of abandoned cropland area to total cropland area (0–1) | 0.043 | 0.154 | 0 | 1 |
| New agricultural operating entities | Is there a professional operator, family farm, agricultural cooperative, or farming company in the village? (yes = 1, no = 0) | 0.670 | 0.470 | 0 | 1 |
| Gender | Is the head of the household male? (yes = 1, no = 0) | 0.849 | 0.358 | 0 | 1 |
| Age | Age of the head of household | 53.603 | 10.674 | 16 | 69 |
| Education | Did the head of the household attend high school? (yes = 1, no = 0) | 0.120 | 0.324 | 0 | 1 |
| Dependency ratio | Dependency ratio of children and the elderly (0–5) | 0.349 | 0.478 | 0 | 5 |
| Family size | Number of family members | 3.642 | 1.708 | 1 | 13 |
| Off-farm employment | Ratio of off-farm employment in the household (0–1) | 0.222 | 0.296 | 0 | 1 |
| Land size | Household cropland area per capita (mu) | 2.982 | 6.089 | 0.001 | 360 |
| Land fragmentation | Number of cropland plots | 5.601 | 6.083 | 1 | 120 |
| Farm assets | Value of domestic livestock and machinery (unit: Yuan) | 5010.964 | 20350.150 | 0 | 500,000 |

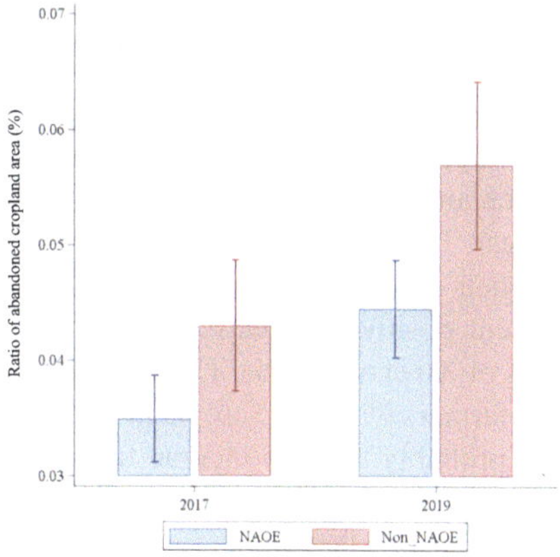


**(a) Bar chart**

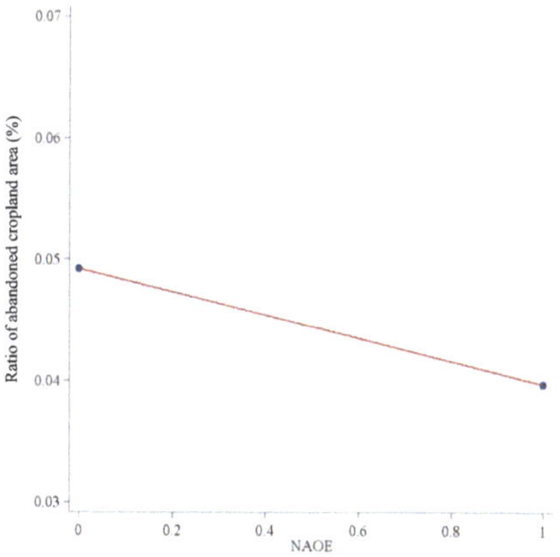


**(b) Scatter chart**

**Fig. 7.2** Correlation between NAOE and cropland abandonment

## 7.4 Impact of NAOE on Cropland Abandonment

### *7.4.1 Main Results*

Table 7.3 presents the estimates using panel Tobit models. Column (1) includes no control variables. On this basis, columns (2) and (3) accumulate individual characteristics and family characteristic variables, respectively. Note that the estimated coefficients are not straightforward for the panel Tobit model. Therefore, we calculated and reported the results of the average marginal effects for a better interpretation. In all three models, the estimated coefficients for NAOE are −0.013, significant at the 1% level. This suggests that omitted variables are unlikely to disturb the above estimates. Regardless of the inclusion of control variables, NAOE always has a significant inhibitory effect on cropland abandonment. Specifically, owing to the presence of NAOE in villages, the ratio of abandoned cropland areas in rural China decreased by 1.3%. The average abandonment ratio over the sample period is 4.3%, which means that from 2017 to 2019, the presence of NAOE is to reduce cropland abandonment by approximately 30.2% ($1.3/4.3 \times 100$).

Among the control variables, male household heads are less likely to abandon their cropland, possibly because they are generally more physically energetic than women. Age and its squared coefficients share an inverse and significant relationship, implying a nonlinear relationship between the age of the household head and cropland abandonment. Specifically, before the age of 50 years ($-0.007/(-2 \times 0.00007)$), the probability of householders abandoning cropland decreases due to increased energy and experience. Once they reach or exceed this age, their likelihood of abandoning cropland increases because of reduced physical fitness (Zhang et al., 2014). Education appears to negatively affect cropland abandonment, suggesting that more educated household heads have better agricultural management skills than less educated ones and are therefore less likely to abandon their cropland (Zheng et al., 2023b). The dependency ratio significantly exacerbates cropland abandonment, whereas family size significantly reduces cropland abandonment. These findings indicate that labor-poor households are more likely to abandon their cropland (Zheng & Qian, 2022). The variable representing off-farm employment positively affects cropland abandonment, which is consistent with the findings of Xu et al. (2019). The negative and significant coefficient of land size implies that farmers with more cropland resources do not easily abandon their cropland. This is probably because income from these cropland areas can sustain their livelihoods (Wang et al., 2023). The coefficient of land fragmentation is positive and significant, suggesting that more fragmented plots are more likely to abandon cropland due to high agricultural production costs (Zheng et al., 2023b). The results show that farm assets significantly reduce farmers' cropland abandonment. This can be explained by the fact that households with more farm assets have higher agricultural productivity and enthusiasm for agriculture, and are, therefore, less likely to abandon cropland (Deng et al., 2019).

**Table 7.3** NAOE and cropland abandonment: Baseline results

| | Ratio of abandoned cropland area to total cropland area | | |
|---|---|---|---|
| | (1) | (2) | (3) |
| NAOE | −0.013*** | −0.013*** | −0.013*** |
| | (0.004) | (0.004) | (0.004) |
| Gender | | −0.022** | −0.013** |
| | | (0.006) | (0.006) |
| Age | | −0.007*** | −0.007*** |
| | | (0.001) | (0.001) |
| Age$^2$ | | 0.00008*** | 0.00007*** |
| | | (0.000) | (0.000) |
| Education | | −0.014** | −0.016** |
| | | (0.007) | (0.007) |
| Dependency ratio | | | 0.017*** |
| | | | (0.005) |
| Family size | | | −0.004** |
| | | | (0.001) |
| Off-farm employment | | | 0.037*** |
| | | | (0.008) |
| Land size | | | −0.003*** |
| | | | (0.001) |
| Land fragmentation | | | 0.004*** |
| | | | (0.000) |
| Farm assets (log) | | | −0.004*** |
| | | | (0.001) |
| Mean of dependent variable | 0.043 | 0.043 | 0.043 |
| Observations | 15,680 | 15,680 | 15,680 |
| Log likelihood | −4937.216 | −4904.019 | −4738.085 |

*Notes* ***, **, and * denote significance at the 1%, 5%, and 10% levels, respectively; Delta-method standard errors are presented in parentheses

## 7.4.2 Robustness Checks

We performed various additional robustness checks to confirm the reliability of the previous estimates. The corresponding estimates are listed in Table 7.4.

First, we re-estimated Eq. (7.2) by replacing the original NAOE dummy variable with the logarithm of the NAOE number. Column (1) shows that after redefining the core independent variable, NAOE still contributes to reducing the occurrence of cropland abandonment by farmers. Moreover, the greater the number of NAOE

**Table 7.4** NAOE and farmland abandonment: Robustness checks

| | Replacing X | Replacing Y | Replacing model | Replacing sample | Adding variables |
|---|---|---|---|---|---|
| | (1) | (2) | (3) | (4) | (5) |
| NAOE | | −0.032*** | −0.010*** | −0.011*** | −0.010** |
| | | (0.010) | (0.003) | (0.004) | (0.004) |
| Number of NAOEs (log) | −0.010*** | | | | |
| | (0.002) | | | | |
| Village traffic | | | | | −0.008*** |
| | | | | | (0.003) |
| Village economy | | | | | −0.007*** |
| | | | | | (0.002) |
| Control variables | Yes | Yes | Yes | Yes | Yes |
| Observations | 15,680 | 15,680 | 15,680 | 14,499 | 15,060 |
| Log likelihood | −4729.330 | −5999.595 | – | −4553.720 | −4522.883 |
| R-squared | – | – | 0.027 | – | – |

*Notes* ***, **, and * denote significance at the 1%, 5%, and 10% levels, respectively; Delta-method standard errors and robust standard errors are presented in parentheses. Village traffic is measured by the number of roads from the village to the county, while the village economy is gauged by the annual disposable income per capita, scored from 1 (less than 1000 yuan) to 9 (more than 50,000 yuan)

in villages, the less likely farmers are to abandon their croplands. This estimate somewhat alleviates the endogeneity problem caused by measurement errors.

Second, referring to Zheng and Qian (2022), I further used the logarithm of the abandoned cropland area to replace the abandoned cropland ratio. As shown in column (2), regardless of whether the dependent variable is replaced, the estimated coefficient of NAOE is significantly negative at the 1% level. This finding is consistent with that in Table 7.3, which once again demonstrates NAOE's positive role in reducing cropland abandonment.

Third, I applied the panel random effects model instead of the panel Tobit model without considering the truncation feature of the dependent variable observations. Column (3) indicates a slight decrease in the estimated coefficient for NAOE compared with column (3) of Table 7.3. However, it remains significantly negative at the 1% level, indicating that previous estimates are robust and that the Tobit model is not undervalued.

Fourth, although the data in this study are primarily a sample of farm households, they are theoretically unlikely to be NAOEs under CFD's sampling strategy. However, to rule out this suspicion, I also tried to employ a sample of smallholder farmers with a farming area of less than 25 mu for a robust estimation[3] when CFD could not identify whether the samples were NAOEs. Column (4) shows that NAOE still significantly reduces cropland abandonment.

Finally, we considered the village traffic and economy variables in conjunction with the availability of data to mitigate the interference of such omitted variables at the village level. Column (5) confirms that accounting for these village-level variables, the inverse association between NAOE and cropland abandonment persists.

In conclusion, the above analyses from different perspectives support the baseline estimates in Table 7.3 for various dimensions, confirming the negative relationship between NAOE and cropland abandonment.

### 7.4.3 Endogeneity Discussion

Endogeneity problems caused by measurement bias and missing variables can be avoided by replacing the core independent variable and adding control variables. However, whether there is an endogeneity problem due to selection bias in this study is worthy of further discussion. To this end, we used a propensity score matching (PSM) approach to re-estimate the impact of NAOE on cropland abandonment. To obtain accurate estimates, we employed three commonly used matching methods: nearest neighbor (NN) matching within caliper ($n = 4, r = 0.05$), radius matching ($r = 0.05$), and kernel matching (bandwidth = 0.03). Results in Table 7.5 show that the average treatment effect (ATT) for NAOE remains positive and significant regardless of the matching method used. This indicates that our findings are highly consistent with previous estimates, even in the face of a potential selection bias.

### 7.4.4 Mechanism Analysis

We further explored the underlying mechanisms after confirming the negative correlation between NAOE and cropland abandonment. As noted earlier, we examined the effects of NAOE on land leases, machinery adoption, technical guidance, and the sale of agricultural products to uncover the channels through which NAOE affects cropland abandonment. Specifically, land leases were defined as whether farmers rented out the land (yes = 1, no = 0). Machinery adoption was defined as whether farmers adopted machinery for agricultural production (yes = 1, no = 0). Technical guidance was defined as whether farmers received technical guidance on agricultural production (yes = 1, no = 0). Agricultural product sales were defined as whether farmers sold agricultural products (yes = 1, no = 0).

[3] Whether the farming area is more than 25 mu is an important criterion for distinguishing large-scale farmers in China's third national agricultural census.

**Table 7.5** NAOE and cropland abandonment: PSM estimates

| PSM methods | Ratio of abandoned cropland area to total cropland area | | ATT | S.E. | T-value | Common support | |
|---|---|---|---|---|---|---|---|
| | Treat | Control | | | | Treat | Control |
| NN matching within caliper (n = 4, r = 0.05) | 0.040 | 0.048 | −0.008*** | 0.003 | −2.82 | 10,498 | 5178 |
| Radius matching (r = 0.05) | 0.040 | 0.049 | −0.009*** | 0.003 | −3.47 | 10,498 | 5178 |
| Kernel matching (bandwidth = 0.03) | 0.040 | 0.050 | −0.010*** | 0.003 | −3.64 | 10,496 | 5178 |

*Notes* ***, **, and * denote significance at the 1%, 5%, and 10% levels, respectively

Table 7.6 provides the estimates of the mechanism analysis. The results show that NAOE significantly increases the likelihood of farmers leasing land, obtaining technical guidance, and selling agricultural products. To be specific, column (1) shows that farmers are 6.3% more likely to rent out their land in villages with NAOEs than those without NAOEs; thus, Hypothesis 1 is confirmed. The likely reason is that NAOEs tend to be market-oriented; their demand for land is relatively high; therefore, farmers with idle cropland are more likely to rent out. As shown in column (3), NAOE increases farmers' access to technical guidance by 4.1%, possibly due to its technical advantages and assistance. Thus, Hypothesis 3 is confirmed. As farmers' agricultural skills improve, their agricultural productivity increases accordingly, making them less likely to abandon their cropland. As demonstrated in column (4), NAOE is significantly associated with a 2.3% increase in the probability of sales of agricultural products, supporting Hypothesis 4. This is mainly due to NAOE's diversified sales channels, which indirectly help farmers solve the problem of difficult sales of agricultural products. Unblocking farmers' sales channels for agricultural products makes them less likely to abandon cropland due to insufficient income from difficult sales. However, the results in column (2) indicate that NAOE has an insignificant impact on farmers' adoption of machinery. Thus, Hypothesis 2 is not supported. One possible explanation is that agricultural production is seasonal, and if a season is missed, it leads to lower yields. Therefore, NAOE's machinery is mainly used for domestic agricultural production and has a smaller radiation effect on other agricultural operators.

**Table 7.6** NAOE and cropland abandonment: Mechanism analysis

| | Land lease | Machinery adoption | Technical guidance | Products sale |
|---|---|---|---|---|
| | (1) | (2) | (3) | (4) |
| NAOE | 0.063*** | −0.003 | 0.041*** | 0.023** |
| | (0.006) | (0.005) | (0.006) | (0.009) |
| Control variables | Yes | Yes | Yes | Yes |
| Observations | 15,680 | 13,713 | 13,679 | 13,491 |
| R-squared | 0.095 | 0.686 | 0.030 | 0.071 |

*Notes* ***, **, and * denote significance at the 1%, 5%, and 10% levels, respectively; Robust standard errors are presented in parentheses. For consistency, all models here are panel random effects models

### 7.4.5 Further Discussion

Different types of NAOEs have different survival logic and comparative advantages; therefore, their impact on cropland abandonment may differ. Consequently, I separately investigated the basic situation of farmers abandoning their cropland under a certain NAOE in their village. As illustrated in Fig. 7.3, apart from farming companies, the other three types of NAOEs, including professional operators, family farms, and agricultural cooperatives, negatively impact cropland abandonment. A possible reason for this is that compared with other types of NAOEs, agricultural companies are more profit-oriented, especially those from outside the village, who usually prioritize maximizing their profits when making decisions (Huang & Liang, 2018). Additionally, agricultural cooperatives have the most prominent inhibitory effect on cropland abandonment, possibly due to the close link between agricultural cooperatives and smallholder farmers (Ma & Zhu, 2020). Conversely, professional operators have the weakest inhibitory effect on cropland abandonment, potentially due to their relatively small-scale operations and lack of significant radiation capacity.

## 7.5 Heterogeneous Effects of NAOE on Cropland Abandonment

We previously demonstrated a negative correlation between NAOE and cropland abandonment. However, owing to obvious differences between regions, villages, and households in rural China, whether this relationship is established remains to be explored. Given this, I analyzed the heterogeneous effects of NAOE on cropland abandonment using the macro-meso-micro dimensions mentioned above.

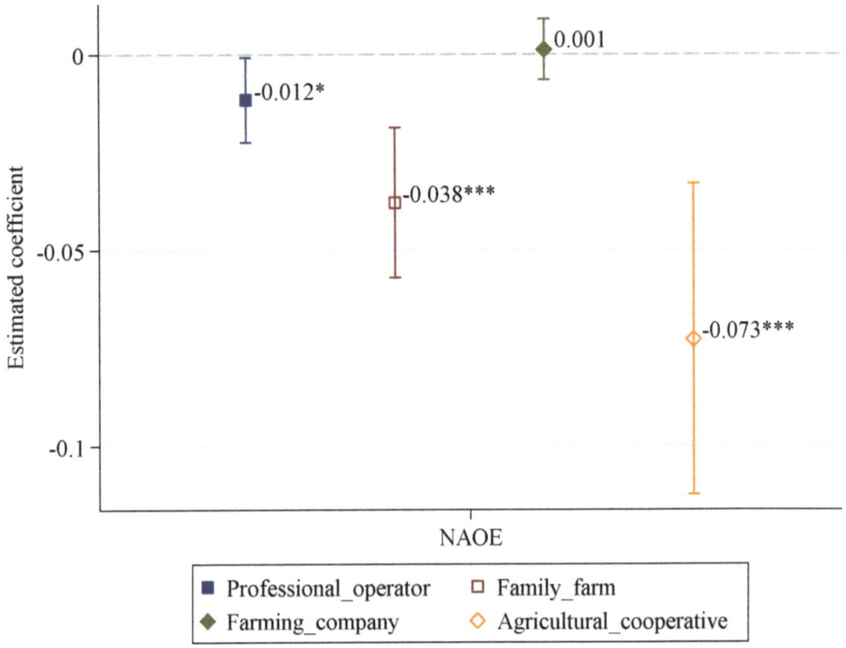


**Fig. 7.3** NAOE and cropland abandonment: Analysis based on different NAOE types. (*Notes* In all models, the control group for a particular type of NAOE is smallholder farmers)

### *7.5.1 Variance Results by Different Regions*

In addition to the direct influence of the control variables in Table 7.3, NAOE's effect on cropland abandonment may be moderated by other factors, particularly geographic and topographical characteristics. Considering the increasing level of China's economic development from west to east, as well as the geographical differences between the eastern, central, and western regions, we employed subsamples of the three regions for estimation according to the division criteria of the National Bureau of Statistics of China.[4] Simultaneously, farmers' land use behavior varies greatly due to the difficulty of agricultural production in mountains and plains (Xu et al., 2019). Therefore, subsamples under both terrain conditions were used for the estimation.

Figure 7.4 plots the grouped regression results based on Eq. (7.1). The figure on the left shows that the estimated coefficients of NAOE in central and western China are negative and significant, while those in the eastern region are insignificant. One possible reason is that the eastern region is the most economically developed, local NAOE numbers tend to be saturated, and their marginal effect on cropland abandonment is slightly insufficient. Conversely, NAOE numbers in the central and

[4] http://www.stats.gov.cn/zt_18555/zthd/sjtjr/dejtjkfr/tjkp/202302/t20230216_1909741.htm#:~:text=%.

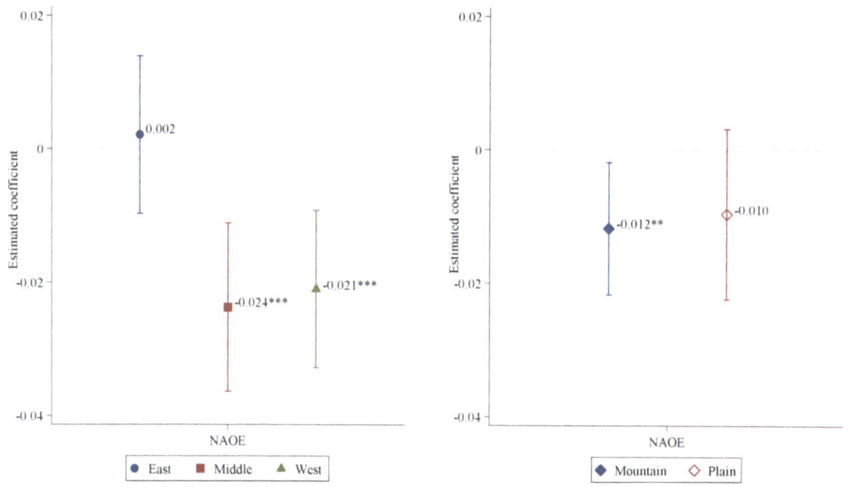


**(a) Geographic grouping** **(b) Topographic grouping**

**Fig. 7.4** NAOE and cropland abandonment: Regional heterogeneity

western regions are relatively small. Therefore, in the context of rural-urban labor migration, NAOEs are more needed to operate idle cropland. On the right side of the figure, we can observe that NAOE mainly has a significant inhibitory effect on cropland abandonment in mountainous areas, but not in plain areas. This may be explained by the fact that cropland in the plains is less difficult and easier to cultivate than in the mountains; thus, even without NAOE, smallholder farmers in the surrounding areas will likely lease unused cropland.

### 7.5.2 *Variance Results by Different Villages*

Like other developing countries, land tenure insecurity is prominent in rural China. In China, the source of land tenure insecurity is land redistribution among village farmers due to population changes under the Household Responsibility System. To improve land tenure security, the Chinese government has repeatedly prohibited land redistribution and introduced two landmark reforms. The first is the *Property Law of the People's Republic of China*, introduced in 2007, which directly treated farmers' land rights as more exclusive property rights rather than creditors' rights. The second is a new round of land certification implemented nationwide in 2013, which required farmers to legally issue land certificates (Zheng & Qian, 2022). As such, I discussed the heterogeneous effects, focusing on whether villages have carried out land certification and distribution since 2013 and 2007, respectively.

Figure 7.5 presents the estimated results for different security rights. As shown on the left, NAOE helps curb cropland abandonment in villages with certified land

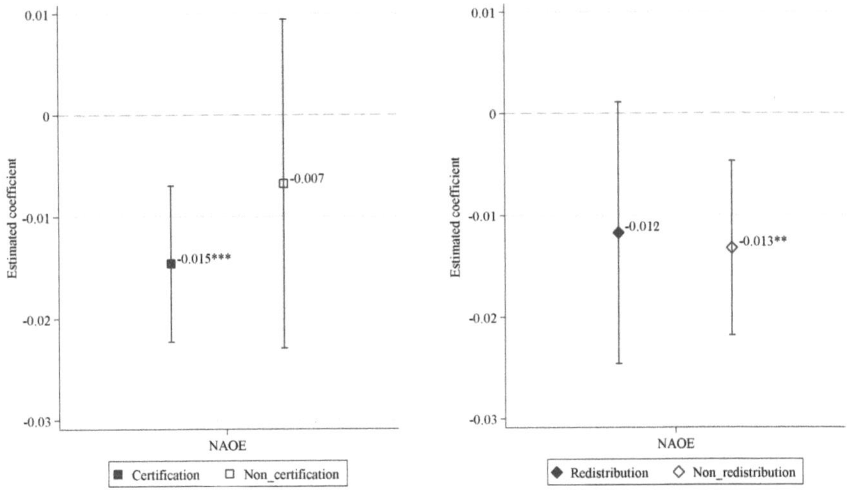


**(a) Land certification grouping** **(b) Land redistribution grouping**

**Fig. 7.5** NAOE and cropland abandonment: Village heterogeneity

but has little effect on villages without certified land. As shown on the right, NAOE reduces cropland abandonment in villages where land redistribution has not occurred in the past, but has no impact on villages where it has occurred. This may be because villages that have not been redistributed or certified are generally more secure regarding land tenure. Consequently, NAOEs prefer to operate on an agricultural scale in such villages, which prevents farmers from abandoning their cropland.

### *7.5.3 Variance Results by Different Households*

Given the conditions of land resources, household human resource endowments—the quantity and quality of labor—usually have a direct impact on agricultural production. Particularly in the rural-urban transformation process, the shortage of agricultural labor due to off-farm employment and aging is often a common challenge for cropland abandonment in developing countries. For such consideration, following Zheng et al. (2023b), I examined the heterogeneous effects of NAOE on cropland abandonment under labor quantity and quality conditions. Specifically, based on whether the number of working-age members in the household was greater than the average of the whole sample, it was divided into a group with more workers and a group with fewer workers. According to whether the health status of the working-age members of the household was better than the average of the whole sample, it was divided into a better health group and a poorer health group.

Figure 7.6 shows the estimated results for various human resource endowments. Regarding the labor quantity grouping, NAOE exerts a significant inhibitory effect on

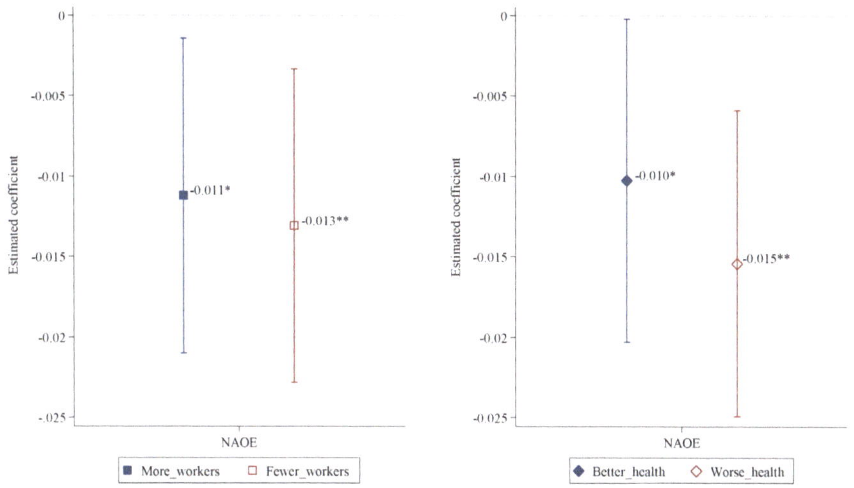


**(a) Labor quantity grouping** **(b) Labor quality grouping**

**Fig. 7.6** NAOE and cropland abandonment: Household heterogeneity

cropland abandonment in both groups. However, this effect is slightly stronger in the group with fewer workers than that with more workers. For the labor quality grouping, the NAOE coefficients in both groups are negative and significantly different from zero. However, the impact appears slightly higher in the poorer health group than in the better health group. These findings suggest that farmers with inferior human resources benefit more from the NAOE than those with superior human resources. Nevertheless, this disparity in human resources has largely disappeared, possibly due to the rapid spread of social services in agriculture (Qing et al., 2023).

## 7.6 Conclusions and Discussion

### *7.6.1 Conclusions*

In the rural-urban transformation, many rural workers constantly migrate to cities to participate in secondary and tertiary industries, leading to a growing concern about cropland abandonment. This could challenge local food security, as less cropland is used for food production. To eradicate hunger, ensure food security, promote sustainable agriculture, and ultimately achieve the global Sustainable Development Goals, it is essential to contain abandoned croplands, strengthen cropland quantity protection, and promote the sustainable use of croplands. Against this background, this study empirically investigates the impacts, underlying mechanisms, and heterogeneous effects of NAOE on farmers' cropland abandonment from the perspective of agricultural operators, using the 2017 and 2019 CFD and panel Tobit Models.

The empirical results reveal that the cultivation of NAOEs in villages could help deter farmers from abandoning their cropland; this estimate remained valid after a series of robustness checks. Specifically, due to the role of NAOE, the ratio of abandoned cropland area to total cropland area in rural China has decreased by approximately 30% in two years. Compared with farming companies, the contributions of the other three types of NAOEs, such as professional operators, family farms, and agricultural cooperatives, are more significant. The mechanism tests imply that NAOEs have significantly reduced the incidence of cropland abandonment by facilitating land leasing, providing technical guidance, and promoting the sale of agricultural products. However, the mechanism for adopting agricultural machinery has not been established. Heterogeneity analysis further indicates that the effects of NAOEs on cropland abandonment vary significantly across regions, villages, and households. At the regional level, NAOEs mainly inhibit the abandonment of cropland in central and western China and mountainous areas. At the village level, NAOEs mainly benefit villages that have not reallocated land and have certified land. At the household level, NAOE's effect on households with poorer human resource endowments is slightly higher than that of households with better human resource endowments.

### *7.6.2 Policy Implications*

Sustainable development is an eternal proposition in human society. From a developmental perspective, using limited and scarce land resources to feed a growing population is a practical challenge for countries worldwide. In this regard, our findings have significant implications for policymakers. First, various types of NAOEs should be established to eliminate the driving mechanisms behind farmers' cropland abandonment. In particular, other countries can develop one or more types of NAOEs according to their conditions and make full use of their positive roles in promoting land leasing, providing technical guidance, and facilitating the sale of agricultural products. Confronted with an aging rural population and an escalating rural exodus, the question of who will cultivate land in China is becoming increasingly critical. There is also an urgent need to vigorously establish various types of NAOE to ensure food security, especially to support returning migrant workers in establishing NAOEs. Second, it is imperative to enhance farmers' access to agricultural machinery to alleviate labor shortages in agricultural production. Notably, NAOEs cannot provide mechanical services to farmers, possibly due to the constraints of the farming season. Therefore, I recommend fostering agricultural social service organizations, increasing subsidies for agricultural machinery, and enhancing the agricultural social service market to meet the future needs of farmers. Third, countries should focus on the heterogeneity of regions, villages, and households to devise targeted solutions to curb cropland abandonment. At the regional level, emphasis should be placed on addressing the issue of cropland abandonment in the less-developed and mountainous regions. From a village perspective, enhancing the security of property rights is crucial for preventing negative impacts on cropland abandonment. Supporting smallholder farmers, especially those with limited human capital, is essential to this strategy.

### 7.6.3 Research Deficiencies and Prospects

Owing to research focus and data limitations, future research can be further developed in the following areas. First, a comparison of NAOEs across countries is needed to identify similarities and differences. Although NAOE is a specific term defined by the Chinese government for professional operators, family farms, farming companies, and agricultural cooperatives, these agricultural operating entities can be found in other countries as well (Candemir et al., 2021; Klepac & Hampel, 2017; Lowder et al., 2021). Second, this study focuses on the role of NAOEs in cropland abandonment from a micro-household perspective. Therefore, future studies can provide more empirical evidence from higher macro levels, such as counties, cities, and provinces. Third, there is a need to investigate the additional impacts of NAOEs on land use, such as land productivity, land intensification, and land-scale management. A comprehensive assessment of the impact of NAOEs on land use will enable a detailed examination of the benefits and disadvantages for smallholder farmers and NAOEs, as well as the design of complementary and mutually reinforcing agricultural development policies.

## References

Anderson, K., & Strutt, A. (2014). Food security policy options for China: Lessons from other countries. *Food Policy, 49*, 50–58.

Andrianarimanana, M. H., Yongjian, P., & Rabezanahary Tanteliniaina, M. F. (2023). Assessment of the importance of climate, land, and soil on the global supply for agricultural products and global food security: Evidence from Madagascar. *Food Policy, 115*, 102403.

Campbell, J. E., Lobell, D. B., Genova, R. C., & Field, C. B. (2008). The global potential of bioenergy on abandoned agriculture lands. *Environmental Science & Technology, 42*, 5791–5794.

Candemir, A., Duvaleix, S., & Latruffe, L. (2021). Agricultural cooperatives and farm sustainability—a literature review. *Journal of Economic Surveys, 35*, 1118–1144.

Deininger, K., Savastano, S., & Carletto, C. (2012). Land fragmentation, cropland abandonment, and land market operation in Albania. *World Development, 40*, 2108–2122.

Deng, X., Xu, D., Zeng, M., & Qi, Y. (2019). Does internet use help reduce rural cropland abandonment? *Evidence from China. Land Use Policy, 89*, 104243.

Díaz, G. I., Nahuelhual, L., Echeverría, C., & Marín, S. (2011). Drivers of land abandonment in southern Chile and implications for landscape planning. *Landscape and Urban Planning, 99*, 207–217.

Elbakidze, M., & Angelstam, P. (2007). Implementing sustainable forest management in Ukraine's Carpathian Mountains: The role of traditional village systems. *Forest Ecology and Management, 249*, 28–38.

FAO, I., UNICEF, WFP, WHO. (2023). *The state of food security and nutrition in the world 2023, urbanization, agrifood systems transformation and healthy diets across the rural-urban continuum*, Rome.

FAOSTAT, 2018. Food and agriculture organization corporate statistical database.

Fu, H., Peng, Y., Zheng, L., Liu, Q., Zhou, L., Zhang, Y., Kong, R., & Turvey, C. G. (2022). Heterogeneous choice in WTP and WTA for renting land use rights in rural China: Choice experiments from the field. *Land Use Policy, 119*, 106123.

Han, Z., & Song, W. (2019). Spatiotemporal variations in cropland abandonment in the Guizhou-Guangxi karst mountain area. *China. Journal of Cleaner Production, 238*, 117888.

Hasegawa, T., Sakurai, G., Fujimori, S., Takahashi, K., Hijioka, Y., & Masui, T. (2021). Extreme climate events increase risk of global food insecurity and adaptation needs. *Nature Food, 2*, 587–595.

Huang, Z., & Liang, Q. (2018). Agricultural organizations and the role of farmer cooperatives in China since 1978: Past and future. *China Agricultural Economic Review, 10*, 48–64.

Ito, J., Nishikori, M., Toyoshi, M., & Feuer, H. N. (2016). The contribution of land exchange institutions and markets in countering farmland abandonment in Japan. *Land Use Policy, 57*, 582–593.

Klepac, V., & Hampel, D. (2017). Predicting financial distress of agriculture companies in EU. *Agricultural Economics, 63*, 347–355.

Li, Z. (2017). China's agricultural basic operating system. In Z. Li (Ed.), *Reform and development of agriculture in China* (pp. 65–79). Springer Singapore.

Lieskovsky, J., & Lieskovska, D. (2021). Cropland abandonment in Slovakia: Analysis and comparison of different data sources. *Land-Basel, 10*.

Liu, G., Ma, Z., Guo, S., Deng, X., Song, J., & Xu, D. (2023). How does farmers' differentiation affect farmland abandonment from the perspective of land attachment and generational differences? Evidence from Sichuan Province. *China. Environmental Development, 48*, 100924.

Liu, Y., Heerink, N., Li, F., & Shi, X. (2022). Do agricultural machinery services promote village farmland rental markets? Theory and evidence from a case study in the North China plain. *Land Use Policy, 122*, 106388.

Lowder, S. K., Sánchez, M. V., & Bertini, R. (2021). Which farms feed the world and has farmland become more concentrated? *World Development, 142*, 105455.

Ma, W., & Zhu, Z. (2020). A note: Reducing cropland abandonment in China—do agricultural cooperatives play a role? *Journal of Agricultural Economics, 71*, 929–935.

Ma, W., Zhu, Z., & Zhou, X. (2022). Agricultural mechanization and cropland abandonment in rural China. *Applied Economics Letters, 29*, 526–533.

Meyfroidt, P., Schierhorn, F., Prishchepov, A. V., Müller, D., & Kuemmerle, T. (2016). Drivers, constraints and trade-offs associated with recultivating abandoned cropland in Russia, Ukraine and Kazakhstan. *Global Environmental Change, 37*, 1–15.

Müller, D., Leitão, P. J., & Sikor, T. (2013). Comparing the determinants of cropland abandonment in Albania and Romania using boosted regression trees. *Agricultural Systems, 117*, 66–77.

Olabisi, M., Tschirley, D. L., Nyange, D., & Awokuse, T. (2021). Does trade protectionism promote domestic food security? Evidence from Tanzanian edible oil imports. *Global Food Security, 28*, 100470.

Qing, C., Zhou, W., Song, J., Deng, X., & Xu, D. (2023). Impact of outsourced machinery services on farmers' green production behavior: Evidence from Chinese rice farmers. *Journal of Environmental Management, 327*, 116843.

Qiu, T., Luo, B., & He, Q. (2020). Does land rent between acquaintances deviate from the reference point? Evidence from rural China. *China & World Economy, 28*, 29–50.

Queiroz, C., Beilin, R., Folke, C., & Lindborg, R. (2014). Farmland abandonment: Threat or opportunity for biodiversity conservation? A global review. *Frontiers in Ecology and the Environment, 12*, 288–296.

Shuai, S., & Fan, Z. (2020). Modeling the role of environmental regulations in regional green economy efficiency of China: Empirical evidence from super efficiency DEA-Tobit model. *Journal of Environmental Management, 261*, 110227.

Tadesse, G., Abate, G. T., & Ergano, K. (2019). The boundary of smallholder producers' cooperatives: A conceptual and empirical analysis. *Journal of Agricultural Economics, 70*, 529–549.

Tobin, J. (1958). Estimation of relationships for limited dependent variables. *Econometrica, 26*, 24–26.

Tseng, T.-W. J., Robinson, B. E., Bellemare, M. F., Ben Yishay, A., Blackman, A., Boucher, T., Childress, M., Holland, M. B., Kroeger, T., Linkow, B., Diop, M., Naughton, L., Rudel, T., Sanjak, J., Shyamsundar, P., Veit, P., Sunderlin, W., Zhang, W., & Masuda, Y. J. (2021). Influence of land tenure interventions on human Well-being and environmental outcomes. *Nature Sustainability, 4*, 242–251.

Wang, Y., Yang, A., & Yang, Q. (2023). The extent, drivers and production loss of farmland abandonment in China: Evidence from a spatiotemporal analysis of farm households survey. *Journal of Cleaner Production, 414*, 137772.

Xu, D., Deng, X., Huang, K., Liu, Y., Yong, Z., & Liu, S. (2019). Relationships between labor migration and cropland abandonment in rural China from the perspective of village types. *Land Use Policy, 88*, 104164.

Yan, J., Yang, Z., Li, Z., Li, X., Xin, L., & Sun, L. (2016). Drivers of cropland abandonment in mountainous areas: A household decision model on farming scale in Southwest China. *Land Use Policy, 57*, 459–469.

Zavalloni, M., D'Alberto, R., Raggi, M., & Viaggi, D. (2021). Farmland abandonment, public goods and the CAP in a marginal area of Italy. *Land Use Policy, 107*, 104365.

Zhang, Y., Li, X., & Song, W. (2014). Determinants of cropland abandonment at the parcel, household and village levels in mountain areas of China: A multi-level analysis. *Land Use Policy, 41*, 186–192.

Zheng, L., Li, L., Zhao, Z., & Qian, W. (2023a). Does land certification increase farmers' use of organic fertilizer? Evidence from China. *Journal of Land Use Science, 18*, 39–54.

Zheng, L., & Qian, W. (2022). The impact of land certification on cropland abandonment: Evidence from rural China. *China Agricultural Economic Review, 14*, 509–526.

Zheng, L., Su, L., & Jin, S. (2023b). Reducing land fragmentation to curb cropland abandonment: Evidence from rural China. *Canadian Journal of Agricultural Economics/Revue canadienne d'agroeconomie, 71*, 355–373.

# Chapter 8
# Farmland Water Conservancy Project and Cropland Abandonment

**Abstract** Against the backdrop of rapid industrialization and urbanization, cropland abandonment has emerged as a major challenge threatening global food security and constraining the sustainable development of agriculture. Endowed with earmarked funds and the characteristic of inclusive benefits, farmland water conservancy project can directly improve agricultural production conditions, therefore help address the issue of cropland abandonment and provide crucial support for consolidating the foundation of food security. Thus, this chapter employs unbalanced panel data from the 2017 and 2019 China Rural Household Panel Survey (CRHPS) and adopts a panel two-way fixed effects (TWFE) model to empirically examine the impact of farmland water conservancy project on cropland abandonment. Results show that farmland water conservancy project facilities significantly curbed cropland abandonment, resulting in a 7.5% decrease in the average abandonment rate among farming households. This effect is primarily achieved through channels such as increasing agricultural production income and reducing production and transaction costs. However, this effect is also moderated by household resource endowments and regional economic development, both of which lead to heterogeneity in the suppression impact of the projects. Specifically, among households with higher agricultural dependency, less per capita arable land, and villages in economically underdeveloped areas or farther from county seats, farmland water conservancy project facilities exert a more pronounced suppression effect on cropland abandonment, while this stronger effect is not observed among other households and villages. Based on these findings, this study proposes focusing on the role of water conservancy facilities, blocking the conditions that lead to cropland abandonment, and tailoring measures to local conditions and individual households. This approach will help achieve the organic integration of sustainable agricultural development and food security.

**Keywords** Farmland water conservancy project · Cropland abandonment · Farm economics · Food security · Sustainable agricultural development

 
L. Zheng, *Cropland Abandonment in Rural China*, Resources, Environment and Agricultural Development, https://doi.org/10.1007/978-981-95-8287-7_8

## 8.1 Introduction

As the material foundation of human survival, food serves as a "ballast stone" for sustaining economic stability and underpinning national development (Timmer, 2000). Its security is not only associated with the basic livelihood and well-being of domestic populations but also exerts far-reaching transnational impacts amid globalized agricultural trade (Ben Hassen & El Bilali, 2022; Koren, 2018). However, the current global food security landscape remains grim, with food shortages and unequal access to food persisting as severe challenges. According to the FAO's *The State of Food Security and Nutrition in the World 2025* report (FAO et al., 2025), approximately 638 million people worldwide faced hunger in 2024, accounting for 8.2% of the global population—far from the 2030 Sustainable Development Goal of "Zero Hunger." Meanwhile, the issue of unequal food access is prominent: low-income countries and impoverished groups confront significantly higher hunger risks than other populations (Ivanic & Martin, 2008). They struggle to afford healthy diets and are vulnerable to food price volatility and supply chain disruptions, trapping them in a vicious "food scarcity-poverty" cycle (Fanzo et al., 2021). Alarmingly, while a large global population still faces hunger threats, cropland—the core carrier of food production—is simultaneously under the threat of abandonment (Subedi et al., 2022). This supply-demand contradiction further exacerbates the uncertainty surrounding food security.

As a unique phenomenon emerging at a certain stage of economic development and urbanization, cropland abandonment has evolved from an initially localized issue in developed countries such as Europe, the United States, and Japan (Fayet et al., 2022; Mather, 2001; San Roman Sanz et al., 2013) into a prominent hazard threatening global food security (Abolina & Luzadis, 2015; Deng et al., 2019). Over the nearly three decades from 1992 to 2020, global abandoned cropland reached 100 million hectares, accounting for approximately 6% of the total cropland area, with one-third located in Asia (Zheng et al., 2023b). Against this backdrop, addressing cropland abandonment and safeguarding food production have become a global consensus for maintaining food security (Estel et al., 2015)—a priority particularly critical for China, a country with a large population and limited cropland. The problem of cropland abandonment in China is not trivial. Survey data indicates that between 1990 and 2020, the number of households abandoning cropland increased nearly 15-fold, with their proportion rising from 1.3% to 21% (Wang et al., 2023). In China, annual grain losses caused by cropland abandonment amount to approximately 7.94 billion kilograms, sufficient to feed around 19.85 million people (Guo et al., 2023)—indirectly confirming the practical significance of addressing this issue.

To ensure national food security, China has implemented incentive measures such as grain subsidies and strict prohibitions on unreasonable cropland use. However, the overall focus of governance still leans toward restrictive measures, including grid-based supervision and dynamic remote sensing monitoring (Song et al., 2025; Wang et al., 2020). Such measures not only incur high costs but also fail to address the root causes of cropland abandonment, often falling into the trap of market distortion. This essentially shifts a substantial share of cropland protection costs onto farmers (Lichtenberg & Ding, 2008). Exploring reasonable and effective governance measures has thus become an urgent priority to curb the expansion of cropland abandonment. Compared with generalized governance approaches, farmland water conservancy project directly targets the protection and sustainable utilization of cropland itself, thereby meriting full attention. Farmland water conservancy project is not merely engineering investments; as an economic instrument, they can reshape cost-benefit dynamics while stabilizing irrigation guarantees and improving production conditions. Whether this approach—replacing constraints with empowerment—can stimulate farmers' endogenous motivation and mitigate conflicts between macro governance objectives and micro-subject interests is a practical question that this study seeks to answer through theoretical and empirical analyses.

Existing research has yielded relatively abundant findings regarding the influencing factors of cropland abandonment and corresponding governance strategies. Literature exploring these factors typically adopts the subsistence rationality and economic rationality framework to elucidate the link between farmers' decision-making logic and cropland abandonment. At the economic rationality level, advancing urbanization and industrialization have driven large-scale rural labor migration to non-agricultural sectors (Abolina & Luzadis, 2015; Zheng, 2024b), raising labor opportunity costs. This is compounded by climate change, ecological and environmental pollution (Liu et al., 2025; Salazar-Espinoza et al., 2015), land fragmentation and quality degradation (Deininger et al., 2012; Terres et al., 2015; Yan et al., 2016; Zheng et al., 2023a), inadequate infrastructure, and rural population aging (Ren et al., 2023). Collectively, these factors result in low agricultural comparative returns (Zheng et al., 2025a), which constitute the core economic drivers of cropland abandonment. At the subsistence rationality level, the long-term security function of land further exacerbates cropland abandonment: to maintain tenure rights (Besley, 1995; Deininger & Jin, 2006), some farmers choose to leave their cropland fallow rather than transfer it. Corresponding to these drivers, existing research has proposed two targeted governance strategies: first, enhancing agricultural returns by improving production conditions and increasing access to socialized services (Zheng, 2024a) to strengthen farmers' cultivation incentives; second, advancing land tenure reforms (Vu & Goto, 2020; Zheng & Qian, 2021) to protect farmers' land property rights (Olagunju et al., 2023). Regrettably, few scholars have recognized the potential value of farmland water conservancy project. Existing literature indicates that backward production conditions and insufficient supporting facilities (Renkow et al., 2004) often amplify the negative effects of cropland abandonment: on one hand, they directly increase cultivation costs, reduce land productivity, and weaken economically driven cultivation willingness (Gou et al., 2025); on the other hand, fragmented plots and inadequate facilities diminish the attractiveness of land transfers, making it difficult for farmers to find transferees even when willing to transfer (Gebru et al., 2019; Rahman, 2010; Teklu & Lemi, 2004)—ultimately forcing them to abandon cropland. Given that farmland water conservancy project helps improve farming conditions, these findings suggest that such projects are of great significance for the effective governance of cropland abandonment.

Currently, quantitative research on the relationship between farmland water conservancy project and cropland abandonment remains scarce. Another strand of literature closely related to this study focuses on the agricultural production effects of high-standard farmland construction and land consolidation. For instance, Du et al. (2018) evaluated the effectiveness of land consolidation projects using 250-m time-series MODIS NDVI remote sensing data from 2001 to 2013, focusing on the impact of land improvement on agricultural productivity. They found that most projects effectively enhanced or stabilized agricultural productivity: approximately 60% directly boosted productivity, and over 78% achieved either enhancement or stabilization. Crucially, the core driver of productivity improvement was not increased per-unit yield but expanded cultivation area and higher multiple cropping indices. This finding indirectly confirms that land consolidation expands cultivation scale by inhibiting cropland abandonment and activating marginal land. Based on 2024 survey data from 1,125 farmers in Sichuan Province, Xu et al. (2025) employed a Probit model to examine the impact of high-standard farmland construction on farmers' grain cultivation behavior. They found that high-standard farmland construction significantly promotes grain cultivation through five key pathways: facilitating land transfers (including transfers of high-standard farmland itself and driving transfers of surrounding plots), promoting the adoption of agricultural machinery and production services, and directly reducing cropland abandonment rates. The study also revealed that this effect is more pronounced in areas with abundant socialized service resources or flat terrain.

However, while these studies provide literature support for this research, they leave room for further advancement. First, high-standard farmland construction is to some extent a black box, making it difficult to clarify its micro-mechanisms of impact on cropland abandonment. As a macro policy, it typically involves comprehensive projects integrating multiple measures—including water conservancy facilities, land consolidation, road maintenance, and even tenure adjustments. This makes it impossible to isolate the impact of individual measures on cropland abandonment, particularly that of farmland water conservancy project, which is critical for agricultural production. Their specific impact on cropland abandonment remains unclear. Second, strong endogeneity exists between high-standard farmland construction and cropland abandonment, undermining the credibility of estimation results. On one hand, previous studies failed to identify the temporal sequence of these two phenomena, making it difficult to determine causal direction—reverse causality is a prominent issue. On the other hand, these studies primarily rely on cross-sectional data and Probit models, which inevitably suffer from omitted variable bias. Finally, the external validity of previous research is questionable. Current studies on the impact of high-standard farmland construction on cropland abandonment mostly use samples from selected provinces, lacking verification with large-scale, nationally representative data. Moreover, as a macro policy, high-standard farmland construction is often subject to selection bias: theoretically, not all plots can be included, and thus not all farmers can benefit. In contrast, farmland water conservancy project typically features "universal village-wide benefits" with earmarked funds, making them theoretically more inclusive.

In light of these considerations, this study employs panel data from the China Rural Household Panel Survey (CRHPS) and a panel two-way fixed effects model to empirically examine the impact of farmland water conservancy project on farmers' cropland abandonment. Furthermore, the potential marginal contributions of this study are reflected in three aspects: First, it extends the focus from high-standard farmland construction to farmland water conservancy project, directly examining the role of the latter, accurately identifying their impact on cropland abandonment and underlying mechanisms, unpacking the policy black box of high-standard farmland construction, and targeting solutions to the "last mile" challenge in cropland abandonment governance. Second, it leverages the intertemporal matching feature of the survey data—linking village farmland water conservancy project in the previous year to farmers' cropland abandonment in the current year—to avoid potential reverse causality. It also uses a panel two-way fixed effects model to address underlying omitted variable issues, enhancing the credibility of research findings. Third, it fully exploits the advantages of large-scale, nationally representative data to explore the heterogeneity of farmland water conservancy projects' impact on cropland abandonment from both the micro perspective of differences in farmers' resource endowments and the macro perspective of regional economic development disparities. This identifies the conditions under which farmland water conservancy project inhibits cropland abandonment, providing empirical evidence and policy references for promoting effective, context-specific governance of cropland abandonment.

## 8.2 Theoretical Basis and Analytical Framework

Social-Ecological Systems (SES) theory, proposed by Ostrom (1990) in Governing the Commons, originates from research on common-pool resource (CPR) governance. It challenges the pessimistic assumptions of the "tragedy of the commons" and emphasizes cross-scale interactions and dynamic feedback between social and ecological systems (Liu et al., 2024). Cropland abandonment is essentially the result of dynamic interactions between the social system (farmers' decisions, governance strategies) and the ecological system (cropland resources, natural conditions). Its core contradiction lies in the compatibility between the efficiency of public resource governance, farmers' rational decision-making, and the sustainable utilization of cropland. Existing research often focuses on the impact of single factors (e.g., agricultural subsidies) on cropland abandonment, lacking a systematic analysis of the "governance strategy-micro decision-resource status" relationship. Consequently, it struggles to reveal the underlying mechanisms through which farmland water conservancy project inhibits cropland abandonment. Grounded in SES theory, this study integrates the "cost-benefit" analysis paradigm with the "rational smallholder" theory (Schultz, 1964) to construct a chain-interaction framework: "Governance Subsystem (external incentives and constraints)—Actor Subsystem (cost-benefit perception)—Resource Subsystem (cropland utilization equilibrium).” Its intrinsic operational mechanism is as follows:

(1) The Governance Subsystem takes farmland water conservancy project as the core variable, focusing on their incentive and constraint effects derived from the upgraded supply of productive public goods. As an inclusive public policy with earmarked funds, farmland water conservancy project strengthens foundational safeguards: by improving irrigation facilities and optimizing cultivation conditions, they provide stable hydrological and operational environments for agricultural production, forming key external constraints and incentive sources that influence farmers’ cropland utilization decisions.
(2) As core actors in cropland utilization, farmers’ decision-making follows the “rational economic man” hypothesis. Changes in the supply of farmland water conservancy project within the Governance Subsystem systematically reshape the cost-benefit structure of their cropland utilization. This reshaping primarily unfolds through two dimensions—return enhancement and cost reduction—ultimately altering farmers’ behavioral choices. From the perspective of return enhancement, farmland water conservancy project boosts cultivation returns through both direct output gains and economies of scale. First, direct output gains: stable irrigation conditions significantly increase the yield level of high-quality cropland (Prishchepov et al., 2013) and drive growth in output rates (Hao et al., 2024). Second, increasing returns to scale: improved water conservancy infrastructure provides the foundational conditions for agricultural mechanization. The high marginal returns of mechanized operations incentivize farmers to expand cultivation scale (Hayami & Kawagoe, 1989), achieving a cumulative scale effect on returns. From the perspective of cost reduction, water conservancy projects lower cultivation costs through both production and transaction links, effectively addressing labor shortage issues and forming a synergistic effect with return enhancement: At the production cost level, farmland water conservancy project enhances farmers’ willingness to adopt capital-intensive technologies such as mechanized tillage and high-quality seed breeding, fostering a factor substitution effect of capital for labor (Li et al., 2015). At the transaction cost level, farmland water conservancy project reduces information asymmetry, risk premiums, and contract enforcement costs in land transfers by stabilizing cultivation returns and reducing production uncertainty, thereby enhancing farmers’ willingness to participate in land transfers. The superposition of cost reduction and return enhancement further widens the profit gap between cultivation/transfer and abandonment, curbing farmers’ tendency toward cropland abandonment.
(3) From the perspective of the comprehensive effects of farmland water conservancy project, the improved cultivation conditions brought about by such projects will prompt farmers to re-examine the Resource Subsystem, and the increased returns and reduced costs will incentivize them to choose cultivation over cropland abandonment. Meanwhile, due to the improved cultivation

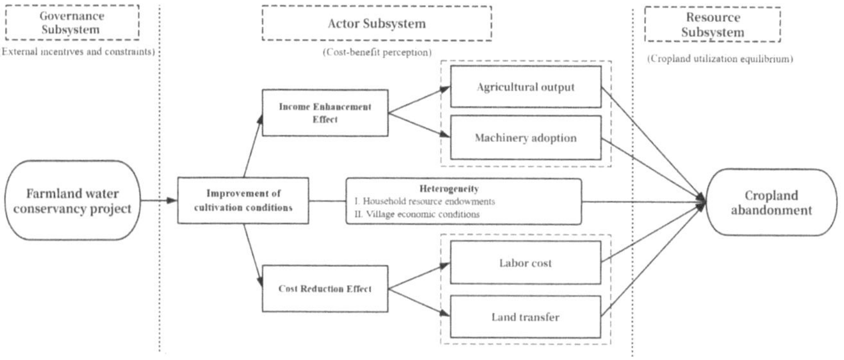


**Fig. 8.1** Analytical framework

conditions, cropland that was previously difficult to transfer and thus had to be abandoned will attract new market demand. As a result, even if farmers do not intend to cultivate their own cropland, others will cultivate it through land transfers.

In summary, as illustrated in Fig. 8.1, farmland water conservancy project theoretically exerts a significant inhibitory effect on farmers' cropland abandonment behavior. Specifically, such projects influence farmers' cropland abandonment decisions through multiple channels, including increasing cropland yield per unit area, facilitating the adoption of agricultural machinery, reducing labor input, and promoting land transfers.

However, in reality, the interactions among the three subsystems may not follow a unidirectional linear transmission but instead form a "positive driving-negative constraining" dynamic: the endowments of the Resource Subsystem and the heterogeneity of the external environment can inversely constrain farmers' cost-benefit perceptions, ultimately leading to differentiated effects of farmland water conservancy project on cropland abandonment. This interactive differentiation effect is specifically reflected in two dimensions: First, differentiation at the farmer level. Farmers' cropland utilization decisions are simultaneously influenced by the interaction between household resource endowments and external contexts, resulting in heterogeneous inhibitory effects of water conservancy facilities on cropland abandonment. Agricultural dependency serves as the core dimension of differentiation: households with higher agricultural dependency have a larger proportion of agricultural income in their income structure, making the impact of cropland returns on household welfare more significant. Consequently, they are more sensitive to the increase in cropland returns brought by improved water conservancy facilities, leading to a more prominent inhibitory effect on cropland abandonment. Heterogeneity also exists in farm size (Fan & Chan-Kang, 2005): smallholder farmers have small and highly fragmented cropland plots, and the improvement of water conservancy facilities can effectively reduce irrigation costs and increase unit yields, thereby alleviating the incentives for cropland abandonment with a more obvious inhibitory effect. In contrast, most large-scale farmers have already realized mechanized cultivation and large-scale operations, with low willingness to abandon cropland, so the inhibitory effect of farmland water conservancy project on their cropland abandonment is limited. Second, differentiation at the regional level. The level of village economic development exerts a moderating effect on the inhibitory effect of farmland water conservancy project on cropland abandonment by changing farmers' opportunity costs and the resource allocation environment. For example, in villages with higher per capita income, off-farm employment opportunities are more abundant, which raises farmers' expectations for non-agricultural income and correspondingly increases the opportunity cost of cropland, potentially weakening the inhibitory effect of the increased cropland returns brought by water conservancy facilities on cropland abandonment. Additionally, the distance from county centers also leads to differences in the effect of inhibiting cropland abandonment: suburban villages benefit from more developed land transfer markets, higher availability of agricultural machinery and socialized services, thus exhibiting a stronger inhibitory effect on cropland abandonment (Li et al., 2024).

## 8.3 Research Design

### *8.3.1 Data Sources*

The data used in this study were sourced from the China Rural Household Panel Survey (CRHPS) database of Zhejiang University, selecting unbalanced panel data covering two waves in 2017 and 2019. As an authoritative micro-database in China's rural research field, CRHPS features a scientific sampling design and extensive sample coverage, providing high-quality data support for studying rural microeconomic behaviors. The survey adopts a stratified, three-stage sampling design proportional to population size (PPS), which can effectively avoid sampling bias; the final sample covers 29 provinces (excluding Hong Kong, Macao, Taiwan, Xinjiang, and Tibet) nationwide, accurately reflecting characteristics at the rural, urban, provincial, and national levels, and endowing the research conclusions with certain generalizability.

To accurately identify the impact of farmland water conservancy project on farmers' cropland abandonment behavior, this study conducted standardized data cleaning with the following steps. First, preliminary screening and merging of data were performed. Since questionnaires before 2017 did not include variables related to the degree of cropland abandonment and the variable of cropland abandonment area had serious missing values, only data from 2017 and 2019 were selected. Second, the research objects were focused on. At the village level, only samples with rural administrative attributes were retained, excluding interfering factors such as land expropriation expectations in areas like urban-rural junctions and distant suburban areas. At the household level, since cropland abandonment is a household decision, only the head-of-household sample was retained for each family, and the age group was controlled to the labor force age range (16–69 years old) to exclude the interference of cropland abandonment caused by capacity constraints on the core relationship. Finally, multi-dimensional characteristics were matched. Variables related to household and village characteristics were matched based on household codes and village codes, and missing values of covariates were uniformly deleted. Ultimately, 20,916 farmer household samples distributed across 29 provinces nationwide were obtained, providing nationally representative microdata support for subsequent empirical analysis.

### 8.3.2 *Variable Selection and Descriptive Statistics*

Drawing on existing literature and aligned with the research theme, the main variables are selected as follows:

(1) Dependent Variable: Cropland abandonment. This binary variable is constructed based on the indicator of the current year's cropland abandonment degree of the surveyed farm households in the original questionnaire: When the household's cropland abandonment degree is 2 (partial abandonment) or 3 (complete abandonment), the household is determined to have the behavior of abandoning cropland, and the variable is assigned a value of 1; otherwise, when the abandonment degree is 1 (no abandonment), the variable is assigned a value of 0 (Zheng, 2024b). This variable directly reflects the actual state of farmers' cropland utilization. In this study, households with cropland abandonment behavior accounted for 9.9% of the total sample, while non-abandonment samples accounted for 90.1%. The overall characteristics are consistent with micro-survey data such as the China Labor-force Dynamics Survey (CLDS) and the China Social Survey (CSS) (Chen et al., 2025), which further verifies the representativeness of the sample and the quality of the data.
(2) Core Independent Variable: Farmland water conservancy project. This variable is derived from the responses of surveyed village cadres in the original questionnaire regarding whether the village has undertaken farmland water conservancy project since 2016, and it is also a binary discrete variable. Since the survey inquired about farmland water conservancy project from the previous year and the data used in this study begins in 2017, the variable is assigned a value of 1 if the village undertook such project since 2016, and 0 otherwise. In this study, approximately 32.8% of villages nationwide carried out farmland water conservancy project during the observation period.
(3) Control Variables: To mitigate the problem of omitted variables, this study refers to the practice of Zheng et al. (2023a) and selects control variables at three levels to further control other factors affecting farmers' cropland abandonment behavior. Specifically, the control variables at the household head level include the household head's age (sample distributed between 16 and 69 years old,

with an average of 51.83), marital status, health status, and education level (Dabara & Chiwuzie, 2022; Zheng, 2024b); the control variables at the household level include the household dependency ratio (non-working-age population/working-age population), per capita household cropland area, household off-farm employment status (ratio of members engaged in off-farm work), and the logarithm of total household income (Peng et al., 2021; Xu et al., 2019); the control variables at the village level include variables reflecting village economic characteristics, such as the logarithm of village per capita income and the number of new types of business entities in the village (Vaz et al., 2023; Zheng et al., 2025; Zheng, 2024a). The above variables cover individual, household, and village-level factors affecting farmers' decisions on cropland abandonment. Additionally, the definitions and descriptions of the above-mentioned variables are presented in Table 8.1.

### 8.3.3 Empirical Strategy

Given the panel data characteristics of the research sample, this study employs a two-way fixed effects (TWFE) model for estimation. This approach controls for time-invariant individual fixed effects and time-specific fixed effects common to all cross-sectional units, thereby effectively mitigating potential omitted variable issues. Specifically, the econometric model is specified as follows.

$$Abandonment_{vit} = \beta_0 + \beta_1 FWCP_{vt\text{-}1} + \gamma \boldsymbol{X}_{vit,t\text{-}1} + \sigma_i + \varphi_t + \mu_{vit} \tag{8.1}$$

where the subscript $i$ represents the head of the farm household, $t$ denotes the survey year, and $v$ indicates the village where the household resides. *Abandonment* is a binary variable, where 1 indicates that the farm household has engaged in cropland abandonment behavior, and 0 indicates otherwise. *FWCP* (Farmland Water Conservancy Project) is a dummy variable indicating whether the village where the household resides has implemented a farmland water conservancy project since 2016. It takes a value of 1 if such a project was carried out, and 0 otherwise. $\boldsymbol{X}$ is a vector of control variables as mentioned earlier, primarily including characteristics at the individual, household, and village levels that may simultaneously affect both the implementation of farmland water conservancy project and cropland abandonment behavior. $\beta_0$ is the constant term; $\beta_1$ and $\gamma$ are the coefficients to be estimated; $\sigma_i$ represents household-fixed effects, which control for time-invariant differences across farm households; $\varphi_t$ represents time-specific fixed effects, which eliminate unobserved factors common to all farm households in a given year; and $\mu_{vit}$ is the random error term capturing other unobserved and unexplained shocks.

**Table 8.1** Variable definition and descriptive statistics ($N = 20{,}916$)

| Variables | Definition | Mean | SD | Min | Max |
|---|---|---|---|---|---|
| Abandonment behavior | Whether farm households abandon cropland (yes = 1, no = 0) | 0.099 | 0.299 | 0 | 1 |
| Abandonment degree | Degree of cropland abandonment: None = 1, partial = 2, complete = 3 | 1.151 | 0.480 | 1 | 3 |
| FWCP | Whether the village has undertaken farmland water conservancy project since 2016 (yes = 1, no = 0) | 0.328 | 0.469 | 0 | 1 |
| Age | Age of household head | 51.830 | 12.590 | 16 | 69 |
| Marriage | Marital Status: Married = 1, unmarried = 0 | 0.845 | 0.361 | 0 | 1 |
| Health | Physical status: Very good = 1, good = 2, average = 3, bad = 4, very bad = 5 | 2.816 | 1.057 | 1 | 5 |
| Education | Educational level: Illiteracy = 1, primary school = 2, junior high school = 3, senior high school = 4, vocational high school = 5, junior college = 6, bachelor = 7, master or above = 8 | 2.679 | 1.153 | 1 | 8 |
| Dependency ratio | Ratio of children and the elderly members (0—1) | 0.352 | 0.481 | 0 | 5 |
| Off-farm employment | Ratio of members engaged in off-farm work (0—1) | 0.245 | 0.275 | 0 | 1 |
| Land size | Household cropland area per capita (mu) | 2.310 | 3.360 | 0 | 15 |
| Household income | Logarithm of total household income (yuan) | 10.030 | 1.467 | 0 | 15.2 |
| Village economy | Logarithm of village per capita income (yuan) | 8.809 | 1.002 | 0 | 11.51 |
| Village agriculture | Number of new agricultural operating entities in villages (e.g., family farms, farming companies, etc.) | 3.801 | 5.826 | 0 | 41 |

*Note* 1 mu = 1/15 hectare

## 8.4 Empirical Results

### 8.4.1 Baseline Results

As mentioned above, we employ a two-way fixed effects (TWFE) model to identify the impact of farmland water conservancy project (FWCP) on cropland abandonment. Table 8.2 presents the corresponding benchmark regression results. Column (1) includes only the core independent variable (FWCP), household-fixed effects, and time-fixed effects. Building on this, columns (2), (3), and (4) sequentially incorporate control variables reflecting individual, household, and village characteristics, respectively. Across all four models, regardless of the inclusion of control variables, the absolute value of the FWCP coefficient remains stable between 0.073 and 0.075, with statistical significance at the 1% level ($p < 0.01$). This indicates that village-level farmland water conservancy project reduces the probability of cropland abandonment by approximately 7.4% points, exerting a significant inhibitory effect on cropland abandonment. Furthermore, as the TWFE model fully controls for household- and time-fixed effects, it effectively eliminates interference from unobservable factors—such as time-invariant household characteristics and year-specific shocks. Consequently, the inhibitory effect of such projects on cropland abandonment demonstrates robust reliability, consistent with theoretical expectations.

Regarding control variables, from the perspective of household head characteristics, rural population aging and the consequent decline in health status are significant drivers of cropland abandonment ($p < 0.01$). This aligns with the findings of Zhang et al. (2014), suggesting that older or less healthy household heads exhibit significantly reduced farming capacity and willingness to invest in production, thereby directly increasing the probability of cropland abandonment. At the household level, the coefficient of per capita cropland area is significantly positive. This result confirms that labor shortages impose direct constraints on land utilization, as insufficient labor directly leads to the abandonment of some marginal croplands (Zheng et al., 2023a). Amid rising agricultural opportunity costs, households typically prioritize cultivating more productive plots while neglecting marginal lands that are remote or less fertile, ultimately forcing these plots into fallow. Additionally, other control variables are not the primary focus of this study and are omitted due to space limitations.

### 8.4.2 Robustness Check

To ensure the robustness of the previously presented estimation results, as shown in Table 8.3, this study conducts robustness tests using three methods.

First, to eliminate the impact of measurement bias, we replace the dependent variable—originally a dummy variable for "whether farm households abandon cropland"—with an ordinal categorical variable for "degree of cropland abandonment" (1 = not abandoned, 2 = partially abandoned, 3 = completely abandoned). The results

**Table 8.2** FWCP and cropland abandonment: Benchmark regression

| | Dependent variable: Whether farm households abandon cropland | | | |
|---|---|---|---|---|
| | (1) | (2) | (3) | (4) |
| FWCP | −0.073***<br>(0.025) | −0.074***<br>(0.025) | −0.075***<br>(0.025) | −0.075***<br>(0.025) |
| Age | | 0.043***<br>(0.004) | 0.042***<br>(0.004) | 0.041***<br>(0.005) |
| Marriage | | 0.074**<br>(0.035) | 0.076**<br>(0.035) | 0.076**<br>(0.035) |
| Health | | 0.020***<br>(0.006) | 0.021***<br>(0.006) | 0.021***<br>(0.006) |
| Education | | −0.001<br>(0.010) | −0.002<br>(0.010) | −0.002<br>(0.010) |
| Dependency ratio | | | −0.020<br>(0.018) | −0.019<br>(0.018) |
| Off-farm employment | | | 0.037<br>(0.027) | 0.037<br>(0.027) |
| Land size | | | 0.006***<br>(0.002) | 0.006***<br>(0.002) |
| Household income | | | 0.000<br>(0.004) | 0.000<br>(0.004) |
| Village economy | | | | −0.011<br>(0.007) |
| Village agriculture | | | | 0.000<br>(0.001) |
| Household-fixed effect | Yes | Yes | Yes | Yes |
| Time-fixed effect | Yes | Yes | Yes | Yes |
| Obs | 20,916 | 20,916 | 20,916 | 20,916 |
| R-squared | 0.890 | 0.891 | 0.891 | 0.891 |

*Notes* ***, **, and * denote significance at the 1%, 5%, and 10% levels, respectively; Robust standard errors, clustered at the household level, are shown in parentheses

in column (1) show that the coefficient of the farmland water conservancy project variable is −0.106, which is significantly negative at the 5% level. This indicates that the core conclusion is largely unaffected by the measurement method of the dependent variable, and the negative relationship between farmland water conservancy project and cropland abandonment persists.

Second, considering the potential correlation of random disturbance terms among farmers within the same village, we further adjust the clustering level from the household to the village level. The results in column (2) show that after adjusting the clustering level, there is no substantial change in either the economic significance or statistical significance of the core explanatory variable. Farmland water conservancy

**Table 8.3** FWCP and cropland abandonment: Robustness checks

| | Redefining Y | Adjusting the cluster | Adding variable |
|---|---|---|---|
| | (1) | (2) | (3) |
| FWCP | −0.106**<br>(0.041) | −0.075**<br>(0.034) | −0.086***<br>(0.028) |
| Control variables | Yes | Yes | Yes |
| Household-fixed effect | Yes | Yes | Yes |
| Time-fixed effect | Yes | Yes | Yes |
| Province × Time-fixed effect | No | No | Yes |
| Obs | 20,916 | 20,916 | 20,916 |
| R-squared | 0.892 | 0.891 | 0.892 |

*Notes* ***, **, and * denote significance at the 1%, 5%, and 10% levels, respectively; Robust standard errors, clustered at the household level, are shown in parentheses

project still plays a positive role in reducing farmers' cropland abandonment, which reaffirms the stability of the estimation results.

Finally, to rule out potential interference from factors that vary simultaneously across provinces and over time—such as provincial land policies and weather conditions (Ward & Shively, 2015)—we further incorporate province-time cross fixed effects into Eq. (8.1). As shown in column (3), under this stricter fixed-effect specification, the negative impact of farmland water conservancy project remains statistically significant. This indicates that even when considering the interference of potential spatio-temporal confounding factors, farmland water conservancy project still helps reduce farmers' cropland abandonment.

The above results show that across the three robustness tests, the core finding that farmland water conservancy project can significantly reduce the probability of cropland abandonment holds true in an empirical sense. This indicates that the conclusion will not change due to variations in indicator measurement, clustering levels, and omitted variables, demonstrating strong reliability. It further supports the positive role of village-level farmland water conservancy project in promoting the sustainable utilization of cropland.

### *8.4.3 Endogeneity Discussion*

Overall, the endogeneity issues faced in this study are likely relatively weak. On one hand, the core independent variable used in this study—village-level farmland water conservancy project in the year preceding the survey—is relatively exogenous. Strictly speaking, decisions on village-level farmland water conservancy project typically depend on regional agricultural development plans and fiscal support capacity, and are highly unlikely to be influenced by farmers' cropland abandonment behavior in the current year. In other words, there is theoretically no significant reverse causality between farmland water conservancy project and farmers' cropland abandonment decisions. On the other hand, the TWFE model employed in this study has effectively controlled for unobservable factors at the household and time levels, significantly reducing omitted variable bias, including those related to farmer capabilities, preferences, and macro policies. The stability of the previous regression results further corroborates the reliability of the conclusions: in the benchmark regression, as control variables were progressively added, the impact coefficient of the core independent variable remained consistently stable within the range of −0.073 to −0.075; in the robustness tests, the coefficient after adjusting the clustering level was −0.075, and the coefficient after incorporating province-time cross fixed effects was −0.086. There were no substantial changes in the absolute values of the coefficients or their statistical significance, indicating that the interference of omitted variable issues on the estimation results is minimal.

### 8.4.4 Mechanism Test

Previous findings have demonstrated that farmland water conservancy project significantly reduces the probability of farmers' cropland abandonment. As theoretically analyzed, does this imply that farmland water conservancy project reshapes the cost-benefit structure of agricultural operators through channels such as increased agricultural output, adoption of agricultural machinery, reduced labor input, and promotion of land transfer, thereby curbing farmers' cropland abandonment behavior? To address this question, we use agricultural output, agricultural machinery adoption, labor input, and land transfer as the dependent variables respectively, and continue to employ the TWFE model to identify the mechanism through which farmland water conservancy project affects cropland abandonment. Detailed results are presented in Table 8.4.

As shown in column (1), farmland water conservancy project exhibits a significantly positive impact on agricultural output. Compared with villages that have not carried out farmland water conservancy projects, the average agricultural output per mu in villages that have implemented such projects increases by 11.6%, and this estimate is statistically significant at the 1% level. This is aligned with the research of Gatti et al. (2021), indicating that farmland water conservancy project effectively improves cropland production efficiency by optimizing cultivation conditions. Furthermore, the increase in output per unit area reduces the probability of farmers abandoning cropland.

The estimation in Column (2) shows that farmland water conservancy project has a significantly positive impact on farmers' adoption of agricultural machinery, increasing the average value of per mu agricultural machinery investment by 10.5%. This result is basically consistent with the findings of Nguyen and Warr (2020), implying that improved farmland water conservancy supporting facilities provide necessary conditions for agricultural mechanization operations, thereby helping farmers increase economic returns through large-scale cultivation. In turn, the

**Table 8.4** FWCP and cropland abandonment: Mechanism analysis

| | Agricultural output | Machinery adoption | Labor cost | Land transfer |
|---|---|---|---|---|
| | (1) | (2) | (3) | (4) |
| FWCP | 0.116***<br>(0.028) | 0.105***<br>(0.029) | 0.038*<br>(0.020) | 0.006***<br>(0.002) |
| Control variables | Yes | Yes | Yes | Yes |
| Observations | 8,844 | 7,865 | 11,788 | 17,789 |
| R-squared | 0.198 | 0.121 | 0.483 | 0.157 |

Notes: ***, **, and * denote significance at the 1%, 5%, and 10% levels, respectively; Robust standard errors, clustered at the household level, are shown in parentheses; Agricultural output (yield per mu) and agricultural machinery adoption (per mu machinery investment value) are both expressed in logarithmic form to reflect elastic relationships between variables. Labor input specifically refers to the per mu labor force, encompassing both hired workers and household-owned labor. Land transfer here specifically denotes the act of farmers transferring cultivated land to new types of business entities, provided that the transfer year is ≥ the survey year. This ensures that only land transfers occurring after the completion of farmland water conservancy project are counted, thereby identifying the causal effect of farmland water conservancy on land transfer decisions

increased economic returns brought by mechanization encourage farmers to choose cultivation rather than abandon cropland.

It can be found from the estimation results in column (3) that farmland water conservancy project significantly increases farmers' agricultural labor input. This differs from the findings of Nguyen and Warr (2020), and the possible reason is that farmland water conservancy project improves cultivation conditions, enhance farmers' enthusiasm for production investment, and prompt farmers who originally planned to abandon cropland to choose to resume cultivation, thereby increasing the supply of agricultural labor.

Estimates from column (4) indicate that farmland water conservancy project significantly enhances the probability of farmers transferring out cropland by 0.6%. A plausible explanation is that farmland water conservancy project improves cultivation conditions, promotes contiguous land consolidation, thereby reducing agricultural production costs and transaction costs (Ito et al., 2016; Leimer et al., 2022), and attracting more land transferees. As a result, cropland that was previously forced to be abandoned due to transfer difficulties can be reused, and the probability of cropland abandonment is correspondingly reduced.

### *8.4.5 Heterogeneity Analysis*

Affected by individual farmers' characteristics and the environments of their respective villages, the impact of farmland water conservancy project on cropland abandonment may not be homogeneous in practice but rather exhibit significant heterogeneity. Intuitively, potential moderating factors can be categorized into two main types: (1)

Differences in resource endowments at the household level, such as the degree of family agricultural dependence and the scale of cropland operation; (2) Differences in economic conditions at the village level, such as the level of village economic development and the geographical location of the village. Building on this, this section will integrate the theoretical analysis presented earlier and, from the perspective of the feedback effect of the Resource Subsystem on the Actor Subsystem, and empirically reveal the heterogeneity of the impact of farmland water conservancy project on cropland abandonment.

#### 8.4.5.1 Heterogeneity at the Household Level

Regarding household resource endowments, households were divided into a higher and a lower agricultural dependence group based on whether the proportion of agricultural laborers in the household exceeded the median of the full sample. They were also categorized into a smallholder group and a large-scale farmer group according to whether the household's cropland area exceeded the median of the full sample. The relevant estimation results are presented in Table 8.5.

The results in columns (1) and (2) show that the estimated coefficient of farmland water conservancy project on cropland abandonment is significantly negative for households with higher agricultural dependence, while it is not significant for those with lower dependence. A plausible explanation is that households with higher agricultural dependence have a close binding between their livelihoods and agricultural production, making them more sensitive to improvements in production conditions (Liu et al., 2023); in contrast, households with lower agricultural dependence are more likely to obtain income through off-farm employment, resulting in a higher opportunity cost of agricultural production. The increase in agricultural returns brought by improved farmland water conservancy is difficult to effectively

**Table 8.5** FWCP and cropland abandonment: Household heterogeneity

| | Dependent variable: Whether farm households abandon cropland | | | |
|---|---|---|---|---|
| | Agricultural dependency | | Farm size | |
| | (1) Higher | (2) Lower | (3) Large-scale | (4) Smallholder |
| FWCP | −0.087**<br>(0.037) | −0.046<br>(0.047) | −0.001<br>(0.034) | −0.155***<br>(0.040) |
| Control variables | Yes | Yes | Yes | Yes |
| Household-fixed effect | Yes | Yes | Yes | Yes |
| Time-fixed effect | Yes | Yes | Yes | Yes |
| Obs | 10,119 | 10,293 | 10,296 | 10,473 |
| R-squared | 0.932 | 0.910 | 0.926 | 0.935 |

*Notes* ***, **, and * denote significance at the 1%, 5%, and 10% levels, respectively; Robust standard errors, clustered at the household level, are shown in parentheses

change their agricultural operation decisions, hence the effect of inhibiting abandonment is relatively weak. Columns (3) and (4) indicate that the estimated coefficient of farmland water conservancy project on cropland abandonment is insignificant for large-scale farmers, while the coefficient is significantly negative for smallholder farmers with less cropland. This phenomenon can be partially explained as follows: large-scale farmers usually have relatively complete production supporting conditions, and the level of cropland abandonment is inherently low, so the marginal effect brought by improved farmland water conservancy is limited; in contrast, smallholder farmers' cropland is characterized by high fragmentation and great potential for yield improvement. The improvement of farmland water conservancy facilities can solve the irrigation difficulties of scattered plots, effectively reduce irrigation costs, and thus form a stronger inhibitory effect on cropland abandonment. This result also indirectly confirms the inclusive value of farmland water conservancy project in land conservation, providing important support for curbing cropland abandonment among smallholder farmers.

#### 8.4.5.2 Heterogeneity at the Village Level

Concerning village economic conditions, villages were categorized into economically developed and economically underdeveloped groups based on whether their per capita income exceeded the median of the full sample. Villages were further classified into remote suburban and suburban villages according to whether their distance from the county seat exceeded the median of the full sample. The corresponding estimation results are presented in Table 8.6.

Results in columns (1) and (2) indicate that, affected by the level of village economic development, the inhibitory effect of farmland water conservancy project on cropland abandonment is more pronounced in economically underdeveloped

**Table 8.6** FWCP and cropland abandonment: Village heterogeneity

| | Dependent variable: Whether farm households abandon cropland | | | |
|---|---|---|---|---|
| | Village economy | | Village location | |
| | (1) Developed | (2) Underdeveloped | (3) Exurban | (4) Suburban |
| FWCP | −0.014<br>(0.030) | −0.111*<br>(0.059) | −0.024<br>(0.033) | −0.166***<br>(0.042) |
| Control variables | Yes | Yes | Yes | Yes |
| Household-fixed effect | Yes | Yes | Yes | Yes |
| Time-fixed effect | Yes | Yes | Yes | Yes |
| Obs | 10,443 | 9,615 | 8,134 | 10,119 |
| R-squared | 0.920 | 0.877 | 0.883 | 0.932 |

*Notes* ***, **, and * denote significance at the 1%, 5%, and 10% levels, respectively; Robust standard errors, clustered at the household level, are shown in parentheses

villages. A possible explanation for this phenomenon is that in economically developed villages, even if farmland water conservancy project increases agricultural income, this income may still be lower than the opportunity cost of farmers engaging in non-agricultural industries. In such cases, farmers still tend to choose high-return off-farm employment, thereby weakening the inhibitory effect of farmland water conservancy project on cropland abandonment. In contrast, in economically underdeveloped villages, the increase in agricultural income brought by improved farmland water conservancy facilities is more likely to exceed costs, effectively curbing cropland abandonment. Estimates in columns (3) and (4) indicate that compared with remote suburban villages, farmland water conservancy project has a more obvious inhibitory effect on cropland abandonment in suburban villages. This may be because the agricultural socialized service system in suburban villages is usually more advanced, and the land transfer market is also more active. In this case, the improvement of farmland water conservancy facilities not only complements the existing socialized services to further reduce agricultural production costs but also optimizes cultivation conditions, attracting more agricultural operators to transfer-in land, thereby indirectly reducing cropland abandonment.

## 8.5 Extended Analysis

The preceding analysis has confirmed the effectiveness of farmland water conservancy project in curbing cropland abandonment. However, the validity of this proposition largely rests on the universal benefit nature of such projects—that is, farmland water conservancy project can basically cover all households or plots in a village. If, in reality, these projects only benefit a small number of households or plots, they will further widen the gap in cultivation conditions between prime cropland and marginal cropland. Under such circumstances, farmers typically allocate more household resources to prime cropland rather than marginal cropland. Moreover, when the net return of marginal cropland is lower than the opportunity cost of alternative choices such as off-farm employment for farmers, farmers may even choose to abandon marginal cropland and switch to non-agricultural employment instead. This indicates that farmland water conservancy project does not necessarily promote the effective governance of cropland abandonment, but may even exacerbate it (Bavorová et al., 2023).

To verify the validity of this competing hypothesis, constrained by the inaccessibility of plot-level data, we attempt to use three proxy variables—variance of village land area, number of plots, and village terrain—to indirectly reflect marginal cropland. We then employ a panel moderating effect model to examine the differences in the impact of farmland water conservancy project on cropland abandonment across plots with varying degrees of differentiation. Specifically, first, the variance of village land area is mainly measured by the difference between the maximum and minimum contracted land areas of all households in the village; a larger variance indicates that there are plots with extremely small areas in the village, which are more likely to become marginal cropland. Second, the number of plots is directly represented by the number of plots operated by the household; under China's Household Responsibility System, the land area per household is roughly equivalent, so a larger number of plots usually means more potential marginal cropland for the household. Finally, village terrain is a dummy variable, assigned a value of 1 if it is mountainous and 0 if it is plain. Generally speaking, due to restricted cultivation conditions, cropland in mountainous areas and other terrains is more likely to become marginal cropland.

Table 8.7 reports the estimation results for the competing hypothesis. Column (1) shows that the estimated coefficient of farmland water conservancy project is significantly negative, while the coefficient of its interaction term with the range of village land area is insignificant. This indicates that farmland water conservancy project indeed helps curb cropland abandonment, and after the implementation of village-level farmland water conservancy project, there is no phenomenon where marginal plots experience exacerbated cropland abandonment due to their size disadvantage. Column (2) shows that the estimated coefficient of farmland water conservancy project is significantly negative, but the interaction term between it and the number of household plots fails to pass the significance test. This also largely rules out the possibility that households with multiple plots exacerbate cropland abandonment due to the high management costs of marginal plots. Column (3) estimates reveal that the coefficient of farmland water conservancy project is insignificant, while the coefficient of its interaction term with mountainous areas is significantly negative. This indicates that the inhibitory effect of farmland water conservancy project on cropland abandonment is stronger in mountainous areas. This result not only rejects the hypothesis of exacerbated marginal plot abandonment but also shows that due to the improvement of farmland water conservancy facilities, the inhibitory effect on cropland abandonment is even more prominent for cropland in mountainous areas. In summary, the competing hypothesis that farmland water conservancy project exacerbates marginal plot abandonment has not received empirical support. It is evident that farmland water conservancy project has universal benefits, directly improving the cultivation conditions of all cropland; even the inherent disadvantages of remote locations and poor quality are partially mitigated through the improvement of water conservancy facilities, enabling the net return of farmers cultivating marginal plots to remain above the threshold that ensures cropland is not abandoned. Therefore, the research finding that farmland water conservancy project helps curb cropland abandonment is robust, and its positive value in land conservation and sustainable land utilization should be highly prioritized in the future.

**Table 8.7** FWCP and cropland abandonment: Extended analysis

| | Dependent variable: Whether farm households abandon cropland | | |
|---|---|---|---|
| | (1) | (2) | (3) |
| FWCP | −0.077***<br>(0.026) | −0.072*<br>(0.038) | −0.025<br>(0.029) |
| FWCP × Variance of village land area | 0.000<br>(0.000) | | |
| FWCP × Number of plots | | 0.001<br>(0.002) | |
| FWCP × Village terrain | | | −0.089*<br>(0.047) |
| Control variables | Yes | Yes | Yes |
| Household-fixed effect | Yes | Yes | Yes |
| Time-fixed effect | Yes | Yes | Yes |
| Obs | 20,916 | 16,249 | 17,971 |
| R-squared | 0.016 | 0.018 | 0.017 |

*Notes* ***, **, and * denote significance at the 1%, 5%, and 10% levels, respectively; Robust standard errors, clustered at the household level, are shown in parentheses

## 8.6 Conclusions and Policy Implications

### *8.6.1 Conclusions*

Ensuring food security is a shared concern for all nations worldwide. Strengthening farmland protection oriented toward food security provides critical support for sustainable agricultural development. In farmland conservation efforts, apart from focusing on issues such as cropland non-agriculturization and cropland non-grain cultivation, the problem of cropland abandonment highlighted in the process of urbanization and industrialization also deserves attention. Compared with macro policies such as high-standard farmland construction, farmland water conservancy project has more prominent advantages in improving cultivation conditions due to its extensive coverage, and theoretically helps curb the expansion of farmers' cropland abandonment. Based on the unbalanced panel data from the 2017 and 2019 waves of the China Rural Household Panel Survey (CRHPS), this study empirically examines the impact of farmland water conservancy project on farmers' cropland abandonment behavior, and obtains the following key findings:

First, farmland water conservancy project exerts a significant positive effect in curbing farmers' cropland abandonment. Empirical results indicate that farmland water conservancy project can effectively reduce cropland abandonment, lowering the probability of farmers' cropland abandonment by approximately 7.4%. This provides a practical policy tool for farmland protection and food security guarantee.

Second, enhancing agricultural returns and reducing agricultural costs constitute the core mechanisms through which farmland water conservancy project curbs cropland abandonment. Specifically, due to the improvement of cultivation conditions, farmland water conservancy project can, on the one hand, increase agricultural production returns through pathways such as improving agricultural output and promoting the adoption of agricultural machinery, thereby enhancing farmers' enthusiasm for agricultural production; on the other hand, it can effectively reduce agricultural production costs and transaction costs, facilitate land transfer, and significantly reduce the possibility of farmers' cropland abandonment.

Third, the impact of farmland water conservancy project on cropland abandonment is also moderated by farmers' resource endowments and regional external conditions. Specifically, this effect is more pronounced among farmer groups with high agricultural dependency and small-scale operations, and is also more obvious in villages with lower per capita income and closer proximity to county centers. This provides important references for the targeted implementation of policies.

### 8.6.2 Policy Implications

The findings of this study carry significant policy implications. The valuable experience from China can provide decision-making references for other countries also facing the problem of cropland abandonment.

First, focus on farmland water conservancy project and synergistically improve the policy system. The problem of cropland abandonment is particularly prominent in marginal cropland, and the improvement level of farmland water conservancy facilities directly determines the cultivation value of such cropland. Compared with previous macro policies, farmland water conservancy project has a wider coverage and is easier to implement. However, during the implementation process, it is necessary to strengthen the policy synergy effect, synchronously plan and advance farmland water conservancy project with projects such as land leveling, high-standard farmland renovation, and field road hardening, systematically improve cultivation conditions, and reduce the farming difficulty for farmers and the threshold for land transfer.

Second, block the occurrence conditions of cropland abandonment and optimize the cost-benefit structure. The core of whether farmland water conservancy project can effectively curb cropland abandonment lies in building a cultivation ecosystem characterized by "high returns and low costs." In the future, it is necessary to take farmland water conservancy project as the starting point, make synergistic efforts from two directions of improving agricultural returns and reducing agricultural costs, and economically block the incentives for cropland abandonment. In terms of improving returns, relying on water conservancy guarantees to improve socialized services, integrate resources such as agricultural machinery leasing and land cultivation services, solve technical problems of smallholder farmers, and encourage the development of high-efficiency agriculture by virtue of water conservancy advantages. In terms of cost control, on the one hand, improve the level of mechanization through technological empowerment to reduce unit output costs; on the other hand, build regional cropland transfer service platforms to reduce the management costs and transfer concerns of farmers caused by scattered plots and labor shortages, and encourage them to transfer cropland to new business entities such as professional cooperatives and large-scale grain producers through entrusted operation, equity participation and dividend sharing.

Third, implement targeted construction strategies based on local conditions and household characteristics. The governance of cropland abandonment is a systematic project that needs to avoid the limitations of a single restrictive policy. It is necessary to establish a differentiated policy combination centered on farmland water conservancy project, integrating public product empowerment with incentive guidance, so as to achieve "adjusting measures to local conditions and formulating policies according to households." For smallholder farmers, subsidize agricultural machinery operations, carry out water conservancy technical training and subsidize facility upgrades to reduce the threshold for use; when new business entities take over marginal cropland, provide special subsidies for water-saving facilities to support large-scale operations. In areas with better economic conditions, relying on technological advantages, on the basis of improving farmland water conservancy facilities, focus on developing intelligent irrigation systems, integrate digital agricultural service resources, and further improve the utilization efficiency and income effect of farmland water conservancy facilities; in areas with weak economic foundations and major grain-producing areas, while promoting the construction of small-scale farmland water conservancy facilities, it is necessary to increase financial transfer payments, and finally achieve the dual goals of ensuring food security and improving agricultural operation efficiency, and promote the organic unity of sustainable agricultural development and food security guarantee.

## References

Abolina, E., & Luzadis, V. A. (2015). Abandoned agricultural land and its potential for short rotation woody crops in Latvia. *Land Use Policy, 49*, 435–445.

Bavorová, M., Ullah, A., Nyendu, D., & Prishchepov, A. V. (2023). Determinants of farmland abandonment in the urban-rural fringe of Ghana. *Regional Environmental Change, 23*, 122.

Ben Hassen, T., & El Bilali, H. (2022). Impacts of the Russia-Ukraine war on global food security: Towards more sustainable and resilient food systems? *Foods, 11*, 2301.

Besley, T. (1995). Property rights and investment incentives: Theory and evidence from Ghana. *Journal of Political Economy, 103*, 903–937.

Chen, M., Han, Q., Zhang, C., & Chen, J. (2025). Valuing the effect of Capital goes to countryside on cropland abandonment: Evidence from rural China. *Habitat International, 156*, Article 103299.

Dabara, D. I., & Chiwuzie, A. (2022). Female-Led agrarian households and the question of sustainable land and food security in an emerging economy: Evidence from Tula Baule. *Habitat International, 120*, Article 102512.

Deininger, K., & Jin, S. (2006). Tenure security and land-related investment: Evidence from Ethiopia. *European Economic Review, 50*, 1245–1277.
Deininger, K., Savastano, S., & Carletto, C. (2012). Land fragmentation, cropland abandonment, and land market operation in Albania. *World Development, 40*, 2108–2122.
Deng, X., Xu, D., Zeng, M., & Qi, Y. (2019). Does internet use help reduce rural cropland abandonment? Evidence from China. *Land Use Policy, 89*, Article 104243.
Du, X., Zhang, X., & Jin, X. (2018). Assessing the effectiveness of land consolidation for improving agricultural productivity in China. *Land Use Policy, 70*, 360–367.
Estel, S., Kuemmerle, T., Alcántara, C., Levers, C., Prishchepov, A., & Hostert, P. (2015). Mapping farmland abandonment and recultivation across Europe using MODIS NDVI time series. *Remote Sensing of Environment, 163*, 312–325.
Fan, S., & Chan-Kang, C. (2005). Is small beautiful? Farm size, productivity, and poverty in Asian agriculture. *Agricultural Economics, 32*, 135–146.
Fanzo, J., Haddad, L., Schneider, K. R., Béné, C., Covic, N. M., Guarin, A., Herforth, A. W., Herrero, M., Sumaila, U. R., & Aburto, N. J. (2021). Rigorous monitoring is necessary to guide food system transformation in the countdown to the 2030 global goals. *Food Policy, 104*, Article 102163.
Fayet, C. M., Reilly, K. H., Van Ham, C., & Verburg, P. H. (2022). What is the future of abandoned agricultural lands? A systematic review of alternative trajectories in Europe. *Land Use Policy, 112*, Article 105833.
Gatti, N., Baylis, K., & Crost, B. (2021). Can irrigation infrastructure mitigate the effect of rainfall shocks on conflict? Evidence from Indonesia. *American Journal of Agricultural Economics, 103*, 211–231.
Gebru, M., Holden, S. T., & Tilahun, M. (2019). Tenants' land access in the rental market: Evidence from northern Ethiopia. *Agricultural Economics, 50*, 291–302.
Gou, F., Liang, W., Liu, Y., Fu, B., Wang, Z., Zhang, W., Chen, Z., Yan, J., Li, J., & Lv, Y. (2025). Large-scale ecological infrastructures enhance the productivity of agro-socio-ecological systems by reducing soil erosion in the Loess Plateau. *Journal of Environmental Management, 373*, Article 123751.
Guo, A., Yue, W., Yang, J., Xue, B., Xiao, W., Li, M., He, T., Zhang, M., Jin, X., & Zhou, Q. (2023). Cropland abandonment in China: Patterns, drivers, and implications for food security. *Journal of Cleaner Production, 418*, Article 138154.
Hao, S., Wang, G., Yang, Y., Zhao, S., Huang, S., Liu, L., & Zhang, H. (2024). Promoting grain production through high-standard farmland construction: Evidence in China. *Journal of Integrative Agriculture, 23*, 324–335.
Hayami, Y., & Kawagoe, T. (1989). Farm mechanization, scale economies and polarization: The Japanese experience. *Journal of Development Economics, 31*, 221–239.
Ito, J., Nishikori, M., Toyoshi, M., & Feuer, H. N. (2016). The contribution of land exchange institutions and markets in countering farmland abandonment in Japan. *Land Use Policy, 57*, 582–593.
Ivanic, M., & Martin, W. (2008). Implications of higher global food prices for poverty in low-income countries 1. *Agricultural Economics, 39*, 405–416.
Koren, O. (2018). Food abundance and violent conflict in Africa. *American Journal of Agricultural Economics, 100*, 981–1006.
Leimer, K., Levers, C., Sun, Z., & Müller, D. (2022). Market proximity and irrigation infrastructure determine farmland rentals in Sichuan Province, China. *Journal of Rural Studies, 94*, 375–384.
Li, R., Chen, J., & Xu, D. (2024). The impact of agricultural socialized service on grain production: Evidence from rural China. *Agriculture, 14*, 785.
Li, Y., Long, H., & Liu, Y. (2015). Spatio-temporal pattern of China's rural development: A rurality index perspective. *Journal of Rural Studies, 38*, 12–26.
Lichtenberg, E., & Ding, C. (2008). Assessing farmland protection policy in China. *Land Use Policy, 25*, 59–68.

Liu, J., Fang, Y., Wang, G., Liu, B., & Wang, R. (2023). The aging of farmers and its challenges for labor-intensive agriculture in China: A perspective on farmland transfer plans for farmers' retirement. *Journal of Rural Studies, 100*, Article 103013.

Liu, L., Wang, L. J., Ma, S., Hao, Y., Hu, H., & Jiang, J. (2025). Unraveling the Dual impacts of urbanization on agricultural habitats: A telecoupling perspective from Zhejiang Province, China. *Land Degradation & Development, 36*(18), 6367–6379.

Liu, R., Zhang, L., Tang, Y., & Jiang, Y. (2024). Understanding and evaluating the resilience of rural human settlements with a social-ecological system framework: The case of Chongqing Municipality. *China. Land Use Policy, 136*, Article 106966.

Mather, A. (2001). *The transition from deforestation to reforestation in Europe, Agricultural technologies and tropical deforestation* (pp. 35–52). CAB International Wallingford UK.

Nguyen, H. Q., & Warr, P. (2020). Land consolidation as technical change: Economic impacts in rural Vietnam. *World Development, 127*, Article 104750.

Olagunju, K. O., Olagunju, K. A., Ogunniyi, A. I., Omotayo, A. O., & Oyetunde-Usman, Z. (2023). To own or not to own? Land tenure security and production risk in small-scale farming. *Land Use Policy, 127*, Article 106584.

Ostrom, E. (1990). *Governing the commons: The evolution of institutions for collective action.* Cambridge University Press.

Peng, J., Chen, J., Su, C., Wu, Z., Yang, L., & Liu, W. (2021). Will land circulation sway "grain orientation"? The impact of rural land circulation on farmers' agricultural planting structures. *PLoS ONE, 16*, Article e0253158.

Prishchepov, A. V., Müller, D., Dubinin, M., Baumann, M., & Radeloff, V. C. (2013). Determinants of agricultural land abandonment in post-Soviet European Russia. *Land Use Policy, 30*, 873–884.

Rahman, S. (2010). Determinants of agricultural land rental market transactions in Bangladesh. *Land Use Policy, 27*, 957–964.

Ren, C., Zhou, X., Wang, C., Guo, Y., Diao, Y., Shen, S., Reis, S., Li, W., Xu, J., & Gu, B. (2023). Ageing threatens sustainability of smallholder farming in China. *Nature, 616*, 96–103.

Renkow, M., Hallstrom, D. G., & Karanja, D. D. (2004). Rural infrastructure, transactions costs and market participation in Kenya. *Journal of Development Economics, 73*, 349–367.

Salazar-Espinoza, C., Jones, S., & Tarp, F. (2015). Weather shocks and cropland decisions in rural Mozambique. *Food Policy, 53*, 9–21.

San Roman Sanz, A., Fernandez, C., Mouillot, F., Ferrat, L., Istria, D., & Pasqualini, V. (2013). Long-term forest dynamics and land-use abandonment in the Mediterranean mountains, Corsica, France. *Ecology and Society, 18*(2).

Schultz, T. W. (1964). *Transforming traditional agriculture.* New Haven and London: Yale University Press.

Song, H., Li, X., Zhang, F., Gu, P., Chen, Y., Wu, H., Xin, L., Lu, Y., Liu, Y., & Wang, X. (2025). Understanding the spatial distribution patterns and dominant determinants of farmland abandonment in China. *Habitat International, 156*, Article 103298.

Subedi, Y. R., Kristiansen, P., & Cacho, O. (2022). Drivers and consequences of agricultural land abandonment and its reutilisation pathways: A systematic review. *Environmental Development, 42*, Article 100681.

Teklu, T., & Lemi, A. (2004). Factors affecting entry and intensity in informal rental land markets in Southern Ethiopian highlands. *Agricultural Economics, 30*, 117–128.

Terres, J.-M., Scacchiafichi, L. N., Wania, A., Ambar, M., Anguiano, E., Buckwell, A., Coppola, A., Gocht, A., Källström, H. N., & Pointereau, P. (2015). Farmland abandonment in Europe: Identification of drivers and indicators, and development of a composite indicator of risk. *Land Use Policy, 49*, 20–34.

Timmer, C. P. (2000). The macro dimensions of food security: Economic growth, equitable distribution, and food price stability. *Food Policy, 25*, 283–295.

FAO, IFAD, UNICEF, WFP & WHO. (2025). The State of Food Security and Nutrition in the World 2025 – Addressing high food price inflation for food security and nutrition. Rome. https://doi.org/10.4060/cd6008en

Vaz, E., Damasio, B., Bacao, F., Shaker, R. R., & Penfound, E. (2023). Urban habitats and food insecurity: Lessons learned throughout a pandemic. *Habitat International, 135*, Article 102779.
Vu, H. T., & Goto, D. (2020). Does awareness about Land Tenure Security (LTS) increase investments in agriculture? Evidence from rural households in Vietnam. *Land Use Policy, 97*, Article 104721.
Wang, Y., Li, X., Xin, L., & Tan, M. (2020). Farmland marginalization and its drivers in mountainous areas of China. *Science of the Total Environment, 719*, Article 135132.
Wang, Y., Yang, A., & Yang, Q. (2023). The extent, drivers and production loss of farmland abandonment in China: Evidence from a spatiotemporal analysis of farm households survey. *Journal of Cleaner Production, 414*, Article 137772.
Ward, P. S., & Shively, G. E. (2015). Migration and land rental as responses to income shocks in Rural China. *Pacific Economic Review, 20*, 511–543.
Xu, D., Chen, M., & Li, R. (2025). How high-standard farmland construction can affect farmers' grain cultivation behavior: Evidence from rural China. *Habitat International, 160*, Article 103384.
Xu, D., Deng, X., Huang, K., Liu, Y., Yong, Z., & Liu, S. (2019). Relationships between labor migration and cropland abandonment in rural China from the perspective of village types. *Land Use Policy, 88*, Article 104164.
Yan, J., Yang, Z., Li, Z., Li, X., Xin, L., & Sun, L. (2016). Drivers of cropland abandonment in mountainous areas: A household decision model on farming scale in Southwest China. *Land Use Policy, 57*, 459–469.
Zhang, Y., Li, X., & Song, W. (2014). Determinants of cropland abandonment at the parcel, household and village levels in mountain areas of China: A multi-level analysis. *Land Use Policy, 41*, 186–192.
Zheng, L. (2024a). Big hands holding small hands: The role of new agricultural operating entities in farmland abandonment. *Food Policy, 123*, Article 102605.
Zheng, L. (2024b). Does off-farm work induce farmland abandonment? Evidence from China. *China Agricultural Economic Review, 16*, 664–682.
Zheng, L., & Qian, W. (2021). The impact of land certification on cropland abandonment: Evidence from rural China. *China Agricultural Economic Review, 14*, 509–526.
Zheng, L., Su, L., & Jin, S. (2023a). Reducing land fragmentation to curb cropland abandonment: Evidence from rural China. *Canadian Journal of Agricultural Economics/revue Canadienne D'agroeconomie, 71*, 355–373.
Zheng, Q., Ha, T., Prishchepov, A. V., Zeng, Y., Yin, H., & Koh, L. P. (2023b). The neglected role of abandoned cropland in supporting both food security and climate change mitigation. *Nature Communications, 14*, 6083.
Zheng, L., Jin, S., & Su, L. (2025a). Of nothing comes nothing: The impact of agricultural comparative return on cropland abandonment. *Journal of Rural Studies, 119*, Article 103759.
Zheng, L., Bin, Y., Qian, W. (2025b). Making up for the deficiency: The role of agricultural subsidy reform in cropland abandonment. *Land Degradation & Development*, 1–15. https://doi.org/10.1002/ldr.70278

# Chapter 9
# Agricultural Subsidy Reform and Cropland Abandonment

**Abstract** Cropland abandonment, a global economic and social trend spurred by rapid rural-urban transformation, has particularly affected China in recent years. Although it is widely believed that agricultural comparative returns primarily drive cropland abandonment, few scholars have explored the blocking effect of agricultural subsidies in this process. Based on CLDS large-scale farm-level panel data, this chapter employs a PSM-DID model to examine the overall effects, mechanisms and heterogeneity of agricultural subsidy reform on cropland abandonment. Results show that agricultural subsidy reform significantly reduced cropland abandonment, resulting in a 1.7% decrease in the proportion of cropland abandoned by farmers. The effect is mainly achieved by increasing the availability and income of agricultural subsidies. However, this effect is also moderated by agricultural comparative return and land titling, both of which weaken the impact of agricultural subsidy reform on cropland abandonment. Moreover, among farmers living in mountainous areas or lacking agricultural machinery, agricultural subsidy reform is negatively associated with cropland abandonment, while this relationship is not observed among other farmers. These insights into the role of agricultural subsidy reform in cropland abandonment can be leveraged to ensure food security in various countries.

**Keywords** Agricultural subsidy reform · Cropland abandonment · Agricultural comparative return · Food security · Sustainable agricultural development

## 9.1 Introduction

Humanity's primary concern in the twenty-first century is to address the paradoxical relationship between increased population growth and reduced food supply (Ward & Pulido-Velazquez, 2008). Cropland serves as a material carrier for food production, and its abandonment can significantly reduce food output, posing a threat to food

This chapter has been published. For more details, please see: Zheng, L., Bin, Y., Qian, W. Making up for the deficiency: the role of agricultural subsidy reform in cropland abandonment. Land Degradation & Development, 2025, 1–15. https://doi.org/10.1002/ldr.70278.



L. Zheng, *Cropland Abandonment in Rural China*, Resources, Environment and Agricultural Development, https://doi.org/10.1007/978-981-95-8287-7_9

security (Zheng et al., 2023b). For instance, in China, the annual area of abandoned cropland is about 23,400 $km^2$, resulting in a loss of about 7.94 billion kilograms of grain per annum, which could feed 19.85 million people (Guo et al., 2023). This indicates the urgent need to curb cropland abandonment to ensure food security. Particularly, in light of the COVID-19 pandemic, the global food security situation has not improved (Berdegué et al., 2024; Zheng & Qian, 2022), with the 2023 State of Food Security and Nutrition in the World report indicating that 2.4 billion people worldwide are unable to consistently access food, accounting for approximately 29.6% of the world's population, of which about 900 million are severely food insecure. It is estimated that by 2030, nearly 600 million people worldwide will still face hunger. Thus, reducing cropland abandonment to ensure food security has become an increasingly urgent and globally recognized challenge (FAO, 2023).

Cropland abandonment is a crucial manifestation of land use and cover change, and refers to the state of dormant or abandoned cropland for a certain period due to a lack of effective cultivation or management measures (Deng et al., 2019; Díaz et al., 2011; Ojha et al., 2022). Currently, it appears in various countries and has gradually evolved into a global economic and social phenomenon. For example, developed countries such as France (San Roman Sanz et al., 2013), Switzerland (Price et al., 2015), and Japan (Ito et al., 2016), as well as developing countries such as Albania (Deininger et al., 2012), Argentina (Izquierdo & Grau, 2009), Chile (Díaz et al., 2011), Nepal (Ojha et al., 2022), and China (Zheng, 2024a) are facing different degrees of cropland abandonment issues. Moreover, with the intensification of agriculture, industrialization, urbanization, and globalization continuing, the abandonment of cropland may even accelerate (Crawford et al., 2024).

To reduce cropland abandonment, a growing body of research has extensively discussed its driving determinants: (i) natural factors such as natural disasters and climate conditions, terrain and topography (Yan et al., 2016), land fragmentation (Zheng et al., 2023b), soil pollution and damage (Díaz et al., 2011); (ii) economic factors such as off-farm employment (Xu et al., 2019b), high agricultural costs (Lieskovsky & Lieskovska, 2021), and low agricultural returns (Wang et al., 2023); (iii) political factors such as political conflicts (Meyfroidt et al., 2016); (iv) institutional factors such as the incomplete reform of land systems (Deininger et al., 2012), restricted land transfer rights and insecure land tenure (Zheng & Qian, 2022) and (v) technological factors such as agricultural machinery (Ma et al., 2022) and the internet (Deng et al., 2019). Among these factors, low agricultural returns are the fundamental reason why farmers abandon cropland (Wang et al., 2023). If agricultural production is unprofitable for farmers, it directly exacerbates cropland abandonment. In this sense, increasing agricultural subsidies is theoretically an effective measure to reduce farmers' cropland abandonment. However, there is limited research directly exploring the causative relationship between the two, possibly due to the potential reverse causality, where some farmers may choose to continue farming to receive subsidies.

To the best of our knowledge, only two studies have indirectly mentioned the potential role of agricultural subsidies (as a control variable) when exploring the impact of other variables on cropland abandonment. Nevertheless, the findings of these studies are inconsistent. Specifically, Wang et al. (2022) based on a sample of 5,479 farmers from the 2017 Chinese Family Database (CFD) and using logistic and Tobit models to estimate found that agricultural subsidies have no impact on cropland abandonment; while Díaz et al. (2011) based on 2,472 farm samples from Chile in 1985 and 2007 and using logit models found that agricultural subsidies significantly reduce farmers' cropland abandonment behavior. It is possible that these studies did not address potential endogeneity issues related to agricultural subsidies, which led them to reflect only correlational rather than causal relationships, resulting in widely differing estimation results. Clearly, to obtain more credible estimates, it is necessary to find an appropriate exogenous shock in agricultural subsidies. Fortunately, China's agricultural subsidy reform since 2015 has provided a clever opportunity for observation. Therefore, this study matches the pilot counties of agricultural subsidy reform with the nationally representative panel data, and employs a propensity score matching (PSM) and difference-in-differences (DID) approach that accounts for causal inference design, to empirically examine the policy effect of agricultural subsidy reform on farmers' cropland abandonment.

Compared with existing research, this study offers several possible contributions to understanding the role of agricultural subsidy reform in farmers' cropland abandonment. First and foremost, this study is one of the first to thoroughly analyze the effect, mechanism, and potential diversity of this phenomenon, filling a critical gap in the field. Additionally, the study design is unique, treating agricultural subsidy reform as a quasi-natural experiment and utilizing a large-scale panel dataset and econometric techniques such as PSM-DID models. This design allows a more precise assessment of the quantitative relationship between agricultural subsidy reform and cropland abandonment, ultimately yielding more credible results. Finally, unlike focusing on the various drivers of cropland abandonment, this study is one of the few empirical studies that directly quantifies its solutions. The insights provided by this study can be instrumental in shaping effective land use policies to maintain food security.

The remainder of the study proceeds as follows. Section 9.2 introduces background on China's agricultural subsidy system, and elaborates on how agricultural subsidy reform affects cropland abandonment. Section 9.3 describes the data and variables, and discusses the empirical strategies employed. Section 9.4 presents the empirical results. Section 9.5 performs the expansion analysis. Section 9.6 concludes with policy implications.

## 9.2 Background and Theoretical Analysis

### *9.2.1 Historical Evolution of China's Agricultural Subsidy System*

Agriculture is a weak industry affected by the interaction and superposition of natural and market risks. When there are fluctuations in risk, it is easy to reduce grain production, reduce farmers' operating income, dampen farmers' enthusiasm for production, and harm national food security and national economic development. Consequently, governments worldwide commonly provide agricultural subsidies to enhance the international competitiveness of agriculture. These subsidies represent the most crucial and frequently used policy tools in agricultural support and protection frameworks.

Since the founding of the People's Republic of China in 1949, with the transformation from rural to urban areas and changes in the relationship between industry and agriculture, China's agricultural subsidy system has undergone four stages. In the first stage (1949–1978), farmers not only did not receive agricultural subsidies, but also had to contribute to the agricultural surplus. The government obtained agricultural surplus value to support industrial development by collecting farm taxes from farmers and using policy tools such as the scissors gap. In the second stage (1978–2004), farmers paid agricultural taxes to the government and also received protection from the government on agricultural prices. The government protected the purchase price of grain by gradually opening up the grain market, implementing a special grain project reserve system and a grain purchase protection price policy, and protecting the purchase price of grain to protect the purchase price of grain, thus ensuring farmers' production income. In the third stage (2004–2015), farmers not only did not have to pay agricultural taxes, but also received agricultural subsidies regardless of whether they were engaged in agricultural production. The government has reduced farmers' production costs and increased farmers' enthusiasm for production by abolishing agricultural taxes and providing farmers with subsidies for improved seeds, direct subsidies for growing grains, comprehensive subsidies for agricultural materials, and subsidies for the purchase of agricultural machinery. In the fourth stage (2015-up to now), only farmers who were engaged in agricultural production could receive agricultural subsidies. Through the implementation of the reform of the agricultural subsidy system, the government has combined the three subsidies of comprehensive subsidies for agricultural materials, subsidies for improved crop seeds, and direct subsidies for growing grains into agricultural support and protection subsidies, and distributed them to farmers who are truly engaged in agricultural production.

Among them, comprehensive subsidies for agricultural materials refer to a direct subsidy system implemented by the government for farmers to purchase agricultural means of production (including chemical fertilizers, diesel fuel, seeds, and agricultural machinery). Under the premise of comprehensively considering the cost and income of farmers' grain planting, through comprehensive direct subsidies for agricultural materials invested in production, farmers can ensure relatively stable income from growing grains, protect their enthusiasm for grain production, and promote national food security. Improvement seed subsidies are subsidies provided by the government to farmers who choose high-quality crop seeds to promote farmers to improve the quality of agricultural products. Direct grain subsidies mainly refer to subsidies given directly to farmers by the state according to certain subsidy standards and the actual sown area of grain to improve farmers' production enthusiasm, protect comprehensive grain capacity, ensure national food security, and increase farmers' income.

In May 2015, the Ministry of Finance and the Ministry of Agriculture of China issued the *Guiding Opinions on Adjusting and Improving the Three Agricultural Subsidy Policies*, endorsing the launch of a new pilot program for reform of the agricultural subsidy system in five provinces, including Anhui, Shandong, Hunan, Sichuan, and Zhejiang. Among them, Shandong, Hunan, Sichuan, and Zhejiang are piloting throughout the province, and Anhui is piloting in six districts and counties, including Yongqiao District, Huaiyuan County, Linquan County, Fengyang County, Jinzhai County, and Guangde County. In April 2016, the Ministry of Finance and the Ministry of Agriculture of China further issued the *Notice on Fully Launching the Reform of the Agricultural Three Subsidies* based on summarizing the pilot experience, requiring a new round of agricultural subsidy system reform to be implemented nationwide. The main contents of this round of subsidy reform are as follows: First, in terms of subsidy objects, adhere to the principle that whoever farms the land will receive subsidies and agricultural subsidies will be directly given to farmers who are truly engaged in agricultural production. Second, in terms of subsidy methods, the original comprehensive subsidies for agricultural materials, subsidies for good crops, and direct subsidies for growing grains are combined into agricultural support and protection subsidies and are required to be distributed to farmers at one time before June 30 each year. Third, in terms of subsidy rules, agricultural subsidies are linked to the protection of cultivated land capacity. During the implementation of the policy, each province mainly determines the subsidy amount based on the area of contracted cultivated land on the farmers' land title certificate. However, the cultivated land that has been abandoned or changed in use is not included in the subsidy area.

According to statistics, China's new round of agricultural subsidy reform covered 220 million farmers and nearly 1.30 billion mu (1 mu = 1/15 hectare) of contracted land. The average subsidy per mu is about 95 yuan (1 pound = 9.12 yuan), and the average subsidy per household is about 564 yuan.[1] This has increased farmers' incomes, mobilized farmers' enthusiasm for production, and expanded the policy space to support agricultural development and increase farmers' incomes. At the same time, the new round of agricultural subsidy reform has unified the review and issuance procedures of the original subsidy funds, reduced the work of multi-caliber and multi-verification of planting areas at the grassroots level, and reduced administrative management costs and policy implementation costs. According to local government workers, the original subsidies need to be issued more than 20

[1] https://www.mof.gov.cn/zhengwuxinxi/caijingshidian/zgcjb/202109/t20210916_3753468.htm.

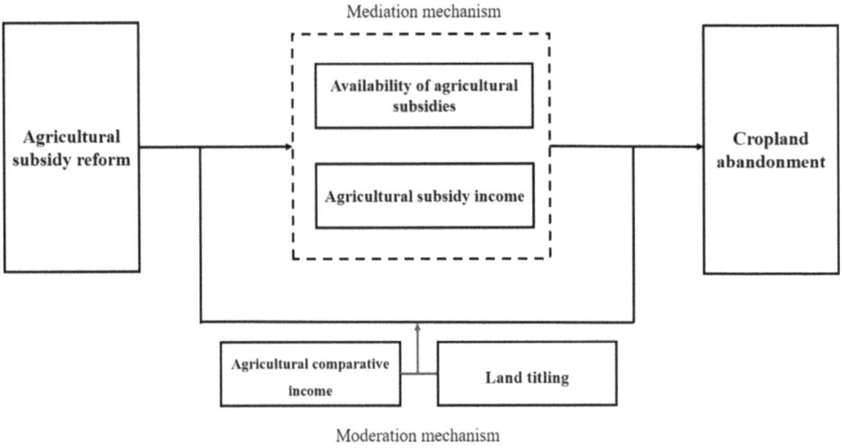


**Fig. 9.1** Theoretical framework of agricultural subsidy reform on cropland abandonment

times before and after the issuance,[2] and only once after the merger, which greatly saves time and costs and improves work efficiency. In addition, the new round of agricultural subsidy reform has advanced the subsidy issuance time to the first half of the year (during agricultural production) and made it clear that abandoned land and changed uses are not included in the scope of subsidies. This will help ease farmers' financial constraints, improve land capacity, and enhance the sustainable development capacity of agricultural production.

## 9.2.2 *Agricultural Subsidy Reform and the Abandonment of Cropland by Farmers*

Considering that the new round of agricultural subsidy reform may not only affect farmers' cropland abandonment through some potential channels, but may also be accompanied by other factors. Therefore, to systematically analyze the underlying mechanisms of agricultural subsidy reform on farmers' cropland abandonment, this study will conduct an in-depth analysis from the perspective of mediation and moderation mechanisms (Fig. 9.1).

### 9.2.2.1 Analysis on the Mediation Mechanism of Agricultural Subsidy Reform Affecting Cropland Abandonment

Low income for agriculture is the main reason farmers abandon cropland (Wang et al., 2023). Whether farmers receive agricultural subsidies and how much agricultural

---

[2] http://politics.people.com.cn/n1/2016/0508/c1001-28332866.html.

subsidies they receive may affect their enthusiasm for production. In theory, the new round of agricultural subsidy reform can reduce the occurrence of cropland abandonment by improving the availability of agricultural subsidies and increasing the income of agricultural subsidies.

In particular, reform of agricultural subsidies may reduce the probability of farmers abandoning their cropland by improving the availability of agricultural subsidies. Before the reform of agricultural subsidies, farmers' agricultural subsidies mainly included comprehensive subsidies for agricultural materials, subsidies for improved crop seeds, and direct subsidies for growing grains. Under this system, due to inconsistent subsidy standards for different types of agricultural subsidies, a wide range of departments involved, numerous work links and issuance procedures, and relatively high transaction costs for policy implementation, farmers not only have difficulty obtaining agricultural subsidies on time, but may also be unable to receive agricultural subsidies due to the mistakes by government staff. Moreover, due to the lack of unified subsidy credentials, the difficulty of supervision in the policy implementation process is more prominent, resulting in farmers' agricultural subsidies being corrupt or misappropriated by some illegal officials (Zheng & Qian, 2022). Fortunately, the new round of agricultural subsidy reform combines the three subsidies of comprehensive agricultural material subsidy, crop planting subsidy, and direct grain planting subsidy into one, and mainly based on the contracted area, the subsidy will be distributed to farmers who have the right to contract cropland at one time before agricultural production. This will help improve the availability of agricultural subsidies to farmers, encourage them to become actively involved in agricultural production, and reduce the abandonment of cropland. Based on the above discussion, this paper proposes the following hypothesis:

H1: Agricultural subsidy reform improves the availability of agricultural subsidies.

Simultaneously, reform of agricultural subsidies may also reduce the possibility of farmers abandoning their cropland by increasing income from agricultural subsidies. According to the new round of agricultural subsidy reform, there are two main sources for the growth of farmers' agricultural subsidy income: First, in addition to the original comprehensive subsidies for agricultural materials, subsidies for good crops and direct subsidies for growing grains, the government has also included the pilot funds for subsidies for large grain farmers and the incremental funds for original three types of agricultural subsidies into the new unified agricultural subsidies, expanding the capital pool of agricultural subsidies; Second, under the original institutional framework, farmers need to pay the cost of agricultural production before they can obtain the corresponding agricultural subsidies. Currently, regardless of whether farmers purchase agricultural means of production and high-quality agricultural seeds, as long as they are still engaged in agricultural production, they can receive agricultural subsidies. Therefore, for farmers engaged in agricultural production, in general, the agricultural subsidies they receive will increase slightly compared to before the reform (Fan et al., 2023). As increased agricultural subsidies ease financial constraints, farmers are less likely to abandon cropland. Based on the above discussion, this paper proposes the following hypotheses:

H2: Agricultural subsidy reform increases agricultural subsidy income.

#### 9.2.2.2 Analysis on the Moderation Mechanism of Agricultural Subsidy Reform Affecting Cropland Abandonment

During the rural-urban transformation, farmers have more opportunities to go out to work, and the opportunity cost of farming has risen. Consequently, agricultural comparative income has become a key factor in farmers' land use decisions. At the same time, under the new round of the agricultural subsidy system, the land area on the land title certificate has become an important credential for the government to issue agricultural subsidies. Therefore, the acquisition of agricultural subsidies, in practice, is also closely related to land titling. In the above sense, the impact of agricultural subsidy reform on abandoned cropland may also be moderated by agricultural comparative income and land titling.

Specifically, the impact of agricultural subsidy reform on cropland abandonment may also be moderated by agricultural comparative income. Generally speaking, if agricultural comparative income is higher, i.e., agricultural income is not less than non-agricultural income, then they are more likely to engage in agricultural production; conversely, farmers are more likely to abandon cropland (Ma & Zhu, 2020). Under the influence of the new round of agricultural subsidy reform, due to additional agricultural subsidy income, farmers with higher agricultural comparative income will work harder to engage in agricultural production; for farmers with lower agricultural comparative income, off-farm employment is a more rational choice. However, the participation of family members in off-farm employment will lead to a decrease in family agricultural labor, thus increasing the possibility of abandoning cropland. Nevertheless, once the sum of agricultural income and agricultural subsidy income is not less than non-agricultural income, some farmers who go to cities to engage in off-farm employment may also return to the countryside to continue agricultural production. As a result, the return of agricultural labor reduces the likelihood of farmers abandoning cropland accordingly. In the above sense, compared to farmers with lower agricultural comparative income, agricultural subsidy reform has less impact on farmers with higher agricultural comparative income. Based on this, this paper proposes the following hypothesis:

H3: Agricultural comparative income weakens the impact of agricultural subsidy reform on cropland abandonment.

At the same time, the impact of agricultural subsidy reform on cropland abandonment may also be moderated by land titling. Previous studies have pointed out that, subject to the transaction costs of policy implementation, the issuance of agricultural subsidies in China is largely distributed according to the land area recorded in land title certificates, so these certificates enhance the availability of agricultural subsidies to some extent (Zheng & Qian, 2022). Therefore, for farmers with land title certificates, since the land title certificate is the certificate for the issuance of agricultural subsidies before and after the agricultural subsidy reform, they are relatively less affected by agricultural subsidies; for farmers without land title certificates, before the agricultural subsidy reform, the issuance of agricultural subsidies, including comprehensive subsidies for agricultural materials, subsidies for good crop planting, and direct subsidies for grain planting, has little to do with land title certificates, but now it matters and uses land areas on the certificate. Without land title certificates, it may mean that the actual operating area needs to be measured, so they will minimize cropland abandonment. In the above sense, compared to farmers without land title certificates, the impact of agricultural subsidy reform on farmers with land title certificates is smaller. Based on this, this paper proposes the following hypotheses:

H4: Land titling weakens the impact of agricultural subsidy reform on cropland abandonment.

## 9.3 Research Design

### *9.3.1 Data Sources*

The data utilized for this study were derived from the China Labor-force Dynamics Survey (CLDS), a nationally representative longitudinal survey of China's labor force that seeks to monitor current situations and shifts in China's social economy. It targets the working-age population aged 15–64 and employs a multi-stage clustering, stratification, probability-to-scale (PPS) sampling method to collect multifaceted information on population structure, household property and income, household consumption, agricultural production, land use, etc. To meet the research requirements, this study effectively matches the manually collected pilot of agricultural subsidy reform with the three rounds of the CLD database in 2014, 2016, and 2018. Thereafter, the relevant data screening involves the following steps: (1) removing samples from urban areas, leaving only samples from rural areas; (2) discarding samples with no cropland in the home; (3) eliminating samples with rural heads above 70; (4) erasing samples with missing values in the selected variables; and (5) eradicating samples with unsuccessful matching of propensity scores. After the above data cleansing, this study finally uses 14,220 valid farm households from 26 provinces in China for analysis.

### 9.3.2 Descriptive Statistics

Table 9.1 presents descriptive statistics for the selected variables in the empirical analysis. In terms of dependent variables, the results show that 8.7% of the surveyed farmers abandoned cropland, and the abandoned cropland area accounted for 5.4% of the total cropland. Regarding the key independent variable, 40.4% of farmers surveyed in the sample period were affected by the new round of agricultural subsidy reform. As far as the control variables are concerned, the average age of heads of household was 51 years old, and most of them had only attended junior high school. On average, there were approximately five farm household members, 66.3% of whom were in good health. The average dependency ratio was 22 per cent, indicating that about one-fifth of farm households had children and the elderly. Averagely, a farm household surveyed was endowed with 1.57 mu of cropland area per capita. In our sample, farmer's wage income accounted for 34.2% of their total income, suggesting that part of rural labor was engaged in off-farm employment. In addition, each sample village had an average of 3,292 mu of cropland area, and the per capita income of the sample village was approximately 10,000 yuan.

### 9.3.3 Empirical Strategies

As a common research method for assessing policy effects, the difference-in-difference method (DID) has been widely used in the social sciences (Callaway & Sant'Anna, 2021). The DID model has various advantages, especially for panel data samples. It can not only take advantage of the exogeneity of independent variables, but also control the impact of individual heterogeneity of some unobservable variables on dependent variables. According to DID's setting principle, a treatment group subject to policy intervention and a control group not subject to policy intervention are constructed. When controlling for other factors, researchers can assess the net effect of the specific policy by comparing changes in outcomes for the treated group before and after the policy intervention with changes in outcomes for the matched control group over the same period.

The DID approach requires a completely random selection between the treatment group and the control group, otherwise, there will be large biases in the estimation results. However, for this study, the reform of agricultural subsidies implemented in China in 2015 may have been selected for some reason, such as the higher value of local agricultural output. To alleviate the endogeneity problems caused by the selection bias of the agricultural subsidy pilot reform, we adopted the propensity score matching (PSM) method before applying DID. Numerous studies have suggested that PSM in combination with DID may help address the additional selection bias associated with unobservable time-invariant heterogeneity (Heckman et al., 1997). Following the PSM-DID research design, this study matches farmers affected by the agricultural subsidy reform intervention (treatment group) with farmers without

**Table 9.1** Variable definition and descriptive statistics ($N = 14{,}220$)

| Variables | Definition | Mean | SD | Min | Max |
|---|---|---|---|---|---|
| Abandonment ratio | Ratio of abandoned cropland to total cropland (0—1) | 0.054 | 0.203 | 0 | 1 |
| Abandonment behavior | Whether cropland is abandoned (yes = 1, no = 0) | 0.087 | 0.282 | 0 | 1 |
| Subsidy reform | Has there been a new round of agricultural subsidy reform since 2015? (yes = 1, no = 0) | 0.404 | 0.491 | 0 | 1 |
| Age | Age of household head | 51.043 | 10.742 | 15 | 70 |
| Education | Education of household head: Illiteracy = 1, primary school = 2, junior high school = 3, senior high school = 4, college or above = 5 | 2.544 | 0.980 | 1 | 5 |
| Family health | Ratio of healthy family members (0—1) | 0.663 | 0.341 | 0 | 1 |
| Dependency | Ratio of children and the elderly members (0—1) | 0.220 | 0.217 | 0 | 1 |
| Family size | Number of family members | 4.507 | 1.996 | 1 | 18 |
| Land size | Household cropland area per capita (mu) | 1.573 | 3.653 | 0.003 | 112.5 |
| Off-farm work | Ratio of off-farm income in total income (0—1) | 0.342 | 0.421 | 0 | 1 |
| Village land | Cropland area of the village (mu) | 3292 | 5771 | 5 | 65,675 |
| Village economy | Annual per capita income of the village (10,000 yuan) | 1.085 | 1.473 | 0.1 | 15 |

such intervention (control group), building a counterfactual framework to effectively reduce the impact of selectivity bias on the accuracy of parameter estimation. Specifically, we draw on Zheng and Qian's (2022) research, choose the commonly used one-to-one neighbor caliper matching method ($n = 1$, $r = 0.05$), and utilize agricultural subsidy reform as the treatment variable, the proportion of cropland abandoned by farmers as the outcome variable, and all the control variables listed in Table 9.1 as covariates. Finally, a logit model is adopted to estimate the propensity score.

Figure 9.2 shows the change in the standard deviation of each covariate before and after matching. Results indicate that after matching, the bias for most covariates decreases to below 10% and aggregates around the value of 0. This suggests that matching improves comparability between treatment and control groups, with no systematic differences observed between them, thus passing the balance test. Figure 9.3 further provides the distribution of propensity scores for these two groups. Results show that after PSM, most samples fall within the common support domain, satisfying the common support hypothesis. The above evidence supports that the

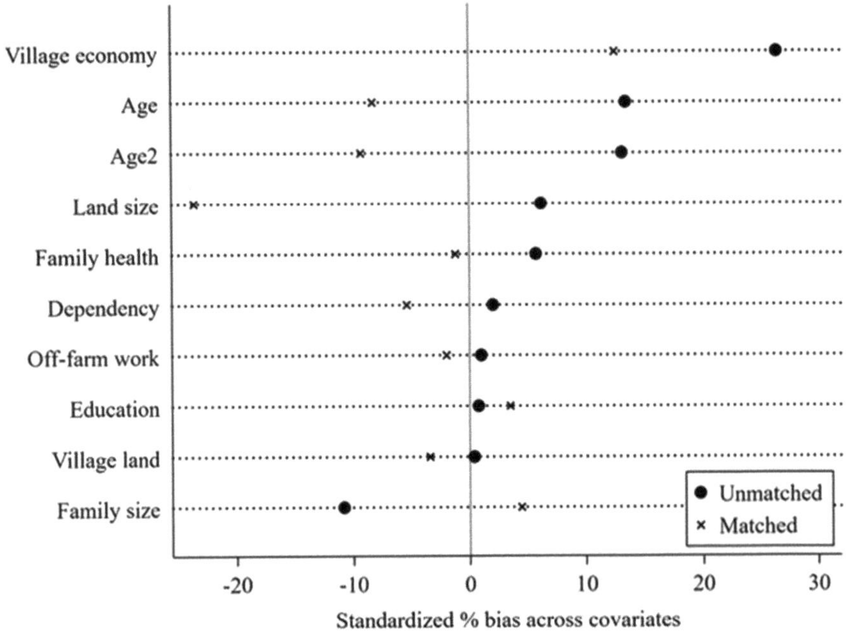


**Fig. 9.2** Standardized bias before and after PSM

matching method adopted in this study is reasonable and reliable, and further DID estimation can be performed.

To further mitigate the potential interference of unobservable factors on estimation results, a staggered DID model based on PSM is applied in this study to evaluate the impact of agricultural subsidy reform on cropland abandonment. The proposed model takes into account both household-fixed and time-fixed effects, along with observable variables commonly discussed in the literature. Specifically, the model can be expressed as follows:

$$Abandonment_{ijt} = \alpha_0 + \alpha_1 Subsidy_{jt} + \alpha_2 Z_{ijt} + \sigma_i + \varphi_t + \mu_{ijt} \tag{9.1}$$

where subscripts *i*, *j*, and *t* represent the farm household, the province where the farm household is located, and the survey year, respectively. Consistent with Ma and Zhu (2020) $Abandonment_{it}$ denotes the ratio of abandoned cropland to total cropland, and its value ranges from 0 to 1. $Subsidy_{jt}$ represents the reform of agricultural subsidies. If the province *j* implements agricultural subsidy reform in year *t*, then for *t* not less than 2015, the value of $Subsidy_{jt}$ is 1, and 0, otherwise. $Z_{ijt}$ is a vector of the control variables mentioned in Table 9.1. We select them based on research objectives, existing literature, and data availability. Specifically, we include the age of the head of household and its quadratic term (Zheng et al., 2023b), the level of education of the head of household (Wang et al., 2023; Zavalloni et al., 2021), family health (Wang et al., 2022), dependency (Zheng & Qian, 2022), family size (Deng

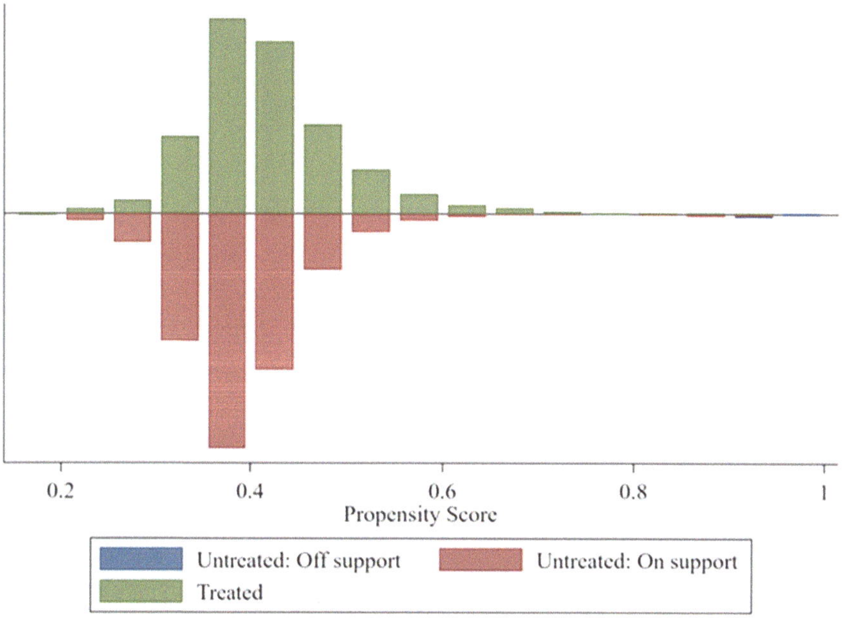


**Fig. 9.3** Common support hypothesis testing

et al., 2019; Zavalloni et al., 2021), land size (Wang et al., 2023), off-farm work (Xu et al., 2019b), land and economic characteristics of the village (Zheng & Qian, 2022; Zheng et al., 2023b). $\alpha_0$ is the constant term. $\alpha_1$, $\alpha_2$ are the parameters to be estimated. $\sigma_i$ refers to the household-fixed effect that controls for household-specific time-invariant factors such as farmers' abilities and preferences; and $\varphi_t$ depicts the time-fixed effect that captures the household-invariant time-varying factors such as macroeconomic conditions or national policies. Additionally, $\mu_{ijt}$ is the random disturbance term accounting for additional unexplained shocks that impact cropland abandonment.

### *9.3.4 Correlation Between Agricultural Subsidy Reform and Cropland Abandonment*

Before the formal empirical analysis, we attempt to draw a scatter plot of agricultural subsidy reform and cropland abandonment to explore the potential relationship between the two. As shown in Fig. 9.4, over the sample period, the fit line of the agricultural subsidy reform group (treatment group) is significantly lower than that of the non-agricultural subsidy reform group (control group), indicating that

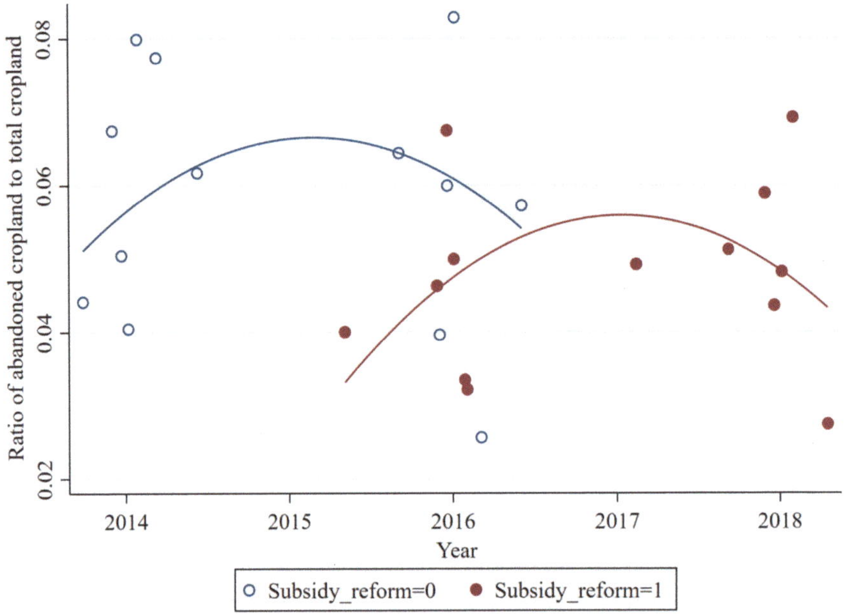


**Fig. 9.4** Agricultural subsidy reform and cropland abandonment: Scatter plot

farmers affected by agricultural subsidy reform have a relatively low rate of cropland abandonment. Consequently, preliminary evidence shows that there is a negative correlation between agricultural subsidy reform and cropland abandonment.

## 9.4 Empirical Results

### *9.4.1 Main Results*

Benchmark regression results based on the PSM-DID model are presented in Table 9.2. Specifically, column (1) reports the estimate for the agricultural subsidy reform variable when controlling household-fixed effects and time-fixed effects. Columns (2) and (3) further include individual- and household-level time-varying variables, respectively. Column (4) adds village-level time-varying controls based on column (3). In all four models, the estimated coefficients on agricultural subsidy reform are negatively significant at the 5% significance level, and there are few changes. Taking column (4) as an example, the coefficient on agricultural subsidy reform is −0.017, indicating that the rate of cropland abandonment among farmers affected by the reform of agricultural subsidies is approximately 1.7% lower than the rate among farmers unaffected by the reform. Since the average cropland abandonment rate during the sample period was 5.4%, according to the above estimates, from

2014 to 2018, the reform of agricultural subsidies reduced cropland abandonment in rural China by about 31.5% (1.7/5.4 × 100).

Concerning control variables, we did not observe significant effects of age, education, and family size on cropland abandonment, which may be due to small changes in the sample period and the inclusion of both household and time-fixed effects in the model. However, the negative and significant coefficient on family health implies that farmers with healthier members have enough energy to engage in agricultural production (Zheng & Qian, 2022). Dependency appears to have a positive and significant impact on cropland abandonment, indicating that farm households with more elderly people and children often lack sufficient youth labor to carry out farming

**Table 9.2** Agricultural subsidy reform and cropland abandonment: Baseline results

| | Ratio of abandoned cropland area to total cropland area | | | |
|---|---|---|---|---|
| | (1) | (2) | (3) | (4) |
| Subsidy reform | −0.018** (0.008) | −0.018** (0.008) | −0.017** (0.008) | −0.017** (0.008) |
| Age | | −0.003 (0.003) | −0.002 (0.003) | −0.002 (0.003) |
| $Age^2$ | | 0.000 (0.000) | 0.000 (0.000) | 0.000 (0.000) |
| Education | | 0.004 (0.005) | 0.004 (0.005) | 0.004 (0.005) |
| Family health | | | −0.017* (0.010) | −0.016* (0.010) |
| Dependency | | | 0.055* (0.029) | 0.055* (0.029) |
| Family size | | | −0.002 (0.005) | −0.001 (0.005) |
| Land size | | | 0.001* (0.001) | 0.001* (0.001) |
| Off-farm work | | | 0.017* (0.010) | 0.017* (0.010) |
| Village land | | | | 0.000* (0.000) |
| Village economy | | | | −0.001 (0.004) |
| Household-fixed effect | Yes | Yes | Yes | Yes |
| Time-fixed effect | Yes | Yes | Yes | Yes |
| Mean of dependent variable | 0.054 | 0.054 | 0.054 | 0.054 |
| Obs | 14,220 | 14,220 | 14,220 | 14,220 |
| R-squared | 0.748 | 0.748 | 0.749 | 0.749 |

*Notes* ***, **, and * denote significance at the 1%, 5%, and 10% levels, respectively; Delta-method standard errors are presented in parentheses activities (Zheng, 2024a). As a result, such households are more likely to abandon their cropland. Land size and village land significantly exacerbate cropland abandonment, which is highly consistent with Deng et al. (2019). This is probably because households or villages with abundant land resources are less interested in some marginal plots of land and are therefore more likely to be abandoned. The negative and significant coefficient for off-farm work suggests that the shortage of agricultural labor caused by off-farm work leads to cropland abandonment (Xu et al., 2019b). The village economy has an insignificant effect on cropland abandonment, which may be due to the combined effect of positive and negative forces. For example, economically developed villages may either reduce low-return agricultural production or develop modern agriculture by adopting advanced technologies and agricultural socialization services.

### *9.4.2 Robustness Checks*

We employed the following four methods to validate the robustness of the aforementioned estimates, with the corresponding results presented in Table 9.3.

First, in the benchmark model, for the treatment group setting in 2015, we mainly selected a sample of 5 provinces in Anhui, Shandong, Hunan, Sichuan, and Zhejiang according to the pilot arrangement of the Chinese government's agricultural subsidy reform. However, it is important to acknowledge that at the same time, there were also three provinces, Tianjin, Shanghai and Henan, independently conducting provincial-level agricultural subsidy reform pilots regarding the requirements of the Chinese government's agricultural subsidy reform. To avoid potential measurement errors,

**Table 9.3** Agricultural subsidy reform and cropland abandonment: Robustness checks

| | Replacing X | Replacing Y | Replacing sample | Replacing model |
|---|---|---|---|---|
| | (1) | (2) | (3) | (4) |
| Subsidy reform | | −0.022**<br>(0.011) | −0.019**<br>(0.009) | −0.102***<br>(0.027) |
| Subsidy reform + | −0.019**<br>(0.009) | | | |
| Control variables | Yes | Yes | Yes | Yes |
| Household-fixed effect | Yes | Yes | Yes | No |
| Time-fixed effect | Yes | Yes | Yes | No |
| Observations | 14,220 | 14,220 | 13,608 | 14,220 |
| Log likelihood | — | — | — | −4592.062 |
| Wald chi2 | — | — | — | 178.13 |
| R-squared | 0.749 | 0.736 | 0.750 | — |

*Notes* ***, **, and * denote significance at the 1%, 5%, and 10% levels, respectively; Delta-method standard errors and robust standard errors are presented in parentheses samples from the autonomous pilot provinces were incorporated into the 2015 treatment group and the agricultural subsidy reform variable was redefined (labeled subsidy reform + ) for re-estimation. The results in column (1) show that the estimated coefficient for agricultural subsidy reform closely aligns with the estimated results in column (4) of Table 9.2, and is negatively significant at the 5% level.

Second, we used whether farmers abandoned cropland to replace the original ratio of abandoned cropland to total cropland, and performed a robustness test by redefining the dependent variable. As demonstrated in column (2) of the table below, the alternative to the dependent variable reveals that agricultural subsidy reform significantly mitigates the likelihood of cropland abandonment by 2.2%. It is again noted that the findings are consistent with baseline results.

Third, as land lessees tend to be commercial-oriented agricultural producers, regardless of whether they receive agricultural subsidies, they are theoretically unlikely to abandon cropland. To eliminate this potential interference, we excluded sample farmers with land lease behavior for re-estimation. The results in column (3) suggest that the estimated results differ little from the baseline results in Table 9.2. Therefore, the previously identified negative association between agricultural subsidy reform and cropland abandonment remains robust.

Finally, 91.3% of the farmers in the sample used in this study did not abandon cropland, suggesting that there may be a lower censoring problem in the cropland abandonment variable. As such, we adopted a panel Tobit model that accounts for censored issues to re-estimate Eq. (9.1). From the average marginal effect reported in column (4), there appears to be a negatively correlated and significant association between agricultural subsidy reform and cropland abandonment.

Overall, the findings from the above models are basically consistent with those in Table 9.2, indicating that agricultural subsidy reform significantly mitigates cropland abandonment. This highlights the robustness of prior estimates across various scenarios.

### 9.4.3 Placebo Test

To exclude interference from other unobservable factors in the estimation results, we further conducted a placebo test using the "Permute" command in Stata software by randomly assigning provinces to implement agricultural subsidy reforms. Following the specification provided in column (4) of Table 9.2, we randomly selected 500 times from the original sample for DID estimation. Figure 9.5 illustrates the kernel density map of these 500 estimations along with the baseline estimate, −0.017. The results show that the estimators generated by random sampling are centered around zero, and differ from the baseline estimate value. Consequently, the negative and significant effects of agricultural subsidy reform on cropland abandonment in this study are not incidental or influenced by unobserved factors, reaffirming the robustness of the previously established baseline results.

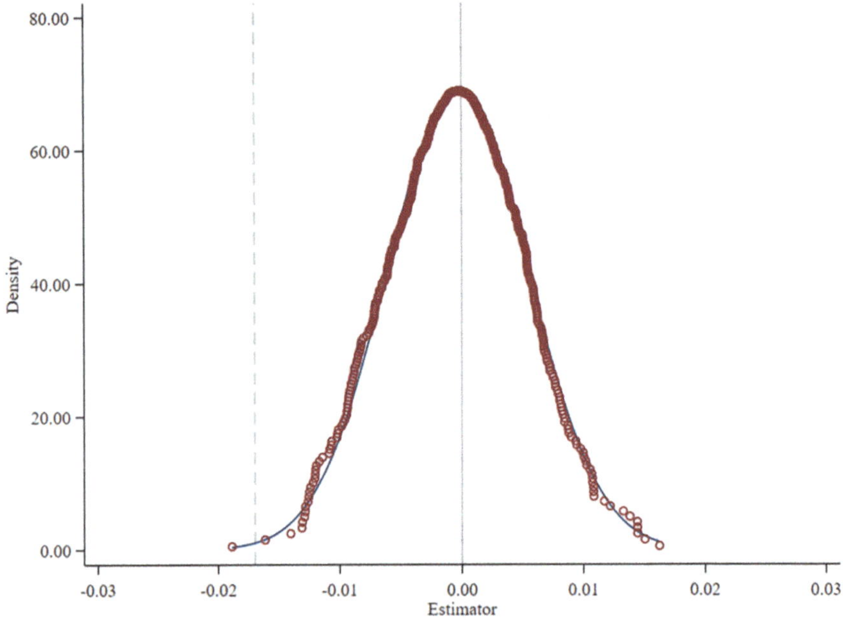


**Fig. 9.5** Agricultural subsidy reform and cropland abandonment: Placebo test

### *9.4.4 Mechanism Analysis*

Based on the above theoretical analysis, we investigated the mechanisms underlying the negative relationship between agricultural subsidy reform and cropland abandonment through both mediation and moderation mechanisms, respectively.

As for the mediation mechanism, we mainly examined whether agricultural subsidy reform can reduce cropland abandonment due to low agricultural income by improving the availability of agricultural subsidies and agricultural subsidy income. Specifically, the availability of agricultural subsidies is defined as whether farmers received agricultural subsidies (yes = 1, no = 0), and agricultural subsidy income is defined as the natural logarithm of agricultural income received by farmers (yuan). The corresponding estimates are presented in Table 9.4. The results show that agricultural subsidy reform is positively correlated with the availability of agricultural subsidies and agricultural subsidy income, and hypotheses 1 and 2 are confirmed. Owing to the reform of agricultural subsidies, farmers' availability of agricultural subsidies and income from agricultural subsidies increased by 9.1% and 39.8% ($(e^{0.335} - 1) \times 100\%$), respectively. This increased farmers' income and enthusiasm for farming, resulting in a decrease in cropland abandonment (Díaz et al., 2011).

Regarding the moderation mechanism, we mainly assessed whether the negative correlation between agricultural subsidy reform and cropland abandonment was moderated by agricultural comparative income and land titling. Specifically, agricultural comparative income is defined as whether farmers' agricultural income was

**Table 9.4** Agricultural subsidy reform and cropland abandonment: Mediation mechanism

| | Availability of agricultural subsidies | Agricultural subsidy income |
|---|---|---|
| | (1) | (2) |
| Subsidy reform | 0.091***<br>(0.020) | 0.335***<br>(0.110) |
| Control variables | Yes | Yes |
| Household-fixed effect | Yes | Yes |
| Time-fixed effect | Yes | Yes |
| Observations | 14,220 | 14,220 |
| R-squared | 0.743 | 0.758 |

*Notes* ***, **, and * denote significance at the 1%, 5%, and 10% levels, respectively; Robust standard errors are presented in parentheses. For consistency, all models here are panel random effects models

no less than non-agricultural income (yes = 1, no = 0), while land titling is defined as whether farmers obtained land title certificates (yes = 1, no = 0). The corresponding estimates are detailed in Table 9.5. As shown in column (2), agricultural comparative income weakens the impact of agricultural subsidy reform on cropland abandonment products, supporting Hypothesis 3. Specifically, the effect of agricultural subsidy reform on cropland abandonment is −0.007 (−0.026 + 0.019) for farmers with higher agricultural comparative income, and −0.026 for farmers with lower agricultural income. The likely reason is that agricultural subsidy reform has increased the income of agricultural subsidies, and hence, farmers with lower agricultural incomes do not have to go out to work to make a living. Simultaneously, the results in column (3) indicate that land titling weakens the impact of agricultural subsidy reform on cropland abandonment; thus, Hypothesis 4 is confirmed. Specifically, the effect of agricultural subsidy reform on cropland abandonment is −0.004 (−0.034 + 0.030) for farmers with land title certificates, and −0.034 for farmers without land title certificates. One possible explanation is that after the reform of agricultural subsidies, land title certificates have become a crucial credential for farmers to access agricultural subsidies, amplifying the impact on farmers without such certificates.

## 9.5 Extended Analysis

### *9.5.1 Rule Out Potential Alternative Explanations*

In the previous mechanism analysis, it was determined that agricultural subsidy reform has exerted a positive impact on availability and income from agricultural subsidies, potentially reducing cropland abandonment. However, this hypothesis relies on the assumption that farmers receiving agricultural subsidies primarily use

**Table 9.5** Agricultural subsidy reform and cropland abandonment: Moderation mechanism

| | Ratio of abandoned cropland area to total cropland area | | |
|---|---|---|---|
| | (1) | (2) | (3) |
| Subsidy reform | −0.017**<br>(0.008) | −0.026***<br>(0.010) | −0.034***<br>(0.013) |
| Subsidy reform × Agricultural comparative income | | 0.019*<br>(0.011) | |
| Subsidy reform × Land titling | | | 0.030**<br>(0.014) |
| Control variables | Yes | Yes | Yes |
| Household-fixed effect | Yes | Yes | Yes |
| Time-fixed effect | Yes | Yes | Yes |
| Obs | 14,220 | 14,220 | 12,033 |
| R-squared | 0.749 | 0.749 | 0.771 |

*Notes* ***, **, and * denote significance at the 1%, 5%, and 10% levels, respectively; Delta-method standard errors are presented in parentheses

this income for agricultural production rather than for daily consumption. To test this, Table 9.6 provides an estimate of the impact of agricultural subsidy reform on agricultural production inputs and household consumption expenditures, respectively. Among them, agricultural production inputs are measured by the natural logarithm of these inputs (yuan), while household consumption expenditures are measured by the natural logarithm of these expenditures (yuan). As illustrated in column (1), the coefficient of the agricultural subsidy reform variable is −0.528, indicating a reduction in agricultural production input of about 41.0% ($(e^{-0.528} - 1) \times 100\%$) for farmers affected by the reform. This may stem from the reduced financial burden on farmers for agricultural production following the receipt of subsidies. Simultaneously, the absence of a significant change in household consumption expenditure in column (2) may suggest that these subsidies are not being used for farmers' daily consumption. To sum up, we have reason to believe that the reform of agricultural subsidies has effectively reduced cropland abandonment.

### 9.5.2 *Reducing the Impact of Cropland Abandonment on Agricultural Output and Productivity*

Previous estimates fully demonstrate that agricultural subsidy reform significantly reduces cropland abandonment. The next question is, to what extent does cropland abandonment affect agricultural production? To answer this question, this study

**Table 9.6** Agricultural subsidy reform and cropland abandonment: Extended analysis I

| | Agriculture production input | Household consumption expenditure |
|---|---|---|
| | (1) | (2) |
| Subsidy reform | −0.528***<br>(0.139) | 0.085<br>(0.055) |
| Household-fixed effect | Yes | Yes |
| Time-fixed effect | Yes | Yes |
| Control variables | Yes | Yes |
| Observations | 14,220 | 14,220 |
| R-squared | 0.843 | 0.739 |

*Notes* ***, **, and * denote significance at the 1%, 5%, and 10% levels, respectively; Robust standard errors are presented in parentheses. For consistency, all models here are panel random effects models

employed limited data to explore the impact of cropland abandonment on total agricultural output value (yuan, logarithm) and agricultural productivity (total agricultural output value/total agricultural input). The estimates in Table 9.7 show that cropland abandonment reduces both the total value of agricultural output and agricultural productivity, regardless of the inclusion of control variables. For instance, in column (2), the estimated coefficient of the abandonment ratio variable is −5.28, indicating that for every one percentage increase in the cropland abandonment rate of farmers, the total agricultural output value decreases by approximately 42.2% ($(e^{-0.549} - 1) \times 100\%$). Combined with the estimates outlined in Table 2, agricultural subsidy reform during 2014–2018 prevented a decline of approximately 13.3% (42.2% × 31.5%) in agricultural output value that would have resulted from cropland abandonment.

**Table 9.7** Agricultural subsidy reform and cropland abandonment: Extended analysis II

| | Agricultural output value | | Agricultural productivity | |
|---|---|---|---|---|
| | (1) | (2) | (3) | (4) |
| Abandonment ratio | −0.547***<br>(0.198) | −0.549***<br>(0.197) | −0.386**<br>(0.174) | −0.300*<br>(0.177) |
| Control variables | No | Yes | No | Yes |
| Household-fixed effect | Yes | Yes | Yes | Yes |
| Time-fixed effect | Yes | Yes | Yes | Yes |
| Observations | 14,220 | 14,220 | 14,220 | 14,220 |
| R-squared | 0.859 | 0.860 | 0.784 | 0.784 |

*Notes* ***, **, and * denote significance at the 1%, 5%, and 10% levels, respectively; Robust standard errors are presented in parentheses

### *9.5.3 Heterogeneous Effects by Machinery and Topography*

In addition to low agricultural returns, labor shortages stemming from the outflow of agricultural workers are also considered a key driver of cropland abandonment (Xu et al., 2019b). Considering the positive role of machinery in replacing labor and the fact that the use of machinery is subject to topography, we further conducted heterogeneous analyses from the grouping of terrain and machinery (Zheng et al., 2023b). We specifically divided the sample into two groups, based on whether the farmer resided in plain areas (yes = 1, no = 0), and created two additional groups according to whether the farmer owned agricultural machinery (yes = 1, no = 0). The corresponding results are presented in Table 9.8.

Columns (1) and (2) show that the estimated coefficients of agricultural subsidy reform in plains are significantly negative, while those in mountains are insignificant. This can be explained in part by the fact that farming conditions in mountainous areas are worse than on the plains, making it difficult for agricultural subsidies to cover the high labor costs of agricultural production. Columns (3) and (4) indicate that agricultural subsidy reform reduces the incidence of cropland abandonment among farmers owning agricultural machinery, but has little effect on those without such equipment. The likely reason is that farmers with agricultural machinery do not have to worry about labor shortages for farming, while farmers without machinery can reduce cropland abandonment by purchasing agricultural machinery after receiving agricultural subsidies.

**Table 9.8** Agricultural subsidy reform and cropland abandonment: Extended analysis III

| | Ratio of abandoned cropland area to total cropland area | | | |
|---|---|---|---|---|
| | (1) Plains | (2) Mountains | (3) With machine | (4) Without machine |
| Subsidy reform | −0.030** (0.013) | −0.014 (0.013) | 0.003 (0.016) | −0.023** (0.010) |
| Observed difference | −0.016* | | −0.026*** | |
| Empirical p-value | 0.076 | | 0.000 | |
| Control variables | Yes | Yes | Yes | Yes |
| Household-fixed effect | Yes | Yes | Yes | Yes |
| Time-fixed effect | Yes | Yes | Yes | Yes |
| Obs | 6052 | 8168 | 2321 | 11,899 |
| R-squared | 0.811 | 0.768 | 0.837 | 0.760 |

*Note:* *** $p < 0.01$, ** $p < 0.05$, * $p < 0.1$. Robust standard errors, clustered at the household level, are shown in parentheses

## 9.6 Conclusions and Policy Implications

### 9.6.1 Conclusions

Supporting and protecting agriculture, which is a global concern, is no exception in both developed and developing countries. However, despite its critical role as a key agricultural support and protection strategy, its effects on cropland abandonment have not received sufficient attention. Given this, our study examines the quantitative relationship between agricultural subsidy reform and cropland abandonment.

Using large-scale farm-level data from CLDS and the PSM-DID model, we quantify that China's new round of agricultural subsidy reform since 2015 has resulted in a significant reduction the proportion of cropland abandoned by farmers. The reliability of these findings is confirmed by various robustness checks (i.e., redefining dependent and core independent variables, using subsamples, and replacing regression models), placebo tests, and the exclusion of potential alternative explanations. Specifically, the reform of agricultural subsidies reduced farmers' cropland abandonment rate by approximately 1.7%, and this effect is mainly achieved by improving the availability and income of agricultural subsidies. Nevertheless, this effect is also moderated by agricultural comparative income and land titling, both of which weaken the impact of agricultural subsidy reform on cropland abandonment. Further analysis shows that cropland abandonment led to a decline in both the value of agricultural output and agricultural productivity, while agricultural subsidy reform recovered about 13.3% of the total loss of agricultural output value during the sample period. Additionally, heterogeneity analysis reveals that among farmers who live in plains or lack agricultural machinery, agricultural subsidy reform is negatively correlated with cropland abandonment, while this relationship is not observed among other farmers.

### 9.6.2 Policy Implications

In recent years, rapid industrialization and urbanization worldwide have triggered a surge in rural labor migration to cities. This has increased the opportunity cost of farming, thereby reducing its relative profitability. Consequently, there has been growing concern about cropland abandonment. Since cropland is the material carrier of food production, reducing its abandonment is essentially a strategy to safeguard food security.

In this regard, China's reform practices and empirical findings hold significant reference value for policymakers worldwide. First, the government should advance reform of the agricultural subsidy system, increase agricultural output, and enhance farmers' enthusiasm for farming. In this process, China's experience highlights three key considerations: (i) Consolidation of multiple subsidies from different sources within a designated department to reduce transaction costs in implementation and improve fiscal fund efficiency; (ii) Utilizing information technology to ensure that subsidies reach farmers truly engaged in agricultural production, thereby preventing misappropriation; (iii) Disbursing subsidies in advance each spring to free farmers from financial constraints and alleviate credit restrictions in agricultural production.

Second, it is essential to enhance the accessibility and benefit levels of agricultural subsidies, strengthen their guiding role in agriculture, and minimize the costs of farming. Particular emphasis should be placed on actively directing agricultural subsidies toward agricultural production rather than daily consumption, fully leveraging their positive impact in curbing the abandonment of cropland abandonment. To this end, the government may differentiate agricultural subsidies from other transfer payments (such as pensions) and establish incentives and restraint mechanisms for agricultural subsidies to ensure their dedicated use.

Third, it is crucial to enhance the level of comparative income in agriculture, to keep the gap between farm and non-farm incomes within a reasonable range, and to make agriculture a more attractive and promising industry. Concurrently, it is worth coordinating reforms to the land tenure system, expanding the scope of use of land title certificates, and transforming these certificates into documents that cover agricultural subsidy disbursement, land leasing, and land conservation. This approach will better coordinate and advance the reform of agricultural subsidy systems.

Finally, there is a need to increase support for farmers in mountainous areas and those lacking agricultural machinery. Specific measures should be implemented to develop small and medium-sized agricultural machinery adapted to agriculture in mountain regions, while providing appropriate subsidies to farmers purchasing such equipment. This approach will help fully leverage the positive role of agricultural subsidy systems in promoting inclusive rural development.

### *9.6.3 Research Deficiencies and Prospects*

Agricultural subsidies and cropland abandonment are among the most pressing issues facing countries worldwide. This study aims to spark further discussion and attract greater scholarly attention. However, due to limitations in data availability and scope, this research offers only a preliminary exploration of the quantitative association between agricultural subsidies and abandoned croplands, as well as the underlying mechanisms involved. Looking ahead, several key areas warrant further collaborative investigation by the global academic community. First, it is essential to examine how different types of agricultural subsidies influence cropland abandonment. Agricultural subsidies can be categorized according to policy frameworks—such as green box and amber box measures—or by form, including direct versus indirect subsidies, production-linked versus circulation-based support, and variations in beneficiary groups and delivery mechanisms. Understanding the differential impacts of these types of subsidies can enhance the precision and effectiveness of subsidy policies, thereby supporting sustainable land use. Second, there is a need to systematically quantify and evaluate the outcomes of existing cropland abandonment mitigation strategies. A review of previous literature reveals that while extensive research has focused on identifying drivers of cropland abandonment, relatively few studies have assessed the effectiveness of management measures implemented. The real-world effectiveness of interventions such as land rental markets and farmland water conservancy infrastructure remains subject to empirical validation. Finally, comprehensive assessments of the broader socioeconomic and environmental implications of agricultural subsidy reforms are required. In theory, such reforms not only directly affect agricultural productivity, but also indirectly influence labor migration patterns and the rural-urban transformation process.

## References


Berdegué, J. A., Castillo, M. J., Gómez, I., Gordillo, G., Navea, J., Rojas, I., & Yáñez, R. (2024). The importance of assets for coping with COVID-19 and other shocks. *Global Food Security, 40*, Article 100732.

Crawford, C. L., R. A. Wiebe, H. Yin, V. C. Radeloff, & Wilcove, D. S. (2024). Biodiversity Consequences of Cropland Abandonment. *Nature Sustainability, 7*(12): 1596–1607. https://doi.org/10.1038/s41893-024-01452-1.

Callaway, B., & Sant'Anna, P. H. C. (2021). Difference-in-differences with multiple time periods. *Journal of Econometrics, 225*, 200–230.

Deininger, K., Savastano, S., & Carletto, C. (2012). Land fragmentation, cropland abandonment, and land market operation in Albania. *World Development, 40*, 2108–2122.

Deng, X., Xu, D., Zeng, M., & Qi, Y. (2019). Does internet use help reduce rural cropland abandonment? *Evidence from China. Land Use Policy, 89*, Article 104243.

Díaz, G. I., Nahuelhual, L., Echeverría, C., & Marín, S. (2011). Drivers of land abandonment in Southern Chile and implications for landscape planning. *Landscape and Urban Planning, 99*, 207–217.

Fan, P., Mishra, A. K., Feng, S., Su, M., & Hirsch, S. (2023). The impact of China's new agricultural subsidy policy on grain crop acreage. *Food Policy, 118*, Article 102472.

FAO, I., UNICEF, WFP, WHO. (2023). *The state of food security and nutrition in the World 2023, Urbanization, agrifood systems transformation and healthy diets across the rural-urban continuum.*

Guo, A., Yue, W., Yang, J., Xue, B., Xiao, W., Li, M., He, T., Zhang, M., Jin, X., & Zhou, Q. (2023). Cropland abandonment in China: Patterns, drivers, and implications for food security. *Journal of Cleaner Production, 418*, Article 138154.

Heckman, J. J., Ichimura, H., & Todd, P. E. (1997). Matching as an econometric evaluation estimator: Evidence from evaluating a job training programme. *The Review of Economic Studies, 64*, 605–654.

Ito, J., Nishikori, M., Toyoshi, M., & Feuer, H. N. (2016). The contribution of land exchange institutions and markets in countering farmland abandonment in Japan. *Land Use Policy, 57*, 582–593.

Izquierdo, A. E., & Grau, H. R. (2009). Agriculture adjustment, land-use transition and protected areas in Northwestern Argentina. *Journal of Environmental Management, 90*, 858–865.

Lieskovsky, J., & Lieskovska, D. (2021). Cropland abandonment in Slovakia: Analysis and comparison of different data sources. *Land-Basel, 10*(4), 334.

Ma, W., & Zhu, Z. (2020). A Note: Reducing Cropland Abandonment in China—Do agricultural cooperatives play a role? *Journal of Agricultural Economics, 71*, 929–935.

Ma, W., Zhu, Z., & Zhou, X. (2022). Agricultural mechanization and cropland abandonment in rural China. *Applied Economics Letters, 29*, 526–533.

Meyfroidt, P., Schierhorn, F., Prishchepov, A. V., Müller, D., & Kuemmerle, T. (2016). Drivers, constraints and trade-offs associated with recultivating abandoned cropland in Russia, Ukraine and Kazakhstan. *Global Environmental Change, 37*, 1–15.

Ojha, R. B., Atreya, K., Kristiansen, P., Devkota, D., & Wilson, B. (2022). A systematic review and gap analysis of drivers, impacts, and restoration options for abandoned croplands in Nepal. *Land Use Policy, 120*, Article 106237.

Price, B., Kienast, F., Seidl, I., Ginzler, C., Verburg, P. H., & Bolliger, J. (2015). Future landscapes of Switzerland: Risk areas for urbanisation and land abandonment. *Applied Geography, 57*, 32–41.

San Roman Sanz, A., Fernandez, C., Mouillot, F., Ferrat, L., Istria, D., & Pasqualini, V. (2013). Long-term forest dynamics and land-use abandonment in the Mediterranean mountains, Corsica, France. *Ecology and Society, 18*.

Wang, J., Cao, Y., Fang, X., Li, G., & Cao, Y. (2022). Does land tenure fragmentation aggravate farmland abandonment? Evidence from big survey data in rural China. *Journal of Rural Studies, 91*, 126–135.

Wang, Y., Yang, A., & Yang, Q. (2023). The extent, drivers and production loss of farmland abandonment in China: Evidence from a spatiotemporal analysis of farm households survey. *Journal of Cleaner Production, 414*, Article 137772.

Ward, F. A., & Pulido-Velazquez, M. (2008). Water conservation in irrigation can increase water use. *Proceedings of the National Academy of Sciences, 105*, 18215–18220.

Xu, D., Deng, X., Huang, K., Liu, Y., Yong, Z., & Liu, S. (2019b). Relationships between labor migration and cropland abandonment in rural China from the perspective of village types. *Land Use Policy, 88*, Article 104164.

Yan, J., Yang, Z., Li, Z., Li, X., Xin, L., & Sun, L. (2016). Drivers of cropland abandonment in mountainous areas: A household decision model on farming scale in Southwest China. *Land Use Policy, 57*, 459–469.

Zavalloni, M., D'Alberto, R., Raggi, M., & Viaggi, D. (2021). Farmland abandonment, public goods and the CAP in a marginal area of Italy. *Land Use Policy, 107*, Article 104365.

Zheng, L. (2024a). Big hands holding small hands: The role of new agricultural operating entities in farmland abandonment. *Food Policy, 123*, Article 102605.

Zheng, L. (2024b). Does off-farm work induce farmland abandonment? Evidence from China. *China Agricultural Economic Review, 16*, 664–682.

Zheng, L. (2024c). Those with constant property rights have perseverance: China's land tenure reform promotes environment-friendly farming practices. *Humanities and Social Sciences Communications, 11*, 763.

Zheng, L., Li, L., & Jin, S. (2025). Opening the village door: China's agricultural e-commerce facilitates the transformation of land rental markets. *Agricultural Economics, 56*(4), 622-636. e70010

Zheng, L., Li, L., Zhao, Z., & Qian, W. (2023a). Does land certification increase farmers' use of organic fertilizer? Evidence from China. *Journal of Land Use Science, 18*, 39–54.

Zheng, L., & Qian, W. (2022). The impact of land certification on cropland abandonment: Evidence from rural China. *China Agricultural Economic Review, 14*, 509–526.

Zheng, L., Su, L., & Jin, S. (2023b). Reducing land fragmentation to curb cropland abandonment: Evidence from rural China. *Canadian Journal of Agricultural Economics/revue Canadienne D'agroeconomie, 71*, 355–373.

# Chapter 10
# Land Tenure Reform and Cropland Abandonment

**Abstract** Expropriation and occupation of croplands are essential in protecting land quantity during rapid urbanization, and so is reducing cropland abandonment during agricultural production; therefore, it deserves close attention. In this regard, this chapter utilizes nationally representative panel data from the 2017 and 2019 China Rural Household Panel Survey (CRHPS), and staggered difference-in-differences (DID) model, to explore how the land tenure reform helps in protecting land quantity during agricultural production by estimating the influence of land certification on cropland abandonment, its mechanisms, and its heterogeneous effects among groups at the provincial, community, and household levels. Results show that land certification significantly contributes to the protection of land quantity during agricultural production, and it reduces the area of abandoned croplands by at least 4%. This effect is mainly achieved by improving soil fertility, promoting land transfer, increasing the availability of agricultural subsidies, and raising agricultural income. However, while land certification benefits farmers in non-major grain-producing areas and western regions, in plain, remote, and non-politically central villages, and farmers who have not undergone land transfer or land adjustment, it is not beneficial for others. This study enriches the applicability of the property rights theory in the Chinese context, and provides Chinese evidence for other developing countries to strengthen the protection of land quantity, by deepening the reform of the land tenure system under different circumstances.

**Keywords** Land tenure reform · Cropland abandonment · Land certification · Land economics · Food security

This chapter has been published. For more details, please see: Zheng, L., Qian, W. The impact of land certification on cropland abandonment: Evidence from rural China. China Agricultural Economic Review, 2022, 14(3): 509–526.



L. Zheng, *Cropland Abandonment in Rural China*, Resources, Environment and Agricultural Development, https://doi.org/10.1007/978-981-95-8287-7_10

## 10.1 Introduction

In the twenty-first century, the greatest challenge facing humankind is how to deal with two opposing trends: population increase and limited food supply (Ward & Pulido-Velazquez, 2008). According to the latest estimates from the Food and Agriculture Organization (FAO) of the United Nations, from 2014 to 2019, the number of people suffering from starvation increased by nearly 10 million each year, and the number of chronically underfed people has risen by about 60 million during this period. Worse still, due to the rapid spread of the coronavirus disease 2019 (COVID-19), the number of chronically hungry people worldwide may exceed 130 million by the end of 2020 (FAO, 2020). With irreversible population growth, the global food crisis is likely to become more serious (Lambin & Meyfroidt, 2010; Xu et al., 2019).

Since human beings began practicing an agricultural civilization, it has been widely believed that cropland is a major carrier of food production (Zavalloni et al., 2021). To guarantee food security, a certain amount of available cropland must be maintained (Alonso-Sarría et al., 2016). However, with the development of the economy and the subsequent rural–urban labor migration, the abandonment of cropland has gradually become a global social and economic phenomenon in recent decades (Gellrich et al., 2007; Levers et al., 2018). According to incomplete statistics, since the beginning of the twentieth century, the total area of abandoned cropland worldwide has reached approximately 3,850,000 to 4,720,000 $km^2$ (Campbell et al., 2008), which has had significant negative impacts on food security among countries. As such, cropland abandonment has attracted widespread attention from scholars (Queiroz et al., 2014), and abundant literature has been produced in this regard.

Several driving factors, including biophysical features and socioeconomic characteristics, affect the abandonment of cropland. Specifically, existing studies have shown that unsuitable environmental conditions (e.g., steep landforms, poor soil fertility, land fragmentation, and remote areas), low agricultural income, insufficient agricultural labor (e.g., labor migration, off-farm employment, and high dependency ratio), imperfect land rental market, and lack of agricultural policy incentives may lead to cropland abandonment by farmers (Baumann et al., 2011; Han & Song, 2019; Lieskovský et al., 2015; Prishchepov et al., 2013; Sikor et al., 2009; Zhang et al., 2014; Zhang et al., 2018; Xu et al., 2019). In addition, the land tenure system is also an important factor influencing the abandonment of cropland, which cannot be ignored. Based on remote sensing data from 1989 to 2000, Alix-Garcia et al. (2012) found that cropland abandonment in Poland and Slovakia can be partly explained by the reform of the land tenure system, while cropland abandonment in the border areas of Ukraine was mainly caused by the incomplete reform of the land tenure system. Macro data from the Soviet Union also indicated that incomplete or inadequate land reforms have resulted in the abandonment of extensive croplands (Prishchepov et al., 2013). However, there are relatively few quantitative studies based on micro-farmer household data that explore the relationship between land tenure system reform and cropland abandonment (Prishchepov et al., 2013; Saint-Macary et al., 2010), especially the reform of land certification (Zheng & Luo, 2019). Relevant research on land tenure systems mainly discusses the economic effects, focusing on land transfer, investment, and credit (Feder & Nishio, 1998), while the ecological effects are rarely studied (Feng et al., 2019).

Fortunately, the reform of the land tenure system in China provides a good observation window for the impact of land certification on cropland abandonment. Marked by the No. 1 Document of the Communist Party of China Central Committee in 2013, the Chinese government launched a new round of land certification reform programs nationwide, aiming to strengthen the protection of farmers' land property rights and grant farmers' increased property rights. Compared with the reforms in other countries, the new round of land certification reform in China has two main characteristics. First, it is massive. According to statistics from the Third National Agricultural Census, there were as many as 207.43 million farmers in China in 2016. The reform required full implementation of land certification to ensure that every farmer received a land certificate that was accurate in size, clear in ownership, and fully functional. Second, China's reform is state-led. The reform of land certification was led by the Ministry of Agriculture and Rural Affairs of China and implemented by local governments at all levels. It had a strict timetable and required the country to complete the registration and issuance of the land certificate in five years.

In fact, discussing the relationship between land certification and cropland abandonment is of great practical significance and theoretical value in the context of China. On the one hand, similar to the economic structural transformation of developed countries, China now is currently experiencing rapid industrialization, urbanization, and economic globalization (Robinson & Carson, 2015; Yang et al., 2018). In this process, the issue of cropland abandonment has become increasingly serious (Xu et al., 2019; Yan et al., 2016; Zhang et al., 2018). On the other hand, China is a developing country with the largest population in the world. In the context of economic globalization and the COVID-19 pandemic, China's food demand has a significant impact on the global food market (Deng et al., 2019). If China cannot guarantee its food security and take effective measures to deal with cropland abandonment, this may inevitably have a huge impact on the world's food market and even cause food panic in countries worldwide (Yan et al., 2009). Therefore, it is of informational value for other countries to find out how to leverage land quantity protection through land reform (Lichtenberg & Ding, 2008), prevent farmers' cropland from being abandoned and thereby build a strong food security barrier. Moreover, whether it is from a practical or theoretical perspective, the abandonment of cultivated land is not a new phenomenon in China, while land certification is. However, the only two relevant Chinese studies that use cross-sectional data (Luo et al., 2017; Zheng & Luo, 2019), not only fail to fully explore the causal relationship between land certification and cropland abandonment, but also greatly restrict the dissemination of knowledge on this subject. Given this, our study uses nationally representative panel data from the China Rural Household Panel Survey (CRHPS) and a staggered difference-in-differences (DID) model to empirically test the impact of land certification on the area of cropland abandonment, and eventually provides empirical evidence of the land tenure system reform promoting the protection of land quantity.

Compared with the two directly related Chinese studies, the possible marginal contributions of this paper are mainly reflected in the following aspects: First, existing studies have not distinguished the specific time of land certification when measuring the new round of land certification, but China has conducted multiple rounds of land certification since the reform and opening up (Zheng et al., 2021). There will be measurement errors in doing so, and this paper can use the time of land certification to scientifically identify the new round of land certification. Second, when the existing research discusses the impact of land certification on cropland abandonment, it mainly focuses on whether farmers have abandonment behavior but lacks attention to the area of abandoned croplands. Restraining the expansion of abandonment areas is an important part of the protection of land quantity. This paper focuses on the impact of land certification on the area of croplands abandoned by farmers, and uses whether or not farmers have abandoned and the ratio of cropland abandonment as a robustness test, to deepen related research and dialogue with existing research. Third, existing studies mainly investigate the impact of land certification on cropland abandonment in general, and lack the heterogeneity analysis of the role of land certification in different situations. In contrast, this paper will further examine the heterogeneity of land certification from the dimensions of the province, community, and household. Fourth, existing studies mainly use cross-sectional data from a small number of provinces of China in 2014, and it is difficult to control unobservable factors at the farmer level. However, this paper uses panel data from 29 provinces across the country in 2017 and 2019, and adopts a staggered DID model. Not only the samples are relatively new, but also the endogenous problems that may be caused by missing variables can be dealt with, making the conclusions more credible.

The remainder of this paper is organized as follows. Section 10.2 presents a review of the relevant literature and the theoretical analysis. Section 10.3 describes the data and establishes the empirical model. Section 10.4 presents our empirical results. Section 10.5 carries out heterogeneity analysis. Finally, Sect. 10.6 provides the conclusions and proposes policy recommendations.

## 10.2 Literature Review and Theoretical Analysis

The land tenure system is an institutional arrangement with cropland as the core. There are numerous factors that affect the abandonment of cropland. Whether it is natural, economic, or social, most of them are related to the land tenure system to some degree. In the context of the massive rural–urban labor migration (Chen et al., 2014), four factors—soil fertility, land transfer, agricultural subsidies, and agricultural income—become the main obstacles to the protection of land quantity, which is especially obvious in a situation of insecure property rights (Abolina & Luzadis, 2015; Deininger et al., 2012; Gellrich et al., 2007; Zheng & Luo, 2019). Therefore, enhancing the security of land property rights through land certification can improve the constraint conditions of land utilization to a certain extent to reduce cropland abandonment.

### 10.2.1 Land Certification, Soil Fertility, and Cropland Abandonment

Poor soil fertility is a direct factor in cropland abandonment by farmers (Alix-Garcia et al., 2012; Bakker et al., 2005). Generally, crop yields are relatively low in plots with poor soil fertility (Sluiter & De Jong, 2007). To obtain an average yield, farmers need to invest more time and energy (Gallart & Llorens, 2003; Rudel & Fu, 1996). Therefore, for rational farmers, it may be more economical to abandon instead of cultivate poor croplands (MacDonald et al., 2000; Rey Benayas et al., 2007). In particular, when farmers are insecure about their land property rights, the option of abandoning the cropland becomes more obvious (Saint-Macary et al., 2010), primarily because land tenure security is often associated with positive long-term behavior. If farmers cannot expect to recover their full investment from future income (Roth & Haase, 1998), they are likely to give up the cropland that has poor soil fertility (Yao, 2000). Fortunately, land certification can address the farmers' insecure status of property rights (Kassa, 2014), and enhance their security about land property rights (Zheng et al., 2020). Once the farmers' croplands are certified, their expectations will become more stable (Wang et al., 2015). In this case, farmers are likely to take long-term measures, including the use of organic fertilizers to improve soil fertility (Huang & Ji, 2012), which can further help reduce abandonment of croplands.

### 10.2.2 Land Certification, Land Transfer, and Cropland Abandonment

The unavailability of land transfer is an indirect factor contributing to cropland abandonment by farmers (Deininger et al., 2012). In actuality, there is no reason or need for farmers to abandon their croplands. Renting out cropland will not only bring them extra rental income but will also make it easier for them to cultivate the land themselves in the future. Regarding land transfer, there are three possible reasons for cropland abandonment. First, the land transfer market is imperfect (Zhang et al., 2014). Second, the transaction cost of land transfers is greater than the transfer rent (Jin & Deininger, 2009). Finally, farmers worry about losing their cropland after renting it out (Benjamin & Brandt, 2002). Property rights are a prerequisite and the basis for land transfer. Land certification is a form of legal empowerment to issue a legally valid land certificate to farmers, which not only provides legal property rights protection for the land, but also provides tradable property rights certificates for land transfer (Zheng et al., 2020). Land certification helps in reducing information asymmetry and transaction costs (Holden et al., 2007), eliminates farmers' concerns about losing their croplands (Wang et al., 2015) and thus, promotes the development of land transfer markets (Yami & Snyder, 2016). Therefore, land certification can create conditions for land transfer, and thereby help reduce cropland abandonment (Ito et al., 2016).

### 10.2.3 Land Certification, Agricultural Subsidies, and Cropland Abandonment

The low availability of agricultural subsidies is an external motivation for farmers to abandon their cropland (Díaz et al., 2011). Agricultural subsidies are an incentive and a restraining mechanism (Strijker, 2005). With subsidies, farmers' enthusiasm for farming increases; without them, the probability of farmers abandoning their croplands increases (Estel et al., 2015). In rural Chinese society, agricultural subsidies, including grain and seed subsidies, are generally based on the area of croplands as stated on the land certificates (Feng, 2015). In this case, if farmers lack the corresponding land certificate, the possibility of obtaining agricultural subsidies is reduced (Díaz et al., 2011). An important goal of the reform of land certification is to issue farmers their legally valid land certificates that clearly state the croplands' area (Zheng et al., 2020), to protect their land rights and interests (Luo et al., 2017). In this sense, land certification can not only reduce information asymmetry and transaction costs in the implementation of agricultural subsidy policies to make the issuance of agricultural subsidies more accurate (Deininger & Feder, 2009), but also protect farmers' legal rights and interests in obtaining agricultural subsidies, and thereby improve their enthusiasm for agricultural production (Nordin, 2014) and reduce the possibility of cropland abandonment.

### 10.2.4 Land Certification, Agricultural Income, and Cropland Abandonment

An internal motive for farmers to abandon their croplands is the relatively low agricultural income (Chen et al., 2014). The rapid expansion of China's economy, large imports of international agricultural products (Aide & Grau, 2004; Sikor et al., 2009) and continuously rising factor prices (Lieskovský et al., 2015; Rudel & Fu, 1996) have greatly increased the pressure on agricultural income growth (MacDonald et al., 2000; Mullan et al., 2011). It is understandable that if agricultural income continues to be lower than non-agricultural income and cannot be effectively increased, farmers would likely abandon their cropland, especially because of the insecurity of land property rights (Deininger et al., 2012). Through the clear definition and effective protection of property rights, land certification can guarantee farmers' exclusive land use rights, exclusive rights to income, and the liberalization of transactions (Cheung, 1973), which will help stimulate farmers' enthusiasm for agricultural production (Zheng & Luo, 2019). With the economic incentive of property rights, farmers will either increase their agricultural investment (Besley, 1995) or expand the scale of agriculture (Holden et al., 2011) to improve agricultural productivity further (Holden et al., 2009), thereby increasing the level of agricultural income and reducing the probability of cropland abandonment.

In short, once the cropland is certified, the security of land tenure will improve accordingly; farmers will be motivated to improve their soil, be able to lease their cropland, have a certificate to receive agricultural subsidies, and have an incentive to increase agricultural income, thereby reducing the probability of cropland abandonment.

## 10.3 Data, Variables, and Research Design

### *10.3.1 Data Sources*

The data employed in this study are sourced from the 2017 and 2019 CRHPS of Zhejiang University. The dataset adopts a stratified, three-stage sampling method proportional to the population size, and covers 29 provinces (excluding Hong Kong, Macao, Taiwan, Xinjiang, and Tibet) across China. Among them, in the first stage, China's cities and counties are divided into 10 tiers according to per capita GDP, and sample counties (districts, county-level cities) are randomly selected in layers; in the second stage, sample communities (villages) are randomly selected from the sample counties (districts, county-level cities); In the third stage, sample households are randomly selected from the sample communities (villages). It is understood that the follow-up survey in 2019 covered 29 provinces, 170 cities, 345 districts and counties, and 1,360 communities (villages) across the country, with a sample size of 34,643 households from urban and rural areas. The dataset is representative at multiple levels, including rural, urban, provincial, and national levels (Qian, 2020). The official website that presents the data is: http://ssec.zju.edu.cn/sites/main/default.aspx. The CRHPS dataset involves relatively rich information about households in China, including the basic structure of the family, economic condition, agricultural production, land use, and other aspects. Although the land certification information in this paper has been collected since 2015, the information on the area of croplands abandoned by farmers will not be available until 2017. Therefore, we can only use the 15,086 original samples of farmers in 2017 and 2019. Furthermore, considering that there are numerous factors affecting the cropland abandonment, we also retained relevant variables such as individual characteristics, family characteristics, and community characteristics. However, considering that not every household provided all the information on the above variables. We deleted 597 samples with missing information, and the sample loss rate was 3.96%. In the end, we got a non-balanced panel of 14,489 farmers distributed in 29 provinces across the country.

## 10.3.2 Statistical Description

Based on the research objectives of our study and the results of existing studies, the following variables are proposed.

#### 10.3.2.1 Dependent Variable

Unlike the quantity protection of cropland during urbanization, this study mainly investigates the quality protection of cropland during agricultural production, focusing on idle and wasted croplands. This is because non-agricultural conversion of cropland is mainly driven by urbanization, while cropland abandonment mainly depends on the farmers' subjective choice. As users and beneficiaries of croplands, it is important to guide farmers' behavior. Therefore, the area of croplands abandoned by farmers is used as a proxy indicator of the protection of land quantity, and cropland abandonment by farmers and the ratio of cropland abandonment are used for the robustness test. The statistical results in Table 10.1 show that the abandonment ratio in China is currently at 9%, and the average area of abandoned croplands for each farmer is 0.26 mu. This indicates that in areas of China where there is a large population and less land, cropland abandonment by farmers is relatively prominent, and this must be sufficiently addressed.

#### 10.3.2.2 Focus Variable

Referring to Zheng et al. (2020), this study considers land certification as the core independent variable, which is mainly based on the two questions of the questionnaire used. One is, "Did your household have the land management rights certificate?" The other question is, "In which year was the certificate issued?" To identify the new round of land certification accurately instead of using the land certificate in general, this study chooses to consider land management rights certificates issued since 2013 as the standards to measure land certification. The main reason for this choice is that 2013 was the beginning of a new round of land certification in China. More importantly, this state-led reform, for the panel data of farmers, not only effectively avoids the reverse causality problem in econometric model inference, but also reduces the endogenous problem caused by selection bias.

#### 10.3.2.3 Control Variables

Consistent with existing studies, our study mainly controls for individual, household, and community characteristics, which are deemed to influence both land certification and cropland abandonment. Specifically, the individual characteristics are the age and age squared of the householder (Xu et al., 2019; Zheng & Luo, 2019) and the

**Table 10.1** Variable definition and summary statistics ($N$ = 14,489)

| Variables | Definition | Mean | SD | Min | Max |
|---|---|---|---|---|---|
| Abandonment area | Area of abandoned cropland in rural households (mu[a]) | 0.26 | 1.51 | 0 | 50 |
| Abandonment behavior | Whether to abandon cropland (0 = no; 1 = yes) | 0.09 | 0.28 | 0 | 1 |
| Abandonment ratio | The ratio of abandoned areas to total cropland | 0.04 | 0.15 | 0 | 1 |
| Land certification | Since 2013, whether farmers have obtained a certificate for rural land contract management (0 = no; 1 = yes) | 0.56 | 0.50 | 0 | 1 |
| Age | Age of the householder | 53.58 | 10.65 | 16 | 69 |
| Age2 | Age square of the householder | 2984.33 | 1069.20 | 256 | 4761 |
| Health | Physical status: Very good = 1, good = 2, average = 3, bad = 4, very bad = 5 | 2.85 | 1.05 | 1 | 5 |
| Education | Whether the householder has a high school diploma or above (0 = no; 1 = yes) | 0.12 | 0.33 | 0 | 1 |
| Dependency ratio | The dependency ratio of the elderly and children | 0.35 | 0.48 | 0 | 5 |
| Off-farm ratio | Household non-farm employment ratio | 0.22 | 0.26 | 0 | 1 |
| Land size | Per capita contracted land area of the household (mu[a]) | 3.06 | 6.32 | 0.01 | 360 |
| Land number | Number of plots | 5.50 | 5.97 | 0 | 120 |
| Community agriculture | Number of new agricultural operating entities | 7.78 | 83.86 | 0 | 2563 |
| Community economy | The range of per capita disposable annual income (1 = lower than 1000 RMB, 2 = 1000–3000 RMB, 3 = 3000–5000 RMB, 4 = 5000–10,000 RMB, 6 = 15,000–20,000 RMB, 7 = 20,000–30,000 RMB, 8 = 30,000–50,000 RMB, 9 = 50,000-100000RMB) | 3.90 | 1.29 | 1 | 9 |

*Note* 1 mu = 1/15 hectare

**Table 10.2** Relationship between land certification and cropland abandonment: Correlation test

| | The sample group | | Difference (3) = (1)-(2) |
|---|---|---|---|
| | With certificate (1) | Without certificate (2) | |
| Abandoned area | 0.235<br>(0.015) | 0.286<br>(0.023) | −0.051**<br>(0.026) |
| Abandonment behavior | 0.084<br>(0.003) | 0.087<br>(0.003) | −0.003<br>(0.005) |
| Abandonment ratio | 0.039<br>(0.002) | 0.040<br>(0.002) | −0.001<br>(0.002) |

*Notes* ***, **, and * denote significance at the 1%, 5%, and 10% levels, respectively; Standard errors are shown in parentheses

health and education of the householder (Deng et al., 2019; Xu et al., 2019). The main household characteristics include the dependency ratio (Zavalloni et al., 2021; Zhang et al., 2018), off-farm employment ratio (Deng et al., 2019; Xu et al., 2019), per capita contracted land area (Zhang et al., 2018), and number of plots (Luo et al., 2017; Yan et al., 2016). To exclude the influence of time-varying factors at the community level, this study also adopts the number of new agricultural operating entities and the community's prior year per capita disposable annual income, which reflect the development of agriculture and economy at the community level, respectively. The definitions and descriptions of the main variables are presented in Table 10.1.

To investigate further the relationship between land certification and cropland abandonment, Student's t-test is used to compare the differences in cropland abandonment between households with certified and uncertified rights by taking land certificates as the grouping variable.

As shown in Table 10.2, compared with farmers who do not have a land certificate, the cropland area being abandoned by farmers with land certificates is relatively less, and this passed the t-test. Although the cropland abandonment behavior and the abandonment ratio did not pass the t-test, the group results show that the possibility of cropland abandonment of farmers with land certificates is lower than that of farmers without land certificates. This evidence indicates that land certification may have a positive effect on reducing cropland abandonment by farmers, thus strengthening the protection of land quantity.

### *10.3.3 Model Setting*

Considering that the new round of land certification reform initiated by the Chinese government since 2013 has obvious gradual characteristics, it is essentially a quasi-natural experiment. To explore the relationship between the reform of the land tenure system and the protection of land quantity, we designate families that have obtained land certificates as the treatment group, and families that have not obtained land certificates as the control group. We adopt a staggered DID model that is in line with the gradual characteristics of the new round of land certification reform to estimate the impact of land certification on the abandonment of croplands by farmers. The specific benchmark model is set as follows:

$$Abandonment\_area_{it} = \alpha_0 + \beta Certification_{it} + \delta_i + \varphi_t + \varepsilon_{it} \tag{10.1}$$

where subscript $i$ represents the farmer household, and $t$ represents the data collection time. *Abandonment_area* denotes the area of cropland abandoned by farmers. Note that considering the large difference in the abandoned area among farmers, the logarithm of the area of abandoned croplands is taken in the subsequent regression to eliminate potential heteroskedasticity problems and facilitate the interpretation of coefficient estimation. *Certification* represents the land certification variable. If the farmer $i$ obtains the land certificate in year $t$, then for $t >= \tau$, the value of *certification* is 1 and 0 otherwise, where $\tau >= 2013$. $\alpha_0$ is the intercept term; $\delta_i$ represents the fixed effect of farmers that mainly controls for factors such as the ability and preference of farmers; $\varphi_t$ represents the year-fixed effect that mainly controls for the factors related to the protection of land quantity, such as national policies or macroeconomic conditions, which change over time but do not change with the farmers; and $\varepsilon_{it}$ is the random disturbance term.

## 10.4 Empirical Results

### 10.4.1 Baseline Results

Table 10.3 reports the regression results of land certification to cropland abandonment. Using a staggered DID model and a stepwise regression method, columns (1) to (4) represent the comparative benchmark analysis for adding no control variables to gradually adding individual, household, and community characteristics, respectively.

We consider that the random disturbance term among different households in the same community may be correlated. On the one hand, the reform of land certification in China is often promoted by the whole village; the issuance of land certificates is essentially carried out at the same time, and the reform of land certification and land protection may both be affected by the collective's ability regarding land governance and control. As such, land certification at the household level may be interrelated. On the other hand, rural communities belong to an acquaintance society by nature, and there may be a peer effect in the behavior of abandoning cropland among community members. Considering the above, all the regressions' standard errors of clustering are at the community level, unless otherwise specified.

As Table 10.3 shows, the estimated results of the focus variable indicate that land certification has an inhibitory effect on cropland abandonment, and this is statistically significant at the 5% level. Compared with farmers who do not have land certificates,

**Table 10.3** Land certification and cropland abandonment: Basic results

| | The logarithm of the area of abandoned croplands | | | |
|---|---|---|---|---|
| | (1) | (2) | (3) | (4) |
| Land certification | −0.046**<br>(0.020) | −0.045**<br>(0.020) | −0.043**<br>(0.019) | −0.042**<br>(0.019) |
| Age | | −0.018**<br>(0.007) | −0.020**<br>(0.007) | −0.020**<br>(0.007) |
| Age$^2$ | | 0.000***<br>(0.000) | 0.000***<br>(0.000) | 0.000***<br>(0.000) |
| Health | | 0.017**<br>(0.008) | 0.018**<br>(0.008) | 0.018**<br>(0.008) |
| Education | | −0.061*<br>(0.031) | −0.064**<br>(0.031) | −0.066**<br>(0.031) |
| Dependency ratio | | | 0.053**<br>(0.021) | 0.053**<br>(0.021) |
| Off-farm ratio | | | 0.069**<br>(0.036) | 0.068*<br>(0.036) |
| Land size | | | 0.007**<br>(0.003) | 0.007**<br>(0.003) |
| Land number | | | 0.007***<br>(0.002) | 0.007***<br>(0.002) |
| Community agriculture | | | | −0.000*<br>(0.000) |
| Community economy | | | | −0.012***<br>(0.005) |
| Household-fixed effect | Yes | Yes | Yes | Yes |
| Time-fixed effect | Yes | Yes | Yes | Yes |
| Obs | 14,489 | 14,489 | 14,489 | 14,489 |
| Adj-R$^2$ | 0.272 | 0.275 | 0.288 | 0.289 |

*Notes* ***, **, and * denote significance at the 1%, 5%, and 10% levels, respectively; Robust standard errors clustered at the community level are presented in parentheses

the area of abandoned cropland by farmers with land certificates is lower by about 4%, on average. Moreover, the results in columns (1) to (4) indicate that regardless of the inclusion of control variables, the estimated results remain robust. These results imply that land certification has a positive effect on the protection of land quantity in China, and that it can effectively inhibit the abandonment of croplands.

At the same time, the results in column (4) of Table 10.3 also show that the control variables have a significant impact on cropland abandonment. Specifically, for the individual characteristics, there is a U-shaped relationship between the age of the householder and the area of abandoned cropland, and the results indicate that improvement of the householder's health and education levels may reduce the abandoned area. These results are consistent with the previous research conducted by Deng et al. (2019). Considering family characteristics, the results indicate that the dependency ratio, off-farm ratio, land size, and land number may increase the area of abandoned croplands. These findings are broadly consistent with those of previous studies (Xu et al., 2019; Yan et al., 2016; Zhang et al., 2018). Regarding community characteristics, the results indicate that the greater the number of new farmers and the higher the income level of farmers in the community, the smaller the area of cropland abandoned by farmers. A possible explanation is that when a community has more market-oriented farmers and higher per capita income, cropland resources become relatively scarce and thus, are more likely to be used.

## *10.4.2 Robustness Test*

To verify the positive effect of land certification on inhibiting cropland abandonment further, robustness tests are conducted.

### 10.4.2.1 Addition of an Interaction Item Between Time and Province

The previous results do not take into account the possible impacts that change with time and province, such as pilot policies, extreme weather, natural disasters, and some other factors related to cropland abandonment. As such, the interaction term between time and province is further added to a follow-up regression.

The results in Table 10.4 show that after adding the interaction terms of province and time, the estimated coefficient of land certification remains significantly positive and slightly higher than the estimated results in Table 10.3. This suggests that the role of land certification in reducing cropland abandonment cannot be ignored, and it is necessary to leverage the protection of land quantity.

### 10.4.2.2 The Dependent Variables: Abandonment Behavior and Abandonment Ratio

The farmers' cropland abandonment behavior and the ratio of the area of cropland abandoned by farmers are also important indicators of land quantity protection (Deng et al., 2019; Zheng & Luo, 2019). As shown in Table 10.5, regardless of whether control variables are added, the regression coefficients of land certification remain significantly negative, this indicates that land certification has a significant inhibitory effect on cropland abandonment.

**Table 10.4** Land certification and cropland abandonment: Robustness test I

| | The logarithm of the area of abandoned croplands | | | |
|---|---|---|---|---|
| | (1) | (2) | (3) | (4) |
| Land certification | −0.053**<br>(0.022) | −0.052**<br>(0.022) | −0.051**<br>(0.022) | −0.050**<br>(0.021) |
| Individual characteristics | | Yes | Yes | Yes |
| Household characteristics | | | Yes | Yes |
| Community characteristics | | | | Yes |
| Household-fixed effect | Yes | Yes | Yes | Yes |
| Time-fixed effect | Yes | Yes | Yes | Yes |
| Province * time | Yes | Yes | Yes | Yes |
| Obs | 14,489 | 14,489 | 14,489 | 14,489 |
| Adj-$R^2$ | 0.266 | 0.269 | 0.281 | 0.282 |

*Notes* ***, **, and * denote significance at the 1%, 5%, and 10% levels, respectively; Robust standard errors clustered at the community level are presented in parentheses; The control variables in column (4) of this Table are the same as those in column (4) of Table 10.3

**Table 10.5** Land certification and cropland abandonment: Robustness test II

| | Abandonment behavior | | Abandonment ratio | |
|---|---|---|---|---|
| | (1) | (2) | (3) | (4) |
| Land certification | −0.028**<br>(0.013) | −0.026**<br>(0.013) | −0.014**<br>(0.007) | −0.013*<br>(0.007) |
| Control variables | | Yes | | Yes |
| Household-fixed effect | Yes | Yes | Yes | Yes |
| Time-fixed effect | Yes | Yes | Yes | Yes |
| Obs | 14,489 | 14,489 | 14,489 | 14,489 |
| Adj-$R^2$ | 0.336 | 0.348 | 0.349 | 0.356 |

*Notes* ***, **, and * denote significance at the 1%, 5%, and 10% levels, respectively; Robust standard errors clustered at the community level are presented in parentheses; The control variables are the same as in column (4) of Table 10.3

#### 10.4.2.3 Application of the Propensity Score Matching-Difference-In-Differences Model

Because this study only has two periods of panel data, it is difficult to conduct an acceptable parallel trend test. Therefore, to exclude or alleviate the situation in which parallel trend may not be satisfied, the PSM-DID model is used here to make it easier for individuals in the treatment group and the control group to have the same time trend under the condition of the same given covariates. Specifically, we first select the commonly used "one-to-one" neighbor matching method and set the caliper range to 0.05. Second, we specify land certification as the treatment variable and the logarithm

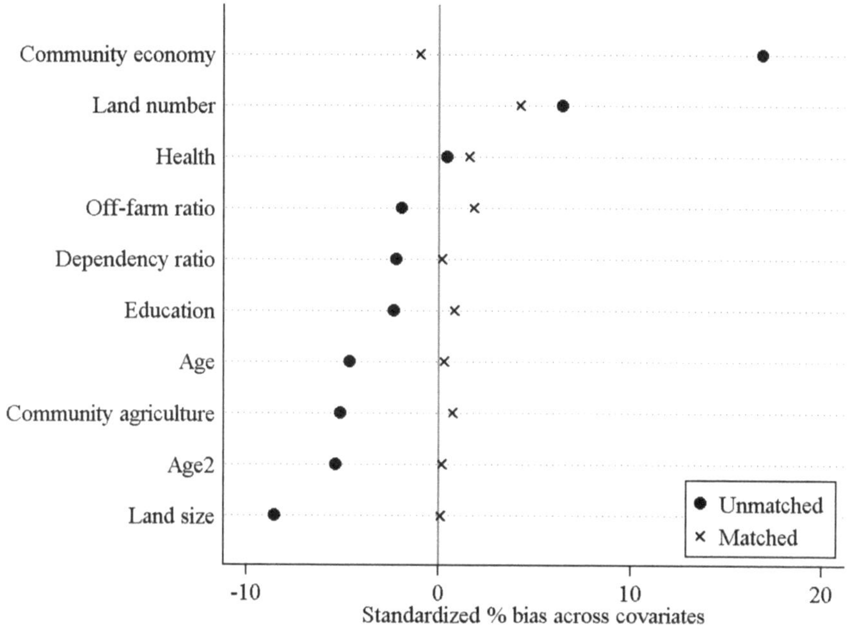


**Fig. 10.1** Standardization bias before and after matching

of the area of abandoned cropland as the outcome variable. Finally, after adding all the control variables in Table 10.1, the logit model is used to estimate the propensity scores.

The standardized deviation diagram (Fig. 10.1) reveals that after propensity score matching, the standardized deviations of all control variables have a corresponding degree of reduction; their values are significantly less than 10%, and they are all near the 0 value. This means that there is no systematic difference between the treatment and control groups after matching, thus satisfying the balance test. Therefore, we further delete five samples not in the common support domain and then use the DID model to perform another estimation. Table 10.6 shows that the estimated results using the PSM-DID model are almost the same as those obtained using the DID model (Table 10.3). This proves once again that land certification helps strengthen the protection of land quantity and significantly reduces the area of cropland abandoned by farmers.

#### 10.4.2.4 Mainly Considering the Agricultural Region Samples

Considering that the Inner Mongolia Autonomous Region, Shanxi Province, Qinghai Province, and Gansu Province predominantly comprise grassland vegetation, with animal husbandry as the predominant type of agriculture, the mechanism of land certification for these places may differ. Therefore, the above-mentioned provinces

**Table 10.6** Land certification and cropland abandonment: Robustness test III

| | The logarithm of the area of abandoned croplands | | | |
|---|---|---|---|---|
| | (1) | (2) | (3) | (4) |
| Land certification | −0.046**<br>(0.020) | −0.045**<br>(0.020) | −0.043**<br>(0.019) | −0.042**<br>(0.019) |
| Individual characteristics | | Yes | Yes | Yes |
| Household characteristics | | | Yes | Yes |
| Community characteristics | | | | Yes |
| Household-fixed effect | Yes | Yes | Yes | Yes |
| Time-fixed effect | Yes | Yes | Yes | Yes |
| Obs | 14,484 | 14,484 | 14,484 | 14,484 |
| Adj-$R^2$ | 0.272 | 0.275 | 0.288 | 0.288 |

*Notes* ***, **, and * denote significance at the 1%, 5%, and 10% levels, respectively; Robust standard errors clustered at the community level are presented in parentheses; The entire regression is estimated using the PSM-DID model

are excluded here and only agricultural samples dominated by the planting industry are retained.

The results in Table 10.7 show that regardless of whether control variables are added, the regression coefficients of land certification remain significantly negative and are not significantly different from the results in Table 10.3. This further confirms that land certification has a positive effect on reducing the area of abandoned croplands and can significantly inhibit abandonment of croplands.

**Table 10.7** Land certification and cropland abandonment: Robustness test IV

| | The logarithm of the area of abandoned croplands | | | |
|---|---|---|---|---|
| | (1) | (2) | (3) | (4) |
| Land certification | −0.040**<br>(0.019) | −0.039**<br>(0.019) | −0.038**<br>(0.019) | −0.038**<br>(0.019) |
| Individual characteristics | | Yes | Yes | Yes |
| Household characteristics | | | Yes | Yes |
| Community characteristics | | | | Yes |
| Household-fixed effect | Yes | Yes | Yes | Yes |
| Time-fixed effect | Yes | Yes | Yes | Yes |
| Obs | 12,959 | 12,959 | 12,959 | 12,959 |
| Adj-$R^2$ | 0.259 | 0.262 | 0.270 | 0.270 |

*Notes* ***, **, and * denote significance at the 1%, 5%, and 10% levels, respectively; Robust standard errors clustered at the community level are presented in parentheses

### 10.4.3 Placebo Test

We further verify whether the estimated results of this study are driven by non-observable factors at the provincial, community, and household levels, and the year, etc. The test method of Cai et al. (2016) is used as a reference, and the placebo test is conducted here for a virtual certification time randomly assigned by the province. Specifically, this study randomly selects any year from 2009 to 2019 for the 29 provinces in China as the year of land certification and then conducts a random sampling 500 times. After controlling for the age, age squared, health, education, dependency ratio, off-farm ratio, land size, land number, community agriculture, community income, household-fixed effect, and time-fixed effect, the staggered DID model is used for estimation, and we finally draw out the distribution of 500 estimated coefficients and their related $p$-values.

Figure 10.2 shows that the mean value of the estimated coefficients of land certification is concentrated around point 0, which is obviously different from the real estimated value of −0.042 in column (4) of Table 10.3. The corresponding p-values of most of the coefficient estimates are also greater than 0.1, thus rejecting the assumption that there is no difference with the real estimated result. This indicates that the results of our study are not biased and are unlikely to be affected by unobvious factors at the provincial, community, and household levels, and the year.

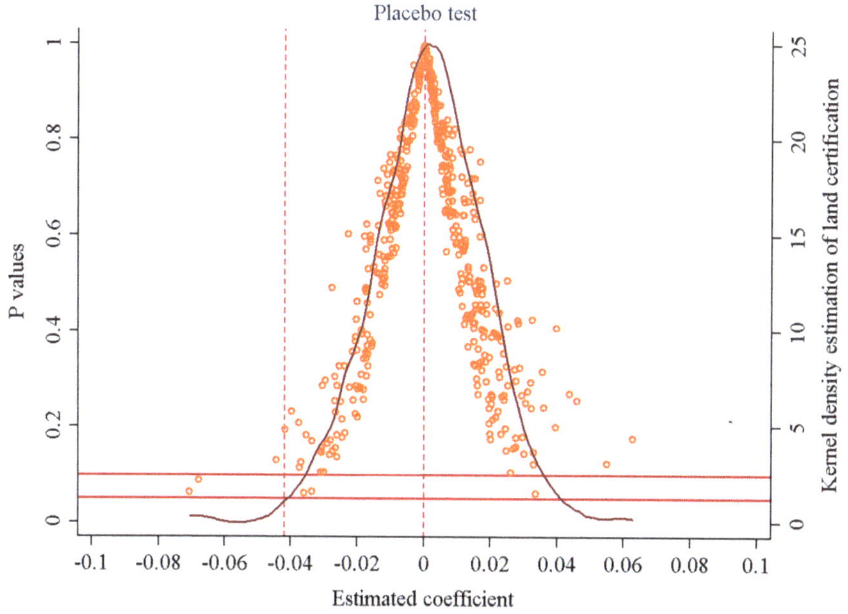


**Fig. 10.2** Land certification and cropland abandonment: Placebo test *Note* The figure is a combination of the estimation coefficient of the land certification, the scatter diagram of its corresponding p-value, and the kernel density estimation curve of the coefficient

### *10.4.4 Endogeneity Discussion*

Endogenous problems are mainly caused by reverse causality, selection bias, missing variables, and measurement errors. Regarding the first two factors, since China's land certification reform is state-led and compulsively promoted, the possibility of reverse causality and selection bias at the household level is relatively small. As for the last two factors, they have been addressed by adding control variables and by replacing the dependent variables in the staggered DID model separately. In addition, the PSM-DID model estimation and placebo test also confirm the robustness of the estimation results. Therefore, endogeneity has been controlled for, to a certain extent.

### *10.4.5 Mechanism Analysis*

As pointed out in the literature, poor soil fertility, unavailability of land transfer, lack of agricultural subsidies, and low agricultural income may lead to cropland abandonment. If so, can land certification improve the conditions concerning cropland abandonment by issuing land certificates with legal effects and multiple economic uses to farmers? This is the mechanism question that this study aims to answer.

The results in Table 10.8 show that land certification creates favorable conditions for improving soil fertility, promoting land transfer, improving the availability of agricultural subsidies, and increasing agricultural income, and it has positive and significant promoting effects on these aspects. These results imply that land certification mainly helps restrain the expansion of abandoned croplands through the above-mentioned channels, and eventually plays a positive role in protecting land quantity.

## 10.5 Heterogeneity Analysis

Considering the heterogeneity of provinces, communities, and households, there may be differences in the influence of land certification on the area of abandoned croplands. Therefore, it is necessary to explore the effects of land certification under different circumstances further.

### *10.5.1 At the Province Level: The Impact of Land Certification on the Area of Abandoned Croplands*

In this section, the effects of land certification on the abandoned croplands in different provinces are investigated from two dimensions: crop regions and geographical

**Table 10.8** The mechanism of land certification on cropland abandonment

| Mechanism | Dependent variable | Model | Land certification | Control variables | Obs | Wald chi$^2$ | Pseudo-R$^2$/ Adj-R$^2$ |
|---|---|---|---|---|---|---|---|
| Use of organic fertilizer | Whether to use organic fertilizer (0 = no; 1 = yes) | Logit | 0.077*** (0.007) | Yes | 14,489 | 373.65 | 0.133 |
| Land transfer | Whether to transfer the land (0 = no; 1 = yes) | Logit | 0.035*** (0.006) | Yes | 14,489 | 486.33 | 0.252 |
| Agricultural subsidies | Whether one gets agricultural subsidies (0 = no; 1 = yes) | Logit | 0.077*** (0.009) | Yes | 14,489 | 269.25 | 0.120 |
| Agricultural income | The logarithm of agricultural income | Fe | 0.270* (0.143) | Yes | 14,489 | — | 0.537 |

*Notes* ***, **, and * denote significance at the 1%, 5%, and 10% levels, respectively; Standard errors are presented in parentheses; The control variables are the same as in column (4) of Table 10.3; The logit model reports average marginal effects

regions. As shown in Table 10.9, in terms of crop regions, land certification has a restraining effect on the area of abandoned croplands in non-major grain-producing areas, but has no effect on major grain-producing areas. The reason may be that major grain-producing areas shoulder the responsibility of ensuring national food security, and the government has both high economic incentives and strong administrative constraints on the farmers. Therefore, regardless of whether land certification has been completed, the possibility of farmers using their cropland is relatively high.

Meanwhile, regarding geographical regions, land certification can reduce the area of abandoned croplands in the western region, but has no effect in the eastern and central regions. A possible explanation is that compared with the western region, the eastern and central regions have more developed economies and more off-farm employment opportunities; thus, land certification is not as attractive to these farmers.

## 10.5.2 At the Community Level: The Impact of Land Certification on the Area of Abandoned Croplands

Table 10.10 reports the community heterogeneity of the impact of land certification on the area of abandoned croplands. Considering the natural geography, land

**Table 10.9** Land certification and cropland abandonment: Province heterogeneity

| | The logarithm of the area of abandoned croplands | | | | |
|---|---|---|---|---|---|
| | Crop regions | | Geographical regions | | |
| | Major grain- producing areas | None | East | Middle | West |
| Land certification | −0.020<br>(0.020) | −0.063**<br>(0.032) | −0.008<br>(0.019) | −0.035<br>(0.047) | −0.096**<br>(0.039) |
| Control variables | Yes | Yes | Yes | Yes | Yes |
| Household-fixed effect | Yes | Yes | Yes | Yes | Yes |
| Time-fixed effect | Yes | Yes | Yes | Yes | Yes |
| Obs | 7572 | 6917 | 5774 | 4239 | 4476 |
| Adj-$R^2$ | 0.252 | 0.287 | 0.420 | 0.187 | 0.322 |

*Notes* ***, **, and * denote significance at the 1%, 5%, and 10% levels, respectively; Robust standard errors clustered at the community level are presented in parentheses; The control variables are the same as in column (4) of Table 10.3; Crop regions are divided according to the standards of the former State Administration of Grain of China, and the major grain-producing areas include Liaoning, Jilin, Heilongjiang, Inner Mongolia, Hebei, Henan, Shandong, Hunan, Hubei, Sichuan, Anhui, Jiangxi, and Jiangsu, while the other provinces are non-major grain-producing areas. Geographically, the regions are divided according to the standards of the National Bureau of Statistics of China: the eastern region includes Beijing, Tianjin, Hebei, Shanghai, Jiangsu, Zhejiang, Fujian, Shandong, Guangdong, Hainan, Heilongjiang, Jilin, and Liaoning; the central region includes Shanxi, Anhui, Jiangxi, Henan, Hubei, and Hunan; and the rest of the provinces belong to the western region

certification mainly has a positive effect on curbing cropland abandonment in plain communities, but has no significant effect on mountainous communities. The main possible reason is that croplands in mountainous communities are not only of relatively low quality, but also are relatively inconvenient to cultivate (Prishchepov et al., 2013). Regardless of whether the cropland is certified, the level of use of cropland in mountainous communities is difficult to change in a short period.

From the perspective of economic location, land certification can help reduce cropland abandonment in remote villages, but has no effect on suburban villages. A possible explanation is that it is more convenient to enter the city; therefore, farmers who live in suburban villages are more likely to engage in off-farm employment, which implies that land certification has little effect on their land use behavior.

Regarding the political centrality of a location, land certification mainly has a positive effect on the protection of land quantity in non-politically central communities, but has no significant effect on politically central communities. This may be due to the fact that politically centered villages are relatively close to the township government, regardless of whether the cropland is certified; thus, farmers are unlikely to abandon their cropland under the supervision of the township government.

**Table 10.10** Land certification and cropland abandonment: Community heterogeneity

| | The logarithm of the area of abandoned croplands | | | | | |
|---|---|---|---|---|---|---|
| | Terrain | | Economic location | | Political location | |
| | Mountains | Plains | Village | Suburb | < 7 km | > = 7 km |
| Land certification | −0.042<br>(0.044) | −0.043**<br>(0.020) | −0.048**<br>(0.020) | 0.113<br>(0.127) | −0.018<br>(0.022) | −0.074**<br>(0.031) |
| Control variables | Yes | Yes | Yes | Yes | Yes | Yes |
| Household-fixed effect | Yes | Yes | Yes | Yes | Yes | Yes |
| Time-fixed effect | Yes | Yes | Yes | Yes | Yes | Yes |
| Obs | 3989 | 10,500 | 14,134 | 355 | 7203 | 7286 |
| Adj-$R^2$ | 0.264 | 0.362 | 0.287 | 0.445 | 0.336 | 0.206 |

*Notes* ***, **, and * denote significance at the 1%, 5%, and 10% levels, respectively; Robust standard error clustered at the community level are presented in parentheses; The control variables are the same as in column (4) of Table 3; The division of locations in terms of political centrality is mainly based on whether the distance between the village committee and the township government seat is greater than the mean value

### *10.5.3 At the Household Level: The Impact of Land Certification on the Area of Abandoned Croplands*

To investigate the difference in the impact of land certification on the area of abandoned croplands under different types of farmer households, this study uses land transfer-in, land transfer-out, and land adjustment as grouping variables to conduct subsample regression.

The results in Table 10.11 indicate that first, land certification has no effect on the area of abandoned croplands for transfer-in households, but has a significant inhibitory effect on the area of abandoned croplands for non-transfer-in households. This is mainly because the cost of abandoning croplands faced by transfer-in households is much higher than that of non-transfer-in households because they must pay rent for the transferred land. Regardless of whether the cropland is certified, they are more likely to choose farming the land instead of abandoning it.

Second, land certification significantly reduces the area of abandoned croplands by non-transfer-out households but does not have a significant impact on transfer-out households. The likely reason is that compared with non-transfer-out households, transfer-out households meet the conditions to transfer the remaining cropland that cannot be cultivated by themselves to others. Therefore, regardless of whether the cropland is certified, no land will be abandoned.

Third, land certification significantly reduces the area of croplands abandoned by farmers who have not undergone land adjustment, but it has no significant impact on farmers who have undergone land adjustment. The possible explanation is that for farmers who have undergone land adjustment, regardless of whether the land certification has been completed, they may have a distrustful attitude toward land

**Table 10.11** Land certification and cropland abandonment: Household heterogeneity

| | The logarithm of the area of abandoned croplands | | | | | |
|---|---|---|---|---|---|---|
| | Land transfer-in | | Land transfer-out | | Land adjustment | |
| | Transfer-in | None | Transfer-out | None | Adjustment | None |
| Land certification | −0.004<br>(0.026) | −0.050**<br>(0.023) | −0.019<br>(0.043) | −0.046**<br>(0.022) | −0.029<br>(0.026) | −0.051*<br>(0.029) |
| Control variables | Yes | Yes | Yes | Yes | Yes | Yes |
| Household-fixed effect | Yes | Yes | Yes | Yes | Yes | Yes |
| Time-fixed effect | Yes | Yes | Yes | Yes | Yes | Yes |
| Obs | 2,428 | 12,061 | 3,109 | 11,378 | 5,433 | 7,668 |
| Adj-$R^2$ | 0.306 | 0.265 | 0.252 | 0.300 | 0.366 | 0.223 |

*Notes* ***, **, and * denote significance at the 1%, 5%, and 10% levels, respectively; Robust standard errors clustered at the community level are presented in parentheses; The control variables are the same as in column (4) of Table 10.3; Since part of the missing values were difficult to complete, the observed samples of the latter two groups were slightly lower than 14,489

tenure security. Since land adjustments have been previously implemented, they are likely to continue in the future; thus, the security of land tenure remains uncertain.

## 10.6 Conclusions and Policy Implications

### *10.6.1 Conclusions*

In the post-pandemic era, food security based on the protection of the amount of cropland has become increasingly important. The protection of property rights is the foundation of land protection. It is realistic and inevitable to rationally use every inch of cropland and curb cropland abandonment by strengthening the land tenure system reform, especially in the case of the insecurity of land tenure. Issuing land certificates with legal effect and multiple economic uses to farmers may improve land tenure security, curbing the expansion of cropland abandonment areas. This study uses nationally representative data from the 2017 and 2019 CRHPS and adopts a staggered DID model to examine the impact of land certification on cropland abandonment.

The results of the study reveal that land certification significantly inhibits cropland abandonment and contributes to the protection of land quantity. Compared with farmers with no land certificates, those with land certificates have less cropland to abandon. This estimation result remains stable even after a series of robustness tests. The mechanism test reveals that the inhibiting effect of land certification on cropland abandonment is mainly realized by improving soil fertility, promoting land transfer, increasing the availability of agricultural subsidies, and raising the level of agricultural income. Further analysis indicates that the influence of land certification on cropland abandonment is heterogeneous at the provincial, community, and household levels. From a regional perspective, land certification has a significant inhibitory effect on the area of cropland abandoned by farmers in non-major grain-producing areas and western regions, but has no significant impact on other regions of China. From a community perspective, land certification has a significant restraining effect on the croplands abandoned by farmers in plain, remote, and non-politically central villages, but has no significant effect on other types of villages. From the perspective of households, land certification significantly reduces the area of croplands abandoned by farmers who have non-transferred and unadjusted land, while the impact on other farmers is not significant. These findings have important policy implications for countries facing both cropland abandonment and land tenure insecurity issues.

### *10.6.2 Policy Implications*

Cultivated land, as the material resource and endowment basis of grain production, is critical to safeguarding national food security, especially in the post-pandemic era. Cropland is extremely valuable, and we cannot afford to waste it. Various factors affect farmers' cropland abandonment behavior, such as poor soil fertility, unavailability of land transfers, too little agricultural subsidies, and too low agricultural income, all of which, to some extent, relate to insecurity of land tenure. Empirical evidence from rural China has shown that a clear definition and effective protection of property rights can help curb cropland abandonment. Similar to the situation in China's rural areas, most developing countries face both problems of cropland abandonment and insecure land tenure (Deininger et al., 2012). According to statistics, half of the developing countries lack a formal land tenure system, and the ratio of issuing land certificates is less than 50% (Feng et al., 2019).

One who has property needs perseverance. The reform of the land tenure system should enhance the land protection behavior of farmers through the reform of land certification and promote the sustainable use of cropland. At present, most developing countries need to strengthen the construction of the land tenure system, carry out land certification reform, and issue farmers with clearly defined and legally effective land certificates. Concurrently, efforts should also be made to promote the diversified use of land certificates after the completion of land certification reform—in China and other developing countries. For example, land certificates have a positive role in improving soil quality, promoting land transfer, increasing agricultural income, and serving as the basis for subsidies. In addition, considering the heterogeneity of different provinces, communities, and households, it is necessary to adopt measures according to local conditions. For example, in economically developed provinces, efforts should be made to train professional farmers, increase agricultural subsidies, and improve agricultural income. In mountainous villages, the government should take measures to strengthen the construction of agricultural infrastructure and improve agricultural production conditions. For farmers who have experienced land adjustment, it is also necessary to further enhance the security of land tenure through legal empowerment.

## References

Abolina, E., & Luzadis, V. A. (2015). Abandoned agricultural land and its potential for short rotation woody crops in Latvia. *Land Use Policy, 49*, 435–445.

Aide, T. M., & Grau, H. R. (2004). Globalization, migration, and Latin American ecosystems. *American Association for the Advancement of Science, 305*(5692), 1915–1916.

Alix-Garcia, J., Kuemmerle, T., & Radeloff, V. C. (2012). Prices, land tenure institutions, and geography: A matching analysis of farmland abandonment in post-socialist Eastern Europe. *Land Economics, 88*, 425–443.

Alonso-Sarría, F., Martínez-Hernández, C., Romero-Díaz, A., Cánovas-García, F., & Gomariz-Castillo, F. (2016). Main environmental features leading to recent land abandonment in Murcia region (Southeast Spain). *Land Degradation & Development, 27*, 654–670.

Bakker, M. M., Govers, G., Kosmas, C., Vanacker, V., Van Oost, K., & Rounsevell, M. (2005). Soil erosion as a driver of land-use change. *Agriculture, Ecosystems & Environment, 105*, 467–481.

Baumann, M., Kuemmerle, T., Elbakidze, M., Ozdogan, M., Radeloff, V. C., Keuler, N. S., Prishchepov, A. V., Kruhlov, I., & Hostert, P. (2011). Patterns and drivers of post-socialist farmland abandonment in Western Ukraine. *Land Use Policy, 28*, 552–562.

Benjamin, D., & Brandt, L. (2002). Property rights, labour markets, and efficiency in a transition economy: The case of rural China. *Canadian Journal of Economics/revue Canadienne D'économique, 35*, 689–716.

Besley, T. (1995). Property rights and investment incentives: Theory and evidence from Ghana. *Journal of Political Economy, 103*, 903–937.

Cai, X., Lu, Y., Wu, M., & Yu, L. (2016). Does environmental regulation drive away inbound foreign direct investment? Evidence from a quasi-natural experiment in China. *Journal of Development Economics, 123*, 73–85.

Campbell, J. E., Lobell, D. B., Genova, R. C., & Field, C. B. (2008). The global potential of bioenergy on abandoned agriculture lands. *Environmental Science & Technology, 42*, 5791–5794.

Chen, R., Ye, C., Cai, Y., Xing, X., & Chen, Q. (2014). The impact of rural out-migration on land use transition in China: Past, present and trend. *Land Use Policy, 40*, 101–110.

Cheung, S. N. (1973). The fable of the bees: An economic investigation. *The Journal of Law and Economics, 16*, 11–33.

Deininger, K., & Feder, G. (2009). Land registration, governance, and development: Evidence and implications for policy. *The World Bank Research Observer, 24*, 233–266.

Deininger, K., Savastano, S., & Carletto, C. (2012). Land fragmentation, cropland abandonment, and land market operation in Albania. *World Development, 40*, 2108–2122.

Deng, X., Xu, D., Zeng, M., & Qi, Y. (2019). Does internet use help reduce rural cropland abandonment? *Evidence from China. Land Use Policy, 89*, Article 104243.

Díaz, G. I., Nahuelhual, L., Echeverría, C., & Marín, S. (2011). Drivers of land abandonment in Southern Chile and implications for landscape planning. *Landscape and Urban Planning, 99*, 207–217.

Estel, S., Kuemmerle, T., Alcántara, C., Levers, C., Prishchepov, A., & Hostert, P. (2015). Mapping farmland abandonment and recultivation across Europe using MODIS NDVI time series. *Remote Sensing of Environment, 163*, 312–325.

Feder, G., & Nishio, A. (1998). The benefits of land registration and titling: Economic and social perspectives. *Land Use Policy, 15*, 25–43.

Feng, H. F. (2015). The train of thought and measure of agricultural subsidy system reform. *Issues in Agricultural Economy*, 8–10 (in Chinese).

Feng, L., Zhang, M. H., & Li, Y. X. (2019). The effect of land certificate in rural land title registration: Mechanism, conditions and empirical tests. *China Land Science*, 39–494 (in Chinese).
FAO, I., UNICEF, WFP, WHO. (2020). *The state of food security and nutrition in the world 2020*. Rome.
Gallart, F., & Llorens, P. (2003). Catchment management under environmental change: Impact of land cover change on water resources. *Water International, 28*, 334–340.
Gellrich, M., Baur, P., Koch, B., & Zimmermann, N. E. (2007). Agricultural land abandonment and natural forest re-growth in the Swiss mountains: A spatially explicit economic analysis. *Agriculture, Ecosystems & Environment, 118*, 93–108.
Han, Z., & Song, W. (2019). Spatiotemporal variations in cropland abandonment in the Guizhou-Guangxi karst mountain area. *China. Journal of Cleaner Production, 238*, Article 117888.
Holden, S. T., Deininger, K., & Ghebru, H. (2009). Impacts of low-cost land certification on investment and productivity. *American Journal of Agricultural Economics, 91*, 359–373.
Holden, S. T., Deininger, K., & Ghebru, H. (2011). Tenure insecurity, gender, low-cost land certification and land rental market participation in Ethiopia. *The Journal of Development Studies, 47*, 31–47.
Holden, S. T., Deininger, K., & Ghebru, H. (2007). *Impact of land certification on land rental market participation in Tigray region, Northern Ethiopia.*
Huang, J. K., & Ji, X. Q. (2012). The verification of the right to use farmland and farmers' long-term investment in farmland. *Management World, 9*, 76–81 (in Chinese).
Ito, J., Nishikori, M., Toyoshi, M., & Feuer, H. N. (2016). The contribution of land exchange institutions and markets in countering farmland abandonment in Japan. *Land Use Policy, 57*, 582–593.
Jin, S., & Deininger, K. (2009). Land rental markets in the process of rural structural transformation: Productivity and equity impacts from China. *Journal of Comparative Economics, 37*, 629–646.
Kassa, W. (2014). Land titling and investment in Tanzania: An empirical investigation. Available at SSRN 2480216.
Lambin, E. F., & Meyfroidt, P. (2010). Land use transitions: Socio-ecological feedback versus socio-economic change. *Land Use Policy, 27*, 108–118.
Levers, C., Schneider, M., Prishchepov, A. V., Estel, S., & Kuemmerle, T. (2018). Spatial variation in determinants of agricultural land abandonment in Europe. *Science of the Total Environment, 644*, 95–111.
Lichtenberg, E., & Ding, C. (2008). Assessing farmland protection policy in China. *Land Use Policy, 25*, 59–68.
Lieskovský, J., Bezák, P., Špulerová, J., Lieskovský, T., Koleda, P., Dobrovodská, M., Bürgi, M., & Gimmi, U. (2015). The abandonment of traditional agricultural landscape in Slovakia-analysis of extent and driving forces. *Journal of Rural Studies, 37*, 75–84.
Luo, M. Z., Liu, K., & Zhu, W. J. (2017). Does right confirmation reduce Farmland abandonment–An empirical analysis of PSM from the questionnaire survey of farmers in Sichuan, Henan and Shanxi. *Journal of Agrotechnical Economics*, 15–27 (in Chinese).
MacDonald, D., Crabtree, J. R., Wiesinger, G., Dax, T., Stamou, N., Fleury, P., Lazpita, J. G., & Gibon, A. (2000). Agricultural abandonment in mountain areas of Europe: Environmental consequences and policy response. *Journal of Environmental Management, 59*, 47–69.
Mullan, K., Grosjean, P., & Kontoleon, A. (2011). Land tenure arrangements and rural–urban migration in China. *World Development, 39*, 123–133.
Nordin, M. (2014). Does the decoupling reform affect agricultural employment in Sweden? Evidence from an exogenous change. *Journal of Agricultural Economics, 65*, 616–636.
Prishchepov, A. V., Müller, D., Dubinin, M., Baumann, M., & Radeloff, V. C. (2013). Determinants of agricultural land abandonment in post-Soviet European Russia. *Land Use Policy, 30*, 873–884.
Qian, W., & Crowley-Vigneau. (2020). *The economy of Chinese rural households*. Springer.
Queiroz, C., Beilin, R., Folke, C., & Lindborg, R. (2014). Farmland abandonment: Threat or opportunity for biodiversity conservation? A global review. *Frontiers in Ecology and the Environment, 12*, 288–296.

Rey Benayas, J. M., Martins, A., Nicolau, J. M., & Schulz, J. J. (2007). Abandonment of agricultural land: An overview of drivers and consequences. *CABI Reviews*, 14.
Robinson, G. M., Carson, D. A. (2015). *Handbook on the globalisation of agriculture.* Edward Elgar Publishing.
Roth, M., & Haase, D. (1998). Land tenure security and agricultural performance in Southern Africa. USAID.
Rudel, T., & Fu, C. (1996). A requiem for the southern regionalists: Reforestation in the South and the uses of regional social science. *Social Science Quarterly*, 804–820.
Saint-Macary, C., Keil, A., Zeller, M., Heidhues, F., & Dung, P. T. M. (2010). Land titling policy and soil conservation in the northern uplands of Vietnam. *Land Use Policy, 27*, 617–627.
Sikor, T., Müller, D., & Stahl, J. (2009). Land fragmentation and cropland abandonment in Albania: Implications for the roles of state and community in post-socialist land consolidation. *World Development, 37*, 1411–1423.
Sluiter, R., & de Jong, S. M. (2007). Spatial patterns of Mediterranean land abandonment and related land cover transitions. *Landscape Ecology, 22*, 559–576.
Strijker, D. (2005). Marginal lands in Europe–causes of decline. *Basic and Applied Ecology, 6*, 99–106.
Wang, H., Riedinger, J., & Jin, S. (2015). Land documents, tenure security and land rental development: Panel evidence from China. *China Economic Review, 36*, 220–235.
Ward, F. A., & Pulido-Velazquez, M. (2008). Water conservation in irrigation can increase water use. *Proceedings of the National Academy of Sciences, 105*, 18215–18220.
Xu, D., Deng, X., Huang, K., Liu, Y., Yong, Z., & Liu, S. (2019). Relationships between labor migration and cropland abandonment in rural China from the perspective of village types. *Land Use Policy, 88*, Article 104164.
Yami, M., & Snyder, K. A. (2016). After all, land belongs to the state: Examining the benefits of land registration for smallholders in Ethiopia. *Land Degradation & Development, 27*, 465–478.
Yan, H., Liu, J., Huang, H. Q., Tao, B., & Cao, M. (2009). Assessing the consequence of land use change on agricultural productivity in China. *Global and Planetary Change, 67*, 13–19.
Yan, J., Yang, Z., Li, Z., Li, X., Xin, L., & Sun, L. (2016). Drivers of cropland abandonment in mountainous areas: A household decision model on farming scale in Southwest China. *Land Use Policy, 57*, 459–469.
Yang, Y., Liu, Y., Li, Y., & Du, G. (2018). Quantifying spatio-temporal patterns of urban expansion in Beijing during 1985–2013 with rural-urban development transformation. *Land Use Policy, 74*, 220–230.
Yao, Y. (2000). The system of farmland in China: An analytical framework. *Social Sciences in China*, 54–65 (in Chinese).
Zavalloni, M., D'Alberto, R., Raggi, M., & Viaggi, D. (2021). Farmland abandonment, public goods and the CAP in a marginal area of Italy. *Land Use Policy, 107*, Article 104365.
Zhang, Q., Song, C., & Chen, X. (2018). Effects of China's payment for ecosystem services programs on cropland abandonment: A case study in Tiantangzhai Township, Anhui, China. *Land Use Policy, 73*, 239–248.
Zhang, Y., Li, X., & Song, W. (2014). Determinants of cropland abandonment at the parcel, household and village levels in mountain areas of China: A multi-level analysis. *Land Use Policy, 41*, 186–192.
Zheng, L. Y., Qian, W. R., & Li, Y. Y. (2020). The influence of rural land certificate on farmers' entrepreneurship: An empirical analysis based on CRHPS. *Journal of Agrotechnical Economics*, 17–30 (in Chinese).
Zheng, L. Y., Qian, W. R., Liu, Q., & Guo, X. L. (2021). The impact of the new round of farmland certification on the ecological protection of cultivated land: Taking the application of chemical fertilizers and pesticides as examples. *Chinese Rural Economy*, 76–93 (in Chinese).
Zheng, W. L., & Luo, B. L. (2019). The impact of farmland ownership certification on farmland abandonment: Based on the property rights incentive. *Journal of Shanghai University of Finance and Economics*, 90–99 (in Chinese).

# Chapter 11
# Key Findings and Future Agenda

**Abstract** The abandonment of cropland has become a global socioeconomic issue, and its potential negative impacts on food security and sustainable agricultural development cannot be overlooked. As one of the world's most populous developing countries, China's cropland abandonment problem and its governance warrant close attention. In the era of globalization, the economic ties among nations are becoming increasingly intertwined. Effectively addressing China's cropland abandonment not only benefits its own development but also makes a significant contribution to global food security and sustainable agricultural development. This book employs nationally representative farm-level panel data from the China Rural Household Panel Survey (CRHPS) and the China Labor-force Dynamics Survey (CLDS). It integrates modern econometric methods to empirically examine the driving factors and governance measures of cropland abandonment by farm households within the "People-Land-Money-Rights" framework. The findings indicate that cropland abandonment by farmers in rural China is ultimately influenced by four key factors: off-farm employment, land fragmentation, agricultural comparative return, and land tenure insecurity. Moreover, the cultivation of new agricultural operating entities, the construction of farmland water conservancy projects, agricultural subsidy system reforms, and land tenure reforms can effectively mitigate the negative impact of these factors on cropland abandonment. However, while this book provides a systematic study of cropland abandonment, future research could be deepened in the following directions: First, utilizing big data and geographic information system (GIS)-based methods to reveal the spatiotemporal patterns of cropland abandonment; second, employing machine learning and system simulation approaches to predict future trends in cropland abandonment; third, using multidimensional long-panel data to comprehensively assess the impacts of cropland abandonment; Fourth, delve deeper into other drivers of cropland abandonment and corresponding governance measures. Fifth, design a comprehensive policy framework that balances food security with sustainable development and encompasses the governance of cropland abandonment.

**Keywords** Cropland abandonment · Food security · Land economics · Key findings · Future agenda



L. Zheng, *Cropland Abandonment in Rural China*, Resources, Environment and Agricultural Development, https://doi.org/10.1007/978-981-95-8287-7_11

The abandonment of cropland has become a global socioeconomic issue, and its potential negative impacts on food security and sustainable agricultural development cannot be overlooked. As one of the world's most populous developing countries, China's cropland abandonment problem and its governance warrant close attention. In the era of globalization, the economic ties among nations are becoming increasingly intertwined. Effectively addressing China's cropland abandonment not only benefits its own development but also makes a significant contribution to global food security and sustainable agricultural development.

## 11.1 Key Findings

This book employs nationally representative farm-level panel data from the China Rural Household Panel Survey (CRHPS) and the China Labor-force Dynamics Survey (CLDS). It integrates modern econometric methods—including the staggered difference-in-differences (DID) model, propensity score matching-difference-in-differences (PSM-DID) model, panel Tobit model, two-way fixed effects (TWFE) model, and panel high-dimensional fixed-effects model—to empirically examine the driving factors and governance measures of cropland abandonment by farm households within the "People-Land-Money-Rights" framework. The study yields several significant findings.

**(1) Off-farm employment raises cropland abandonment risk due to labor shortage, with effects varying by region, market access and household worker count**

In the context of large-scale labor migration in rural China, current off-farm employment leads to an increase in the probability and area of cropland abandoned due to insufficient agricultural labor. However, off-farm employment does not harm farm households in plain areas, or villages with land rental markets, abundant agricultural labor, and agricultural machinery, while abandon their cropland than those in other areas. Additionally, when the number of off-farm workers in a household exceeds two, the probability and area of cropland abandonment will miraculously decline, as the household will no longer live entirely on agriculture. This study fills the gap in clarifying the relationship between off-farm employment and cropland abandonment, and identifies scenarios where off-farm employment may not cause cropland abandonment through multiple dimensions, providing insights into the governance of cropland abandonment during rural-urban transformation in developing countries.

**(2) Land fragmentation exacerbates cropland abandonment due to high labor costs and rental difficulties, with heterogeneous impacts across groups and rent-in scenarios**

Land fragmentation has a significant and positive relationship with cropland abandonment. The mechanism analysis reveals that this relationship is due to high labor costs and difficulties in renting out the fragmented land. The heterogeneity analysis indicates that farmers with poor human capital and those living in non-plain areas are at a higher risk of abandoning their cropland due to land fragmentation. Furthermore, the association between land fragmentation and cropland abandonment tends to vary across different land rent-in scenarios. For instance, an increase in the number of plots in the case of land rent-in is not necessarily associated with cropland abandonment. These findings are conducive to correcting the underestimation of the role of land fragmentation in cropland abandonment, and their implications may be extended to various countries.

**(3) Agricultural comparative return increases abandoned cropland proportion via reduced investment/input, with effects moderated by rural markets and agricultural subsidies**

Agricultural comparative return (ACR) has a positive impact on the proportion of abandoned cropland area to total cropland area, with an average coefficient of 0.016. This effect is mainly achieved through reductions in long-term land investment, agricultural capital input, and agricultural labor input. Nevertheless, it is also moderated by the effects of rural factor markets and government agricultural subsidies. In particular, the agricultural machinery market, the land rental market, and the level of agricultural subsidies can weaken ACR's negative impact on land use, while current agricultural subsidies have little effect. These findings also reveal that the effects of ACR on cropland abandonment vary significantly across geographical regions, grain areas, and terrain zones. Specifically, ACR is not harmful to households in northeastern and central China or major grain-producing areas, while it harms others. Overall, this study provides a better understanding of the quantitative relationship between ACR and cropland abandonment in rural China, and valuable insights for other developing countries in formulating targeted measures to curb cropland abandonment in low ACR situations.

**(4) Land tenure insecurity exacerbates cropland abandonment via suppressed capital investment, labor input and land transfer, with effects varying by income and generation and moderated by institutions**

Land tenure insecurity significantly exacerbates cropland abandonment, increasing the proportion of abandoned cropland by an average of 0.70 percentage points. This effect is primarily driven by the fact that land tenure insecurity suppresses agricultural capital investment, reduces agricultural labor input, and impedes land transfer, thereby accelerating the spread of cropland abandonment. However, the impact of land tenure insecurity on cropland abandonment exhibits heterogeneity across horizontal income differentiation and vertical intergenerational disparities. Specifically, the adverse effects are more pronounced among higher-income farmers and the older generation, whereas lower-income farmers and the younger generation remain largely unaffected. Furthermore, formal institutions—exemplified by land certification—help mitigate the adverse effects of land tenure insecurity on cropland abandonment, while informal institutions, represented by village regulations, prove ineffective. Accordingly, future efforts should focus on strengthening the land tenure system, improving factor allocation efficiency, implementing tailored policies for different farm household groups, and advancing institutional coordination. This integrated approach will help alleviate the negative impacts of land tenure insecurity on land utilization and promote the sustainable development of agriculture.

**(5) New agricultural operating entities lower cropland abandonment ratio via land leasing, technical guidance, and product sales, with stronger benefits in specific regions/households**

New agricultural operating entities (NAOEs)—professional operators, family farms, and agricultural cooperatives—are negatively and significantly correlated with the ratio of abandoned cropland areas. The cultivation of NAOEs in villages could help deter farmers from abandoning their cropland. This effect is achieved through channels such as promoting land leasing, providing technical guidance, and facilitating the sale of agricultural products. Moreover, relative to farming companies, the contributions of the other three types of NAOEs, are more significant. Additionally, the effects of NAOEs on cropland abandonment vary significantly across regions, villages, and households. NAOEs benefit more from China's central and western regions, mountainous areas, villages with better land tenure security, and households with poorer human resource endowments. These findings provide valuable insights for policymakers to ensure food security and promote sustainable development by cultivating various large-scale farmers.

**(6) Farmland water conservancy projects curb cropland abandonment by 7.5% via income boost and cost reduction, with effects varying by household endowment and regional development**

Farmland water conservancy project (FWCP) facilities significantly curbed cropland abandonment, resulting in a 7.5% decrease in the average abandonment rate among farming households. This effect is primarily achieved through channels such as increasing agricultural production income and reducing production and transaction costs. However, this effect is also moderated by household resource endowments and regional economic development, both of which lead to heterogeneity in the suppression impact of the projects. Specifically, among households with higher agricultural dependency, less per capita arable land, and villages in economically underdeveloped areas or farther from county seats, farmland water conservancy project facilities exert a more pronounced suppression effect on cropland abandonment, while this stronger effect is not observed among other households and villages. Based on these findings, this study proposes focusing on the role of water conservancy facilities, blocking the conditions that lead to cropland abandonment, and tailoring measures to local conditions and individual households. This approach will help achieve the organic integration of sustainable agricultural development and food security.

**(7) Agricultural subsidy reform cuts cropland abandonment by 1.7% via more accessible, higher subsidy income, with effects moderated by ACR/land titling and varying by region/machinery access**

Agricultural subsidy reform significantly reduced cropland abandonment, resulting in a 1.7% decrease in the proportion of cropland abandoned by farmers. The effect is mainly achieved by increasing the availability and income of agricultural subsidies. However, this effect is also moderated by agricultural comparative return and land titling, both of which weaken the impact of agricultural subsidy reform on cropland abandonment. Moreover, among farmers living in mountainous areas or lacking agricultural machinery, agricultural subsidy reform is negatively associated with cropland abandonment, while this relationship is not observed among other farmers. These insights into the role of agricultural subsidy reform in cropland abandonment can be leveraged to ensure food security in various countries.

**(8) Land certification reduces cropland abandonment by at least 4% (and protects land quantity) via soil improvement, land transfer, and higher subsidies/income, with heterogeneous regional/group impacts**

Land certification significantly contributes to the protection of land quantity during agricultural production, and it reduces the area of abandoned croplands by at least 4%. This effect is mainly achieved by improving soil fertility, promoting land transfer, increasing the availability of agricultural subsidies, and raising agricultural income. However, while land certification benefits farmers in non-major grain-producing areas and western regions, in plain, remote, and non-politically central villages, and farmers who have not undergone land transfer or land adjustment, it is not beneficial for others. This study enriches the applicability of the property rights theory in the Chinese context, and provides Chinese evidence for other developing countries to strengthen the protection of land quantity, by deepening the reform of the land tenure system under different circumstances.

## 11.2 Future Agendas

There is no end to practice and no limit to research. Practice and research in the field of cropland abandonment are inherently ongoing processes. Although this book offers a systematic examination of the driving factors behind cropland abandonment through the analytical framework of "People-Land-Money-Rights," and employs large-scale farm-level panel data combined with advanced econometric techniques to comprehensively assess the effectiveness of existing policy interventions, numerous aspects of this complex issue remain underexplored. These gaps call for sustained and collaborative efforts from the global research community to deepen understanding and advance knowledge toward sustainable land utilization. In light of these considerations, this book therefore concludes by proposing five future research agendas on cropland abandonment, which are intended to serve as references—and welcome critical feedback—for scholars and practitioners interested in this topic.

**(1) Revealing spatio-temporal patterns of cropland abandonment using big data and GIS-based analysis**

Cropland abandonment exhibits intricate spatio-temporal dynamics that vary across regions and time periods. Big data technologies enable the integration of vast datasets encompassing farmers' behavioral patterns, land use changes, and environmental conditions, thereby establishing a robust empirical foundation for analysis. Geographic Information Systems (GIS) facilitate precise mapping of the spatial distribution of abandoned cropland and, through spatio-temporal coupling analyses, allow for the identification of diffusion trajectories, spatial agglomeration patterns, and interactions with key natural factors such as topography, soil quality, and climatic variability. For instance, big data analytics may reveal strong correlations between the onset of cropland abandonment in specific regions and the timing of rural labor outmigration, while GIS-based visualization and modeling can further demonstrate that such abandoned lands are predominantly located in remote, mountainous areas characterized by poor transportation access and limited water availability. A thorough understanding of these spatio-temporal evolution patterns is essential for identifying high-risk zones, enabling proactive and geographically targeted policy interventions, mitigating the expansion of abandonment, and ultimately supporting evidence-based decision-making for the sustainable management of agricultural land resources.

**(2) Predicting the future evolution of cropland abandonment using machine learning and system simulation approaches**

Accurately forecasting the future trajectory of cropland abandonment is essential for the formulation of effective governance strategies. Machine learning algorithms can identify underlying patterns from historical data and generate predictions about future trends through automated learning processes. For example, by constructing models such as random forests or neural networks and incorporating variables including farmer demographics, land quality indicators, and policy parameters, these models can produce probabilistic forecasts of cropland abandonment across different time horizons. System simulation techniques, on the other hand, enable the modeling of dynamic interactions within agricultural systems under varying scenarios of policy intervention and market fluctuation. For instance, simulating the effects of different subsidy levels in land transfer policies allows researchers to observe corresponding changes in farmers' cultivation decisions and overall trends in the extent of abandoned cropland. Together, these predictive methodologies offer forward-looking insights that support evidence-based policymaking, enabling proactive planning and timely implementation of preventive measures to mitigate large-scale cropland abandonment, thereby safeguarding national food security and ecological sustainability.

**(3) Comprehensive assessment of the impacts of cropland abandonment using multidimensional long-panel datasets**

The consequences of cropland abandonment are multifaceted, spanning production, livelihoods, ecology, and broader economic, social, and environmental dimensions. Leveraging long-panel datasets across multiple spatial and administrative levels—such as individual farmers, villages, counties, provinces, and cross-border regions—enables a robust analysis of the longitudinal dynamics of these impacts. In agricultural production, abandonment may result in declining soil fertility and structural imbalances in crop output. At the household level, it can negatively affect farmers' income and overall quality of life. Ecologically, it may alter ecosystem structure and function, with potential repercussions for biodiversity. Economically, widespread abandonment could hinder regional agricultural growth; socially, it may exacerbate rural labor imbalances and accelerate the decline of rural communities; environmentally, it increases risks of soil erosion and land degradation, including desertification. By developing a comprehensive evaluation framework and applying quantitative methods to long-term panel data, researchers can systematically assess the full range of adverse outcomes associated with cropland abandonment. Such an approach provides a solid empirical foundation for designing integrated governance strategies that balance economic development, social equity, and environmental protection, ultimately supporting the sustainable use of cropland resources.

**(4) In-depth investigation of additional driving factors and governance measures for cropland abandonment**

Beyond established natural and economic determinants, several emerging factors significantly influence cropland abandonment. One critical factor is the maturity and efficiency of the land transfer market. A well-functioning and regulated land transfer system facilitates the consolidation of fragmented plots into larger, more viable farming units managed by professional operators, thereby enhancing land utilization efficiency and reducing abandonment. The advancement of agricultural socialized services (ASS) also offers promising solutions. Services such as contracted farming and mechanized agricultural operations can reduce production costs and labor burdens, thereby strengthening farmers' willingness to continue cultivating their land. Furthermore, the integration of digital information technologies—including precision agriculture and the Internet of Things (IoT) in agriculture—can improve both productivity and management accuracy, increasing farmers' reliance on cropland and discouraging disengagement. In-depth research into these evolving drivers and policy instruments enables a multidimensional understanding of the issue and supports the development of a holistic governance framework. This comprehensive approach not only addresses the root causes of abandonment but also contributes to the broader goal of advancing agricultural modernization.

**(5) Designing an integrated policy system for cropland abandonment governance that balances food security and sustainable development**

Effective governance of cropland abandonment requires a systematic, coordinated, and adaptive policy framework that reconciles immediate food security needs with long-term sustainability goals. Ensuring stable food supply is fundamental to national stability, while sustainable agricultural development is crucial for maintaining ecological integrity and securing future food production. An effective policy system must therefore integrate economic, social, and environmental considerations to achieve synergy between short-term interventions and long-term strategic objectives. For example, financial incentives—such as subsidies for seeds, fertilizers, or conservation practices—can be implemented to encourage farmers to resume cultivation of abandoned land and enhance their motivation to farm. Simultaneously, policies should promote environmentally sound agricultural practices, such as crop rotation and intercropping, to preserve soil health and protect ecosystems. Moreover, the policy framework should allow for regional differentiation, accommodating variations in natural endowments, socioeconomic conditions, and local stakeholder needs. In economically advanced regions, greater investment in agricultural technological innovation may be prioritized to boost productivity; in ecologically vulnerable areas, ecological compensation mechanisms could be emphasized to support restoration efforts. By establishing a balanced and flexible governance system that simultaneously advances food security and sustainable development, policymakers can effectively address current challenges related to cropland abandonment while laying the groundwork for resilient, inclusive, and environmentally responsible agricultural systems.

MIX
Papier aus verantwortungsvollen Quellen
Paper from responsible sources
FSC® C105338

If you have any concerns about our products,
you can contact us on
**ProductSafety@springernature.com**

In case Publisher is established outside the EU,
the EU authorized representative is:
**Springer Nature Customer Service Center GmbH**
**Europaplatz 3, 69115 Heidelberg, Germany**

Printed by Libri Plureos GmbH
in Hamburg, Germany